Jacques Lacan

06/08/01

transitions

General Editor: Julian Wolfreys

Published Titles
NEW HISTORICISM AND CULTURAL MATERIALISM John Brannigan
POSTMODERN NARRATIVE THEORY Mark Currie
CHAUCER TO SHAKESPEARE, 1337–1580 SunHee Kim Gertz
MARXIST LITERARY AND CULTURAL THEORIES Moyra Haslett
JACQUES LACAN Jean-Michel Rabaté
LITERARY FEMINISMS Ruth Robbins
MILTON TO POPE, 1650–1720 Kay Gilliland Stevenson
DECONSTRUCTION•DERRIDA Julian Wolfreys

Forthcoming Titles
TERRY EAGLETON David Alderson
JULIA KRISTEVA AND LITERARY THEORY Megan Becker-Leckrone
BATAILLE Fred Bothing and Scott Wilson
NATIONAL IDENTITY John Brannigan
HÉLÈNE CIXOUS: WRITING AND SEXUAL DIFFERENCE Abigail Bray
GENDER Alison Chapman
IDEOLOGY James Decker
QUEER THEORY Donald E. Hall
POSTCOLONIAL THEORY Claire Jones
ROLAND BARTHES Martin McQuillan
POSTMODERNISM•POSTMODERNITY Martin McQuillan
ALTHUSSER Warren Montag
RACE Brian G. Niro
MODERNITY David Punter
PSYCHOANALYSIS AND LITERATURE Andrew Roberts
SUBJECTIVITY Ruth Robbins
TRANSGRESSION Julian Wolfreys
FORMALIST CRITICISM AND READER-RESPONSE THEORY
    Kenneth Womack and Todd Davis

SIDNEY TO MILTON, 1580–1660 Marion Wynne Davies
POPE TO WOLLSTONECRAFT, 1713–1786 Moyra Haslett
BURKE TO BYRON, 1790–1830 Jane Stabler
DICKENS TO TROLLOPE, 1837–1884 Julian Wolfreys
PATER TO FORSTER, 1873–1924 Ruth Robbins
IMAGE TO APOCALYPSE, 1910–1945 Jane Goldman
ORWELL TO THE PRESENT, 1945–1999 John Brannigan

---

transitions Series
Series Standing Order ISBN 0–333–73684–6
(*outside North America only*)

You can receive future titles in this series as they are published by
placing a standing order. Please contact your bookseller or, in case of
difficulty, write to us at the address below with your name and address,
the title of the series and the ISBN quoted above.

Customer Services Department, Macmillan Distribution Ltd
Houndmills, Basingstoke, Hampshire RG21 6XS, England

---

transitions

Jacques Lacan

Psychoanalysis and the Subject of Literature

Jean-Michel Rabaté

palgrave

First published 2001 by
PALGRAVE
Houndmills, Basingstoke, Hampshire RG21 6XS and
175 Fifth Avenue, New York, N.Y. 10010
Companies and representatives throughout the world

PALGRAVE is the new global academic imprint of
St. Martin's Press LLC Scholarly and Reference Division and
Palgrave Publishers Ltd (formerly Macmillan Press Ltd).

ISBN 0–333–79304–8 hardback
ISBN 0–333–79305–6 paperback

This book is printed on paper suitable for recycling and
made from fully managed and sustained forest sources.

A catalogue record for this book is available
from the British Library.

Library of Congress Cataloging-in-Publication Data
Rabaté, Jean-Michel, 1949–
    Jacques Lacan : psychoanalysis and the subject of literature /
Jean-Michel Rabaté.
        p. cm.
    Includes bibliographical references and index.
    ISBN 0-333–79304–8 (cloth)— ISBN 0–333–79305–6 (pbk.)
        1. Psychoanalysis and literature. 2. Lacan, Jacques, 1901—
    –Contributions in criticism. I. Title. II. Title: Last word. III. Title.

 801'.92–dc21   00-033296

10   9   8   7   6   5   4   3   2   1
10 09 08 07 06 05 04 03 02 01

Printed in China

Contents

General Editor's Preface   vii

Abbreviations   ix

Acknowledgements   xi

1. Lacan from L to Z , or 'Against Interpretation'   1

2. Lacan from A to L: Basic Lacanian Issues and Concepts   11

3. The Theory of the Letter: *Lituraterre* and Gide   29

4. Poe's 'Purloined Letter'   42

5. *Hamlet* and the Desire of the Mother   54

6. *Antigone*: Between the Beautiful and the Sublime   69

7. Sade: Subverting the Law   85

8. *Ravishing* Duras, or the Gift of Love   115

9. Tragedies and Comedies of Love: from Plato to Claudel and Genet   135

10. Joyce's *Jouissance*, or a New Literary Symptom   154

11. Conclusion   183

Notes and References   186

Annotated Bibliography   200

Index   222

General Editor's Preface

Transitions: *transition-em*, n. of action. 1. A passing or passage from one condition, action or (rarely) place, to another. 2. Passage in thought, speech, or writing, from one subject to another. 3. **a**. The passing from one note to another **b**. The passing from one key to another, modulation. 4. The passage from an earlier to a later stage of development or formation ... change from an earlier style to a later; a style of intermediate or mixed character ... the historical passage of language from one well-defined stage to another.

The aim of *transitions* is to explore passages, movements and the development of significant voices in critical thought, as these voices determine and are mediated by acts of literary and cultural interpretation. This series also seeks to examine the possibilities for reading, analysis and other critical engagements which the very idea of transition – such as the transition effected by the reception of a thinker's oeuvre and the heritage entailed – makes possible. The writers in this series unfold the movements and modulations of critical thinking over the last generation, from the first emergences of what is now recognised as literary theory. They examine as well how the transitional nature of theoretical and critical thinking is still very much in operation, guaranteed by the hybridity and heterogeneity of the field of literary studies. The authors in the series share the common understanding that, now more than ever, critical thought is in a state of transition and can best be defined by developing for the student reader an understanding of this protean quality. As this *tranche* of the series, dealing with particular critical voices, addresses, it is of great significance, if not urgency, that the texts of particular figures be reconsidered anew.

This series desires, then, to enable the reader to transform her/his own reading and writing transactions, by comprehending past developments as well as the internal transitions worked through by particular literary and cultural critics, analysts, and philosophers. Each book in the series offers a guide to the poetics and politics of such thinkers, as well as interpretative paradigms, schools, bodies of thought, historical and cultural periods, and the genealogy of particular concepts, while transforming these, if not into tools or methodologies, then into conduits for directing and channelling thought. As well as transforming the critical past by interpreting it from the perspective of the present day, each study enacts transitional readings of critical voices and well-known literary texts, which are themselves conceivable as having been transitional and influential at the moments of their first appearance. The readings offered in these books seek, through close critical reading and theoretical engagement, to demonstrate certain possibilities in critical thinking to the student reader.

It is hoped that the student will find this series liberating because rigid methodologies are not being put into place. As all the dictionary definitions of the idea of transition suggest, what is important is the action, the passage, of thought, of analysis, of critical response, such as are to be found, for example, in the texts of critics whose work has irrevocably transformed the critical landscape. Rather than seeking to help the reader locate him/herself in relation to any particular school or discipline, this series aims to put the reader into action, as readers and writers, travellers between positions, where the movement between poles comes to be seen as of more importance than the locations themselves.

Julian Wolfreys

Abbreviations

I. Works by Jacques Lacan

E   *Ecrits* (Paris: Seuil, 1966).

E/S   *Ecrits: A Selection*, transl. A. Sheridan (New York: Norton, 1977).

KS   'Kant with Sade', transl. J. Swenson, October n°51 (M.I.T. Press, Winter 1989) pp. 55–75.

FFC   *Seminar XI, The Four Fundamental Concepts of Psychoanalysis*, transl. A. Sheridan (London: Penguin, 1979).

HMD 'Homage to Marguerite Duras, on *Le Ravissement de Lol V. Stein*', transl. P. Connor, in *Duras by Duras* (San Francisco: City Lights, 1987) pp. 122–9.

L   'Lituraterre', *Littérature* n°3 (Paris: Larousse, October 1971) pp. 3–10.

O24   'Le Séminaire: *Hamlet*.' in *Ornicar?* n°24 (Paris, 1981) pp. 7–31.

O25   'Le Séminaire: *Hamlet*.' in *Ornicar?* n°25 (Paris, 1982) pp. 13–36.

S1   *Seminar I, Freud's Papers on Technique*, transl. J. Forrester (New York: Norton, 1998).

S2   *Seminar II, The Ego in Freud's Theory and in the technique of Psychoanalysis*, transl. S. Tomaselli and J. Forrester (New York: Norton, 1998).

S3   *Seminar III, Psychoses*, transl. R. Crigg (New York: Norton, 1993).

S5   *Seminar V, Les Formations de l'Inconscient* (Paris: Seuil, 1998).

S7   *Seminar VII, The Ethics of Psychoanalysis*, transl. D. Porter (New York: Norton, 1992).

S8   *Seminar VIII, Le Transfert* (Paris: Seuil, 1991).

S17   *Seminar XVII, L'Envers de la Psychanalyse* (Paris: Seuil, 1991).

S20   *Seminar XX: On Feminine Sexuality, The Limits of Love and Knowledge 1972–73* transl. B. Fink (New York: Norton, 1998).

T   *Television; A Challenge to the Psychoanalytic Establishment*, ed. Joan Copjec and transl. D. Hollier, R. Krauss and A. Michelson (New York: Norton, 1990).

II. Other Works

EYS   Slavoj Zizek, *Enjoy your Symptom!* (New York: Routledge, 1992).

FW   James Joyce, *Finnegans Wake* (London: Faber, 1939).

JAL   *Joyce avec Lacan*, edited by Jacques Aubert (Paris: Navarin, 1987).

LP   *Literature and Psychoanalysis. The Question of Reading: Otherwise*, edited by Shoshana Felman (Baltimore: Johns Hopkins University Press, 1982).

PP   *The Purloined Poe: Lacan, Derrida and Psychoanalytic Reading* edited by John P. Muller and William. J. Richardson (Baltimore: Johns Hopkins University Press, 1988).

RLS   Marguerite Duras, *The Ravishing of Lol Stein* transl. R. Seaver (New York: Pantheon, 1966).

Acknowledgements

The author and publishers wish to thank the following for permission to use copyright material: Jaques Lacan (transitions and annotations by James B. Swenson, Jr), for 'Kant with Sade', *October*, 61 (Winter, 1989), pp. 55–104 © 1990 by October Magazine Ltd and the Massachusetts Institute of Technology (this translation only); Jaques Lacan for excerpts from *Seminar Book VII – The Ethics of Psychoanalysis* by Jaques Lacan, edited by Jacques-Alain Miller, translated by Dennis Porter, © 1986 by Les Editions du Seuil, English translation © 1992 by W. W. Norton & Co. (used by permission of W. W. Norton & Company Inc. and Routledge). Every effort has been made to trace all the copyright-holders, but if any have been inadvertently overlooked the publishers will be pleased to make the necessary arrangement at the first opportunity.

1 Jacques Lacan, from L to Z, or 'Against Interpretation'

The focus of this volume is Lacan's contribution to literary studies, or more properly, what could be called Lacan's theory of literature. While several attempts have recently been made to produce Lacanian readings of literary texts, most of these have proved rather disappointing. Moreover no-one has yet addressed the consistency of Lacan's approach to literature. Excellent books have been written to explain the 'literary' side of Lacan's texts (for instance Malcolm Bowie's brilliant inroads into Lacan's Gongorism and links with Proust) but they tend to be obsessed with the difficulty of Lacan's style. Whereas these attempts are worthwhile, and often very useful, this book takes a different approach: I believe that Lacan was not only a 'user' of literary examples but also a 'reader' of literary texts, and that an entire system of criticism – of a special type – can be found in his seminars and various 'writings'.

Many British and American psychoanalysts who have tried to grapple with the intricacies of Lacan's convoluted style have expressed their regret about the paucity of case studies in his texts. Indeed, apart from one striking exception – a remarkable interview with a psychiatric patient who, among other delusions, believed he was the reincarnation of Nietzsche and Antonin Artaud,[1] – there exists almost nothing in English that testifies to his clinical practice (Lacan's doctoral thesis on paranoia has yet to be translated). And it would be a mistake to think that the missing 'Lacanian case studies' are to be found in the many unpublished seminars: these seminars, often full of gems as they are, seem more concerned with a systematic reading of Freud's basic texts and the development of Lacan's own concepts than with any careful theoretical elaboration based on a few well-chosen cases. And yet, as Lacan notes at the end of the interview with the psychotic patient mentioned above, today's symptoms look less classically Freudian than Lacanian: 'Today we have seen a 'Lacanian' psychosis ... very clearly marked. With these 'imposed speeches', the imaginary, the symbolic and the real.'[2] Before considering to these notions, I wish to note that the relative scarcity of clinical presentations and the curious discretion facing the cases he himself studied, such as the famous Aimée of his thesis, seem to be offset by an almost equivalent increase in literary analyses, as if the lack of case histories was compensated by a wealth of literary and cultural exegeses. Could it be that literature has taken – in the published works – the place of the stricter, more scientific if not always quite verifiable field of clinical studies?

In fact, Lacan's whole effort is aimed at undermining the naiveté of the above question. Not only does he show how much Freud and other practitioners rely on literary effects in many case studies, with all the subsequent narratological problems they entail, but he also follows Freud in the suggestion that there is not opposition but complementarity between the literary domain and 'real cases'. Like Freud, who found in a famous play by Sophocles the doomed hero whose fate could explain a vast array of phenomena, Lacan goes to Joyce's works to discover a new way of understanding the symptom; in *Hamlet* he gains an insight into the way in which a man's desire can remain determined by the wish to solve the riddle of his mother's desire; and in *Antigone* he finds a surprising reversal between ethics and aesthetics that provides him with a motto, a tragic vision and radically new formulations of human desire.

This volume will thus attempt to explain systematically what Lacan has brought to our understanding of literature – poetry, plays and novels – while highlighting the crucial concepts that are brought to bear on fundamental issues in literary texts, of their 'literariness', such as the 'letter', the 'symptom' and *jouissance*. I use the word 'understanding' deliberately, since Lacan does not particularly privilege individual literary texts, and moves effortlessly in his seminars from Dante to Frege, Plato to Gide. He reads them in order to understand something of human nature, which may sound grandiose but it should not be forgotten that his approach is founded on what he constantly calls an 'experience' – the experience of psychoanalysis. What does this consist of? Basically it consists of two persons interacting through language only, engaged as they are in a certain pact (one pays and speaks, the other listens and often remains silent) aiming at the resolution of certain personal difficulties or the transformation of certain inhibitory situations. This experience is an experience of language as living speech, a fundamental factor Lacan always puts to the fore. But it is also an experience of 'writing' or of 'reading' of some kind – not only because Lacan's practice is based on a fresh rereading of Freud's texts, not simply because the analysand's symptoms are organised like a written text, themes to which I shall return, but because the 'experience' of psychoanalysis introduces the two agents into a very complex enmeshing of speech and writing. Lacan's main tenet is that literature provides uniquely significant models that allow both the psychoanalyst and the patient to understand new configurations in dreams, symptoms, parapraxes.

This is why Lacan's lifelong confrontation with literature has always hinged on basic and almost naive questions, such as why do we write? Why do we read? What touches us in this apparently simple process? Why do we enjoy reading certain texts and hate other texts? What is the psychic economy implied by these acts? Where and how are our bodies touched by the 'letters' of literature? One consequence of these fundamental questions is that they imply a radical critique of everything that has been produced under the name of applied psychoanalysis or psychoanalytical criticism. As he states in texts devoted to single authors such as Duras or Joyce, Lacan refuses to psychoanalyse either the author or the works. This would be too easy and would miss the mark. In a foreword to an essay devoted to him, he writes this dense concluding statement in response to what literary criticism usually does with psychoanalysis:

> It is because the Unconscious needs the insistence of writing that critics will err when they treat a written work in the same way as the Unconscious is treated. At every moment, any written work cannot but lend itself to interpretation in a psychoanalytic sense. But to subscribe to this, ever so slightly, implies that one supposes the work to be a forgery, since, inasmuch as it is written, it does not imitate the effects of the Unconscious. The work poses the equivalent of the Unconscious, an equivalent no less real than it, as it forges the Unconscious in its curvature. And for the work, the writer who produces it is no less a forger, if he attempts to understand while it is being produced, as Valéry did when he addressed the new intelligentsia between the wars.[3]

Lacan points to Paul Valéry's attempts to analyse the functioning of his mind when he was writing some famous poems, an effort similar to Poe's famously mythical reconstruction of the genesis of 'The Raven' in *The Philosophy of Composition*. The paradox underlined by Lacan (the writer cannot know what he or she does when writing, since writing is caught up in the effects of the Unconscious, both being a production of writing) implies that one cannot understand the text in a reductive way, as the mere expression of a neurosis for instance. What he does with texts, then, is similar to what he does with patients: he treats 'the symptom as a palimpsest' and tries to understand the 'hole' created by the signifier, into which significations pour and vanish. However in both cases 'interpretation does not have to be true or false. It has to be just'. And Lacan continues his attack on imitation:

> The literary work fails or succeeds, but this failure is not due to the imitating of the effects of the structure. The work only exists in that curvature which is that of the structure itself. We are left then with no mere analogy. The curvature mentioned here is no more a metaphor for the structure than the structure is a metaphor for the reality of the Unconscious. It is real, and, in this sense, the work imitates nothing. It is, as fiction, a truthful structure.[4]

We shall have to reopen the 'Purloined Letter' by Poe and Lacan's systematic exploitation of this text to plumb the depths of the concept of a language that can provide the key to the structure of the unconscious and of a structure that describes the most fundamental codes of society. In this introduction Lacan names three authors he has used at various points of his career in order to invent and refine notions: Poe, with the famous letter whose meaning is never disclosed; Racine, whose *Athalia* he read to reach the concept of the 'quilting point' in Seminar III; and Sartre's political plays. He concludes that, like all these writers, he cannot remain the master of his 'intentions' when he writes.

In order to reconstruct Lacan's theory of literature – and as we have seen, there cannot be a theory without an experience, without a subjective discovery, without a dynamic 'understanding'– it is necessary first to provide a sense of the contemporary context of Lacan's reception in English-speaking countries. I believe that this has been strongly marked by Slavoj Zizek, whose groundbreaking culturalist and political approaches have never really worried about the place of literature in Lacanian theory. After this contextualisation, I shall discuss a number of 'keywords' and 'schemes' that have to be presented in their proper philosophical context. Finally, I shall discuss in some detail a few paradigmatic 'readings' of literary texts by Lacan: Poe's Dupin stories; several plays, including *Hamlet*, *Antigone* and Claudel's Coûfontaine trilogy; Gide's and Genet's works; Marguerite Duras's novels; Sade's novels and political tracts; and Joyce's entire works.

The range of Lacan's literary readings is not immense (his area of interest, nevertheless, was extremely broad and extended into anthropology, philosophy and scientific knowledge), but it does deal with essential texts in the Western canon, from Plato and Aristotle to Joyce and Duras, with inroads into out-of-the-way fields such as feminine mystics, troubadours, Dante, Gide, Genet and Surrealist poetry, all backed by constant reference to Freud's readings. (The Annotated Bibliography at the end of this book surveys Lacan's main texts and lists about twenty useful commentators.) The phrase 'the Last Word' in the title of this book alludes to Lacan's prophetic mode of address, and also to the current controversy about his allegedly 'Christianised' version of Freud's theories. The sequence of the letters of the alphabet will be played with systematically in an attempt to come to terms with what Lacan calls the materiality of writing and of letters. Finally, the 'Last Word' points to Lacan's personal identification with a living voice that was not above toying (playfully, of course, but with a hint of paranoiac delusion of grandeur) with an embodiment of truth. Lacan has often uttered, half-seriously, half-jokingly, 'I the Truth, speak'. We shall question this oracular mode of speech and see how its own material textualisation via writing leads to the placing of a theoretical wedge between the position of an author, a 'founder of discursivity' as Foucault would say, and the attendant delusion of founding a *logos* or dogma. An author needs the agency of 'dead letters' in order to let the 'spirit' – or ghost – survive.

When attempting to describe, or rather to introduce, what might be called a Lacanian poetic, this book will not reopen the various debates on Lacan's theory of rhetorics, his idiosyncratic use of 'metaphor' and 'metonymy' as equivalent to the main Freudian unconscious processes of 'condensation and displacement'; this has been done all too often, and has led to a simplified version of a purely 'structuralist' Lacan whose theses merely add a post-Freudian footnote to Roman

Jakobson's formalist poetics. However one debate I do wish to
address revolves around the function of literature, or more precisely
its status in Lacanian theory, an issue that has opposed Lacan to
Derrida and the Derridians. I shall try to show how, if both Lacan and
Derrida oppose the notion of 'applied psychoanalysis', they disagree
fundamentally about the function of literature. Some questions they
dispute are very broad. Can one reduce literature to truths? Can these
truths be used as examples of a general theory? Is literature as such
amenable to theoretical modelling? Far from voicing a traditional
defence of the 'autonomy' of literature, a literature that would have to
be defended from the encroachments of an imperialist psychoanalytic theory, Derrida resists the idea that one should be allowed to use
literary texts as examples. Here is what he says about a reading of Poe
in Lacan's Seminar (this reading will be presented at some length in
Chapter 4):

> From the outset, we recognize the classical landscape of applied
> psychoanalysis. Here applied to literature. Poe's text, whose status is
> never examined – Lacan simply calls it 'fiction' – finds itself invoked
> as an 'example'. An 'example' destined to 'illustrate', in a didactic
> procedure, a law and a truth forming the proper object of a seminar.
> Literary writing, here, is brought into an *illustrative* position: 'to illus-
> trate' here meaning to read the general law in the example, to make
> clear the meaning of a law or of a truth, to bring them to light in strik-
> ing or exemplary fashion. The text is in the sphere of the truth, and of
> a truth that is taught.[5]

Derrida, then, opposes the undecidability and 'infinity' of literature to
any idealisation that will aim at 'modellising' it in the name of a preestablished truth that will merely confirm its presuppositions.
However, as the two Derridian scholars who have examined Lacan's
theory of language and of the letter critically and at some length
conclude, it is because Lacan's theories do not form a totalising
system that they partly escape this reproach. Lacan's theses do not
just 'exploit' literary examples as so many confirmations of Freudian
insights, for instance, they also, since they present themselves as
fundamentally 'literary', give literature a much more ambiguous role
to play in them and for them: literature cannot be just an 'object'
caught up, traversed or exhibited by a discourse seeking a simple
justification through exemplification, it inhabits the theory from the

start, and makes it tremble, hesitate as to its own status, it ruins the mirage of a pure and clean theory neatly opposed to a few well-chosen examples. In *The Title of the Letter*, Lacoue-Labarthe and Nancy conclude their analysis of Lacan's elaboration on metaphor in the following terms:

> It is certainly not by chance if, along with the usual meaning of the word 'metaphor', Lacan also incorporates the literary genre where we seem to find it most often – namely poetry, and more precisely poetry circumscribed by two references: Hugo and surrealism.... That is, the poetry that we are able to designate, in its own terms, as that of the Word – of Divine Speech or of speech – and of the 'power' or 'magic' of words. An entire poetics of this order and an entire poetic practice of this style indeed subtend Lacan's text, here as elsewhere, in its literary references, its peculiar stylistic effects, and finally its theoretical articulations.[6]

Even if they reach a more critical assessment in the end, pointing out Lacan's equivocations about the role of Heidegger in his discourse and the crucial reference to a truth that is hidden but nevertheless known or implied by the psychoanalyst, they acknowledge that although Lacan is unable to found his own discourse rigorously, moving strategically between a pragmatics of therapy and borrowings from many other theories of philosophy, linguistics, rhetorics, anthropolgy and so on, at least he can be described as an essentially 'literary' theoretician, (or a home-made *bricoleur* of theory, to use Lévi-Strauss's useful term).

Lacoue-Labarthe and Nancy are not blind to the cunning effects derived by Lacan when he advances partly hidden, proffering his 'anti-pedagogy' as a subtler and more powerful form or domination:

> Hence Lacan's search for what he calls ... *formative effects*, a search which commands, on this we must insist, a certain recourse to speech, a certain use of the efficacy proper to speech and, as it were, of its *persuasive* power. This is in fact what animates and governs the entire Lacanian strategy, and accounts, up to a point, for the scrambling, the turns and disruptions which alter the demonstrative thread of his discourse. ... The fact that Lacan seeks to rescue psychoanalysis from a certain orthopedics does not prevent, on the contrary, his project as a whole from being orthopedic. It is, if you will, and *anti-orthopedic* orthopedics, or a counter-pedagogy, which is not unre-

lated, in its critical intention as well, perhaps to the most fundamental aim of philosophy, as a whole, at least since Socrates.[7]

It is clear that Lacan would not deny any of this, and as we shall see in
Chapter 9 he claims a line of descent from Socrates to Freud and
beyond. On the other hand, he would probably not agree with the two
critics when they align him with the project of the Enlightenment:
'Lacan's formation would thus be nothing else, presumably, than
παιδεια itself, or its revival in the *Bildung* of the Enlightenment (with
which Lacan explicitly affiliates himself) and of German Idealism,'[8]
even if, as they note in their reference, the introductory note
to the French *Ecrits* begins with an allusion to the *Lumières*
(Enlightenment), and opposes the deliberate obfuscation that has
been perpetuated in the name of the ego to the 'dawn' of a new
wisdom gained from Freud.[9] For as we shall see in our reading of
'Kant with Sade', Lacan does not hesitate to question the whole
humanistic and anti-humanistic conceptions of the Enlightenment.

The theoretical debate would have to focus on the main rhetorical
or strategic consequences of one central thesis in Lacanian theory:
that there is 'no metalanguage', that is, that truth can never be said
fully in a philosophical or scientific discourse made up of preliminary
definitions, basic concepts and fundamental axioms. As speaking
subjects who inhabit language, we are all plunged, even before our
birth, into a world of linguistic effects that are both momentous in
that they determine our fate, from our first and last names to our most
secret bodily symptoms, and also totally unaccountable, since this
belongs to the Unconscious, or in Lacanian terms, pertains to the
discourse of the Other. As a consequence one should not, for
instance, sum up Freud's basic ideas in a series of topological distinctions, like the usual ternary schema dividing the subject between the
ego, the super-ego and the id, a simplificative view to which he has
often been reduced in Anglo-Saxon countries. The only way to avoid
this ideological reduction to a pat *doxa* is to reopen Freud's texts and
read them carefully, literally.

Does this imply a need to defend literature from the encroachments
of Lacanian psychoanalysis? It might be useful to look at a completely
different approach, that of Slavoj Zizek, who not only accepts the idea
that literature can provide examples to illustrate Lacan's theories and
his own, but also multiplies the use of examples. For him, one might
say that everything can turn into an example, an illustration. There is

a priori no difference in status between literary texts, films, television programmes, cartoons, newspaper articles, stories we have just heard, dreams, jokes, you name it. Since everything belongs to cultural production, everything can be made sense of in the terms provided by Lacan's diagrams. For instance in *Looking Awry* and *Enjoy your Symptom!* we move deftly between Hitchcock's films and pre-Socratic philosophy, Shakespeare's tragedies and Hegel's philosophemes, science-fiction stories and horror movies, film noir and Kafka's parables, anti-Soviet jokes and considerations on current nationalism and pornography, and so on. Lacan provides a set of fundamental analyses or readings, and these are 'verified' or 'applied' through the use of popular culture.

Can this be described as a return to applied psychoanalysis? Yes, in the sense that Freud himself never really hesitated to use jokes, quotes from Shakespeare or Goethe, or the most varied cultural references to make his theoretical points. No, in the sense that one would not find here a systematic programme for the gradual expansion of a 'meta-psychology' or the full deployment of a classical *paideia*. Cultural studies, in this post-Lacanian mode, would tend to bridge the gap between Derrida's awareness that there is 'no outside the text' (*pas de hors-texte*) – or in other words, that is impossible to decide once and for all where a text 'stops' and its 'other' (be it defined as 'life', 'reality', 'the world') begins – and Zizek's insight into the generalised exemplarity and polymorphic relevance of cultural formations. Zizek has found not one but many models with Lacan's concepts, less organised into a system than into a dynamic network of schemes, a jumble of enigmas and paradoxes, showing a progression through various layers of reference and levels of 'modellisation'.

This is why Lacan's style, made up of polyphonic verbal echoes and heterogeneous levels of conceptualisation, should not be streamlined or abolished – it plays an essential role in a discourse that attempts to mime the opacity of the Unconscious while letting us float on the dense sea of words it request as a medium. Above all, this heterogeneous complexity should be usable in such a way that it may be *enjoyed*. This implies that stylistic density should not erect a barrier between the text and the reader but simply force the reader to be more curious, to become aware of the productive role of equivocation, grammatical dislocation and homophonic punning. In short it should invite the reader to experience language not just as an instrumental means of communication, but as an active medium, a site of cultural interaction that enables critical thought and a new sense of political or ethical agency, while, at times, indeed, permitting psychoanalysis to function as a 'talking cure'.

2 Lacan from A to L: Basic Lacanian Issues and Concepts

Like Poe and Mallarmé, with whom he has often been compared, Lacan was ahead of his time, having anticipated trends that we now tend to take for granted. Things changed significantly after the dissolution of his own school just prior to his death in 1981: this controversial figure bequeathed a complex theoretical legacy and an even more tangled institutional situation, with numerous schools created in his name throughout the world. Lacan's famous 'return to Freud' stressed the importance of the culture in which psychoanalysis has to work, and indeed his popularity has grown in recent years in the United States, fundamentally as a result of Zizek's successful attempts to popularise his thought by using Hitchcock, Hollywood and popular culture to explain Lacanian ideas. (See the discussion in the Annotated Bibliography at the end of this book). Zizek has been successful where more classical Lacanians have failed – despite the fact that he does not always avoid repetitiveness and circularity. For Zizek had the productive idea of beginning at the end with Lacan, that is, from the last seminars, taking his cue from a moment when the master was at his most gnomic, speaking enigmatically in mathemes and parables. Zizek managed to make sense of this mode of utterance, illuminating the 'gists' and riddles by examples taken from popular culture, to which they in turn provided a deeper meaning in a constant give and take.

Following Zizek and the important magazine *October,* a whole critical industry has sprouted from Lacan's remarks on the gaze and vision, often applied to film, from the British journal *Screen* to influential essayists such as Kaja Silverman and Laura Mulvey. Slavoj Zizek and Joan Copjec are among the most original critics who have applied these models to film (especially film noir). If one turns to remarks made in Seminar XI in reply to the publication of Merleau-Ponty's posthumous essay *The Visible and the Invisible*, one can follow how Lacan has rewritten and subverted a whole French school of phenomenology (one can think of Sartre's theory of the gaze in *Being and Nothingness*) in the light of the radical decentring brought about by the Unconscious and the big Other. Lacan's central insight – that each picture, each image, holds in various blots or stains a trace of the gaze of the Other as the place from which I cannot see myself but know that I am seen from outside – could be said to have triggered Barthes' idea of the *punctum*: a 'point' from which my specifically personal enjoyment is solicited while also pointing to the space beyond my own death.

However the massive impact of Lacanism on film theory, gender studies and cultural studies has often been at the cost of some important omission or the elision of some dimension, be it literary, clinical or conceptual. If I highlight the literary dimension of Lacan's teaching, it is not to stress the metaphoric style of his often mannered prose or to uncover all the hidden allusions in his dense texts, but to show that most of his important insights entail a revision of literary categories.One can present Lacan as a philosophical or a literary theoretician of psychoanalysis, but my claim here is that he did not use literary or philosophical references as examples or illustrations promoting stylistic indirection or cultural reverberations, but in order to think through and eventually resolve difficult problems. For instance texts such as *Hamlet*, *Antigone* and Claudel's Coûfontaine trilogy, as we shall see, were able to teach him something about the dialectics of desire even more than they allowed him to teach this dialectics via parables to the audiences of his seminars.

Thus after a remarkable commentary on *Antigone* in Seminar VII, he concluded that psychoanalysis would end up by presenting tragedy as a model of knowledge and of ethics. I shall show later how much of Lacan's reading of *Antigone* is in debt to Hegel's *Phenomenology of Spirit*, while exploring other themes that fall outside the conflict between the political and the ethical that both outline, and it is clear that his notion of the 'second death' and the role of beauty in tragedy could not have been reached without a careful textual consideration of *Antigone* and some key texts by Sade. If the final lesson he draws from *Antigone* is that one should not 'yield on one's desire', one can be tempted to see the whole of Lacan's teachings as determined by a 'tragic' approach to desire. Moreover, as we shall also see, Lacan's reading of *Hamlet* represents a systematic critique of Freud's canonical interpretation. By positing a Hamlet who is caught up in his mother's desire until he traverses death and the phallus – thanks to Ophelia and her sad fate – Lacan present a totally original reading of the play that remains very attentive to the interaction of its key signifiers, while working away from the usual interpretation of the play as just another staging of the Oedipus complex.

A good example of these intricate restagings of theoretical issues is provided by the concepts 'Desire' and 'the phallus', terms with which Lacan's theories have been closely associated. I shall try to show in my various readings that his conception of desire is indissociable from a concept of tragedy that he traces back to Sophocles, Shakespeare and Claudel. Conversely the phallus is fundamentally a comical notion since it is intimately bound up with the genre of comedy that begins with Aristophanes, reaches its maturity with Molière and culminates with Jean Genet. Literary genres and categories thus acquire a truth value that cannot be reduced to the mere exemplarity denounced, as we have seen, by Derrida.

In the same way, Lacan's main revolutionary contribution to post-Freudian theory has been to shift the emphasis from the father (whose figure always has frightening features inherited from the domineering and castrating leader of the horde portrayed by Freud) to the mother: in numerous readings of Freud's texts and literary classics (including *Hamlet*), he shows that human desire cannot find its place without questioning its link with the mother's desire. In the genesis of the human subject, it is the mother who can open up the realm of the 'Desire of the Other'. And in his later 'formulas of sexuation' (Seminar XX) there is room for a different sexuality that rejects the norm of the phallus and remains open to the Other. No need, therefore, to believe that he remains caught up in a nostalgic fascination for the phallus, or to understand it just as the 'signifier of lack' to which it has too often been reduced, since the phallus provides an introduction to a fundamentally funny, even ludicrous version of a bloated, excessive, impossible and symptomatic sexuality from which we are saved – but condemned at the same time – because we are 'speaking beings' whose fate has been written in advance. As Lacan wrote in a cryptic preface written in 1976, at a time when Joyce obsessed him: 'A certificate tells me that I was born. I repudiate this certificate: I am not a poet, but a poem. A poem that is being written, even if it looks like a subject.'[1]

In this context, one might be tempted to look to Lacan's own life to gain more leverage on his theories. Elisabeth Roudinesco, in an excellent biography of Lacan,[2] tries to understand Lacan not just as a person but also as a cultural phenomenon. Lacan's legacy has become indistinguishable from his own personality, in a symptomatic repetition of what took place with Freud. An awareness of Lacan's tortured personality will not detract from a balanced appreciation of his real genius, which may not always tally with the official version handed to us by his son-in-law and literary executor. It is important to examine the subjective and institutional logic that led Lacan to invent the 'variable session', thus engaging in shorter and shorter sessions that eventually led to his exclusion from the International Psychoanalytic Association. Throughout his life Lacan maintained a very picturesque and 'symptomatic' profile that marked him off as an outrageous figure, but he knew how to relate to the brightest intellectuals of his time, including Bataille, Kojève, Lévi-Strauss, Jakobson, Heidegger, Merleau-Ponty, Althusser and a group of clever if rather crazy mathematicians. It is indeed time to read the whole of Lacan's works and legacy in a rigorously historical way. Lacan's genius consisted in often thinking against himself, for instance producing a theory of the Unconscious identified with a speaking of truth at a time when he was lying not only to all the women with whom he was engaged but also to the International Psychoanalytic Association about the nature of his clinical practice, or courting simultaneously the recognition of Pope Pius XII and the French Communist Party. A deeper intimacy with this obstinate, histrionic, arrogant man provides a very distinctive glimpse of an atmosphere bristling with intellectual passion, of a world fascinated by the riddles of the Unconscious, desire and the Other.

Roudinesco and other historical commentators have pointed to the need to distinguish between various moments in the elaboration of Lacan's theories. The most elegant formulation is provided by Philippe Julien in *Jacques Lacan's Return to Freud*.[3] Following Julien, one can sketch three main stages of Lacan's theoretical elaboration, each of which is in turn marked by one of the three concepts he eventually managed to knit together. First the 'Imaginary' dominates and corresponds to the 1930s and 1940s, with the analysis of the mirror stage and aggressivity, then the stress falls on the 'Symbolic' in the 1950s and mid-1960s, and is finally relayed by the 'Real', starting in the late 1960s and extending into the 1970s. The final chapters of this book will address the determining role of the 'Borromean knot' that firmly ties the three circles together, until a fourth circle – the 'Symptom' – intervenes to complicate the scheme.

In the 1950s, Lacan's fascination with Saussure is often alluded to as an example of a creative distortion of basic concepts. This is the domain of what Lacan later called his *linguisterie*, not just linguistics but a systematic distortion of Saussurean dichotomies, focusing on the signifier/signified couple. Lacan's stroke of genius consisted less in linking Freud's couple, (condensation and displacement) in the *Interpretation of Dreams* with Jakobson's couple (metaphor/ metonymy), based on the same pathology of aphasia and language trouble, than in allegorising Saussure's 'bar', linking and separating the big S from the small s (while reversing the meaning of the two S's) and making it function as the Freudian bar of repression. This is a familiar story, and we have seen that Lacoue-Labarthe and Nancy provided a philosophical critique of it. Nevertheless one should not forget that Lacan soon encountered the limits of this model, hence his wish to move into a linguistics of the 'enunciation' in which the speaking subject is marked by an elision produced by an enunciation that punctures the 'enounced' or expressed statement. This new conceptual couple, which appeared as early as 1964 in Seminar XI, has too often been ignored. The new linguistics of enunciation does not replace the linguistics of the Signifier however, but adds another level of agency and production.

A similar genealogical approach would be to tackle Lacan from the philosophical angle. Starting with his juvenile admiration for Spinoza, moving on to his infatuation with Hegel, whom he first discovered with Bataille in Kojève's seminar, and then explored with the help of Hyppolite (who provided Lacan with a rigorous concept of the Other and of language as the negation of the 'thing'), going on to a brief flir- tation with Heidegger's second philosophy, in which it is language as Logos that 'speaks Being' (*Die Sprache spricht*), Lacan can indeed be called a philosopher of psychoanalysis. Yet unlike Bion (for whom he had a great admiration) he did not try to align his concepts with those of Locke, Kant or Hegel, but instead continued to criticise philosophy for an original sin that consisted in placing consciousness as the origin of meaning. One might say that Lacan's career was marked by several missed encounters with French phenomenology, leading to a misunderstanding with Merleau-Ponty (who nevertheless remained a personal friend), a break-up with Ricoeur and a fierce battle with

Derrida and Derrida's disciples (including Mikkel Borch-Jakobsen, a gifted 'introducer' to Lacan who at first stressed how philosophically sounder Freud was than Lacan but then turned completely anti-Freudian).[4] This should lead to a revision of Lacan's alleged structuralism, a 1950s philosophical movement that has too often been reduced to scientism and anti humanism. Structuralism does not merely entail a belief in the supremacy of anonymous structures that are integrated in a combinatory system. Moving from Lévi-Strauss to Foucault, one can now place Lacan in a tradition that is less obsessed with subjectless linguistics or kinship systems than with what could be called 'a thinking of the outside' that does not preclude a thinking of history. The important difference is that Lacan has always insisted on the possibility of 'calculating' the position of the subject; thus even if this subject is decentred and divided, the speaking and desiring subject remains at the core of the theory.

In this genealogy one can distinguish various layers in Lacan's archive, in all its confusion and multiplicity. There are three main types of text: the seminars (some published by Le Seuil, others in *Ornicar*, many more circulating as unauthorised versions), which provide a genetic account of Lacan's inventions; the psychoanalytical writings published in *La Psychanalyse* and other professional psychoanalytic journals; and the more belletristic essays, tending towards a literary or philosophical status, many published in *Critique* and later in *Scilicet*. The success of *Ecrits*, published in 1966, was partly due to the mixture of all these genres and tones. For the distinction between these textual sites is not purely descriptive, it regulates different strategies and generates different styles. The usual disjunction between speech and writing very early on acquired a structural function for Lacan, who on the one hand seemed to prefer speech to writing – thus publishing his only real 'book' very late: *Ecrits* was published when he was 65 – while on the other hand peppering his oral seminars with effects that can best be described as 'written', by which I mean not only the numerous graphs, schemes and other figures he drew on a blackboard in order to find an 'oral' inspiration from them, but also the way he would talk, moving from parenthesis to parenthesis, circling around a theme and making a virtue of indirection, allusiveness and paradox.

The difficulty is not restricted to Lacan's 'writings'; even if he sharply distinguished between the 'oral' teaching of his seminars and the published 'writings' which had to be dense, witty and intertextual, this distinction was not water tight since the texts of the seminars were partly written in advance, whereas he expected, as he often said, to find a response to what he had just uttered, if not verbally then at least on the faces of his audience. In a seminar in 1965 Lacan explicitly compared his indirect and digressive progression to a kind of writing: 'Let it be said in passing that if my discourse unfolds from the parenthesis, from suspense and from its closure, then from its often very embarrassed resumption, you should recognize there, once again, the structure of writing.'[5] This is at a time when the signifier is brought closer to writing, since it too creates a 'hole in the real'. In a later statement at Yale University, Lacan insisted that without written documents, no history is possible: 'Without written documents, you know you're in a dream. What the historian must have is a text: a text or a scrap of paper. At all events, there must be somewhere, in an archive, something that certifies in writing and the absence of which makes history impossible.... What cannot be certified in writing cannot be regarded as history.'[6] I shall return later to Lacan's insistence on writing as a foundation, from Freud's earliest insights into a 'scientific psychology' to Joyce's metamorphosis into a fascinating *jouissance* of the ego-as-writing, an insistence made all the more curious by the fact that he also relied on the 'oral history' of his seminars to create and perpetuate his own legend.

This is why it is important to note that the more 'literary' seminars correspond to one crucial decade, which started with the discovery of Poe's 'Purloined Letter' in the spring of 1955, was followed by a discussion of Gide's psychobiography in 1958, moved on to *Hamlet*, a play that allowed Lacan to criticise Freud's Oedipus theory while engaging with a new dialectics of desire in 1959–60, before exploiting the vein of tragedy in *Antigone* in the spring of 1960 and Claudel the following year, all this via readings of texts by Sade (1959–60) and Marguerite Duras in 1965. When Lacan published his *Ecrits* in 1966 he could indeed declare that this inclusive anthology was not only a 'written text' but also, as he would say much later, had to be considered as pure 'literature'.[7] The systematic engagement with literary texts marked the slow transition from what can be described as a rhetorical and structuralist theory of the Symbolic based on the logics of the signifier to a theory of literary language caught between the effects of the written 'knot' or 'hole' and the simply spoken signifier. It took Lacan another ten years (after a series of investigations of logics, mathematics and topology) to 'find' Joyce on his way to the

'Symptom' in 1975. My focus will thus be on what could be called the 'literary turn' in Lacan, or a moment situated half-way between the early 1950s with the stress on rhetorics, Hegelianism and the Name-of-the-Father, and the Lacan of the 1970s, with more and more math-emes, the algebra of the four discourses leading to games with a topology still lacking the Borromean knot.

In the philosophical and literary genealogy just outlined, one might say that Lacan used literary models to move away from the term 'structure' coupled with the 'logics of the signifier', seen as access to the language of the Unconscious determined by metaphorical processes (symptoms) and metonymic processes (desire creating effects along the verbal chain), to a more intense and abrupt confrontation with the Real, with perversion, with the lack in the Other connected with a *jouissance* of the Other. The term Symptom was used more and more systematically by Lacan in the 1970s, not only as a clinical term but also as a literary concept: it seems that the Symptom had taken the place of the Letter of earlier formulations. We have to be clear about what distinguishes a sign from a symptom. While a sign is made up of the two sides we have already encountered, a symptom is not just a sign of something (Dora's persistent cough is not a sign of her having a bad cold, but a symptom that aims at making some sense by embodying her identification both with her father and her father's mistress, through what she imagines as their purely oral love making). Lacan always insisted that a psychoanalytic symptom could be treated by linguistic ambiguity – precisely what Freud failed to do with Dora, to whom he was too eager to announce his 'truth'. This is why Lacan's apparent detour through the works of James Joyce was not a coincidence, nor was his decision to rename Joyce the *sinthome* – a curious portmanteau word that combines 'sin', 'Aquinas', 'tomes' and of course 'the saint' – or saintly man of litera-ture. One may even surmise that Joyce thus functioned as Lacan's alter ego, at least insofar as he presented his own literary ego as the Symptom.

The Real and the Symptom converge in a place that Freud perceived both as a limit to his own practice and as a source of fasci-nation (as he testifies in his purely literary encounter with Schreber): psychosis. Lacan began his career with a bold investigation of para-noia, choosing one case as a starting point for a career that already appeared distinctively different from classical psychiatry. His still untranslated psychiatric thesis on paranoia – *De la psychose para-*

noïque dans ses rapports avec la personnalité (1932) – poses an hermeneutic problem: is Lacan already 'Lacanian' in a thesis that quotes Freud only sparingly and relies on conventional psychiatric nosography and philosophical concepts such as personality? If one should decide that Lacan finds his own concepts and methods only later, then his essay 'Of a question preliminary to any possible treatment of psychosis', coming from his 1955–56 seminar, provides a crucial synthesis of clinical considerations and post-Freudian conceptualisation. The notion of a 'foreclosure' from the Symbolic that precipitates a return to the Real is indeed elaborated after a long confrontation with Schreber's text (especially when Lacan analyses Schreber's 'fundamental language', the *Grundsprache* spoken by God and by birds) and Freud's text on Schreber. Such is also the case with the notion of the Name-of-the-Father and of the paternal metaphor, both of which suggest a radical reworking of the Freudian legacy. This has launched all the fascinating readings of horror movies and science fiction stories with which Zizek illustrates the condition of psychosis as the 'return of the Thing' in the Real (see for instance his *Looking Awry*, 1991).

The symptom is first described as a metaphor (the creative crossing of the bar of repression separating the signified from the signifier) then as an ego: the subject of literature, the writing and written subject will ultimately become a myth for culture. We have reached the enigmatic position of a Joyce, through the notion of 'symptomatic readings', a term that was probably coined by Lacan although it was first conceptualised by Althusser. When he initiated a systematic reading of Karl Marx's *Capital*, the French philosopher Althusser used the concept of 'symptomatic' readings in the hope of finding the epistemological break that would divide the 'pre-Marxist Marx' from the really 'Marxist Marx'. Althusser then engaged in a productive dialogue with Lacan that endured a decade and was instrumental in allowing Lacan at last to address an audience of young and radical philosophers from the Ecole Normale Supérieure. The impact of their collaboration on the institutional history of French psychoanalysis was enormous, and there are many affinities between *Reading Capital* and *Ecrits*. Althusser published one of the earliest introductions to a 'scientific' and 'political' version of Lacanian theory in 1964, when he wrote his 'Freud and Lacan'. In his praise of Lacan, Althusser managed to reconcile Marxists (who had remained quite suspicious of what they saw as Freud's petty-bourgeois attitude) and psychoanaly-

sis. Althusser was very perceptive when he described the inner necessity of Lacan's baroque style as deriving from a deliberate pedagogy:

> having to teach the theory of the unconscious to doctors, analysts or
> analysands, Lacan gives them, in the rhetoric of his speech, the
> mimed equivalent of the language of the unconscious, which, as all
> know, is in ultimate essence 'Witz', pun or metaphor, whether failed
> or successful, the equivalent of what they experience in their practice
> as either an analyst or a patient.[8]

Althusser also calls up the complex strategy of Lacan:

> Whence the contained passion, the impassioned contention of
> Lacan's language, which can live and survive only in a state of alert
> and prepossession: the language of a man already besieged and
> condemned by the crushing strength of threatened structures and
> guilds to anticipate their blows, at least to feign returning them
> before they have been received, thus discouraging the adversary from
> crushing him under its own.[9]

Of course Althusser was soon to express some skepticism and then
disenchantment. In the 1970s, he felt that Lacan was not scientific
enough, that he flirted too much with Hegel, Heidegger and
Wittgenstein, and finally embodied that detestable French tendency
to 'tinker' (*bricoler*) with philosophy. In Althusser's view, Lacan
started very auspiciously by providing psychoanalysis what it lacked
with Freud: a scientific status, provided by Lacan when he stated that:
'The Unconscious is structured like a language'. Unhappily, Lacan did
not rest content with this groundbreaking discovery – he wanted to
become a 'philosopher of psychoanalysis' but was ill-equipped for the
task.

> Lacan was thus playing a double game. To philosophers he brought
> the guarantee of the master who is 'supposed to know' what Freud
> thought. To psychoanalysts he brought the guarantee of the master
> who is 'supposed to know' what thinking (philosophically) means. He
> duped everybody, and quite plausibly, despite his extreme trickiness,
> he duped himself as well.[10]

Ironically the example of Lacan being 'duped' by himself sends us
back to Poe's character Dupin: Althusser mentions the conclusion of

Lacan's seminar on the 'Purloined Letter', which ends with the outrageous statement that 'a letter always arrives at its destination' – a statement that may call up the worst philosophy of destiny, fate or idealistic teleology (this reproach is shared by Althusser and Derrida, as we shall see).

After May 1968, Lacan began to attract more and more of Althusser's former students to his discipleship, at a time when Lacan asserted that it was 'Marx who had invented the symptom', a notion that has been intelligently exploited by Zizek. (Space constraints prevent me from investigating what could be called Lacan's psycho-Marxism of the late 1960s.) From Lacan's personal ties with Althusser to Zizek's highly congenial contributions to issues of contemporary politics, from remarks on subjective alienation that recall a still very Hegelian 'young Marx' to the attempt to posit a Freudian *Mehrlust* (*plus-de-jouir*) that would be an exact equivalent to Marx's *Mehrwert* (surplus value), the connections between Lacan and a structuralist version of Marxism are innumerable and perhaps not completely understood. It is in the theory of the four discourses, elaborated in 1971, that we find Lacan's response to Marxism. The scheme of the four discourses is extremely condensed, and aims at introducing the concept of *plus-de-jouir* into the following tabulation:

$$\begin{array}{cccc}
\text{U} & \text{M} & \text{H} & \text{A} \\
\dfrac{S2}{S1} \to \dfrac{a}{\$} & \dfrac{S1}{\$} \to \dfrac{S2}{a} & \dfrac{\$}{a} \to \dfrac{S1}{S2} & \dfrac{a}{S2} \to \dfrac{\$}{S1} \\
\text{Discourse of} & \text{Discourse of} & \text{Discourse of} & \text{Discourse of} \\
\text{the University} & \text{the Master} & \text{the Hysteric} & \text{the Analyst}[11]
\end{array}$$

This grid is based on a very ancient scheme: it repeats with only minor modifications the basic pattern of the medieval logic of statements, in which one moves from one term to its opposite, then to its negation, and then to the negation of the negation. Thus A and E and I and O are contraries, while A and O and I and E are contradictories in the traditional scheme:

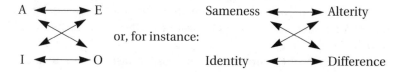

The grid surfaces again with Greimas's semiotic square,[12] before being adapted by Lacan with important variations. Lacan explains that the four corners of his square correspond to four levels of agency, the top line indicating a visible axis of determination, while the bottom line (with a recursive arrow in some variations) is the hidden locus of 'truth' or production. Thus each square or 'quadripode' can be viewed as made up of two fractions articulating the latent (bottom line) and the explicit (top line):

$$\frac{\text{agent}}{\text{truth}} \quad \rightarrow \quad \frac{\text{other}}{\text{production (or loss)}}$$

According to Lacan, S1 is the 'master signifier', S2 is 'unconscious knowledge', the barred S is the old barred subject of desire, and a is not just the old '*objet petit a*', missing as such and causing desire, but also a neo-Marxist equivalent of 'surplus value': 'surplus *jouissance*' or, literally, 'more enjoyment!' (*plus-de-jouir*). Why are there four discourses only, out of the possible 24 provided by the combinatory? The four discourses produce each other, each generating the next discourse by the simple rotation of a quarter circle. There is therefore both a genealogy and a circularity to observe.

These are not clinical categories: they do not overlap with the usual categories of 'the discourse of the obsessional, of the hysteric, of the psychotic or of the perverse'. Lacan was later tempted to add a few more discourses (such as the discourse of capitalism, or the discourse of science), but these four positions allowed him to account for the entire structure of the social link. Science can indeed be associated with the discourse of the Hysteric insofar as it aims at procuring new knowledge, while it is linked to the discourse of the University when this knowledge is merely catalogued and transmitted. Similarly the discourse of capitalism falls under the jurisdiction of the discourse of the Master, since it is also the discourse of power, of the institutions, of the state – although in Seminar XVII Lacan repeatedly told the leftist students who tried to 'subvert' his seminar that if the Soviet or Maoist models of society they admired viewed the domination of the discourse of the university as a dream of the bureaucracy achieving power, they themselves were in quest of a master – and they would have it![13]

Freud had posited three main 'impossible tasks' – to educate, to govern and to heal. Lacan added a fourth one: that of the desiring subject exemplified by the discourse of the hysteric. Freud had famously written: 'It almost looks as if analysis were the third of those "impossible" professions in which one can be quite sure of unsatisfying results. The other two, much older-established, are the bringing-up of children and the government of nations.'[14] Lacan's meta-discourse attempts to identify points of impossibility in four fundamental discursive patterns and to provide a formalisation of what Bourdieu calls the '*socius*' – society seen as a series of significant practices – from one main point of view: psychoanalysis. One should not object that psychoanalysis falls back on the idea of a metalanguage denounced, as we have seen, by Lacan: here the analyst's discourse is only one of four. Here society is caught from the specific angle of psychoanalytic practice, a practice in which everything is by definition reduced to speech and its effects, but also a practice that highlights what is most commonly forgotten in these issues: it stresses the place and function of the subject's enjoyment, asks what is the main signifier that can provide ideals or a programme, and looks for a dialectisation of knowledge (understood as 'unconscious knowledge') and *jouissance* (in the shape of an elusive or impossible object, this 'surplus enjoyment').

If we take literature as an example, we can see how these four discourses can map out the field of literary production and investigation. The Master's discourse on literature is close to Plato's position when he explains that poets should not be allowed in the City, and only military songs are useful in time of war. Or, conversely, this is the position of young researchers who wish quickly to find a 'hot' 'new' theory as a 'handle' that will allow them quickly to gain academic power or prestige. On the other hand the University's discourse consists in putting knowledge above all – knowledge is the main agent to trigger a specific enjoyment. Knowledge is seen as enjoyment in and for itself, without any consideration of the subjective position of the person who puts it to work. The discourse of the Hysteric puts the subject in the first place, but in order to insist upon subjective division and a quest for the master signifier. One signifier will orient all the quest and be taken for the whole truth, love for this key aspect will erase all the rest, in the hope of proving to all theoreticians that they are wrong or lacking in some way. Finally, the discourse of the Analyst aims at letting unconscious enjoyment appear as the main force at work in a text, and sees this as the cause of the division of the subject.

The divided subject will not be reduced to the singular reader as in the discourse of hysteria, but will be the site of a more generalisable reading process (hence the use of literature as made up of ready-made parables and allegories). A master signifier will indeed allow for the production of an unconscious truth about the text. For instance, as we shall see with the reading of *Hamlet*, the pun linking Ophelia to *o-phallos* yields for Lacan a theory of the phallus as a ghost.

As always, Lacan's graphs and schemes aim at providing a particular writing of the subject's interaction with the Other and its objects. They all sketch a more and more comprehensive logic of the divided subject. One can start from the earliest of these graphs, the L schema introduced as early as 1954 in the seminar on the ego, and also in *Ecrits*.[15] It seems to be the main graph from which all other graphs and mathemes derive. Presenting a Z rather than an L, it provides a clear depiction of the zigzag of unconscious desire, a desire that structures the subject (S) from the locus of the Other (O) through the mediation of objects (o') and the ego (o).[16]

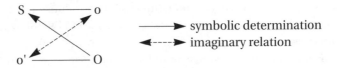

Note that the subject is not yet barred here, but is already distinguished from the ego, seen as a projection. This is the easiest and simplest of Lacan's many schemes, and it gives visual support to the idea that the subject is determined by the Unconscious as the locus of the Other while being mystified by what it takes as its whole world: the imaginary realm dominated by the interaction between the ego and the objects of desire. This is the scheme that underpins the Poe reading, to which we shall return.

The S became barred in Seminar V (1957-58) to indicate that the subject is split (as Freud had shown when he talked about *Ichspaltung* in a late text), and in 1958–59, at the time of the *Hamlet* reading, Lacan multiplied the terms that refer to this division: *Spaltung*, fading, cut, *refente*, *éclipse*, *Verwerfung*, ellipsis, abolition, *évanouissement* and so on. In the 1962–63 Seminar X on anxiety the divided subject is the subject of fantasy while in Seminar XI, on the 'Four Fundamental Concepts of Psychoanalysis', the subject is divided between utterance and statement. There the division of the subject is

pushed further, since Lacan now states that a subject is only represented by a signifier and for another signifier (inverting the usual
order). The unitary signifier (S1) emerges as the *trait unaire* or mark-
one from S2 as binary knowledge. The S2 is the originary repression
Freud had elaborated: the subject is thus instituted as the certainty of
a 'lack-in-knowledge'. Later S2 becomes the signifier of the subject's
alterity, while S1 is the signifier of its unity. One can see in Lacan a
tendency to rework his schemes over the years, to reelaborate them
until they become so complex that he himself becomes lost in them.
Such is the case with the scheme of *jouissance* at the end of
'Subversion of the Subject and dialectics of desire'. It appears as a
series of mystifying doodles added in the footnotes to the *Hamlet*
seminar and also in *Ecrits*.[17] This graph, which receives new layers of
complexity through four revisions, resembles a corkscrew, with two
superimposed curves bisecting a curious question mark. It attempts
to do too much, situating desire, *jouissance*, castration, the signifier,
the fantasy, primal repression and the voice all on one scheme. It can
be read at many levels, and allegorises so many developments that it
should be treated less as a pedagogical tool or support than as a kind
of writing: here one sees Lacan groping for the mathematical simplicity of the later 'mathemes', when the new conceptual algebra replaces
the tentative and tantalisingly obscure schemes and graphs of the
1960s.

In the final years one can observe a tendency towards greater
simplicity and condensation. The main formulations of the 1970s
tend to correspond to an almost numerological progression. Lacan
seems to be merely counting 1, 2, 3 ... and 4! One corresponds to the
major enigma of Being as One. Lacan repeats 'There's the One' in an
untranslatable idiom (*Y'a d'l'Un*) *that* is supposed to account for the
link between the soul and love in Seminar XX. Two: there are two
sexes, and no subject can be said to be determined by biology alone
as a fate, since the formulas of sexuation show how one can place
oneself either under the sign of castration (defining normal male
sexuality) or in a 'feminine position' of *jouissance* that is not ruled by
castration. Three: there are three registers, and three only – the Real,
the Symbolic and the Imaginary –, and they should ideally be tied
together in a Borromean knot to stressg their complete interdepen-
dence and lack of hierarchy. Four: one has to wait for the fourth ring
of the Symptom or Sigma to appear, which happens with the Joyce
seminar this will be explored in Chapter 10.

In later years Lacan tended to identify more and more with the discourse of female mystics who spoke of God as their ineffable lover. Thus another important issue is female sexuality and the feminist controversy that surrounded Freud's conceptions and then Lacan's apparent bias towards the phallus. In Lacan's Seminars one can find his continuing interest in psychoanalysts such as Riviere and Jones, and it might be contended that he elaborated his idea of the phallus in an attempt to provide an answer to the many questions raised by the debate on Freud in the 1920s. Lacanian psychoanalysis clearly benefited from feminist critique, and one wonders whether Lacan would have come up with his ground-breaking formulas of sexuation in Seminar XX had he not had to deal with the '*psych. et po.*' opposition he met in his own ranks in the early 1970s. Jacqueline Rose asserts very cogently that only psychoanalysis allows women and men to question their political fate as gendered beings. Mitchell and Rose's careful edition of Lacan's essays on feminine sexuality[18] has led to a more balanced account of Lacan's alleged 'phallocentrism' and of the rift with early American feminism. When Lacan announces an 'Other' sexuality that is not under the domination of the phallus, he reflects a line of writers (not all women) who – from Marguerite de Navarre to Marguerite Duras – throw new light on a non-phallic *jouissance*, perhaps a *jouissance* of the whole body, or a *jouissance* of the mystical soul.

This is why Lacanian readings of literature have an important role to play in 'queer' theory, and theoreticians of gender such as Judith Butler and Catherine Millot have shown that if the subject cannot be reduced to the ego, one should not forget that sexual identities are produced by unconscious performative agencies. It is only a determination by the Unconscious that can make sense of the issue of sexual identity, a point that has often been miscontrued in the name of Foucault's notion of power, especially when it is superimposed onto Lacanian paradigms. Lacan's intervention in the discourse of psychoanalysis reminds us that we cannot reduce alterity to social, sexual or ethnic difference: Lacan has always insisted on the fundamental 'uninhabitability' of the world of the Other, except perhaps through writing, in a fiction that bypasses ordinary imaginary processes. One of the important issues raised by Queer theory is acceptance or refusal of the moral condemnation that seems to be attached to the concept of perversion. It is clear that Lacan does not use the term in connection with homosexuality, rather he uses it to describe a structure (for instance when talking of Gide's paedophilia, as we shall see). Here the questions revolve around one main worry: was Lacan perhaps too close to perversion? If his model of desire was elaborated through a meditation on Sade and sadism that barely disguised his fascination for the *divin Marquis*, can Sade can be described as a potential model for Lacan? Sade opened up for Lacan the realm of the *jouissance* of the Other, as we shall see in Chapter 7, a crucial concept that enabled him to revise his entire system in the 1970s. While in traditional Freudian literature, studies of fetishism have played a leading role in what can described as the negation of castration, Lacan focuses more on figures of excess and *jouissance* – as we shall see in the literary field with the figures of Sade and Joyce.

This sends us back to the radical opposition between an indulgent fascination for a *jouissance* that negates the law of castration and a more radical ethics that posits the structuring function of the law. When the subject identifies him- or herself with such a drive object, the cause of desire, what is at stake is a *plus-de-jouir* (surplus enjoyment) for the other body, in the non-knowledge of the *jouissance* of the Big Other's irreducible otherness. If *jouissance* is Lacan's version of 'Beyond the Pleasure Principle', it is important to understand how this concept of *jouissance* remains crucial to his approach to literature. Even if the object of the drive is what Lacan calls his unique invention, under the name of the 'object small a' (*objet petit a*), Lacan's central concept, as Nestor Braunstein has argued,[19] his real 'signature', consists in letting Freud's *Lust* drift from its usual meaning of pleasure to a more and more excessive, perverse, murderous even enjoyment he calls *jouissance*. The term *jouissance* has a complex genealogy in Lacan's seminars, and while it maintains all the meanings of the French word – sexual climax, excessive enjoyment, legal ownership – it has been variously inflected by different commentators. Braunstein has sketched the whole spectrum of the concept and the various uses to which *jouissance* is put in Lacanian theory, which helps us understand how, while the concept originally opposed a desire through which the subject was marked by language, it played a more and more crucial function in the later seminars. Does *jouissance* provide the basis for the only ontology Lacanian psychoanalysis admits of? Since one can speak of a 'feminine *jouissance*', are there several types of *jouissance* or just one? What is the specific *jouissance* of the symptom, which makes us at times hold so dearly to the most crippling disease? The concept is especially fruitful in the handling of clinical cases (for instance in the pathology of drug addiction), but literature provides another privileged field of investigation while offering another haunting question: in what sense can there be a sublimation of *jouissance?*

The idea of 'sublimated *jouissance*' forces us to look closer at what Lacan has to say about the 'letter', and letters in general, as providing a rim, a margin encircling the erotic hole left by *jouissance*. In his analyses of Poe, Gide and Joyce, Lacan identifies the structural function of a letter that never betrays its content but gives shape to the libidinal logic by which the subject is determined. Lacan's reading of Poe's 'Purloined Letter' remains emblematic of his entire strategy, which is why he gave it place of honour in his 1966 *Ecrits*. A few years after the Poe seminar was published, Derrida attacked Lacan on several counts, including for jumping to the conclusion that the circuit of the letter would always close upon itself. Like Althusser, Derrida criticised Lacan's 'idealism' in treating the letter as an allegory of a signifier that would always exemplify a psychoanalytic truth (allegedly reduced to castration). When Barbara Johnson came on the scene she showed how Poe's notion of a quasi-Freudian 'repetition compulsion' had worked on Derrida himself, forcing him to repeat Dupin's and Lacan's oversights, to be 'framed' by their texts even as he was 'framing' Lacan. This could no doubt be applied to Althusser too. Such a vertiginous spiral of commentaries reinscribing a previous straight line into a circuit proves that the letter possesses a logic of its own, a logic fundamentally linked with the Unconscious, understood both as hidden knowledge and as a writing machine. It is this first notion that we must explore.

3 The Theory of the Letter: *Lituraterre* and Gide

Lacan's persistent emphasis on a 'return to Freud' should not be understood as an ideological slogan, as are most returns to an older version of a doctrine are, or as a wish to promote a 'purer' or more radical Freudianism. It is primarily a request for French psychoanalysts to start *reading* Freud. Lacan's central insight is that if Freud is read literally, the main practitioners of the movement Freud founded under the name of psychoanalysis will realise that he is mainly talking about language and not about 'instincts' or 'depth psychology' when plumbing the elusive depths of the Unconscious. Here lies Lacan's revelation, a notion he did not hit upon immediately but crystallised in the early 1950s: language and the Unconscious have a similar structure (with all the misunderstandings that the motto 'The Unconscious is structured *like* a language' can entail). Lacan also set out to read a certain aspect of Freud that had almost disappeared from official psychoanalysis. He first reread the early Freud, who wrote on jokes, dreams and hysteria, a Freud who was caught in *statu nascendi* as it were, as he invented psychoanalysis out of the wild somatisations exhibited by Vienna's beautiful hysterics. Lacan also treated the later Freud very seriously, the Freud who wrote about the *Spaltung* of the subject, about interminable analysis, about culture's discontents, before finally producing a wonderful 'historical novel' about Moses.

If one takes a closer look at Freud's earlier writings, his first models for unconscious processes came close to a sort of psychic 'writing' or an interaction of 'traces' – a notion that was already present in his pre-analytical work on aphasia, where Freud had postulated the agency of some 'paths' that could be written over. But it was in his letter to Fliess of 6 December 1896 (often referred to by Lacan as

Letter no. 52, following the classification of the editors) that he
provided the clearest formulation:

> As you know, I am working on the assumption that our psychical
> mechanism has come about by a process of stratification: the mater-
> ial present in the shape of memory-traces is from time to time
> subjected to a rearrangement in accordance with fresh circumstances
> – is, as it were, transcribed. Thus what is essentially new in my theory
> is the thesis that memory is present not once but several times over,
> that it is registered in various species of 'signs'.[1]

He illustrated this with a schema that describes different 'tran-
scripts' as connected but distinct:[2]

```
                  I          II         III
   Pcpt. ——Pcpt.-s —— Uc. ——— Pc. —— Consc.
    X  X      X  X      X  X      X  X      X  X
      X       X  X      X  X       X         X
```

The first block consists of perception neurones, which register
consciousness without keeping a memory of it; then come (in I) the
neurones that register the perceptions, followed by II the second
reelaboration of these traces in such a way that they become inaccessible to consciousness, and can therefore be called unconscious
traces. In III the neurones of the preconscious intervene and offer a
third transcription with a stress on verbal images and links to the official ego before one reaches simple consciousness.

This is the model Freud elaborated in his 1895 'Project for a scientific psychology', a manuscript he sent to Fliess but never cared to
retrieve. Lacan commented on this text in a number of seminars,
always insisting that it contained the most scientific model of the
Unconscious. It is indeed Freud's most materialist text, since he
hoped to found psychology upon a theory of purely quantitative
processes based on differences between what he called the 'ϕ
neurones' and the 'ψ neurones'. The ϕ neurones are permeable
neurones that perceive the external world, while the ψ neurones
retain traces of these perceptions.[3] Memory is represented by a
process of *Bahnung* – literally 'opening the path' and 'linking' – which
connects certain types of ψ neurones.[3]

Freud seems to have quickly abandoned this speculative drift, for complex reasons but above all because he was immersing himself in the double project of the dream book and his notes on jokes and the Unconscious. However, for Lacan this constituted a crucial text to which he returned again and again, and we see it looming large in Seminar VII's notion of the 'Thing', a concept that comes straight from the *Entwurf*. What this means for Lacan is the idea of an 'archiwriting' of the Unconscious, upon whose basis the later bifurcation of speech and writing can be established. The Unconscious is fundamentally writing, and the battery of these archaic inscriptions antedates the child's first immersion in a 'babble' of half-meaningful signifiers that Lacan calls *lalangue* (one could translate this as 'lallalanguage'). Transference with other speaking beings will nevertheless start with the oral side of language, which is also the element that psychoanalysis primarily exploits.

Freud developed this equivalence between the Unconscious and writing in a number of texts, the most famous of which is probably 'The Mystic Writing Pad', a text very well commented upon by Derrida in *Writing and Difference*.[4] The equivalent of Freud's essay on the Unconscious, presented as a 'writing and erasing' tablet, can be found in Lacan's curious essay on literature, or rather on letters. 'Lituraterre' is a rather difficult text that was written for a special issue of a relatively new quarterly auspiciously called *Littérature*. Lacan's piece has pride of place: it opens the issue, entitled 'Literature and Psychoanalysis' and is printed in more widely spaced type than the essays that follow. His first lines gloss the startling word he uses as his title, 'Lituraterre', a word that does not exist in French and transposes the syllables of 'literature':

> This word can be warranted by Ernout and Meillet's etymological dictionary: *lino, litura, liturarius*. However it came to me from a pun that, it happens, makes sense through its wit [*de ce jeu du mot dont il arrive qu'on fasse esprit*]: the spoonerism returning to my lips, the permutation to my ear.
>
>   This dictionary (just have a look at it) augurs well by allowing the point of departure (departure here means partition) I took in Joyce's equivocation when he (James Joyce, I say) slides from *a letter* to *a litter*, I translate, from a letter to garbage.[5]

Lacan's late style is in evidence here: puns and verbal creations abound (for instance he refers to Mrs McCormick – a would-be benefactress of Joyce who had put a condition to her credit, namely that he should consult with Jung – as 'messe-haine', which combines 'mass' and 'hatred' into a well-meaning but hateful Maecenic patron who implies that one should 'take' psychoanalysis as one would take a shower) and the highly allusive style create a rich and idiosyncratic texture of allusions.

While announcing the systematic confrontation with Joyce a few years later, Lacan is being self-referential in this text, since he keeps returning his readers to his Poe seminar, a seminar in which, his faithful followers will not have forgotten, he referred to Joyce's grouping of literary apostles around him: '"A letter, a litter": in Joyce's circle, they played on the homophony of the two words in English.'[6] This allusion to a recurrent pun in *Finnegans Wake* ('The letter! The litter!')[7] or to a series of practical jokes among Joyce's disciples – remember the last text in *Our Exagmination*, called 'A Litter' (to Mr. germ's Choice) and signed by Vladimir Dixon[8] – points to future evocations of Lacan's meeting with Joyce in the 1975–76 seminar (this will be examined in Chapter 10).

The first note struck by Lacan in this piece is a scathing attack on current psychoanalytic readings:

> For psychoanalysis, the fact that it be appended to the Oedipus, does not qualify it in any way to find its bearing in Sophocles' text. The evocation by Freud of a text by Dostoyevsky is not enough to assert that textual criticism, hitherto a private hunting ground reserved to academics, has received any fresh air from psychoanalysis (*L*, 3–4).

He then opposes the 'ironic' title he gave to his *Ecrits* to previous attempts by literary-minded psychoanalysts to engage with literature: of course they are allowed to do so, but their judgments will not carry more weight because of their profession. He recalls his tactical decision to open *Ecrits* with a reading of Poe's story, and surveys the main elements of his interpretation (we shall return to this issue in Chapter 4). He stresses the curious lack of content of the 'purloined letter', distinguishing the letter from the signifier it carries:

> My criticism, if it can be called literary, can only bear (I hope) on what makes Poe a writer when he gives us such a message about the letter. Clearly, if he does not tell this as such, this is not a defect but an all the more rigorous avowal.

Nevertheless such an elision could not be elucidated by some feature in his psychobiography: it rather appears blocked to us. (Thus, the kind of psychoanalysis that has cleaned up all the other texts of Poe declares here that its housecleaning meets a limit).

No more could my own text be solved by my own psychobiography: as for instance by the wish I reiterate of being at last read correctly. For, in order to think this, one would have to develop what I say that the letter carries so as to *always* reach its destination.

It is sure that, as always, psychoanalysis receives from literature a less psychobiographic conception even when taking repression as its main spring.

For me, if I propose to psychoanalysis the idea of a letter in sufferance, it is because this shows its own failure. And here is where I bring some light: when I invoke the enlightenment, I demonstrate where it makes a *hole*. This is well-known in optics, and the recent physics of the photon is underpinned by it.

This is a method by which psychoanalysis might justify its intrusion better: for if literary criticism could indeed renew itself, it would be because of the presence of psychoanalysis forcing texts to measure up to it, the enigma remaining on the side of psychoanalysis (*L*, 4).

We shall return shortly to the concept of the letter as a hole, but what I would like to underline now is Lacan's staunch refusal to reduce the meaning of any text to a psychobiographical 'housecleaning' (by which the normativisation implied is denounced) and his decision not to be blind to the riddles contained in those literary texts – that is, to read them as literally as possible so as to let them speak of desire, *jouissance* and sublimation and finally touch the core of being: the main riddle remaining after all 'to be or not to be'.

A look at Lacan's references highlights his apparently bold notion that literature consists of holes and erasures. In Latin the plural *literae* signifies writing, epistle, literature, while *literatura* in the singular means writing, grammar, learning or literature. However the latter noun comes from the verb *lino*, whose meaning is contradictory since it calls up 'I smear', 'I cover' or 'I erase'. As Freud indicated in his fascinating 1910 essay 'The Antithetical Sense of Primal Words',[9] the original roots of all languages, from Ancient Egyptian to present-day German and English, contain 'antithetical meanings'. In German, for instance, there are links between *Stimme* (voice) and *stumm* (mute). Literature belongs to this curious category, at least insofar as its roots provide us with a divided image: we see a hand covering a tablet with wax or another inscribable substance, while the same hand, or a different one, is erasing the tablet so that it might register other signs.

As Lacan pursues the image, *literatura* as a signifier leads us closer to the Latin word *litus* – a word that has different meanings: as a noun, the act of smearing or covering a surface; as a participle, the same meaning as *lino*; as another noun, (*litus, litoris*), the 'littoral', a shore or coastline. 'Literature', then, generates a double pun: it suggests both letters and their erasure (a pun that is more obvious in French since one can always hear *rature* – erasure or crossing out – in the very signifier) and the limit or border of a territory, be it the sea, a hole or even another territory. A whole new topography – based on a trip to Japan during which he admired the calligraphy of *kakemono* and was inspired by the rain and clouds seen from an airplane – emerges in Lacan's essay:

> The streaming down [*ruissellement*] is a bunch of features made up of the original stroke and what erases it. As I said: it is from the conjunction of the two that the subject emerges, but when two moments are marked off. One has therefore to distinguish the erasure.
>
> Erasure of no trace that would have been there before, this is what makes a *terre* [earth, soil] of the *littoral*. Pure *litura*, it is the literal. To produce this means reproducing this half without a pair from which the subject subsides. Such is the exploit of this calligraphy...
>
> Between center and absence, between knowledge and *jouissance*, there is a littoral that only turns into a literal because this turn can be taken identically by everyone at any time.[10]

Here the tone of the meditation sounds almost Heideggerian in its wish to conjoin the sky and the earth in a theory of the letter as constitutive of the human subject and sexuality as a whole: the text concludes with an enigmatic reference to an 'it is written' that would underpin sexual rapport. It also refers to the transformation of knowledge into *jouissance* 'through the edge of the hole in knowl-edge'.[11] Much of the essay is an condensed account of Lacan's recent trip to Japan and appears as a sort of anti-*Empire of Signs*, that is, a critique of Barthes' admiration of Japanese calligraphy and writing. Whereas Barthes praised the Zen-like hollowing out of meaning and the parade of pure forms he saw everywhere in Japan, Lacan is wiser to the fact that letters do not point to a pure void of signification but produce a 'hole' in which enjoyment of the most excessive type can lurk.

Lacan returns to this text and points out its imprecisions, in his Seminar XX. He adds the following when discussing the solitude of the speaking 'I':

> That solitude, as a break in knowledge, not only can be written but it is that which is written *par excellence*, for it is that which leaves a trace of a break in being.
>
> That is what I said in a text, certainly not without its imperfections, that I called '*Lituraterre*'. 'The cloud of language', I expressed myself metaphorically, 'constitutes writing.' Who knows whether the fact that we can read [*lire*] the streams I saw over Siberia as the metaphorical trace of writing isn't linked [*lié*] – beware, *lier* [to link] and *lire* consist of the same letters – to something that goes beyond the effect of rain, which animals have no chance of reading as such?[12]

Lacan then explains that this link should be understood as proving right an 'idealism' that is 'related to the impossibility of inscribing the sexual relationship between two bodies of different sexes'.[13] This writing then takes the form of a simple knot, which 'has all the characteristics of writing – it could be a letter'.[14] This letter becomes more and more encompassing until it finally allegorizes the trefoil of Trinity. We are already in the realm of the Borromean knot, whose particularly graceful coils can show without words the enigma of the sexual *non*-rapport.

The letter, be it Roman or Greek or even the loop of an arabesque, circumscribes the edges of the hole that has been left open by *jouissance*, and then closed by the symbolic system. At this point, to avoid being plunged too soon into the convoluted maze of Lacan's late style, an illustration is necessary. The best example is provided by Lacan's discussion of André Gide after the latter deplored the destruction of his correspondence by his wife Madeleine. There are two texts on Gide, one is a long section devoted to perversion in the 5 March 1958 seminar on 'The Formations of the Unconscious', the other is a detailed review of two books on Gide's life, Jean Delay's *Gide's Childhood* and Jean Schlumberger's *Madeleine and André Gide*,[15] a review-essay that Lacan published in the April 1958 issue of *Critique*. This is the most specifically literary essay to be published in *Ecrits*, and as such it deserves our attention. Its subtitle is a good indicator of what is at stake in Gide: 'Gide's youth, or the Letter and Desire' (*E*, 739–64).

The critical review pays homage to Jean Delay as a psychiatrist and literary figure but is more reserved about Schlumberger's book (whose explicit aim is to correct Gide's portrayal of Madeleine). Even though Lacan does not agree with the avowed intention of Delay's psycho-biography, he recognises that by exploring in depth one particular subject, Gide, he can grasp the central core of being, throwing new light on 'the *rapport between man and the letter*'.[16] Delay's two monumental volumes devote some thirteen hundred pages to Gide's life between 1869 and 1895 and try to offer a key to the entire career of this French novelist and essayist. Acknowledging that this enterprise had enjoyed the collaboration of Gide and his family, who had made available all manner of private documents and letters, Lacan calls up the models of Boswell for Johnson and Eckermann for Goethe, and reminds his readers of the fact that Sainte-Beuve, the great nineteenth-century writer who made biographical criticism his speciality (which incurred Proust's indignant critique of the biographical approach to literature in *Against Sainte-Beuve*, thus generating the earliest draft of the entire *Recherche*) has not died in French literary circles, nor has his fundamental tenet: the belief that one can write a 'natural history of spirits' based on scientific principles (*E*, 741).

Lacan does not completely contradict this notion, but he does qualify it: even the Proust example shows that one can hardly separate the matter of the novel from the author's life, but this matter contributes only rough material, and the meaning of the work or 'message' can be founded on delusion and falsification:

> The only thing that counts is a truth derived from what is condensed by the message in its development. There is so little opposition between this *Dichtung* and the *Wahrheit* in its bareness, that the fact of a poetic operation should rather bring us back to a feature that is forgotten about every truth, namely that it is produced as truth [*qu'elle s'avère*] in a structure of fiction. (*E*, 741–2).

And Lacan quotes Gide, who derides de Gouncourt's flatness and timidity in that he thinks he needs 'the proof by adducing the reality' of everything he writes (*E*, 742, n.1).

Lacan concentrates on the interesting absence that Delay mentions as early as the acknowledgments – the absence of the entire correspondence between Gide and his wife. He notes with extraordinary prescience the rise of what would later be called 'genetic criticism' in France, the critical school that dominated the last two decades of the twentieth century and took the 'prepublication draft' as its main object. He sees in Delay's book the promotion of these 'little papers' to the status of literary symptom. Lacan's deference is limited, but his barbs are softened by a subtle stylisation. A few pages later he alludes to the way in which Delay's psychological reconstitution offers a 'marriage of psychology and the letter', to which he gives a 'Blakean title' (by which he alludes, of course, to the *Marriage of Heaven and Hell*), which tends to confirm that the letter entirely dominates psychology (*E*, 747). Delay himself, although not ignorant of psychoanalysis, has refused to produce a work of 'applied psychoanalysis' – an expression that always takes on negative connotations under Lacan's pen. Lacan comments:

> He first rejects what this absurd phrase [applied psychoanalysis] reveals of the confusion reigning there. Psychoanalysis can be applied in a strict sense only as treatment and therefore to a speaking and hearing subject. In this case, it can merely be a psychoanalytic method, proceeding to the deciphering of signifiers without paying any attention to the presupposed existence of the signified. (*E*, 747–8).

Praising Delay's honesty and rigour in the method he follows, Lacan concludes that the biographer has been able to expose the very 'structure of the subject' that psychoanalysis has outlined. Moreover Gide himself had briefly been introduced to psychoanalysis, and even if he remained ironical or skeptical (he called Freud an 'idiot of genius' and made fun of a 'wave of oedipedemics') his works probe the complexities of human sexuality with a rare candour.

Gide's ambivalence about his wife is acknowledged almost shockingly in the text he published after the death of Madeleine, *Et nunc manet in te*.[17] The riddle that Lacan, like Delay and Schlumberger before him, tries to explain is Gide's obstinate desire to marry an older cousin who was like a sister tor him, someone he also wanted to protect from sexual scandal (partly provoked by the cousin's mother, who was known to take lovers and eventually remarried, departing her tightly knit and religiously minded family), even though he had been made aware of his homosexual inclinations in Biskra by Oscar Wilde, Lord Douglas and some other friends. How could Gide, whose sensuality had developed very early and whose homosexuality was never closeted, decide to marry in an almost incestuous union a cousin whose own sexual urges would always remain unsatisfied? Gide believed that there existed a 'mystical love' based on sexual renunciation that he could share with a very religious partner, but the unconsummated marriage exacted its toll on Madeleine, who was kept in the dark as to her husband's real sexuality. In *Et nunc manet in te*, Gide documents how aged in appearance she soon became, so much so that they were often mistaken for mother and son!

While Delay's psychobiography addresses all the elements that contributed to this fateful union, Lacan focuses on a crucial episode that took place in 1918 as a consequence of the deception: Madeleine's decision to burn all Gide's letters to her after he had departed to England with Marc, a young male friend. Gide's reaction to this loss was somewhat excessive: he cried for an entire week and felt as if he had lost a child. 'I am suffering as if she had killed our child'.[18] Lacan compares Gide's crying with 'the wail of a primate's female companion when struck in the belly' (*E*, 761) and equivalent to the gaping hole his wife had dug in herself and him. Madeleine admitted that these letters had been 'her most precious possession' – as Gide had often written as many as ten pages a day to her since their teenage years, the letters, to which both had access, filled a large drawer in a chest – but according to her account, she had needed to 'do something' after he had left with his male lover in order not to go mad or die.[19] Gide betrays his own infatuation with these letters when adding: 'Maybe there never was a more beautiful correspondence.'[20]

Surprisingly, it is a sense of laughter or comedy that seizes Lacan when he surveys this 'disaster' in Gide's life. In Seminar V, he compares Gide's cry with that of Harpagon (Molière's famous miser) for his lost treasure: 'My casket!'[21] He shows how this can be a 'passion', that is, the alienation of desire fetishised in an object. Gide becomes for Lacan a character in one of Molière's plays. Madeleine had already noticed how passion would suddenly distort the features of her husband, as in the scene that took place during their wedding trip to Algiers, when Gide, sitting next to his wife, would once in a while go to the window and furtively caress the arms and shoulders of playfully seductive little Arab boys. 'You looked like a criminal or a madman' she finally confided to him.[22] Lacan refuses to treat this as a serious metamorphosis, stressing the function of laughter in the process. I shall return to Lacan's conception of comedy and its links with what he sees as the fundamentally theatrical presentation of the phallus, but limit my remarks to the diagnosis he gives about Gide.

In Lacan's reading, Gide's 'perversion' does not come from his sexual desire for young boys, but from his desire for the little boy he once was – a 'desired child' who was the object of his aunt's attentions. Lacan draws a little scheme that opposes two triangles:[23]

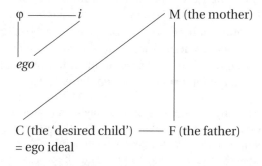

φ ———— i M (the mother)

ego

C (the 'desired child') ——— F (the father)
= ego ideal

The larger triangle sums up the determinations in which the child is caught, with the mother and the father as poles. The smaller triangle is the imaginary set-up of the child, with his own ideal image in i facing the ego and the phallus he will have to be:

> André Gide's perversion consists in this, that he can only constitute himself by being in C ... by submitting himself to this correspondence that is the heart of his work – by being one whose importance increases if he is in his cousin's place, the person whose every thought is turned toward her, the one who literally gives her at every moment what he doesn't have, but nothing more than that – who constitutes himself as a personality only thanks to her.... This wife whom he does not desire becomes the object of a supreme love, and when this object with which he has filled up the hole of a love without desire comes to disappear, he cries out the miserable shout whose connection I have pointed out with the comical cry par excellence, that of the miser – *My casket! My dear casket!* (*S5*, 260–1)

The 'hole of a love without desire' refers of course to the famous letters that will be destroyed.

The review in *Ecrits* equally stresses the laughter inherent in our 'human comedy', as Balzac would say. Just as Harpagon bemoans the disappearance of his casket whereas he ought to investigate his daughter's loss, Gide can only understand what has happened to the strange couple they formed after Madeleine's death: the letters have replaced desire, have been left in the place where desire has vanished. This is not very different from the function of the phallus – a function Lacan is busy exploring in this Seminar, especially when he comments on Joan Riviere's famous article 'On Femininity as Mascarade' (*S5*, 254–5), and which he later takes up in a systematic reading of Jean Genet – (we shall return to this development in Chapter 9).

This is how one can become a 'man of letters', whose 'truth' is also valid for the general reader. Lacan quotes the last page of *Et nunc manet in te*, admitting to an almost deliberate misreading. In 1939 Gide had written the following in his own diary:

> Before leaving Paris, I was able to revise the proofs of my *Diary*. Rereading it, it appears to me that the systematic excision (until my mourning at least) of all the passages concerning Madeleine have in a way *blinded* the text. The few allusions to the secret drama of my life thus become incomprehensible because of the absence of what could throw light on them. Incomprehensible or inadmissible, the image of my mutilated self I give there, offering only, in the burning place of the heart, a hole.[24]

Lacan says that when he first saw this passage he thought Gide was referring to the burnt correspondence, then realised his mistake, but finally concluded that he was nevertheless correct in his assumption since the text also points to the same structural function. This is the point where Gide's famous irony, so visible in many novels, finds a radical limit – the limit of the letter as such. Lacan goes on: 'The letters into which he poured his soul had ... no double. And when their fetishistic nature appears, this provokes the laughter that always accompanies a subjectivity at a loss. Everything ends in comedy, but what will make laughter end?' (*E*, 764).

After a series of allusions to Gide's facility as a writer, Lacan congratulates Delay on the forthcoming *Nietzsche* and concludes with another question: 'It will only stop, this movement, at the rendezvous you already know since you are going toward it, to the question concerning the figure offered by words beyond comedy when it turns into farce: how can one know who, among the tumblers, is holding the real Punchinello?' (*E*, 764) Lest we get lost in this dense tissue of allusions – in which we can identify either the phallus or death as an 'absolute master' who will send Gide back to his cousin's place – a later footnote puts us on the right track: Lacan really alludes to Nietzsche's famous cry of *Ecco, ecco, il vero pulchinello!* when pointing to a cross. If the crucifix is the 'true Punch', parody is everywhere and does not spare even the letter of desire. This is what Nietzsche implies in his last letters, when he writes that he goes round the streets, taps people on the shoulder and tells them: 'Are we happy? I am god, and I made this caricature.'[25] We thus have to go with Lacan, to follow him as he traces the lethal signs left behind by repetition compulsion – and therefore to meet Poe's 'purloined letter'.

4   Poe's 'Purloined Letter'

Lacan's analysis of Poe's 'Purloined Letter' has been glossed so often that one can be seized by a sort of metatextual vertigo, especially after reading the very comprehensive anthology entitled *The Purloined Poe*.[1] However no-one can deny the particular importance of this reading for Lacan, no more than the fact that he decided to open the volume of *Ecrits* with this seminar, thus eliminating any possibility of chronological order. Here is the outline of his programme:

> But if man was reduced to being nothing but the place where our discourse returns, would not the question of: 'what's the point of sending it?' be returned to us?
>
> This is indeed the question posed for us by these new readers whose presence has been an argument when we were pressed to gather these texts [*écrits*].
>
> We will leave them time to adapt to our style by giving the 'Purloined Letter' the privilege of opening their sequence, in spite of the diachronical order. (*E*, 9)

A particularly apt introduction to his style and its intricacies, the Poe seminar also fulfils another purpose. For when he started reading Poe, Lacan could not ignore that he had been preceded by an illustrious figure, someone who was not only one of the founders of the French psychoanalytic movement but also a personal friend of Freud: Marie Bonaparte. Lacan could not have forgotten her monumental psychobiography of Poe, published in 1933 and prefaced by Freud. His short foreword is well worth quoting in full:

> In this book my friend and pupil, Marie Bonaparte, has shone the light of psycho-analysis on the life and work of a great writer with pathologic trends.

Thanks to her interpretive effort, we now realise how many of the characteristics of Poe's works were conditioned by his personality, and can see how that personality derived from intense emotional fixations and painful infantile experiences. Investigations such as this do not claim to explain creative genius, but they do reveal the factors which awaken it and the sort of subject matter it is destined to choose. Few tasks are as appealing as enquiry into the laws that govern the psyche of exceptionally endowed individuals.[2]

Freud clearly condones and even praises the project of psychobiography, confirming that his own approach (as can be seen from his texts on Leonardo, Dostoyevsky and other artists) is indeed devoted to pursuing, through biographical readings, an examination of the links between creation and neurotic or pathological features in creators. Freud's use of the term 'personality' may have sent Lacan back to the title of his own doctoral thesis on paranoia and 'its relation to personality', published in 1932, a year before Bonaparte's book on Poe.

It is clear from what precedes that this 'archaeology' (both in the historical sense of 'earliest works' and in the psychological sense of 'excavatory investigation') corresponds to what Lacan rejects most vehemently in literary criticism. What is interesting in Bonaparte's copious book (more than seven hundred pages) is that she is not content with just presenting an interpretation of the 'life and works' of Poe, as her title says, she also opens up new vistas at the end of her book. The last chapter, entitled 'Poe and the Human Soul', begins with a theoretical section ('Literature: its Function and Elaboration') in which she restates Freud's main tenets on the links between the creator and the Unconscious: she surveys the function of unconscious fantasies and daydreams in literary creation, talks of the links between dreams and works of art, the logic of condensation and displacement, and finally introduces the entire domain of applied psychoanalysis in the field of art and literature. The second section ('Poe's Message to Others') is less predictable as it focuses on Baudelaire as Poe's main heir. Even though she sticks to her psychobiographical approach and provides a condensed version of Baudelaire's life and his passionate and difficult relationship with his mother, she assumes that the French poet found in Poe not only a 'brother-soul' but also someone who gave him the courage to confront his own narcissism, necrophilia and sadism. Poe's ultimate message would thus paradoxically survive in French and not in English, and might be seen as being condensed in Baudelaire's defiant formula: 'What is the eternity of damnation for someone who has found in a single second the infinity of *jouissance*!'[3] One can understand why Derrida was later so attracted to Bonaparte's position: it is less because she has to be defended against Lacan's barely disguised contempt, or because he feels in sympathy with her psychological deductions, but because she opens the infinite world of the library along with that of the Unconscious.

In a sense, Lacan's seminar constitutes a systematic refutation of both Freud and Bonaparte – although he does not admit this as such. In order to investigate this complex dialogism I shall begin by quoting Marie Bonaparte's useful summary of the famous tale – a tale to which she devotes only two pages in her bulky essay, adding in parentheses a few remarks (the trick of this story is that it is impossible to summarise it without grossly distorting it):

> The reader will remember that, in this story, the Queen of France [she is never named as such], like Elizabeth Arnold [Poe's mother], is in possession of dangerous and secret letters [in fact, only one letter is mentioned], whose writer is unknown [in fact the initial of his name is given at the end of the story]. A wicked minister, seeking a political advantage and to strengthen his power, steals one of these letters under the Queen's eyes, which she is unable to prevent owing to the King's presence. This letter must at all costs be recovered. Every attempt by the police fails. Fortunately Dupin is at hand. Wearing dark spectacles with which he can look about him, while his eyes are concealed, he makes an excuse to call on the minister, and discovers the letter openly displayed in a card-rack, hung 'from a little brass knob just beneath the middle of the mantelpiece'.
>
> By a further subterfuge, he possesses himself of the compromising letter and leaves a similar one in its place. The Queen, who will have the original restored to her, is saved.
>
> Let us first note that this letter, very symbol of the maternal penis, also 'hangs' over the fireplace, in the same manner as the female penis, if it existed, would be hung over the cloaca which is here represented – as in the foregoing tales – by the general symbol of fireplace or chimney. We have here, in fact, what is almost an anatomical chart, from which not even the clitoris (or brass knob) is omitted.... The struggle between Dupin and the minister who once did Dupin an 'ill turn' ... represents, in effect, the Oedipal struggle between father

and son, though on an archaic, pregenital and phallic level, to seize possession, not of the mother herself, but of a part; namely, the penis.[4]

This summary is revealing in that only one scene interests Bonaparte – the moment of the discovery of the letter's hiding place. Once the letter is identified with the mother's penis the Freudian mechanism falls into place, and the Oedipal solution intervenes like a very pat *deus ex machina*. Dupin and the Minister just fight out a brotherly rivalry over the mother's body and its coveted 'penis' – or rather, as Lacan shows, the mother's phallus.

Lacan dramatises his rejection of psychocriticism in his two texts on Poe, in which he also systematises and refines his theory of the letter. It is important, however, to distinguish the stakes and strategies of the two texts. The first occurs as a kind of detour in the seminar of 1954–55 on 'The Ego in Freud's Theory and in the Technique of Psychoanalysis'. The second text is a 'rewrite', completed a few months later and used as the general introduction to *Ecrits* (1966). When we read this seminar it looks as if Lacan had come upon Poe's story by chance, since he was at that time interested in automatism and cybernetics. When he first mentions the 'Purloined Letter' he does not concern himself with the allegorical quality of the plot, but focuses on the long excursus in which, in order to explain his method, Dupin recalls his schoolboy days and describes how a young boy of eight would invariably win the game of 'odds or evens' (guessing whether the marbles held in the other person's hand totalled an odd or an even number) by means of systematic identification with his opponent. The first seminars on Poe are in fact occupied by the games of odds or evens that Lacan forces his audience to play. It is only later that Lacan notices the rich potentialities of the story.

Another surprise comes when one notices that the *écrit* constituted by the analysis of Poe stresses its oral status (unlike the Gide or Sade pieces, for instance). We should never forget that this derives from a 'seminar' endowed with a past, a specific communal tradition. Thus Lacan begins *in medias res*, as it were, by writing: 'Our inquiry has led us to the point of recognizing that the repetition automatism [*Wiederholungszwang*] finds its basis in what we have called the *insistence* of the signifying chain' (*PP*, 28). As a note in the French edition of *Ecrits* indicates, the text presents itself as a single seminar session: this seminar was 'pronounced on April 26th, 1955' (*E*, 918), which corresponds to the date given in Seminar II (*The Ego in Freud's Theory*).[5] Lacan gives a detailed reading of Poe, beginning with a series of mathematical speculations concerning odd and even, plus and minus, but the two texts have radically different structures and styles. On the issue of content, two examples should suffice to show there is a method in their stylistic discrepancies. On the question of the 'letter' as opposed to writings, the Seminar offers the following:

> What, after all, is a letter? How can a letter be purloined [*volée*]? To whom does it belong? To whoever sent it or to whoever it is addressed? If you say that it belongs to whoever sent it, what makes a letter a gift? Why does one send a letter? And if you think that it belongs to the recipient, how is it that, under certain circumstances, you return your letters to the person who, for a period in your life, bombarded you with them?
>
> When one considers one of those proverbs attributed to the wisdom of nations – the wisdom of which is thus denominated by antiphrase – one is sure to light upon a stupidity. *Verba volant, scripta manent*. Has it occurred to you that a letter is precisely speech which flies [*vole*]? If a stolen [*volée*] letter is possible, it is because a letter is a fly-sheet [*feuille volante*]. It is *scripta* which *volant*, whereas speech, alas, remains. It remains even when no one remembers it any more. Just as, after five hundred thousand signs in the series of *pluses* and *minuses*, the appearance of α, β, χ, δ will still be determined by the same laws.
>
> Speech remains. You can't help the play of symbols, and that is why you must be very careful what you say. But the letter, for its part, that goes away (*S2*, 197–8).

In the version published in the second issue of *La Psychanalyse* (dated May-August 1956) and later taken up in *Ecrits*, this becomes:

> *Scripta manent*: in vain would they learn from a deluxe-edition humanism the proverbial lesson which *verba volant* concludes. May it but please heaven that writings remain, as is rather the case with spoken words: for the indelible debt of the latter impregnates our acts with its transferences.
>
> Writings scatter to the winds blank cheques in an insane charge. And were there not such flying leaves [*feuilles volantes*], there would be no purloined letters.

But what of it? For a purloined letter to exist, we may ask, to whom does the letter belong? We stressed a moment ago the oddity implicit in returning a letter to him who had but recently given wing to its burning pledge (*PP*, 41).

The second passage concludes with a rather obscure allusion to the Chevalier d'Eon's correspondence, the elucidation of which requires a whole page of notes by the editors (*PP*, 93–4). Condensation, allusiveness and paradoxes thus increase in visibility in the revised version. A crucial difference in wording is also perceptible: whereas Lacan says 'I' in the seminar, he uses the authorial 'we' in the written version (possibly to suggest collective response in an 'open' seminar). Both versions are full of puns and difficult to translate, but the seminar clearly relies on spoken rhetoric when expanding and elaborating on a paradox (here the reversal of the old proverb: *Scripta manent, verba volant*) while the written one sends us back to a complete library (Lacan's own, probably).

A second contrastive analysis provides another clue. We find in the original seminar an early insight into the feminised position occupied by the owner of the letter. Lacan is commenting on the particular way the Minister has disguised the Queen's letter so that the police will not recognise it, and his approach is quite tentative:

> This letter, whose nature we do not know, he has in some way addressed it to himself with its new and false appearance, it is even specified by whom – by a woman of his own standing, who has a diminutive feminine hand – and he has it sent to him with his own seal.
>
> Now this is a curious relation to oneself. The letter undergoes a sudden feminisation, and at the same time it enters into a narcissistic relation – since it is now addressed in this sophisticated feminine hand, and bears his own seal. It's a sort of love-letter he's sent to himself. This is very obscure, indefinable, I don't want to force anything, and in truth if I mention this transformation, it is because it is correlative of something else far more important, concerning the subjective behavior of the minister himself (*S2*, 199).

Lacan makes a diversion at this point but three pages later he returns to the same idea: 'Isn't there some echo between the letter with a feminine superscription and this languishing Paris? ... in order to be in the same position vis-à-vis the letter as the Queen was, in an essentially feminine position, the minister falls prey to the same trick as she did' (*S2*, 202).

It is only at this point in the seminar that Lacan elaborates on what becomes the main conceptual handle in the revised version: the notion that all the characters in the story go round in a circle (or triangle) and systematically exchange their positions one after the other; thus exhausting the permutations allowed by a combinatory system.

The 'written' version appears manifestly denser and tighter. When Lacan recalls Poe's astute remark that the most difficult words to read on a map are not the tiny, closely printed names of cities but large names spread across the expanse of a country or continent, he makes a connection with the idea that the best dissimulation is absolute lack of concealment:

> Just so does the purloined letter, like an immense female body, stretch out across the Minister's office when Dupin enters. But just so does he already expect to find it, and has only, with his eyes veiled by green lenses, to undress that huge body.
>
> And that is why without needing any more than being able to listen in at the door of Professor Freud, he will go straight to the spot in which lies and lives what that body is designed to hide, in a gorgeous center caught in a glimpse, nay, to the very place seducers name Sant'Angelo castle in the innocent illusion of controlling the City from within it. Look! between the cheeks of the fireplace, there's the object already in reach of a hand the ravisher has but to extend.... The question of deciding whether he seizes it above the mantelpiece as Baudelaire translates, or beneath it, as in the original text, may be abandoned without harm to the inferences of those whose profession is grilling (*PP*, 48).

Lacan appends a note to the end of the last sentence with the even more enigmatic remark: 'And even to the cook herself.'

We are obviously in the realm of parody. The discussion of Baudelaire's translation sends us to the right source: it is Marie Bonaparte who is the butt of Lacan's zesty satire, since she corrects Baudelaire's mistranslation in the French text of her essay on Poe. Even if she could be said to have Freud's ear, she is reduced to an ancillary 'cook' or, even worse, to a torturer who 'grills' suspects until they confess to the crimes for which they have been framed. In a sense this previous reading is a blessing: Lacan has been saved from the sin of overinterpretation by the negative example of Marie Bonaparte, who looks too eagerly for equivalences and equations, while also anticipating Lacan's discussion of the penis and the phallus. Although Derrida accuses Lacan of repeating and simplifying Bonaparte's argument, and of missing what constitutes the richness of psychobiographical criticism – that is the possibility of building series of images that migrate from story to story[6] – a number of later critics (among whom Barbara Johnson is the most brilliant) have stressed the fact that Lacan never really 'equates' the letter with a concept or an object. Or rather, he equates the 'purloined letter' with a letter, even with The Letter, and this is where his argument becomes a little more complex.

In the final version of the seminar, the first salient feature of the story is its logical structure, its pattern of almost ironical repetitions. Three scenes are entirely superimposed: in the first scene, which can be called the 'primal scene' of the theft, we have a 'blind' King who embodies the Law but is unable to understand that anything is happening at all, a 'seeing' Queen who suffers and remains impotent while the daring Minister profits from the interaction between the first two. He can put his own letter on the table and leave with the coveted prize, knowing that the Queen cannot ask for it without awaking her spouse's suspicions.

The second scene is the most developed in the story and consists of the doomed efforts by the police to retrieve the letter on behalf of the Queen. This time the 'blind' character is the Prefect of Police and by extension his men who cannot find the letter because they assume that it must be hidden, projecting into reality what they think 'hiding' means, never imagining of course that the letter would be left in full view. The 'seeing' character who cannot do much – in this case at least confronting someone who is his equal, Dupin – is the Minister, who basks in a mistaken assumption of power and in the imaginary security of his possession of the letter. The active agent is Dupin, who can identify with the Minister and reconstruct his mental process (that is, see it all, prepare an exact double of the stolen letter and devise the strategy by which he will distract the Minister).

The third scene corresponds to the theft by Dupin, an act that reverses the first theft. Here the Minister has turned into a 'blind' man, unaware of what is happening, while Dupin, who indeed acts 'signs' his substitution by quoting lines from Crébillon that will surely identify him as soon as the Minister checks the contents of the letter.

Caught up in brotherly rivalry, he seems to be motivated less by feelings of honour or greed (although he will be handsomely paid) than
by the wish to settle an old score. He thus exposes himself to the all-
seeing gaze of the author, Poe, or his readers, including Lacan, who
are placed willy-nilly into the position of a psychoanalyst who needs
to reconstitute the tale's logic and psychical economy so as not to fall
into the trap of allegorising the letter by 'stealing' its meaning or
content.

The strength of such a 'structuralist' scheme is such that it
inevitably forces its own undermining: for who could prevent another
turn of the screw and decide to stop the permutations at this point?
The third triangular pattern cannot provide a resolution to the dialectics of blindness and seeing. That is why, when Derrida accuses Lacan
of translating the contentless letter into a content that would be
summed up by the 'truth', defined by femininity and castration, he
too 'sees' too much, translates too much, reduces the stylistic play of a
text that, as we have seen, is no less 'literary' than Poe's model.

We can now return to the beginning of Lacan's seminar. What
matters in his reading is not the series of imaginary projections each
place entails, but the careful mapping out of a symbolic structure that
determines each subject's position in respect of the others and the
Other. This symbolic structure can be described as a chain of effects
determined by the revolving displacement of a signifier. In Poe's story
the letter allegorises the itinerary of a signifier whose signified
remains inaccessible, if not unimportant. That is why both the
seminar and the written version stress the issue of 'intersubjectivity',
a term that may sound a little dated in Lacan's discourse. However he
always uses it in the sense of 'intersubjective complex' or 'intersubjective repetition', since he means that no 'place' can be described in
isolation from the other two (at least). The places are caught in a
repetitive process that literally ensures that the letter will return to the
same place at the end. Here Derrida is entitled to some doubt as to
the legitimacy of this postulated economy: how can we say with Lacan
that 'a letter always reaches its destination?' Doesn't it happen that
letters are lost, nay stolen, or even destroyed?

Lacan's argument is indissociable from his description of the letter
as a single entity that is 'uncuttable'. In a long semantic analysis that
draws on French idioms, he shows that one can speak of letters in the
plural but one cannot say 'there is letter' (*de la lettre*) or 'there is some
letter' in the same way that one can say 'there is time' or 'there is

some butter here'. The letter, be it singular or plural, if divided or cut into pieces is still a collection of fragments belonging to a letter. This is why the police start from the wrong assumption that the Minister's room can be divided into smaller and smaller units, including all the objects, books, frames, table legs and so on it contains, so that they may be examined with needles, magnifying glasses and all the technical apparatus of scientific detection. They repeat the paradox of Zeno's argument: Zeno demonstrates that if a line is endlessly divisible, then movement is impossible; Achilles can run faster, but he will never catch up with a receding tortoise that he can only approach asymptotically.[7]

In a similar way, a letter in French and English is based on a complex homophony that does not work in other languages, for example German. A letter (*Brief* in German) is made up of letters as so many written signs (*Buchstaben* in German), and even if it has been destroyed – as we have seen in Gide's case – it remains present by its absence as a letter, made 'whole' by the 'hole' Gide keeps in his heart. Lacan refuses to distinguish the three meanings: 'as for the letter – be it taken as typographical character, epistle or what makes a man of letters' (*PP*, 39). At any rate the police prove *a contrario* how the indivisibility of the letter creates its invisibility. They show how the letter can function as a hole: since their categories cannot accommodate an exhibited but reversed and re-signed paper, for them the letter 'is missing in its place' (Lacan uses the phrase by which libraries indicate that a book has been lost, often by simply being misplaced). Seeing everything as something they can divide into smaller units, they miss the single entity that lies in front of their eyes.

Lacan had already conceded that the materiality of the signifier was 'odd' – in Poe's own terms (*PP*, 38). Derrida goes further in his denunciation of Lacan's gesture:

> Now for the signifier to be kept in its letter and thus make its return, it is necessary that in its letter it does not admit 'partition', that one cannot say *some* letter but only a letter, letters, the letter. It is against this possible loss that the statement of the 'materiality of the signifier', that is, about the signifier's indivisible singularity, is constructed. *This 'materiality', deduced from an indivisibility found nowhere, in fact corresponds to an idealization.* Only the ideality of a letter resists destructive division (PP, 194).

What is interesting here is the argument that the alleged 'indivisibility' is 'found nowhere' – precisely an argument that repeats the gesture of those who look for something without finding it. But placing himself strategically on the terrain of empirical evidence (I can always tear a letter into small pieces) Derrida deliberately blinds himself to what was described in the previous paragraph, in fact to the relatively common paradox that the materiality of a single letter may not entail its being present here and now – something that Heidegger had already taught him (and Lacan). There is indeed a process of idealisation in the fact that Lacan constructs a theory of the materiality of the signifier by proffering the concept of a single and indivisible letter, just as there is aprocess of idealisation when one produces a rigorous discourse based on abstract concepts.

If this is relatively simple to explain, Derrida's objections to the letter's very economy – and the implications of a circuit determined by a 'truth' that will always find a phallus as a key-signifier – seem more damaging. Why indeed should the letter always return to its original place? We saw earlier how Althusser expressed the same concern. Does Lacan actually imply that all lost or mislaid letters eventually end up in their rightful owners' hands? If one goes on playing with Lacan's terms, the answer will be 'found': I am the answer, or any reader will be. This is what Zizek demonstrates in the first chapter of *Enjoy your Symptom!*, a chapter aptly entitled: 'Why does a *Letter* always arrive at its destination?'[8] Attempting to disentangle Derrida's accusation of idealism and teleology, Zizek shows that Lacan's formula can be understood according to three registers: the Real, the Imaginary and the Symbolic. At the imaginary level the phrase 'a letter always reaches its destination' means that 'its destination is wherever it arrives' (*EYS*, 10): in order for anyone to mention the letter, it must have had at least one recipient, even if she or he is not the original addressee.

Zizek uses Pêcheux's analysis of a silly joke to prove his point. If I say 'Daddy was born in Manchester, Mummy in Bristol and I in London: strange that the three of us should have met!', I imply a model of 'fate' that does not bracket off pure chance encounters. Through a similar retrospective effect, if I am in the position where I have to be responsible for the letter, it will have arrived at its destination. At a symbolic level, the circuit of the letter implies the lack of a metalanguage that would allow someone to elaborate a theory of Fate, for instance: fate is entirely contained within the letter itself, whether one sees its possession as tragic, gendered or a blessing. At a real level, the letter contains death or annihilation as one of its hidden messages – and in its very materiality (what could be more 'dead', indeed, than these inert little signs on a piece of paper – as Derrida has often stressed?) The letter becomes an object in excess, a dangerous supplement that has to be put to rest, the uncanny enjoyment of a *jouissance* that has no name and no clear function (*EYS*, 22).

We can now turn to what is either a curious slip of the pen or a deliberate transformation in Lacan's seminar: he quotes several times the lines taken from Crébillon by Dupin, but when he concludes his written text (not in the seminar) he replaces the original *dessin* by *destin*: '*Un destin si funeste, S'il n'est digne d'Atrée, est digne de Thyeste*' (*E*, 40, *PP*, 52). The single change of letter has transformed the 'design' of teleology into a fate determined by repetition. Here again the key seems to lie in ancient tragedy, with the figures of Atreus and Thyestes. As Barbara Johnson has pointed out in her fascinating commentary, Crébillon's play revolves around a letter informing King Atreus of his betrayal by his brother Thyestes. This letter denounces the fact that Atreus's son is really the son of Thyestes and will trigger the usual roll-call of incest, parricide and even cannibalism (*PP*, 235–6). As Johnson also notes, Derrida tried to exceed the frame provided by Lacan but failed to read other parts of the seminar, especially the long mathematical passage not translated in *The Purloined Poe* and only available in the French *Ecrits*.[9] Curiously, Lacan again dates the second part of his seminar as 26 April 1955 (*E*, 44) and inserts in it a series of parentheses that he calls 'the parenthesis of parentheses' (*E*, 54). After which, he writes, the 1955 text resumes (*E*, 57) – a text that in no way corresponds to the text of that session of Seminar II, a text in which, again, Poe only intervenes as the author of speculations on guessing games and identification. I only mention this to illustrate how complex and infinite the imbrication of these textual layers can be. Like Dupin and the Minister, conjoined by Poe's phrase, we have to become 'poets and mathematicians' (*PP*, 17). But in order to bridge the gap between 'mathemes' and textual readings we have to know a little more about what constitutes the very structure of tragedy.

5 *Hamlet* and the Desire of the Mother

Here we shall engage with another seminar, whose focus on desire and its interpretation radically displaces the usual Freudian reading of *Hamlet* as an Oedipus at one remove. It again seems useful to follow Lacan's cautious investigations in a seminar in which he seems at first to be quite respectful of Freud's ideas. I shall try to show how Lacan reaches a different interpretation in several stages, as if he had not completely seen at first that he would contradict both Freud and the Freudian canon.

Lacan was brought to *Hamlet* less by the numerous Freudian allusions than by the fact that in the middle of his 1959 seminar he was reading a series of texts by Ella Sharpe, above all her *Dream Analysis* (1937) and her unfinished notes for an essay on *Hamlet*.[1] When glossing the way she analyses a patient's dream, Lacan is above all interested in translating her insights into his own graph of desire, the blueprint for the complex scheme I have examined in connection with 'Subversion of the Subject and Dialectic of Desire' in *Ecrits*. He concludes that for Sharpe's patient the issue was 'to be or not be the phallus'.[2] Realising that the intertextual overtones of the formula force him to make a detour through Freud's *Hamlet* theory, he sends his audience to Freud's first mention of *Hamlet* – this is in an often quoted letter to Fliess, in which Freud both likens Hamlet's position to that of a male hysteric and links him with Oedipus:

> How can one explain the hysteric Hamlet's phrase: 'So conscience doth make cowards of us all', and his hesitation to avenge his father by killing his uncle, when he himself so casually sends his courtiers to their death and dispatches Laertes so quickly? How better than by the torment roused in him by the obscure memory that he himself had meditated the same deed against his father because of his passion for his mother – 'use every man after his desert, and who should 'scape

whipping?' His conscience is his unconscious feeling of guilt. And are not his sexual coldness when talking to Ophelia, his rejection of the instinct to beget children, and finally his transference of the deed from his father to Ophelia, typically hysterical? And does he not finally succeed, in just the same remarkable way as my hysterics do, in bringing down his punishment on himself and suffering the same fate as his father, being poisoned by the same rival?[3]

Most critics have noted Freud's revealing slip of the pen: he clearly thinks of Polonius – 'dispatched' quickly by Hamlet – when he writes 'Laertes'. Although Lacan does not remark on this, I would suggest that his own interpretation answers precisely to Freud's oversight – as if he had seen in Freud's conceptual hesitation when confronting the role and place of the Rival replacing a dead Father, a slip of the pen that replaces Hamlet's first murder (of Polonius, a murder accomplished in great haste) with the victim of a later duel (also performed in haste and revolving around mistaken objects and identities). Like Ella Sharpe, as we shall see, Lacan stresses the function of haste in interpretation – in the sense of the 'haste to conclude' he elaborated in 'Logical Time.'[4] In this sense the slip of the pen is only a 'parapraxis' in that it precipitates an unconscious interpretation that is too present, therefore too pressing. But I am anticipating...

While the idea of Hamlet as a male hysteric is no doubt highly suggestive in Lacan's mapping of the 'four discourses' – in which the 'discourse of the Hysteric' is presented as relentlessly posing the question of desire – it is just the second part of the thesis that is later developed by Freud in *The Interpretation of Dreams*, and it is important to sketch this in order to see how much Lacan's differs. In *The Interpretation of Dreams*, Freud does not mention Hamlet's hysteria (he is just called a neurotic) because Hamlet, as a character and a play, embodies a new stage of civilization: if *Hamlet* finds its roots in the Oedipus complex, everything has changed:

> the changed treatment of the same material reveals the whole difference in the mental life of those two widely separated epochs of civilization: the secular advance of repression in the emotional life of mankind. In *Oedipus* the child's wishful phantasy that underlies it is brought into the open and realized as it would be in a dream. In *Hamlet* it remains repressed; and – just as in the case of a neurosis – we only learn of its existence from its inhibiting consequences.[5]

This remains Freud's thesis on *Hamlet* throughout, even after he changes his mind about the identity of the author: he confides in a bold footnote added in 1930 that he no longer believes that 'the man from Stratford' was the author of the plays. As the French humorist Alphonse Allais once quipped, Shakespeare never existed: all the famous plays were written by a totally unknown person who just happened to have the same name.

Freud nevertheless often returns to *Hamlet* in later years, but in connection with melancholia rather than hysteria. In 'Mourning and Melancholia' (1915), Hamlet embodies the self-abasement typical of protracted melancholia. Freud quotes the play in a rather humorous passage:

> When in his exacerbation of self-criticism [the patient] describes himself as petty, egoistic, dishonest, lacking in independence, one whose sole aim has been to hide the weaknesses of his own nature, for all we know it may be that he has come very near to self-knowledge; we only wonder why a man must become ill before he can discover truth of this kind. For there can be no doubt that whosoever holds and expresses to others such an opinion of himself – one that Hamlet harboured of himself and all men ['Use every man after his desert, and who should 'scape whipping' (II, 2)] – that man is ill, whether he speaks the truth or is more or less unfair to himself.[6]

We shall see that Lacan uses some important elements taken from the famous opposition between mourning – defined as process through which lack or absence of the loved object is finally accepted after a certain time, and the subject can begin investing new objects with libido – and melancholia, when the subject remains stuck in the position of loss and deploration. Narcissism is the key in this analysis, since the melancholic identifies his or her ego with the abandoned or lost object, an identification that blocks the process and freezes time.

Besides this important character analysis, if one concentrates on plot and structure Freud's psychoanalytical thesis does not change. In his interpretation, *Hamlet* must be understood within a structure provided by Sophocles, with the difference that whereas Oedipus acts and indeed kills his father and sleeps with his mother, Hamlet is inhibited in the revenge expected from him. His inhibition stems from the fact that he unconsciously recognises that his uncle has accom-

plished before him what he most intensely desired: to kill his father
and marry his mother. This is posited as a cornerstone of psychoanalytical dogma, and should escape any reproach of 'psychologisation'
since this derives from a totally unconscious structure.

In his 4 March 1959 seminar, Lacan makes an interesting connection when he moves from Ella Sharpe's dream to the famous passage
in the *Interpretation of Dreams*, in which Freud mentions a patient
who, just after his father's death, relived that sad event in his dreams.
The dream is summed up thus: '*His father was alive once more and
was talking to him in his usual way, but* (the remarkable thing was
that) *he had really died, only he did not know it*'.[7] In order to account
for the apparent absurdity of the dream, Freud needs to connect it
with a 'stirring up of the dreamer's earliest infantile impulses against
his father' and the idea of emotional ambivalence facing dead people.
The full syntax of the unconscious thought the dream contains is
simply: 'he did not know that I wished him to be dead'. A dreamer
who dreams of his own death and the dreamer who dreams of his
father's death have something in common (besides being projections
of Freud's psyche – we know how much the *Interpretation of Dreams*
owes to his own father's death, and Freud's interpretation of *Hamlet*
hinges on the fact that the play was written shortly after the death of
Shakespeare's father): they are haunted by a non-knowledge that
blurs the usual distinctions between life and death. They are forced to
see the deceased as a potential ghost who attests to the tenacious
survival of unconscious desires. Or as Freud often writes, quoting
Horatio, 'there needs no ghost, my Lord' to give news of the inevitable
return of the Unconscious.

While Lacan's interpretation focuses on 'he did not know', he is not
grudging in his admiration for Freud, stressing how 'this approach is
so just, so balanced' and promising that he will not move Hamlet
from the place in which Freud has put him! (*O24*, 10). He then points
to Ella Sharpe's unfinished *Hamlet* book and expresses reservations
about yet another psychobiographical attempt. In a later seminar,
Lacan does not mince his words when dealing with Sharpe's later
Shakespeare essays: 'I wouldn't want to encourage you to produce the
sort of hogwash that psychoanalytic texts are full of. I'm just surprised
that nobody's pointed out that Ophelia is *O phallos*, because you find
other things equally gross, flagrant, extravagant, if you just open the
Papers on Hamlet, which Ella Sharpe unfortunately left unfinished
and which it was perhaps a mistake to publish after her death.'[8] But

the essay Lacan keeps praising is the famous piece Sharpe wrote in 1929 on 'The Impatience of Hamlet'.

Sharpe's provocative thesis is that it is misleading to describe *Hamlet* as the 'tragedy of procrastination'; it makes more sense to characterise it as a 'tragedy of impatience'.[9] By this she means that, in spite of the protracted denouement of the last act, the main symptom exhibited by the play's eponymous hero is melancholia caused by a failed mourning. Mourning demands time, time that is denied to Hamlet and all the other protagonists. This accounts for the curious accelerations in the plot, the various untimely murders of which Hamlet is guilty, until the final general slaughter. There again, time is lacking for a proper account – since Hamlet finally exclaims:

> Had I but time, as this fell sergeant, death,
> Is strict in his arrest, oh I could tell you –
> But let it be (*Hamlet*, V, 2, 314–16).[10]

Lacan and Ella Sharpe agree that Freud's genius lies in the fact that he has gone directly to the core of a 'complex' and has managed to unite 'science and art' as Shakespeare had done.[11] Lacan adds that Freud's insights go beyond those of all his later commentators. He then gives a rapid summary of the play (*O24*, 11–12), stressing how the return of the ghost is linked with the function of the Unconscious as determined by the Big Other. It is because 'the Father did not know that he was dead' that the subject discovers that the Other cannot know, and thus constitutes his own unconscious. However, with a little dig at Freud's theory, Lacan adds: 'Why should the Moderns be more neurotic than the Ancients?' (*O24*, 12) and decides to push the investigation further into textual readings. He then opposes the Ghost in *Hamlet*, who 'knows he is dead', to Oedipus, who 'did not know' and whose tragedy comes from his desire to know the truth. The Oedipian crime has been accomplished unconsciously, whereas in Shakespeare's play it is denounced from the start. Then Lacan examines the core of Freud's argument: Hamlet could not kill Claudius because Claudius is a successful rival, a rival who has dared to do what he did not dare to accomplish (*O24*, 14). The core of the play then becomes less: 'why cannot Hamlet act?' than 'What happens with Hamlet's desire?' There is something wrong with this desire, and the whole play, according to Lacan, could be condensed into what he sees as Hamlet's request: 'Give me my desire back!' What he tries to do, moreover, is to interpret this demand in terms that are not psychological but ontological – Hamlet's whole being is determined by the eclipse of his desire.

Ophelia should throw some light on this desire. Can one say that Ophelia is the object of Hamlet's desire? Not really, since she releases in Hamlet the expression of his 'horror of femininity' (*O24*, 15). Polonius intervenes as a 'wild psychoanalyst' who jumps to hasty conclusions, as we know, when he decides that Hamlet's melancholia has been triggered by a forbidden love for Ophelia. Finally, Lacan too jumps to a conclusion, albeit of a different kind, when he says that 'Hamlet's act is not Oedipus's act, in so far as Oedipus's act underpins his life and turns him into the hero he was before his downfall, as long as he does not know anything. Hamlet, for his part, is from the start guilty of being. For him being is unbearable' (*O24*, 15). In an almost Sartrean analysis, no doubt coloured by Sartre's or Camus's plays, Lacan then quotes the 'To be or not to be' monologue, and goes back to what the Father tells the son when asking for revenge: that he has been killed while a mortal sinner, 'Cut off even in the blossoms of my sin' (*Hamlet*, I, 5, 76). As Lacan notes, Hamlet cannot pay for this debt, he cannot act because something is missing, something akin to castration (*O24*, 17). I have quoted this first seminar at some length in order to emphasise two points: Lacan praises Freud but is clearly eager to replace his Oedipal interpretation by a different logic in which the Other, being and non-being, or more precisely symbolic castration will play a role, however it looks as though his ambivalent groping came from the fact that he had not yet really found the key to his own reading.

The following week (11 March), Lacan returns to historical and contextual issues, mentioning the telling date of 1601, when the play was performed for the first time in London. He opposes Ella Sharpe's book on Hamlet to Jones's famous 1910 essay 'The Oedipus complex: An explanation of the Hamlet mystery', and then surveys all the classicists among the *Hamlet* commentators, including Goethe and Coleridge. He still believes, following Jones at any rate, that *Hamlet* is 'a sort of trap' in which the Oedipus complex and castration have been caught (*O24*, 24). Then, when again summarising the play, he stops at the moment when Hamlet is on the point of dispatching Claudius whom he sees as full of remorse after the 'play' and lost in his prayers (*Hamlet*, III, 3, 72–82). Hamlet cannot kill him, since he knows that his own father is either in Hell or in Purgatory. Lacan comments: 'The whole *to be or not be* is entirely to be found here. He is concerned with the eternal *to be* of Claudius, and this is why he leaves his sword in its sheath' (*O24*, 28). The notion of a 'being' or a 'to be' even after death clearly announces the concept of 'second death', which Lacan will later identify as a key to *Antigone*. Here the analysis shifts from being to desire, since Lacan then adds: 'Let us return to Claudius. Hamlet explains very clearly that he would like to catch him in the excess of his pleasures, that is to say in a rapport with the Queen. The key point is the desire of the mother' (*O24*, 28). Lacan has finally hit upon the key term, and it will serve as a central insight into his reading. Here one can perceive the extent to which Lacan's formula 'the subject's desire is the desire of the Other' displaces the Freudian thesis. Far from saying that Hamlet is motivated by Oedipal rivalry – indeed, as Lacan wonders a few times, how can such an Oedipal pattern explain the endless delay and prevent the revenge? Why would Hamlet not want to kill the uncle precisely because he has accomplished his deepest wishes? Why would one not wish to eliminate a successful rival? – he is saying that the source of the riddle lies in an unfathomable feminine desire.

What Lacan has finally brought to light is the dependence of Freud's Oedipal model upon a psychological reasoning that could be completely reversed:

> What does the psychoanalytic tradition tell us? That everything hinges around the desire for the mother, that this desire is repressed, and that this is the cause for which the hero could not approach the act that is requested of him, namely the revenge against a man who is the current possessor, how illegitimate because a criminal, of the maternal object. If he cannot strike the person who has been pointed out for his vindication, it is because he himself has already committed the crime to be avenged. In as much as there is in the background the memory of an infantile desire for the mother, of the oedipal desire to murder the father, Hamlet would in a sense become an accomplice of the current owner, *beatus possidens*, in his eyes. He could not attack this owner without attacking himself. Is this what they mean? – or he could not attack this possessor without reawakening in himself the old desire, felt as a guilty one, in a mechanism that makes obviously more sense.

> Let us not get fascinated by such a non dialectical scheme. Couldn't we say that everything could be reversed? If Hamlet was to jump

immediately on his father-in-law, could one not say that he finds in this an opportunity to quench his guilt? (*O25*, 19).

Here, Lacan has completely discarded Freud's earliest insight and also, more fundamentally, the intellectual mainspring of his interpretation as being non-dialectical (while he actually seems to believe that he refutes only Jones and Sharpe). The source of Hamlet's inhibition does *not* stem from his desire for his mother, but from his own 'fixation' within his mother's desire. The shift from a subjective genitive (where 'mother's desire' means 'desire for the mother') to an objective genitive ('mother's desire' as her 'desire for another man') has never worked better; it is a 'dialectical' mechanism indeed, whose flexibility is nevertheless limited since it refutes the old Oedipian psychology. This psychology has been replaced by an ontology in which the subject is requested to go beyond his first object and reach an awareness of the place of the big Other as determining desire. I should pause here to add that just a few years later Lacan replaces the notion of 'ontology of desire' by an 'ethics of desire'. The consequences of such a displacement are momentous, not merely for Hamlet the character, but for any subject.

Thus the key scene in the play for Lacan is not, as it is for Ella Sharpe, the play within the play, or the 'mousetrap' with which Hamlet catches the conscience of Claudius, but the following scene, when he has managed to touch his uncle but finally fails with the mother. This is why Lacan comments at some length or the harrowing scene in which Hamlet argues with Gertrude, pointing out that when the ghost says 'O, step between her and her fighting soul' (*Hamlet*, III, 4, 112), this seems to quote the 'between' mentioned by Hamlet in reply to Ophelia's 'You are as good as a chorus': 'I could interpret between you and your love if I could see the puppets dallying' (*Hamlet*, III, 2, 222–4) which of course calls up his earlier bawdy remark pointing to sexuality as one main site of dereliction: 'That's a fair thought to lie between maids' legs' (ibid., 105). Hamlet fails to enter this 'between', this wedge that would give him access to female sexuality. He fails with his mother as he fails with Ophelia, because he measures the limit and weakness of his own desire. This limit is also that of his fantasy: Hamlet does not know what he wants because his fantasy has left him in the lurch. This explains why so much of the seminar is devoted to what could be called a 'grammar of fantasy', in which the barred subject or Hamlet has to learn to link his desire with an object that will 'cause' it, and that will 'bite' on him and force him to act accordingly.

In the next seminar Lacan again quotes a number of commentators. He has read with interest T. S. Eliot's piece in the *Sacred Wood*, and discusses whether or not *Hamlet* can be called a 'good play'. In spite of surface variations, Eliot's interpretation is not that far from Lacan's. Let us remember that for Eliot, *Hamlet* fails as a work of art because Shakespeare has attempted to do too much at once. He agrees with Robertson, another commentator who believes that: 'Shakespeare's *Hamlet*, so far as it is Shakespeare's, is a play dealing with the effect of a mother's guilt upon her son, and that Shakespeare was unable to impose this motive successfully upon the 'intractable' material of the old play.'[12] Eliot's argument, concluding that emotional excess has led to artistic failure, leaves room for the 'pathologist' and points to an 'unconscious knowledge':

> The intense feeling, ecstatic or terrible, without an object or exceed-ing its object, is something which every person of sensibility has known; it is doubtless a study to pathologists. It often occurs in adolescence: ... The Hamlet of Laforgue is an adolescent; the Hamlet of Shakespeare is not, he has not that explanation and excuse. We must simply admit that here Shakespeare tackled a problem which proved too much for him. Why he attempted it at all is an insoluble puzzle; under compulsion of what experience he attempted to express the inexpressibly horrible, we cannot ever know.... We should have, finally, to know something which is by hypothesis unknowable, for we assume it to be an experience which, in the manner indicated, exceeded the facts. We should have to understand things which Shakespeare did not understand himself.'[13]

It is clear the Lacan hopes to rise up to this challenge and provide if not a biographical explanation – quite obviously futile – at least a pattern linking some 'experience' and the ineffable depths to which Eliot alludes. Lacan thus concludes that *Hamlet* is a good play, contrary to Eliot's opinion, precisely because here the riddle of desire, as determined by the locus of the Other, is so well depicted, staged in such an engrossing manner.

To shed more light on the 'inexpressibly horrible' he needs to reopen the issue of Hamlet's dependence on his mother's desire. This is how he sums up his central hypothesis: 'Notice that what Hamlet is affronted to, and all the time, who he struggles with, is a desire. This desire has to be considered where it is in the play. This desire is quite far from his own. It is not his desire for his mother, it is his mother's desire' (*O25*, 20). The key resides in a further decentring of the hero's plight. Just as Eliot performed the curious slip of the pen that made him title his essay 'Hamlet and *his* problems', whereas he wished to treat the play as a text and not as a psychological document (having rightly noticed that all commentators tend to project themselves into the hero, Goethe seeing him as a Werther, and Coleridge as a Coleridge), Lacan addresses 'Hamlet and *its* problems', or better said, '*Hamlet* and *her* problems'. Indeed *Hamlet* as a play is even more crucial for Lacanian theory, since it both articulates how desire and fantasy can work together and how desire is determined by the mother, while fantasy is underpinned by the phallus and the missing, shifting, elusive *objet petit a*. As Lacan sums up on 22 April 1959:

> Our first step in this direction [NB. How to understand the way human subjectivity is determined by the signifier] was to express the extent to which the play is dominated by the Mother as Other, i.e., the primordial subject of the demand. The omnipotence of which we are always speaking in psychoanalysis is first of all the omnipotence of the subject of the first demand, and this omnipotence must be related back to the Mother.[14]

This is why Lacan needs to reread once more the scene of moral torture in which Hamlet tries to make Gertrude renounce Claudius, and notices that it is only when Hamlet seems to have won, forcing his mother to confess 'Oh Hamlet! thou hast cleft my heart in twain' (*Hamlet*, III, 4, 157), when he has admonished her 'go not to mine uncle's bed' (ibid., 160), and when she sounds ready to follow his advice ('What shall I do?', ibid., 181), that suddenly in an enigmatic tirade, he evokes the possibility of sexual betrayal:

> Let the bloat king tempt you again to bed,
> Pinch wanton on your cheek, call you his mouse,
> And let him, for a pair of reechy kisses,
> Or paddling in your neck with his damn'd fingers,
> Make you to ravel all this matter out... (ibid., 182–7)

Hamlet had almost found a discourse that suggested restraint, shame and rejection of the murderous brother, when his discourse appears to collapse, to fall back from this position. Lacan then adds that this confirms Hamlet's earlier intuition about his mother: his mother is a 'real genital woman' who cannot understand mourning (*O25*, 23). She is a 'gaping cunt' who thinks only 'when one has gone, here comes the other' (*O24*, 23). One could say that Hamlet is overwhelmed by his mother's *jouissance*, an excessive enjoyment of genital love-making he is unable to move or budge from its groove.

An almost farcical symptom of the power Gertrude seems to have over her son is provided by the curious exchange that takes place between Hamlet and Claudius when he finally agrees to leave Denmark with Rosencrantz and Guildenstern:

> *Hamlet*: For England?
> *Claudius*: Ay Hamlet.
> *Hamlet*: Good.
> *Claudius*: So it is if thou knew'st our purposes.
> *Hamlet*: I see a cherub that sees them. But come, for England! Farewell dear mother.
> *Claudius*: Thy loving father, Hamlet.
> *Hamlet*: My mother. Father and mother is man and wife, man and wife is one flesh, and so, my mother. Come, for England. (*Hamlet*, IV, 3, 44–9)

Whereas Claudius woodenly and obstinately enacts the consequences of his own speech on fathers (*Hamlet*, I, 2, 87–117), insists upon a literal gendering of authority, Hamlet's 'mad' speech alludes both to Denmark as his 'motherland' and to the riddle of an 'incestuous' couple, which has by then been identified in his mind with the puzzling mother.

This explains why Hamlet only retrieves his desire when, at the end, coming back from his sea trip, he sees Laertes in Ophelia's open tomb: he cannot stand a rival who is better able to express mourning. He recaptures his desire and even signs it as he shouts the passionate cry 'This is I, Hamlet the Dane' (*Hamlet*, V, 1, 223–4). By this time, indeed, Ophelia has become mad and has drowned. Ophelia fulfilled her role as impossible object of desire when she died: she literally embodied the phallic overtones of her name, and chose a string of erotic names for the flowers out of which she wove her funeral garland. Ophelia becomes the phallus – Lacan quotes Homer, who uses *ophelio* to mean 'swell, make bigger' (*O25*, 35) as he describes the phallus in terms that hesitate between comedy and tragedy. If the phallus is that part of the body in which 'vital tumescence' is symbolised (*O25*, 32), then indeed Ophelia's very name condenses this function, while her imaginary role for Hamlet could be evoked in terms of the dire consequences of the sexual act: 'why wouldst thou be a breeder of sinners?' (*Hamlet*, III, 1, 119).

In the following seminar – the first to be translated into English[15] – Lacan elaborates on Ophelia and her crucial function as the object of fantasy according to the following scheme: $ ◊ a. Ophelia is not simply identified with the missing phallus, she is also Hamlet's *objet petit a*: 'What is it that the subject is deprived of? The phallus; and it is from the phallus that the object gets its function in the fantasy, and from the phallus that desire is constituted within the fantasy as its reference' (*LP*, 15). By her agency, the big Other of desire is barred (Ⱥ) when it meets its own lack as φ. Hamlet has lost all interest in the Ophelia he says he 'did love' once. She is a mere symbol who can be associated with other symbols, such as the 'dead men's fingers' to which 'liberal shepherds give a grosser name' (*Hamlet*, IV, 7, 170). Lacan knows that these wild orchids were commonly associated with testicles because of the shape of the roots, or with mandrakes, supposed to have been generated from the sperm of hanged men. 'Ophelia is at this point the phallus exteriorized and rejected by the subject as a symbol signifying life' (*LP*, 23). And one should not forget that at the time of her madness, she intones potentially ribald song fragments:

> Young men will do't if they come to't –
> By Cock, they are to blame.
> Quoth she, 'Before you tumbled me,
> You promised me to wed'. (*Hamlet*, IV, 5, 60–4)

It is indeed fitting that Claudius should ask: 'How long has she been thus?' (ibid., IV, 5, 66).

Here Lacan partly restates Ella Sharpe's thesis about 'the impatience of Hamlet', but within a symbolic logic that is underpinned by the Other, as he describes how, for Hamlet, all actions are determined by 'the time of the Other': 'Hamlet is always at the hour of the Other' (*LP*, 25). This time over which Hamlet has no control is the second manifestation of his having lost his grip on desire: first there was the unshakeable desire of his mother, followed by the fact that his time eludes him until he crosses the limit separating life from death. When he jumps into Ophelia's freshly dug tomb, Hamlet can mourn the *objet a*, escape from the power of his mother's desire and recapture his desire for a lost object – an object not of desire but *in* desire, as Lacan writes (*LP*, 28). The price is of course his own death, a death that finally allows the expected revenge in answer to the ghostly father's demand. Because of the haste evinced by every protagonist, the dead father has reached the kingdom of the dead with an open wound, an open debt. The father appears supported by the barred Other: one hopes that this hole will be closed at the end by a resolution in which death triumphs, in what Mallarmé called Shakespeare's 'sumptuous and stagnant exaggeration of murder'.[16]

This is why Lacan reads very closely the last scene of the duel, noticing a special emphasis in the elaborate descriptions of the swords used by the fighters. The term Shakespeare uses is 'foil' ('Let the foils be brought', *Hamlet*, V, 2, 154) so as to allow for Hamlet's pun: 'I'll be your foil, Laertes. In mine ignorance/Your skill shall like a star i' th' darkest night/Stick fiery off indeed' (ibid., 227–9). While glossing on the prevalence of punning in Shakespeare – which attests to the domination of the signifier over the signified – Lacan rightly surmises that *foil* is derived from *feuille* and means a material such as velvet used to set off jewels in a box, for instance. Hamlet means that Laertes is a better swordsman and more handsome than he is. Lacan draws the conclusion that we have come back to a mirror stage in which Hamlet and Laertes are still caught in an imaginary rivalry (based on a more general deception). The phallus has found its last metamorphosis in the play: like a deadly letter completing its circuit, it will unite Hamlet and Laertes and also the King. 'In this pun there lies ultimately an identification with the mortal phallus' (*LP*, 34). This phallus finally appears as a way of stopping the hole in the real that has opened for Hamlet when he jumped into Ophelia's tomb.

The hole created by death is identical to the hole of the letter of literature: both allow the projection of a missing signifier without which desire cannot find its place:

> Just as what is rejected from the symbolic register reappears in the real, in the same way the hole in the real that results from loss, sets the signifier in motion. This hole provides the place for the projection of the missing signifier, which is essential to the structure of the Other. This is the signifier whose absence leaves the Other incapable of responding to your question, the signifier that can be purchased only with your own flesh and your own blood, the signifier that is essentially the veiled phallus (*LP*, 38).

By a neat structural homology, what is revealed by literature has the most momentous consequences for individual desire.

Here, after a series of detours – indeed he mentions in an aside how his strategy consists in a series of 'concentric strokes' (*LP*, 47) – Lacan finally manages to reconcile his interpretation with the main elements Freudian theory. If *Hamlet* is a 'tragedy of desire' and if it is shown to fail because of insufficient mourning, then the key is a forceful link between mourning and the phallus. Quoting Freud's late text on the decline of the Oedipus complex (1924),[17] Lacan shows that the only way for the subject to accept castration and 'resolve' the Oedipus complex is to 'mourn the phallus': 'the Oedipus complex goes into its decline insofar as the subject must mourn the phallus' (*LP*, 46). The phallus, as Freud sees it in this context, is determined by the narcissism that the subject is ready (or not) to abandon; in Lacan's terminology, it is less an imaginary object than a 'veiled' object that only appears in brief flashes, in sudden 'epiphanies' (*phanies*) (*LP*, 48). Then all the elements fall together:

> And doesn't it seem that this is the point around which Hamlet's action turns and lingers? His astounded spirit, so to speak, trembles before something that is utterly unexpected: the phallus is located here in a position that is entirely out of place in terms of its position in the Oedipus complex. Here, the phallus to be struck at is real indeed. And Hamlet always stops. The very source of what makes Hamlet's arm waver at every moment is the narcissistic connection that Freud tells us about in his text on the decline of the Oedipus complex: one cannot strike the phallus, because the phallus, even the real phallus, is a *ghost* (*LP*, 50).

One cannot kill the phallus because, like Hamlet's king, it is a 'thing of nothing' – it does not exist. Hamlet will be able to desire and kill his two rivals only after he has relinquished all other narcissistic attachments, that is, when he is mortally wounded and knows he is going to die. Laertes and Hamlet can then exchange their mutual blessings, so that other deaths will not follow them (unlike in *Oedipus*, where the tragic *Atè* is perpetuated until the next generation). By positing a Hamlet who is caught up in his mother's desire until he traverses death and the phallus – thanks to Ophelia and her sad fate – Lacan has presented a totally original reading of the play, in an approach that remains very attentive to the network of its key-signifiers, while working away from the usual interpretation of the play as just a modern-day restaging of the Oedipus complex.

As Bruce Fink has indicated in a useful discussion of Lacan's reading of *Hamlet*, Lacan does not wish to interpret the play so much as to learn from it.[18] The play is a universal masterpiece not just because it offers an interesting riddle that we may try to decipher, but also because it teaches us something fundamental about human desire. Reading literature remains a pedagogical process for Lacan, not only because he performs his own readings in front of an audience – and I have tried to give an idea of the detours, obliquities and even strategical repetitions he indulges in – but because any interpretation proposes an interaction in which we as readers are taught something about ourselves (in our connection with language, desire, society, gender and so on) not only insofar as our social beings are concerned, but insofar as our desire is questioned. Freud had already noted that poets had 'preceded' him on the terrain of the unconscious, but he quotes Shakespeare so often that one can say there is a Shakespearian myth at work in psychoanalysis. This Shakespearian myth 'hystericises' us all, forces us to pose again and again the question of desire.

With Lacan, we have moved to an awareness of this unconscious as not simply the obscure part of a knowledge unavailable to the writer (whoever the author of *Hamlet* may have been) but also as an injunction that seems closer to Eliot's concept. Having read or seen *Hamlet* performed on stage we are indeed left with an ethical obligation: the play, the text, posit a demand that we should not remain passive but go on interpreting. Much as when Freud felt the urge to interpret why and how Michelangelo's Moses could exert such a fascination on him, we, as readers of *Hamlet* must 'know something which is by hypothesis unknowable', as Eliot wrote. Having met the Other in 'an experience which exceeds the facts', we have the added burden of trying to understand all those things that Shakespeare (or Freud) could not understand.

6 *Antigone*: Between the Beautiful and the Sublime

If Lacan reads literary texts in order to learn from them, moreover to learn things he would not find in other kinds of text or experience, one can understand why *Antigone* plays such a role in the 1959–60 seminar, 'The Ethics of Psychoanalysis'. It is a commonplace understanding in classical criticism that in this play Sophocles depicts Antigone as a tragic heroine who is ready to die in order to save the unwritten values of the family, values coming directly from the realm of the gods, thus salvaging ethics from any political encroachment. She is taken to state that even if her two brothers died fighting, one for Thebes, the other against Thebes, their fates should not be distinguished in death. This provides Hegel with a central argument in his well-known analysis of the play, an analysis that Lacan acknowledges, even if it is to explore unexpected avenues or even to take a somewhat eccentric route to the play.[1]

Hegel's main thesis has been often restated and at times simplified. It consists in a dichotomy between Creon, who embodies the political values of the city, and Antigone, who embodies the ethical values of the family. Creon wants to honour the defender of Thebes, Eteocles, through proper rites of burial, but he decides to leave Polynices's body unburied, to be devoured by wild beasts in the plain where he fell, which constitutes one of the worst ignominies for the beliefs of the time, and moreover prevents anyone from rendering the same rites to him, upon penalty of death. Antigone defies Creon by conspicuously covering Polynices's body. Hegel states very cogently that these conflicting value systems have equal rights, and how it is from their clash that tragedy is born. When Creon wishes to separate 'the good from the bad' in the name of a logic of inclusion and exclusion, Antigone stresses a more fundamental respect for the dead that admits of no division:

Creon: Attacking his country, while the other defended it.
Antigone: Even so, we have a duty to the dead.
Creon: Not to give equal honour to the good and bad.
Antigone: Who knows? In the country of the dead that may be the
law.
Creon: An enemy cannot be a friend, even when dead.[2]

Hegel's reading goes further, however, when he attempts to make sense of a passage in *Antigone* that has caused a lot of speculation: Antigone seems to distinguish between the universal duty one owes to any dead member of one's family, and her specific relationship with this particular brother. In the poignant lament voiced just before she goes to her tomb, she expresses this very clearly:

It was by this service to your dear body, Polynices,
I earned the punishment which now I suffer,
Though all good people know it was for your honour.
    O but I would not have done the forbidden thing
For any husband or for any son.
For why? I could have had another husband
And by him other sons, if one were lost;
But father and mother lost, where would I get
Another brother? For thus preferring you,
My brother, Creon condemns me and hales me away,
Never a bride, never a mother, unfriended,
Condemned alive to a solitary death.[3]

The passage shocked Goethe to the point that he expressed the wish that some day it would be revealed to be a mere interpolation, as Lacan reminds us (*S7*, 255). Like Hegel, Lacan does not seem so shocked, and he even relishes the 'odour of scandal' these lines contain (*S7*, 256). One of the main issues implied by this 'scandal' concerns the concept of 'generation', both in the sense of the ability to procreate, here refused to Antigone, and in the sense that the succession of generations has been perverted after Oedipus's transgression. Antigone's very name suggests a movement 'against' generation, as if her fate was linked to a deliberate or enforced sterility. In this passage she seems to contradict a universalistic command that would stress respect for the dead whoever they are, administering correct funeral rites and not wishing to strike someone 'beyond death', in the name of a more personal preference for this slain brother. Before jumping ahead to a psychoanalytic reading that would find an incestuous love linking brother and sister,[4] let us see how Hegel interprets this absolute singularity:

> The loss of the brother is therefore irreparable to the sister and her duty towards him is the highest. ... The brother is the member of the Family in whom its Spirit becomes an individuality which turns towards another sphere, and passes over into the consciousness of universality. ... He passes from the divine law, in whose sphere he lived, over to human law. But the sister becomes, or the wife remains, the guardian of the divine law. In this way, the two sexes overcome their (merely) natural being and appear in their ethical significance, as diverse beings who share between them the two distinctions belonging to the ethical substance.[5]

Hegel's reading of *Antigone* thus entails not simply a strict opposition between the city and the individual, but a meditation on what could be called the ethical and political roles of sexual difference, a point that should be remembered when we see how much Creon is afraid of looking weak in front of a woman. 'Better be beaten, if need be, by a man,/Than let a woman get the better of us' (*Antigone*, 144). The family is the site of this transition between the hidden laws coming from the gods and the written or spoken laws of the city. The brother emerges from the family and moves into the public domain, while the sister can choose to remain in the house, as Ismene does, or to go out into the open and act, as Antigone does. Hegel seizes on this and on the subversive factor represented by Antigone: insofar as she is not merely the representative of the unwritten law of the gods, but also of an extreme singularity of desire, she embodies the 'perversion' of the universalist values upon which Creon's order is based:

> Since the community only gets an existence through its interference with the happiness of the Family, and by dissolving [individual] self-consciousness into the universal, it creates for itself in what it suppresses and what is at the same time essential to it an internal enemy – womankind in general. Womankind – the everlasting irony [in the life] of the community – changes by intrigue the universal end of the government into a private end, transforms its universal act into a work of some particular individual, and perverts the universal property of the state into a possession and ornament for the Family.[6]

Thus, in a curious but logical move, Hegel stresses the guilt inherent in Antigone's actions – she indeed transgresses the law knowingly: 'The ethical consciousness must, on account of this actuality and on account of its deed, acknowledge its opposite as its own actuality, must acknowledge its guilt. "Because we suffer we acknowledge we have erred.".'[7]

In this passage Hegel quotes the only line of the play in which Antigone appears to hesitate, for a short instant, as she is on the threshold of death (she has been condemned to be entombed alive). What she says has been glossed by a translator as this: 'If the gods regard this right (sc. that I, though pious, am thought impious), I would confess, having been taught by suffering (according to the maxim (πάθος μάθος) that I have done wrong.'[8] A number of commentators have stressed that this reading gives undue emphasis to a single line, while most of the time Antigone is adamant that she was right to act as she did.[9] Antigone merely hints that she is confident that the gods will finally declare her right to postulate that their decrees should be valued above human laws.

Hegel, who has thus paired off Creon and Antigone as both 'wrong' in some way, concludes that the only possible outcome is the rigorous annihilation of each party:

> The victory of one power and its character, and the defeat of the other, would thus be only the part and the incomplete work which irresistibly advances to the equilibrium of the two. Only in the downfall of both sides alike is absolute right accomplished, and the ethical substance as the negative power which engulfs both sides, that is, omnipotent and righteous Destiny, steps on the scene.[10]

Death is thus indeed the 'absolute master' and the only mediator allowing a movement towards a definition of ethical life (*Sittlichkeit*) as a substance reconciling the universal and the singular in the community.

This detour is necessary to understand why Lacan, if he cannot be called Hegelian in his reading, nevertheless remains quite close to the original insights of the philosopher. In the seminar on the ethics of psychoanalysis, one can follow how Lacan reaches Antigone through Hegel, while openly stating his disagreement and moving on to a different track. The first mention of Sophocles' play appears in a passage in which he discusses Hegel:

A new problem arises for us, one that even Hegel found obscure. For a long time in the *Phenomenology of Spirit*, Hegel tried to articulate the problem of human history in terms of conflicts between discourses. The tragedy of Antigone especially appealed to him because he saw the clear opposition there between the discourse of the family and that of the state. But in my opinion things are much less clear.[11]

He states a few pages later that Hegel considered *Antigone* 'the most perfect' tragedy 'but for the wrong reasons' (*S7*, 240). Lacan's starting point is Hegelian in the sense that he insists that Antigone's position 'relates to a criminal good' (ibid.) and is not dictated simply by the Good. In the same session leading to a systematic confrontation with *Antigone*, Lacan presents a rather devastating critique of the Freudian concept of 'sublimation':

Freud's text is very weak on the topic. The definition he gives of sublimation at work in artistic creation only manages to show us the reaction or repercussion of the effects of what happens at the level of the sublimation of the drive, when the result or the work of the creator of the beautiful reenters the field of goods, that is to say, when they have become commodities. One must recognize that the summary Freud gives of the artist's career is practically grotesque. The artist, he says, gives a beautiful form to the forbidden object in order that everyone, by buying his little artistic product, rewards and sanctions his daring. That is a way of short-circuiting the problem (*S7*, 238).

These remarks, coupled with a critique of Hegel, show the importance of *Antigone*: it is with this play that Lacan will at the same time show an example of the true ethical position, a repudiation of sublimation in the old sense, and praise for a desire based on something else than the good (in the idealist sense defined by classical wisdom since Plato and Aristotle) or the goods (in the sense of a cultural economy that commodifies values and works of art).

This is why he can announce in the following meeting that he has reached a 'turning point' with *Antigone* (*S7*, 243). However the title given to the session is surprising: 'The splendor of Antigone'. Far from stressing, as one might have expected, a guilt Antigone somehow admits of (as did Hegel), which has the effect of fore-grounding Creon's tragic nature, or an innocence that she claims, Lacan admits from the start that one can see only Antigone in the play: she catches all the glances. He does so after a discussion of catharsis or the 'purgation of passions' as the main effect of tragedy, linking Aristotle's *Poetics* to Freud's idea of a 'cathartic method'. Lacan insists that like the Cathars of Provence, who called themselves 'the Pure', the tragic process is centrally concerned with purification or purity. The tragedy of *Antigone*, according to his interpretation, manages to purge or, better, purify us by presenting a brilliant and fascinating image – that of Antigone herself:

> In effect, *Antigone* reveals to us the line of sight that defines desire. This line of sight focuses on an image that possesses a mystery which up till now has never been articulated, since it forces you to close your eyes at the very moment you look at it. Yet that image is at the center of tragedy, since it is the fascinating image of Antigone herself. We know very well that over and beyond the dialogue, over and beyond the question of family and country, over and beyond moraliz- ing arguments, it is Antigone herself who fascinates us, Antigone in her unbearable splendor. She has a quality that both attracts us and startles us, in the sense of intimidates us; this terrible, self-willed victim disturbs us (*S7*, 247).

This is a surprising and original move by Lacan: Antigone is not called upon to allegorise the power of ethics over politics, but is taken primarily as a figure of beauty. At first the shift appears so brutal as to be unwarranted. Lacan nevertheless points out that this is not mere invention, since in the play the Chorus describes Antigone in those terms:

> But glory and praise go with you, lady,
> To your resting-place. You go with your beauty
> Unmarred by the hand of consuming sickness,
> Untouched by the sword, living and free [αυτονομος],
> As none other that ever died before you.[12]

This is said in reply to Antigone's dirge (Κομμος) but goes back to their earlier Ode to Eros. In the *Stasimon* the Chorus curiously praises the power of Love that conquers everything else just after hearing from Creon the manner in which Antigone has been condemned to die. To Creon's parting words ('... or learn at last/What hope there is

for those who worship death') the Chorus replies with a lyrical hymn
to Eros and Aphrodite:

> Where is the equal of Love (Ερος)?
> ... he is here
> In the bloom of a fair face
> Lying in wait;
> And the grip of his madness
> Spares not god or man,
>
> Marring the righteous man,
> Driving his soul into mazes of sin
> And strife, dividing a house.
> For the light that burns in the eyes of a bride of desire
> Is a fire that consumes.
> At the side of the great gods
> Aphrodite immortal
> Works her will upon all.[13]

At this precise point, Antigone enters among guards, and the Chorus
continues:

> But here is a sight beyond all bearing,
> At which my eyes cannot but weep;
> Antigone forth faring
> To her bridal-bower of endless sleep.

The rapid modulations between love and death, harmony and strife,
desire and division are bewildering. Clearly Lacan assumes that
Antigone is the hidden object of the entire song of praise, that the very
strong expression of a 'light that burns in the eyes of a bride of desire'
(εναργης βλεφαρων ιμερος) refers to her fascinating appearance, and
even announces it. This is how he construes this crucial passage:

> And it is from the same place that the image of Antigone appears
> before us as something that causes the Chorus to lose its head, as it
> tells us itself, makes the just appear unjust, and makes the Chorus
> transgress all limits, including casting aside any respect it might have
> for the edicts of the city. Nothing is more moving than that ιμερος
> εναργης, than the desire that visibly emanates from the eyelids of this
> admirable girl.

> The violent illumination, the glow of beauty, coincides with the moment of transgression or of realization of Antigone's *Atè*.... The moving side of beauty causes all critical judgment to vacillate, stop analysis, and plunges the different forms involved into a certain confusion or, rather, an essential blindness.
>
> The beauty effect is a blindness effect (*S7*, 281).

Lacan's allusion to the *Atè* of Antigone that is, her 'evil', her 'harm' or her 'misfortune' – sends us back to the whole Oedipus legend and to the legacy of 'sin' that Antigone has inherited from her father. This is what the Chorus tells her:

> My child you have gone your way
> To the outermost limit of daring
> And have stumbled against Law (Δικας) enthroned.
> This is the expiation
> You must make for the sin of your father.[14]

The Chorus shows the same ambivalence confronting Eros as facing Antigone: Antigone is remarkable for her beauty and her independence, but she has also condemned herself to death by her 'self-will', leading to a self-inflicted punishment ('You are the victim of your self-will' in line 875 echoes negatively the positive praise of her as a 'living and free' – αυτονομος – being in line 821). The Chorus's contradictions respond to what is 'blinding' in Antigone's fate: she embodies desire, an erotic desire, while the object of her desire is dead, and can even be called Death. It is not true to say, as some commentators have, that Lacan identifies with Antigone;[15] on the contrary, he identifies with the fascinated gaze of the Chorus on a heroine whose beauty baffles and seduces them. While admitting to a similar disorientation, Lacan identifies with an audience upon whom tragedy can work its purification, which is why he describes his whole reading of the play as an approach to 'the essence of tragedy' (*S7*, 241). On might even suggest that this passage in the seminar is the equivalent of Nietzsche's *Birth of tragedy*. Lacan is conscious of this proximity, although he distinguishes between a purely Nietzchean reading and his own approach, more influenced by Bataille. He thus says 'There is nothing Dionysiac about the act and the countenance of Antigone. Yet she pushes to the limit the realization of something that might be called the pure and simple desire of death as such. She incarnates that desire' (*S7*, 282).

We can begin to understand the paradoxical link Lacan establishes between her beauty and her ethical function. Antigone fascinates, but creates a fascination that destroys fascination itself. Antigone provides an image that goes beyond itself and that, in this very movement, purifies vision, operates a *catharsis* on the imaginary:

> It is in connection with this power of attraction that we should look for the true sense, the true mystery, the true significance of tragedy – in connection with the excitement involved, in connection with the emotions and, in particular, with the singular emotions that are fear and pity, since it is through their interventions, δι' ελεον και φοβον, through the intervention of pity and fear, that we are purged, purified of everything of that order. And that order, we can now immediately recognize, is properly speaking the order of the imaginary. And we are purged of it through the intervention of one image among others (*S7*, 247–8).

This is the main reason why Lacan refrains from using the term 'sublime' when speaking of Antigone, while showing in his style, in his rhapsodic mode of utterance, the elevating power of Antigone as a character.

By demonstrating concretely how this specific 'beauty' can function as sublime in effect, Lacan deliberately avoids resorting to an analysis of the Kantian sublime in his reading. He refers to Kant repeatedly, but only in order to emphasise the links between the beautiful and desire on the one hand, and the law and negative excess on the other. For instance he shows how Creon is a 'Kantian' ruler when he poses his maxim as universal, and his side of the tragedy points to the dire consequences of universal laws:

> Note that his language is in perfect conformity with that which Kant calls the *Begriff* or concept of the good. It is the language of practical reason. His refusal to allow a sepulcher for Polynices, who is an enemy and traitor to his country is founded on the fact that one cannot at the same time honor those who have defended their country and those who have attacked it. From a Kantian point of view, it is a maxim that can be given as a rule of reason with a universal validity. Thus, before the ethical progression that from Aristotle to Kant leads us to make clear the identity of law and reason, doesn't the

spectacle of tragedy reveal to us in anticipation the first objection? The good cannot reign over all without an excess emerging whose fatal consequences are revealed to us in tragedy (S7, 259).

We will meet again the figure of a 'Sadian' Kant; Antigone's position is first of all a negative one, that of resistance to tyranny. She does not counter with another 'categorical imperative' that would assert something like 'all sisters have a duty to their dead brothers'.

Antigone's positive assertion concerns her desire, a desire that, as we have seen, one might be tempted to reduce to incest, especially in such a loaded Oedipian context. Lacan suggests to the contrary that in *Antigone* incest is merely a figure of singularity. Rather than generalising her close relationship with Polynices as incest, as a more or less universal category defining a certain type of prohibition, we have a trope of absolute singularity that opposes the universality of the law. This singularity is embodied in a woman whose 'beauty' cannot be measured by objective criteria (we should not forget that the actor who played Antigone wore a mask, but Lacan's thesis is that her beauty should be apparent even with a very plain person on stage) but distinguishes her in the eyes of her beholders. This shining and blinding beauty comes as a singular feature linked with the most arbitrary elements (like the shape of one's nose or mouth, the flash in the gaze) that provide both a critique of universalist maxims and a reminder that one cannot truly act without claiming full responsibility for one's desire. In a sense Antigone takes over Hamlet's plight after he has jumped into the open tomb. Which is why she too will be condemned to a 'living death' in a tomb. Antigone acts beyond traditional ethics; she is beyond the good and the goods, she repudiates the usual definition of goodness and escapes any form of commodification of her beauty – she will not marry, she has been subtracted from the circuit of symbolical exchanges.

The reference to Kant's second critique (and not to the *Critique of Judgment*) is thus very revealing: Lacan focuses his reading on the consequences of a collective choice in favour of the good over the beautiful. In respect of Antigone, his avoidance of the concept of sublime is even more striking, given the many sessions devoted earlier in the seminar on ethics to a new definition of sublimation. (Philippe Van Haute has written an excellent essay on sublimation in Lacan's reading of Antigone.)[16] It is necessary to keep in mind the long discussion of the Thing as opposed to the object, and the definition of sublimation as 'raising the object to the dignity of a Thing' – 'The object is elevated to the dignity of the Thing' (*S7*, 112) – at the beginning of the seminar in order to understand what Lacan may be suggesting.

As I shall return to this issue in connection with Sade and Duras (Chapters 7 and 8) I will limit my remarks to what Lacan articulates directly about *Antigone*, a reading in which he does not return to this dichotomy of Thing/object, but discusses a turning point, a conceptual hinge he had observed in Freud: 'It is, I assume, clear to you all that what I am concerned with this year is situated somewhere between a Freudian ethics and a Freudian aesthetics. Freudian aesthetics is involved because it reveals one of the phases of the function of ethics' (*S7*, 159). As Lacan develops this, Freudian aesthetics reveal both that 'the Thing is inaccessible', which is not far from what takes place with *Antigone*, and that the path of sublimation does not cancel out desire. Or to be more precise, Antigone can be said to be both sublime and beautiful in her 'blinding way' precisely because she does not sublimate her own desire, rather she heightens it and charges it with libidinal intensity, even when this desire is a desire for death.

Indeed we have to visualise Antigone's particular fate as accurately as possible. Her being condemned to die a slow death in a tomb (in fact she kills herself, thus preventing Creon from saving her at the end) places her in a curious no-man's land, or in a 'death-in-life', which is congruent with the concept of a 'second death' that Lacan elaborates in respect of Sade. Creon condemns her 'not to live' rather than to die, which allows her to assert her autonomy one last time by committing suicide, a hasty gesture that also triggers the suicide of Haemon, Creon's son and her lover, and of Creon's wife. Like Oedipus, who does not die immediately after the revelation of his identity (as Jocasta does) and who finally dies at Colonnus, Creon cannot kill himself at the end, but is condemned to live on so as to suffer inexpiable remorse: 'I am nothing. I have no life./Lead me away...', he utters plaintively at the end of the tragedy.

Creon's crucial mistake, his *harmartia*, hinges on his belief that he can 'kill his enemy a second time'; here he is not so far from Hamlet, who refrains from killing Claudius when he concludes that this would just be inflicting the 'first death' upon him, and not the 'second death' of the soul, as suffered by his father. Tiresias finally flatly condemns Creon's bad judgment in terms that clearly attack his αυθαδια, that is, his overweening self-confidence, his arrogant overreliance on his own judgment – a term that Aristotle would oppose to the 'happy mean' of balanced judgment: 'Only a fool is governed by self-will [αυθαδια]./ Pay to the dead his due. Wound not the fallen./It is no glory to kill and kill again.'[17] More literally, Tiresias says 'There is no bravery in killing a second time a dead man [θανοντ' επικτανειν]' (l. 1030). Much worse than flogging a dead horse, Creon's wish to pursue his enemy beyond death is a clear symptom of hubris, indicating a transgression, a passing of certain limits in a gesture that disrupts the very polity it pretends to bolster.

Understood in this broader context, Antigone's beauty encapsulates several functions: we have seen how it embodies desire by making it visible ('Ιμερος εναργης is literally desire made visible', *S7*, 268) and how it arrests desire at the same time ('The appearance of beauty intimidates and stops desire', *S7*, 238). This state of 'arrestedness' suggests a more intimate link between beauty and death. Lacan comments on the fact that beauty both attracts outrage and resists it:

> On the one hand, it seems that the horizon of desire may be eliminated from the register of the beautiful. Yet, on the other hand, it has been no less apparent ... that the beautiful has the effect, I would say, of suspending, lowering, disarming desire.... That is not to say that on certain occasions beauty cannot be joined to desire, but in a mysterious way, and in a form that I can do no better than refer to by the term that bears within it the structure of the crossing of some invisible line, i.e., outrage. Moreover, it seems that it is in the nature of the beautiful to remain, as they say, insensitive to outrage, and that this is by no means one of the least significant elements of its structure (*S7*, 238).

Antigone's beauty therefore functions as a screen for fantasy that will also arrest the movement from the first to the 'second death'.

The 'beauty effect', then, derives from the relationship between the hero or heroine and the passage to the limit (*S7*, 286) – a passage that cannot but evoke the sublime. Thus only towards the end of his sessions devoted to Antigone does Lacan approach an analysis of the sublime, but he leaves this to another speaker, Pierre Kaufmann:

> I would, therefore, like today to ask someone to speak about the beautiful who seems to me to be particularly well-equipped to

discuss it in relation to something that I take to be essential for the continuation of my argument; that something is the definition of the beautiful and the sublime as articulated by Kant (*S7*, 286).

A little later he acknowledges that he has not managed to work out a theory of the two concepts, 'to indicate to you the direction taken by our research on the subject of the beautiful and, I would add, the sublime. We haven't yet extracted from the Kantian definition of the sublime all the substance we might' (*S7*, 301). It is perhaps useful to note at this point that Lacan never fulfilled this task, leaving it to Zizek, who brilliantly took up the notion in his *Sublime Object of Ideology*. Zizek was able to show very skilfully how the notion of the sublime leads us from Kant's third critique to Hegel's dialectics of negativity.

This is not what Lacan is doing in this seminar, partly because he is still very close to Heidegger, partly because beauty calls up both a sense of aesthetic arrest and a notion of specifically formal features in a way that the sublime does not. In an important afterthought to the *Antigone* discussion, he uses an anecdote to provide a funny example of the function of beauty. On a visit to London he and his wife had been having breakfast in their hotel when she declared that Professor D, whom they had not seen for years, was staying in the same place. To prove this rather unlikely assertion, she said that she had seen his shoes standing outside one of the rooms in the corridor. Later, Lacan, still skeptical, walked back to his room, and to his surprise he saw the professor slipping out of his room in a dressing gown. He concludes this rather fanciful illustration as follows: 'I find that experience highly instructive, and it is on this basis that I intend to suggest to you the notion of the beautiful' (*S7*, 296). Since he could visualise the professor's shoes '*ohne Begriff*' – quoting Kant's definition of the Beautiful as that which pleases 'immediately and without concept' – these telltale, worn-out 'clodhoppers' suddenly called up Van Gogh's famous shoes, and Heidegger's meditation about them. From the vignette he derives a sense of deidealised beauty, a beauty that does not ask to be sublimated:

> What I am, in effect, attempting to show here is that the beautiful has nothing to do with what is called ideal beauty. It is only on the basis of the apprehension of the beautiful at the very point of the transition between life and death that we can try to reinstate ideal beauty..., and

in the first place the famous human form (S7, 297).

By an astonishing detour, via this pair of old shoes waiting to be polished, we fall back on the question of Antigone's beauty:

> And it is this that leads me to posit the form of the body, and espe-
> cially its image, as I have previously articulated it in the function of
> narcissism, as that which from a certain point of view represents the
> relationship of man to his second death, the signifier of his desire, his
> visible desire.
>
> The central image is to be found in Ιμερος εναργης, which both
> indicates the site of desire insofar as it is desire of nothing, the rela-
> tionship of man to his lack in being, and prevents that site from being
> seen (S7, 298).

This passage indicates that Lacan is distancing himself from his previous fascination with Antigone, although a number of earlier remarks on the heroine heralded this a more negative appraisal: Antigone is called 'inhuman', her dialogue being marked by an 'exceptional harshness', especially in respect of her sister Ismene (S7, 263). She never seems to know pity or fear – the two basic emotions with which tragedy works, and she quickly turns into a willing 'martyr', which puts her in a truly terrifying position facing the other protagonists. Antigone remains 'unshakeable' and 'unyielding' in her resolve (S7, 279), which seems to be the lesson that Lacan draws from the play, especially when he concludes his seminar with his formula of 'ethics': 'First, the only thing one can be guilty of is giving ground relative to one's desire [céder sur son désir]' (S7, 321). If 'catharsis has the sense of purification of desire' (S7, 323), the spectator who sees the sad fate of a tragic heroine or hero realises that 'even for him who goes to the end of his desire, all is not a bed of roses' (S7, 323). Lacan is not advocating a kind of 'heroism' of desire, although it is obvious that Antigone can be seen as a model of constancy and consistency in one's desire.

As Patrick Guyomard notes, the issue of 'yielding' or 'not yielding' to one's desire is not really Antigone's problem; she has made a firm decision, and embraces death so quickly because she knows that this is the best way to avoid losing her resolve. (Guyomard links the fact that Lacan attributes to Oedipus a formidable 'me phunaï', expressing a desire that he wishes 'not to have existed', whereas it is in fact the

Chorus that utters this fateful phrase, to what he calls a second misquote when he seems to believe that it is Antigone who says: 'I will not yield.')[18] However, it might be simpler to assume that Lacan identifies less with Antigone than with the blinded Creon. The only character in *Antigone* who can be said to have been 'purified' by the play's crisscrossing of excesses and hubris is Creon. This is why he cannot die, unlike his wife, his son and Antigone. Without going as far as Jean Bolack, who in a recent book says that Creon is the 'tragic hero' of the play and does not spare his barbs when addressing Lacan's reading,[19] it is clear that if we take the injunction 'Do not yield to your desire' as central, then it is Creon who suffers from it rather than Antigone: he is the one to yield and repent, but too late.

The one problematic assertion made by Lacan concerns what he sees as the origin of the tragic 'evil' or *Até*, namely the desire of the mother. This occurs in a passage in which Antigone is associated with a desire for death:

> What happens to her desire? Shouldn't it be the desire of the Other and be linked to the desire of the mother? The text alludes to the fact that the desire of the mother is the origin of everything. The desire of the mother is the founding desire of the whole structure, the one that brought into the world the unique offspring that are Eteocles, Polynices, Antigone and Ismene; but it is also a criminal desire. Thus at the origin of tragedy and of humanism we find once again an impasse that is the same as Hamlet's, except strangely enough it is even more radical.
>
> No mediation is possible here except that of this desire with its radically destructive character. The fruit of the incestuous union has split into two brothers, one of whom represents power and the other crime. There is no one to assume the crime and the validity of crime apart from Antigone.
>
> Between the two of them, Antigone chooses to be purely and simply the guardian of the being of the criminal as such (*S7*, 282–3).

We should not attack Lacan for unduly blaming poor Jocasta![20] We could indeed discuss endlessly whether or not Oedipus was guilty, and whether it makes sense to condemn Jocasta for a knowledge (and a desire) she might have kept secret. What matters here is not whether Lacan is trying to lay the tragic blame on anyone: on the contrary, all these lines must be read as ones of praise. What interests him is not 'whodunit', even if he points to the desire of the Other as the main cause, but to see the beauty of Antigone in an aura of crime – in short, to portray her as a heroine of Sade.

7 Sade: Subverting the Law

'La Philosophie doit tout dire.' (Philosophy must say everything)[1]

When discussing Sade, one is dealing with a domain that is still rather contentious, the excesses of those who hate him having triggered a sort of hero worship as a response. Indeed thinkers such as Monique David-Ménard and Judith Feher-Gurewich have recently denounced what they see as Lacan's excessive complacency about the French writer.[2] One should never forget that Sade's main dream was to be acclaimed as a popular novelist or playwright, and that he only became a symbol of resistance to oppression because his writings more than his sexual transgresssions sent him to jail for most of his life. I would like to stress here Lacan's extreme prudence when confronting the 'Sade cult', blending fascination, annoyance and reservation when dealing with the 'divine Marquis'. This chapter will show how Sade's figure emerges out of his reading of ethics in Seminar VII, how he forces Lacan to reach the notion of the *'jouissance* of the Other' in Seminar X, before focusing on the difficult essay on Sade in *Ecrits,* namely 'Kant with Sade'.

Sadian genealogies

It is important to remember that Sade's literary fortunes were undergoing a deep sea-change at the time when Lacan became interested in him. In 1953 Simone de Beauvoir had asked provocatively 'Must we burn Sade?', and Blanchot's *Lautréamont et Sade* (1949) had attempted to give meaning to what he called 'Sade's Reason'. Lacan refers approvingly to Blanchot's book in Seminar VII (p. 201), and he mentions Pierre Klossowski's essay, *Sade My Neighbor* (1947) in 'Kant with Sade'.[3] De Beauvoir, Blanchot and Klossowski were not the only ones to help revise the French audience's opinion by forcing them to confront serious theoretical problems within a work that had too often been catalogued under the heading 'pornographic literature' or rejected as a clear example of clinical perversion. In the 1930s Samuel Beckett had been one of the first to dare go beyond this facile rejection when he was asked to translate *One Hundred and Twenty Days of Sodom* for Jack Kahane's Obelisk Press. Although he never completed the translation, here is what Beckett wrote to a friend:

> I have read 1st and 3rd vols. of French edition. The obscenity of surface is indescribable. Nothing could be less pornographical. It fills me with a kind of metaphysical ecstasy. The composition is extraordinary, as rigorous as Dante's. If the dispassionate statement of 600 'passions' is Puritan and a complete absence of satire juvenalesque, then it is, as you say, puritanical and juvenalesque.[4]

Lacan, as we shall see, to some extent shares these feelings, but oscillating more sharply between wonder and annoyance. Let us also recall that Lacan had been asked to write an introduction to 'The Philosophy in the Bedroom', which was part of Sade's collected works published by Editions du Cercle Précieux in 1963. Since the editors found his essay too obscure, he had to content himself with publishing it in *Critique* instead (April 1963) taking his revenge in a zestful note in which he wonders why the editors had again asked him to write on Sade after the success of his *Ecrits*.[5]

Thus when Lacan begins his investigation of the broadest questions of ethics, it is not so surprising to see Sade's name appear. In the 'Outline of the Seminar', Lacan stresses the fact that if psychoanalysis has anything new to say on the topic of ethics, it is because the daily experience of psychoanalysts puts them in touch with the 'universe of transgression' (*S7*, 2). He attributes to his colleague Angelo Hesnard, who had published several essays on crime and psychosis,[6] the phrase 'the morbid universe of transgression' and insists that a psychoanalyst has to confront the lure, the seduction of transgression. Such transgression can be accompanied by a sense of guilt, as illustrated by Freud's quasi-mythical elaborations on the murder of the original father. Psychoanalysis also suggests a productive function of desire, which does not put it in the same camp as the thinkers who attempted to elaborate a 'naturalist liberation of desire' (*S7*, 3). Here Lacan has in mind the libertines of the seventeenth and eighteenth centuries, who saw the 'man of pleasure' as the measure of all things. He notes that the main exponents of such a doctrine always display a sense of defiance when talking about eroticism and libertinage. There has been a failure of a purely naturalistic or positivistic moral theory, since one cannot escape from positing somewhere the big Other as a limit. The grandeur of Sade and some of his contemporaries has been to rise to the level of this demand:

> As the creator of nature, God is summoned to account for the extreme anomalies whose existence the Marquis de Sade, Mirabeau, and Diderot, among others, have drawn our attention to. This challenge, this summoning, this trial by ordeal ought not to allow any other way than the one that was, in effect, realized historically. He who submits himself to the ordeal finds at the end its premises, namely, the Other to whom this ordeal is addressed, in the last analysis its Judge. That is precisely what gives its special tone to this literature, which presents us with the dimension of the erotic in a way that has never been achieved since, never equaled. In the course of our investigations, we definitely must submit to our judgment that which in analysis has retained an affinity with, a relationship to, and a common root with, such an experience (S7, 4).

When Lacan points to the affinity that exists between Sadian excess and psychoanalysis, he does not indicate a complicity but rather a common knowledge that has to do with perversion and *jouissance* insofar they are both determined by the Other. Consequently he refuses to identify the task of psychoanalysis as that of 'taming perverse *jouissance*' – a goal that would only confirm a return to some 'more embracing moralism than any that has previously existed' (S7, 4). Lacan is thus quite alert to the danger of a psychoanalytic 'moral order' that will be later denounced by antipsychiatry and philosophers such as Deleuze and Foucault.

A second reference is as tantalising, since it joins the names of Kant and Sade, although in a very elliptic manner. In the conclusion to his discussion of the Freudian 'Thing' (addressed earlier in this book), Lacan raises the issue of the Ten Commandments, whose function is to regulate the distance between the subject and the Thing (S7, 69). He points to the 'great revolutionary crisis of morality, namely, the systematic questioning of principles there where they need to be questioned, that it, at the level of the imperative' (S7, 70). He then

adds: 'That is the culminating point for both Kant and Sade with relation to the Thing; it is there that morality becomes, on the one hand, a
pure and simple application of the universal maxim and, on the other,
a pure and simple object'(S7, 70). Cryptic and elusive, these insights
need an exemplification to make fuller sense. This is what Lacan does,
although without explicitly naming Sade, when in a later seminar he
criticises Kant's view of moral law.

In a discussion of 'the object and the Thing', Lacan rereads Kant's
Critique of Pure Reason, with its famous double image of a man who is
offered the possibility of spending a night with a woman he desires
while the gallows await him if he satisfies his wish, contrasted with the
same punishment in the case of bearing false testimony against a
friend. Kant concludes that no one would be foolish enough to accede
to an erotic realisation punishable by death, whereas if one was
threatened with the same punishment for perjuring a friend, this
becomes a matter of conscience. Lacan starts to show signs of impatience with the philosopher of Koenigsberg, whose passions may have
been on the weak side, objecting that one just might be able to find
someone who would be crazy enough to accept the first challenge:

> All of which leads to the conclusion that it is not impossible for a man
> to sleep with a woman knowing full well that he is to be bumped off
> on his way out, by the gallows or anything else (all this, of course, is
> located under the rubric of passionate excesses, a rubric that raises a
> lot of other questions); it is not impossible that this man coolly
> accepts such an eventuality on his leaving – for the pleasure of
> cutting up the lady concerned in small pieces, for example (S7, 109).

He adds that the annals of criminology and the newspapers are full of
such stories.

Kant – who thinks that he can rely on some 'reality principle' that in
this case would be determined by the common fear of death, and
therefore would regulate a basic common sense, hinged on a principle of conservation – cannot take into consideration two types of
excess that precisely subvert the reason he wants to erect on this
basis: the excess of object sublimation, and the excess of perverse
enjoyment. After all, someone might wish to remain true to his or her
deepest desires, especially if he or she is a compulsive liar or a serial
killer for instance!

For there is another register of morality that takes its direction from that which is to be found on the level of *das Ding*; it is the register that makes the subject hesitate when he is on the point of bearing false witness against *das Ding*, that it to say, the place of desire, whether it be perverse or sublimated (*S7*, 109–10).

Sade's forceful praise of excessive passions strikes us as the exact antithesis of Kant's universalism: perverse desire embodies the most corrosive parody of the ethical law, and beyond its purely subversive aspect, poses an *a priori* question if it can be shown to question the very foundations of universalism.

Thus it is no surprise to see again the two names linked in a later discussion of 'the death drive':

> Thus by leading you on to the ground of the ethics of psychoanalysis this year, I have brought you up against a certain limit that I illustrated through a confrontation, or heightening of the difference by contrast, of Kant and Sade, however paradoxical that may seem. I have led you to the point of apocalypse or of revelation of something called transgression (*S7*, 207).

Even if this contrast or parallel is merely suggested rather than fully elaborated, it is interesting that Lacan should have no doubt as to its crucial function. The concept of transgression leads him to quote a fable or myth developed by Sade. Lacan quotes a long passage from Sade's novel *Juliette*, in which Pope Pius VI reveals his philosophy of nature. For Sade, nature thrives on destruction, and it is only through crime that man can collaborate in the regeneration of nature. Since war can be called the 'mother of all things', murder is but the social equivalent of what takes place on a much larger scale in the universe as a whole. The passage that attracts Lacan's attention is devoted to the idea of 'second death': 'Murder only takes the first life of the individual whom we strike down; we should also seek to take his second life, if we are to be even more useful to nature. For nature wants annihilation; it is beyond our capacity to achieve the scale of destruction it desires' (*S7*, 211). Without really noting the fact that this is only a fictional character who speaks (and also a perverse and libidinous pope), Lacan likens this notion to Freud's death drive.

In what may look like a paradox, Lacan states that for Freud, as for Sade, the death drive is a 'creationist sublimation' (*S7*, 212) that

assumes an *ex nihilo* foundation. Whereas one might be tempted to
see quite the reverse in both Sade and Freud, namely a naturalist and
evolutionist system of nature, Lacan sees in this a mere disguise for a
subject still present as the meaning of this evolution. Here, Lacan is
clearly rather ironical facing both Sade and Freud:

> I am not telling you that the notion of the death wish in Freud is not
> something very suspect in itself – as suspect and, I would say, almost
> as ridiculous as Sade's idea. Can anything be poorer or more worth-
> less after all than the idea that human crimes might, for good or evil,
> contribute in some way to the cosmic maintenance of the *rerum
> concordia discors*? (*S7*, 212–13).

Rather than enjoying the pantheistic sense of an energy that releases
itself through human actions as well as in spontaneous natural formations, both Sade and Freud are here accused of 'substituting a subject
for Nature' (*S7*, 213).

Finally, Lacan refers this movement to the recurrence of antique
Manicheism: such a nature becomes animated only if it is underwrit-
ten by the hidden struggle between the opposed principles of Good
and Evil, Light and Darkness. Indeed Lacan has read Sade accurately.
In the last volume of the Pauvert edition of *Juliette* used by Lacan, one
libertine exclaims that even if God existed, he could not be conceived
as other than a supremely evil being: 'If it were true that there was a
God, master and creator of the universe, he would indubitably be the
most bizarre, the most cruel, the most evil and the most sanguinary
being...'[7] Therefore he would have to be abhorred, insulted and
rejected – while the same bloody and evil nature would have to be
imitated in all its ravaging excesses! Having placed Sade in a
Manichean tradition – whose effects on courtly love we have seen –
does Lacan imply that Freud is also a latent Manichean? Not exactly,
at least if we follow the drift of a later passage in which Lacan once
more parallels Sade's concept of the second death and Freud's death
drive. He boils down the issue raised by Freud to this:

> How can man, that is to say a living being, have access to knowledge
> of the death instinct, to his own relationship to death? The answer is,
> by virtue of the signifier in its most radical form. ... In truth, it's as
> dumb as can be. Not to recognize it, not to promote it as the essential
> articulation of non-knowledge as a dynamic value, not to recognize

that the discovery of the unconscious is literally there in the form of this last word, simply means that they don't know what they are doing (*S7*, 295).

The last word is of course the word marking death, a word that is always missing from the chain of signifiers. This accounts for the tenacious Sadean fantasy of going beyond the first death – like Hamlet, like Creon. Sade's fantasy involves eternally beautiful victims who are subjected to the most cruelly excessive torture and then dispatched only to be replaced by almost identical victims:

> After all, the human tradition has never ceased to keep this second death in mind by locating the end of our sufferings there; in the same way it has never ceased to imagine a second form of suffering, a suffering beyond death that is indefinitely sustained by the impossibility of crossing the limit of the second death. And that is why the tradition of hell in different forms has always remained alive, and it is still present in Sade in the idea he has of making the sufferings inflicted on a victim go on indefinitely. This refinement is attributed to one of the heroes of his novels, a Sadist who tries to assure himself of the damnation of the person he sends out life into death (*S7*, 295).

One might argue that in Sade's novels, such as *Juliette, Justine* and *Hundred and Twenty Days of Sodom*, most victims are destroyed in great quantity serial manner – to the point where their exact number is the object of obsessive calculations this has been well analysed by Marcel Hénaff[8] – but there is something that links them all in a homogeneous continuum: they all exhibit beauty, the grace of youth, or the 'touching' vulnerability provided by poverty linked with naiveté. These are the typical features of the body upon which Sade's libertines exert their terrifying rages – or use it as a springboard to let their fantasies fly so as to test an even more terrifying indifference or godlike apathy.

Here again, Lacan resorts to a parallel between Sade and Kant to understand what is at stake:

> In the typical Sadean scenario, suffering doesn't lead the victim to the point where he is dismembered and destroyed. It seems rather that the object of all the torture is to retain the capacity of being an indestructible support.... The victims are always adorned not only with all kinds of beauty, but also with grace, which is beauty's finest flower.

How does one explain this necessity, if not by the fact that we need to find it hidden, though imminent, however we approach the phenomenon, in the moving presentation of the victim or also in every form of beauty that is too obvious, too present, so that it leaves man speechless at the prospect of the image that is silhouetted behind it and threatens it.... The forms that are at work in knowledge, Kant tells us, are interested in the phenomenon of beauty, though the object itself is not involved. I take it you see the analogy with the Sadean fantasy, since the object there is no more than the power to support a form of suffering, which is in itself nothing else but the signifier of a limit. Suffering is conceived of as a stasis which affirms that that which is cannot return to the void from which it emerged (*S7*, 261).

Lacan then branches off into a discussion of Christian crucifixion, understood as a fantasy in which one can see 'the apotheosis of sadism' (*S7*, 262), which leads to towering accusations, lumping together missionaries, colonial imperialism and the reduction of desire operated by religion and bureaucracy! We have seen how beauty functioned in the case of Antigone, and its modality in Sade is not so different: a similar purging of the imagination takes place but this time in the name of a perverse fantasy, whose political overtones are highlighted by Lacan – for instance he describes Sade as just a 'country squire, a social example of the degeneration of the nobility at a time when its privileges were about to be abolished' (*S7*, 233). Another long quotation is necessary here to move between all these levels of meaning:

It is nevertheless the case that Sade's extraordinary catalogue of horrors, which causes not only the senses and human possibilities but the imagination, too, to flinch, is nothing at all compared to what will, in effect, be seen on a collective scale, if the great and very real explosion occurs that threatens us all. The only difference between Sade's exorbitant descriptions and such a catastrophe is that no pleasure will enter into the motivation of the latter. Not perverts but bureaucrats will set things off, and we won't even know if their intentions were good or bad. Things will go off by command; they will be carried through according to regulations, mechanically, down the chain of command, with human wills bent, abolished, overcome, in a task that ceases to have any meaning (*S7*, 233).

This apocalyptic tone brings to mind the indictment of bourgeois society and the new type of bureaucracy produced by the type of industrial society one finds in Adorno and Horkheimer when they compare Sade and Kant in their *Dialectic of Enlightenment* – a reference to which I shall soon return. The crucial link here is the idea of a collective law, of a utopian society that agrees to curb its enjoyment in the name of a moral imperative.

> Proclaiming the law of *jouissance* as the foundation of some ideally utopian social system, Sade expresses himself in italics in the nice little edition of Juliette published recently by Pauvert...: 'Lend me the part of your body that will give me a moment of satisfaction and, if you care to, use for your own pleasure that part of my body which appeals to you [*et jouissez, si cela vous plaît, de celle du mien*]. (S7, 202)[9]

Indeed, in the first volume of *Juliette* one finds these italics in a long speech by Delbène, who is presented as an abbess who has turned into a sort of brothel-keeper. What matters here is perhaps less the idea of reciprocity of *jouissance* than its excessive nature – Delbène develops the idea that one cannot put a stop to this erotic enjoyment even though it can trigger all sorts of bad treatment, since the *jouissance* of a body cannot be limited in advance. *Jouissance* in French implies ecstatic erotic enjoyment but also full possession of an object. Sade reiterates this 'law' of *jouissance* at various points in his novel. To sum up his thought, a libertine states: '*Jouissons: telle est la loi de la nature*' (Let us enjoy – such is the law of nature).[10] Lacan sees in this maxim the 'formulation of the fundamental law' of Sade's social vision, and compares it to the psychoanalytic theory of 'part objects', which are often reduced to dismembered bodies, like the mutilated corpses Carpaccio painted in San Giorgio degli Schiavoni in Venice. What stands out, too, with Sade, is the indestructibility of the fantasy when it is located in the Other – with its radicalisation of the idea of eternal suffering.

The conclusion now becomes almost obvious: one can posit Sade's law in terms that are very close to Kant's categorical imperative. For both Kant and Sade toy with a 'formalism' of reason that allows them to posit a principle irrespective of any object to which it might apply. Here is how Lacan grapples with this parallel in his seminar on ethics, in a discussion of how traditional morality fails to justify its own basis once desire has been posited:

The breakthrough is achieved by Kant when he posits that the moral imperative is not concerned with what may or may not be done. To the extent that it imposes the necessity of a practical reason, obligation affirms an unconditional 'Thou shalt.' The importance of this field derives from the void that the strict application of the Kantian definition leaves.

Now we analysts are able to recognize that place as the place occupied by desire. Our experience gives rise to a reversal that locates in the center an incommensurable measure, an infinite measure, that is called desire. I showed you how one can easily substitute for Kant's 'Thou shalt' the Sadean fantasm of *jouissance* elevated to the level of an imperative – it is, of course, a pure and almost derisory fantasm, but it doesn't exclude the possibility of its being elevated to a universal law (*S7*, 315–16).

Here at last is the insight that gave Lacan the theoretical impetus in his 'Kant with Sade' article. We shall explore this now, and also refer to the contemporary seminar on anxiety to investigate some of the questions it tackles.

If Kant *is* Sade, 'is' Sade Kant?

We have just seen how a 'pure and almost derisory fantasm' of absolute *jouissance* can be elevated to the status of a universal law. This is spelled out more systematically at the beginning of 'Kant with Sade': '*Philosophy in the Bedroom* comes eight years after the *Critique of Practical Reason*. If, after having seen that the one accords with the other, we show that it completes it, we will say that it gives the truth of the *Critique*' (*KS*, 56). In this intense and witty piece, Lacan aims to restore Sade's work to 'its diamondlike subversion' (*KS*, 56), promising that Sade will add the erotic spice that might otherwise not be perceptible in Kant's moral philosophy. Kant's 'eroticism' will then surface for the persistent and tenacious reader, with the 'grain of salt which it lacks' (*KS*, 58).

Kant's starting point is the simultaneous disappearance of an object and the emergence of an inner law:

> Let us retain the paradox that it should be at the moment when the subject is no longer faced with any object that he encounters a law, one which has no other phenomenon than something already signifi-

cant, which is obtained from a voice in the conscience, and which, in articulating itself as a maxim, proposes the order of a purely practical reason or of a will (*KS*, 56–7).

This law has no phenomenal object as its correlate, and it has to reign universally and in all cases, otherwise it fails – by a synthetically universal foundation which is glossed jokingly by Lacan with a reference to Jarry's play *Ubu Roi*: 'Long live Poland, for if there were no Poland, there would be no Poles' (*KS*, 57).

Similarly, Sade's universal maxim can be posited as follows: 'I have the right of enjoyment [*jouissance*] over your body, anyone can say to me, and I will exercise this right, without any limit stopping me in the capriciousness of the exactions that I might have the taste to satiate' (*KS*, 58). Indeed everyone will recognise here some black humour, or an imperceptible sliding from the rational to the merely reasonable, and then to the pathological. As Lacan suggests, the subversive impact of such a formulation lies in its debunking any 'reciprocity' that would be taken as an ethical basis for intersubjectivity: 'And one would not want to miss this opportunity to denounce the exorbitant role which is conferred to the moment of reciprocity in structures, notably subjective ones, which are intrinsically resistant to this' (adapted from *KS*, 58). Lacan implies quite clearly here that subjectivity cannot be equated to reciprocity – desire, as the Desire of the Other, has already marked the subjective interpositioning through the law of the signifier, so that any belief in mirror-images from one other to another other will be marked by illusion or distortion. The point of the formulation is precisely its resistance to subjective reversal:

> Whatever it may be, it is already a point in favor of our maxim that it can serve as the paradigm of a statement which excludes as such reciprocity (reciprocity and not trading places).
>
> Any judgment about the infamous order that would enthrone our maxim is thus indifferent to the matter, which is to recognize or refuse it the character of a rule admissible as universal in ethics, the ethics which since Kant is recognized as an unconditional practice of reason (*KS*, 59).

Finally, both Kant's and Sade's maxims entail that the Other be placed in a position of absolute domination over the subject:

Certainly these two imperatives, between which moral experience
can be stretched, to the breaking-point of life, are, in the Sadean
paradox, imposed on us as upon the Other, and not as upon
ourselves.

But this distance only exists at first sight, for the moral imperative
does no less in a latent fashion, since it is from the Other that its
commandment makes its demand on us (*KS*, 59).

This overarching domination finally discloses to us the truth of the
splitting of the subject.

One perceives here the naked revelation of what the parody made
above of the obvious universality of the duty of the depository would
lead us to, namely that the bipolarity by which the moral Law insti-
tutes itself is nothing other than this splitting of the subject which
occurs in any intervention of the signifier: namely that of the subject
of the enunciation from the subject of the statement.... In which the
Sadean maxim, by pronouncing itself from the mouth of the Other, is
more honest than if it appealed to the voice within, since it unmasks
the splitting, usually conjured away, of the subject (adapted from *KS*,
59).

Sade's humorous debunking finally attacks what is usually taken as
the main foundation of democracy, the rights of man and their
universalist ethos. With an untranslatable French pun, Lacan explains
that the installation of subjectivity as a second person disposing of
rights is an imposition of identity – a '*Tu es...*' (You are) – that exposes
its murderous essence through the repressed echo of '*Tuez!*' (Kill! in
the imperative).

Like Kant, Sade forces us to acknowledge that pain is the prime
marker of moral experience. Lacan adds that the only limit for a
Sadean would be a Stoician form of detached contempt – like
Epictetus, he or she would merely exclaim 'See, you broke it' about his
or her own leg when facing the tortures of a master. Sadean pain aims
at shame, at a 'rape in the modesty in the other' (*KS*, 60), or in other
words, at total abandonment by the divided subject confronting the
enjoying Other. This Other will indeed return as Sade's fantasy of an
evil God.

Assuredly Christianity has educated men to pay little attention to the
jouissance of God, and that is how Kant slips by his voluntarism of the

Law-for-the-Law, which really piles it on, so to speak, with respect to the ataraxia of Stoic experience. One might think that Kant is under pressure from what he hears too closely, not from Sade, but from some mystic nearer to home, in the sigh which stifles what he glimpses beyond having seen that his God is faceless: *Grimmigkeit?* Sade says: Being-Supreme-in-Wickedness (*KS*, 61).

Lacan had already digressed in his ethics seminar on Jacob Boehme, the German mystic who used the term *Grimmigkeit* to refer to God's dark and unfathomable wrathfulness. Kant had criticised Boehme and Swedenborg as mystics who had fallen prey to *Schwärmereien* – wild and unaccountable enthusiasm. Can one just expel this 'ghost' of an evil God by saying that it corners *jouissance*, thus depriving the subject of his or her will and obliging the 'henchman' of perverse enjoyment to become a mere slave to mechanical pleasure?

> Desire, which is the henchman of this splitting of the subject, would doubtless put up with being called will-to-*jouissance*. But this appellation would not render desire more worthy of the will which it invokes within the Other, in tempting this will to the extremity of its division from its pathos; for to do this, desire sets forth beaten, promised to impotence (*KS*, 61).

As Lacan elaborates, the Sadean scene of perversion is only fleetingly a scene of pleasure. It aims at triggering *jouissance* in the absence of real desire, and needs a fantasy to sustain it 'by the very discord to which it succumbs' (*KS*, 62). In other words 'fantasy constitutes the pleasure proper to desire' (*KS*, 62). Sade's testimony is therefore crucial in that it allows Lacan to revise his graph of fantasy. Here is the new graph he posits (*KS*, 62):

This is the trajectory of a desire that is sustained by fantasy (barred S – *poinçon* – a) and produces a sinuous 'calculus of the subject with a V for *Volonté* (Will) and an S for the 'raw subject of pleasure' or an unbarred 'pathological subject' projected by the perverse fantasy.

Lacan comments:

> It is thus indeed the will of Kant which is encountered in the place of
> this will which can be called-to-*jouissance* only to explain that it is the
> subject reconstituted from alienation at the price of being no more
> than the instrument of *jouissance*. Thus Kant, in being tortured and
> questioned 'with Sade', that is to say with Sade filling the office (for
> our thought as in his sadism) of an instrument, confesses to what is
> plain to see about the 'What does he want?' which henceforth is
> applicable to anyone (adapted from *KS*, 63).

This graph can provide a deeper logic for the 'forest of fantasies' that
constitute the works of Sade: the point of subjective disappearance or
aphanisis that Jones has introduced into Freudian theory will be
indefinitely postponed in the imagination, in the name of a fantasy
that repetitively revives the spectre of a fully enjoying subject who
would, in turn, only betray the excessive enjoyment of a perverse God.
This is why Lacan mentions once more his theory of beauty as a
barrier to desire, and as a screen onto which the 'second death' can
aim to be projected. The deaths of the victims only insert them into a
mere series of replaceable and expendable items; they add up in a
combinatory programme aiming at an exhaustive exploration of all
possibilities, while the one subject of the fantasy (like Justine) is
monolithic. The only variation that is provided is through the
diversely inventive ways in which the *object a* of fantasy is produced
as a metamorphic and endlessly plastic object of torture.

Lacan is not deluded by the apparent contradictions in Sade's
works, but he does not claim to be a Sadean specialist (as he says,
their problem is that they all tend to become hagiographers). He only
offers a few graphs and concepts ('second death', *jouissance*, desire of
the Other) to make sense of the apparent discrepancies, such as those
that appear between an atheistic praise of perversion and the need to
posit an eternity of suffering going even beyond death. After a disquisition of Buddhism as another response to the universal pain of existence (*KS*, 64), he suggests that Sade projects this very pain into the
Other. He rejects the usual cliché that sadism is the mere inversion or
conversion of masochism, and is adamant in disclaiming that Sadean
subjects 'negate the other': on the contrary – and this is a point to
which we shall return – it is based on a recognition of the Other as
Other. Lacan even supposes that Sade is not entirely 'duped by his

own fantasy' – 'to the extent that the rigor of his thought passes into the logic of his life.' He then gives a resolution of his first scheme by a simple rotation, turning by a quarter of a circle (as he was to do in the theory of the four discourses), which sketches not only the basic fantasy but also Sade's personal fate (KS, 65):

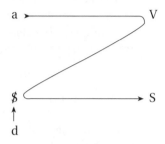

The key-terms have undergone an important change. V remains the 'will-to-*jouissance*' but its position marks absolute despotism: from the Présidente de Montreuil's constant persecution of her hated son-in-law, it has become a moral constraint that sealed off the author's final 'alienation' by incarceration. The full S now represents the friends or helpers who have shown a surprising and 'heroic' devotion to Sade (such as his wife, his sister-in-law, his valet, his second common-law wife when he was in Charenton), and the barred S testifies to the disappearance that Sade had wanted to achieve in his famous will, in which he specified that his body was to be buried in a copse, in the woods of his property at Malmaison:

> The ditch once covered over, above it acorns shall be strewn, in order that the spot become green again, and the copse grown back thick over it, the traces of my grave may disappear from the face of the earth as I trust the memory of me shall fade out of the minds of all men save nevertheless for those few who in their goodness have loved me.[11]

Let us tiptoe away, provisionally leaving the intricate web of allusions and stories that mark 'Kant with Sade' as one of Lacan's most ambitious essays. It is striking that Lacan keeps returning his audience to this text in his later seminars, as if this was a doctrinal point of reference. One seminar in particular deserves some attention since it took place at the time of the publication of the article in *Critique*. In

Seminar X, on anxiety, Lacan returns to the issue of the '*jouissance* of the Other' in a very forceful way. In a seminar of March 1963, he alludes to Sade to show that anxiety in the victim is also one of the aims of the humiliation and torture in which the libertines are engaged. Referring back to his previous seminar on ethics, Lacan reflects on what the sadist looks for in the Other, adding that 'for him, the Other is absolutely essential', so much so that he is led to 'simulate the requirements of the moral law'.[12] He adds an original insight to his previous analysis when focusing on a curious expression in Sade:

> I will leave you to search in *Juliette*, even in *Hundred and Twenty Days*, these few passages where the characters, completely occupied in slaking on those chosen victims their greed for torments, enter into this bizarre, singular and curious trance, indicated, I repeat, on several occasions in the text of Sade, which is expressed in these strange words, in effect that it is necessary for me to articulate here: 'I had,' cries the tormentor, 'I had the skin of the cunt.'
>
> This is not a feature which is obvious along the track of the imaginable, and the privileged character, the moment of enthusiasm, the character of supreme trophy brandished at the high point of the chapter is something which, I believe, is sufficiently indicative of the following: it is that something is sought which is in a way the reverse of the subject [*l'envers du sujet*], which takes on here its signification from this feature of the glove turned inside-out which underlines the feminine essence of the victim.[13]

We shall see how this theme returns in connection with Joyce (Chapter 10). What is important at this point is the notion of a 'reverse' of the subject, just as Lacan later talks of the 'Reverse of Psychoanalysis' (the title of Seminar XVII). The Sadean fantasy aims at turning the subject inside-out in the name of the Other's enjoyment. For this is obviously the counterpart:

> He [the Sadean Libertine] has a relationship with God, this is what is exposed everywhere in Sade's text. He cannot take a step forward without this reference to the supremely wicked being and it is just as clear for him as for the one who is speaking that it is God that is involved.
>
> For his part he goes to all sorts of exhausting trouble, even to the extent of missing his goal, to realise – which, thank God, it has to be

said, Sade spares us having to reconstruct, for he articulates it as such
– to realise the *jouissance* of God.'[14]

In this seminar, interestingly *jouissance* is not completely separated
from its purely sexual meaning; two pages later Lacan talks of the
pervert who comes (*jouit*) at the higest point of anxiety. Whose
anxiety, in the case of the Sadean fantasy? The subject's or the
victim's? All the graphs elaborated by Lacan in this seminar tend to
suggest that the Sadean scenario supposes a full *jouissance* projecting
a full subject (the 'pathological subject') he mentions in 'Kant with
Sade' in the place of the big Other, while the barred subject is
depicted underneath as the subject of desire. Anxiety marks a symptomatic locus between *jouissance* and desire. Or as the conclusion of
'Kant with Sade' makes very clear, desire is the 'other side of the law'
(*KS*, 73) and Sade betrays everywhere his 'submission to the Law'. He
seems for Lacan not to have gone much further than Saint Paul:

> For Sade, we see the test of this, crucial in our eyes, in his refusal of
> the death penalty, which history, if not logic, would suffice to show is
> one of the corollaries of charity.
>   Sade thus stopped, at the point where desire is knotted together
> with the law. If something in him held to the law, in order there to
> find the opportunity Saint Paul speaks of, to be sinful beyond
> measure, who would throw the first stone? But he went no further.
>   It is not only that for him as for the rest of us the flesh is weak, it is
> that the spirit is too prompt not to be lured. The apology for crime
> only pushes him to the indirect avowal of the Law. The supreme
> being is restored in Maleficence (*KS*, 74).

Ironically, it is the final scene in the 'Philosophy in the Bedroom',
when the mother, Madame de Misteval, is condemned by the
perverted daughter Eugénie to be raped (so as to be given syphilis)
and then to have her sex sewn up, that confirms Lacan's negative
diagnosis:

> Be that as it may, it appears that there is nothing to be gained by
> replacing Diotima with Dolmancé, someone whom the ordinary path
> seems to frighten more than is fitting, and who – did Sade see it?–
> closes the affair with a Noli tangere matrem. V...ed [*sic*] and sewn up,
> the mother remains forbidden. Our verdict upon the submission of
> Sade to the Law is confirmed.

Of a treatise truly about desire, there is thus little here, even nothing. What of it is announced in this crossing taken from an encounter, is at most a tone of reason (*KS*, 75).

The ellipses mark an interesting ambiguity, as the translator notes: does Lacan mean *violée* or *voilée*? Is not *Volonté* implied in the last *Vel* ('either-or' in Latin) that attacks the mother's body only to leave it even more intact than before? The last couple of concepts we meet here oppose desire and reason so as to suggest the rationalist limitations of Sade's philosophy – symptomatically, it cannot help but let reason speak whereas it believes, mistakenly, to be launched in the midst of the most transgressive sexual excess. This is an insight that also underpins Adorno's reading of Sade.

The sadism of the law: a genealogy

A few crucial questions still remain. Has Lacan read Adorno and Horkheimer on Kant and Sade, as Roudinesco seems to believe? How can the law be seen as the *jouissance* of the Other? Should one replace Marquis de Sade in his historical context with Klossowski, or is the pairing of Kant with Sade in excess of a philosophical tradition that has been misread, as Monique David-Ménard suggests?[15] In order to find an answer we shall examine the philosophical genealogy of Lacan's 'Kant with Sade'. A number of critics have noted that 'Kant with Sade', written in 1963, owes a lot to Adorno and Horkheimer's groundbreaking parallel between Kant and Sade in their *Dialectic of Enlightenment* (1944).[16]

The thesis of this essay, jointly written in America by two refugees from the Frankfurt school, is relatively simple. Kantian reason leads ineluctably to the calculating rationality of a totalitarian order. Its counterpart is the systematic mechanisation of pleasure in Sade's perverse utopias. *The Critique of Practical Reason* stresses the autonomy and self-determination of the moral subject, and thereby defines the pure form of ethical action. This is how the philosophy of Enlightenment meets global capitalism with a vengeance: any human concern has to be ruled out, what matters is merely the conformity of reason with its own laws, a reason that must then appear abstract and devoid of any object. All 'human' effects are pushed further away from an independent and all powerful reason. Juliette is thus more logical

than Kant when she draws the conclusion that Kant denies: the bourgeois order of society justifies crime, provided crime is regulated by a
rationality that controls all activities and pleasures. The famous
Sadean 'apathy' thus functions like Kant's 'disinterestedness', both
being underpinned by the 'brutal efficiency' of the bourgeois
conquest of the world. The 'right to enjoyment' logically includes an
absolute extension of its field – up to and including my right to enjoy
the bodies of others, and to do with them as I like.

It is nevertheless conceivable, that Lacan never read *Dialectic of
Enlightenment* (1944), since he asserts in 'Kant with Sade' that the link
between the two contemporary thinkers has never been 'noted, to our
knowledge, as such'[17] Lacan usually parades his erudition, and if the
essay had been available to him (it had not yet been translated into
French), I believe that he would have acknowledged it. His analysis is
sufficiently different and lacks any trace of the basic Marxism that
Adorno and Horkheimer evince – one would assume that Lacan
would have paid this kind of debt. But perhaps he is less trying to
disguise philosophical borrowings than sending us back to the more
rightful owner of the basic insight upon which his thesis rests – Freud.

My guess is that Lacan owes his main intuition to Freud's analysis
of sadism and masochism. Freud's thesis in 'The economic problem
of masochism' (1924) is well-known. In this essay, in order to address
a third type of masochism he calls 'moral masochism', Freud presents
Kant's 'categorical imperative' as the most elaborate philosophical
expression that can be given to the concept of the 'cruelty' of the
super-ego. Here is the genesis he sketches:

> This super-ego is in fact just as much a representative of the *id* as of
> the outer world. It originated through the introjection into the ego of
> the first objects of the libidinal impulses in the *id*, namely, the two
> parents, by which process the relation to them was desexualized, that
> is underwent a deflection from direct sexual aims. Only in this way
> was it possible for the child to overcome the Oedipus-complex. Now
> the super-ego has retained essential features of the introjected
> persons, namely their power, their severity, their tendency to watch
> over and to punish.... The super-ego, the conscience at work in it, can
> then become harsh, cruel and inexorable against the ego which is in
> its charge. The categorical imperative of Kant is thus a direct inheri-
> tance from the Oedipus-complex.[18]

A 'perverse couple' is thus created: the sadism of the super-ego and the masochism of the ego go hand in hand, as with these 'Russian character types' (is Freud thinking of the Wolf-man, or of Dostoyievsky's characters here?) who multiply 'sinful acts' in order to be punished by the sadistic conscience. Kant is thus clearly designated by Freud as the accomplice of Sade, precisely because their unlikely coupling poses all the problems associated with civilisation's way of dealing with aggression. Freud shows that it is the renunciation of instinctual gratification that comes first, followed by the creation of morality, and not the reverse as is often assumed.[19]

Before Freud, Hegel's critique of Kant's version of morality in 'The Spirit of Christianity' (1798–99), provides an early negative appraisal of Kantian morality. For Hegel, Kant is the modern successor of Jewish law-givers such Abraham and Moses, who 'exercised their dominion mercilessly with the most revolting and harshest tyranny,... utterly extirpating all life; for it is only over death that unity hovers'.[20] A real stranger to everything, including love, Abraham takes the whole world as his opposite, and he creates a picture of a terrifying God who is also a merciless stranger and the master of a people he reduces to religious slavery. Hegel agrees with Freud in that he sees Moses as more Egyptian than the Egyptians, and the founder of an 'oriental' system of absolute domination: 'Moses sealed his legislation with an oriental beautiful threat of the loss of all pleasure and all fortune. He brought before the slavish spirit the image of itself, namely, the terror of physical force.'[21] Hegel's 'Spirit of Christianity' thus sketches the theological genesis of the castrating father, anticipating on *Moses and Monotheism* by some hundred and fifty years.

Similarly Kant is accused by Hegel of importing a Jewish formalism or 'positivity' of the law into philosophy. For Hegel, Kant misinterprets the Christian commandment 'Love God above everything and thy neighbour as thyself' as a 'command requiring respect for a law which commands love'. This reduction of love to a command is a great perversion according to Hegel, 'because in love all thought of duties vanish'.[22] In these early texts, Hegel extols Jesus for being able to raise love above any type of morality. Jesus does not praise reverence for the laws but announces a self-annulling love, a love that 'exhibits that which fulfills the law but annuls it as law and so is something higher than obedience to law and makes law superfluous'.[23]

Lacan systematically echoes this anti-Kantian feeling, and one find traces as late as the 'Etourdit' text of 1972, in which he speaks of 'the

inept topology that Kant bodied forth by establishing firmly the bourgeois who cannot imagine anything but transcendence in esthetics
and dialectics'.[24] The tonality of this statement betrays a neo-Marxist
irritation quite similar to that of Adorno and Horkheimer. He adds
that 'as soon as meanings are freed ... Kant's statements lose theirs',
confessing that Sade's critique may not be much funnier than Kant's,
but at least it is more logical.[25] This is an important issue to which we
shall return.

As soon as one superimposes this critique of an oriental and Jewish
slavery of the spirit with Hegel's subsequent evocation (in the
Phenomenology of Spirit) of the Terror during the French Revolution,
the circle linking the universality of an absolute law with terror and
death, seen as the absolute master, seems completed. Whether
inspired by Kojève's masterful neo-Marxist reconstruction of Hegel's
early system, or by Hyppolite's more balanced assessment (Lacan
owes to Hyppolite's groundbreaking commentary on the
Phenomenology of Spirit the idea of desire as 'Desire of the Other'),[26]
Lacan remains Hegelian in his vision of morality. If Sade can express
what is hidden behind Kant's law, namely the cruelty of the Other
underpinning the law, then what remains to be understood is the
jouissance of the Other when it forces the subject to go beyond pleasure and the limits of the ego. Such a *jouissance* underlies Sade's
works and goes beyond anything Kant may have to say about pleasure
and displeasure in his second critique.

In other words, and this should have become obvious by now,
Lacan's 1963 essay cannot be reduced to a psychoanalytic or philosophical critique of Kant's moral philosophy: the introduction of
jouissance signals a theoretical excess that forces us to return once
more to Sade's parody of the law.

Sade, sade, çade: or why Sade is not so sad

I shall return to Sade's parody by referring to a passage in Lacan's
Encore seminar, in which he seems to be giving a lesson in practical
Sadism (as one speaks of a 'practical joker') as he unpacks the first
'sentence' he gave his audience, or rather wrote for them on the
blackboard, during their first meeting. Lacan had written: '*Jouissance*
of the Other', 'of the body of the Other who symbolizes the Other, is
not the sign of love'.[27] A week later Lacan returns to this dense

formula, adding that it suggests the notion of an 'enjoying substance'. As we have seen, and as Nestor Braunstein has shown,[28] Lacan's main concept, his real 'signature' might consist less in the invention of the *objet petit a* than in his bifurcated translation of Freud's *Lust* into *plaisir* on the one hand and *jouissance* on the other. Here is the passage:

> Isn't it precisely what psychoanalytic experience presupposes? – the substance of the body, on the condition that it is defined only as that which enjoys itself (*se jouit*). That is, no doubt, a property of the living body, but we don't know what it means to be alive except for the following fact, that a body is something that enjoys itself [or: can be enjoyed, *cela se jouit*].
>
> It enjoys itself only by 'corporizing' the body in a signifying way. That implies something other than the *partes extra partes* of extended substance. As is emphasized admirably by the kind of Kantian that Sade was, one can only enjoy a part of the Other's body, for the simple reason that one has never seen a body completely wrap itself around the Other's body, to the point of surrounding and phagocytizing it. That is why we must confine ourselves to simply giving it a little squeeze, like that, taking a forearm or anything else – ouch!
>
> Enjoying (*jouir*) has the fundamental property that it is, ultimately, one person's body that enjoys a part of the Other's body. [An alternative translation was offered by the translator in a footnote: 'that is the body of the one that enjoys a part of the body of the Other]' (*S20*, 23).

This passage poses several problems, not least of which is the surprising fact that Lacan seems to endow the big Other with a body. As the baffled translator notes on page 4, there seems to be a typographical error in the first 'sentence' – unless we can understand how one body can symbolise the Other. Another complex problem is generated by the tricky reflexive expression '*un corps cela se jouit*', meaning both 'a body enjoys itself' and 'a body is available for your enjoyment'. We have thus moved rapidly from auto-eroticism to the Sadean dogma of the availability of every body for everybody's limitless pleasure. It is interesting to note that Lacan demonstrates the ambivalence by squeezing or pinching hard his own forearm in front of his audience. His 'ouch!' (*ouille!*) stands as the only verifiable marker (a real Jakobsonian shifter, analogous to a personal pronoun) that he has a body, a body that's alive and kicking because it is capable of being enjoyed and of enjoying. It seems that it is crucial to grasp what a paradoxical 'Kantian' such as Sade had seen in order to understand the fundamental issue of *jouissance* in its connection with the body.

As Lacan recapitulates in Seminar XX, the main point of his article 'Kant with Sade' was to prove that 'morality admits that it is Sade' (*S20*, 87) – which should not be understood just as in the English ('a sad thing indeed'), but mediated through the variety of French idioms he details:

> You can write Sade however you like: either with a capital *S*, to render homage to the poor idiot who gave us interminable writings on that subject – or with a lower-case *s*, for in the final analysis that's moral- ity's own way of being agreeable ... – or, still better, you can write it as *çade*, since one must, after all, say that morality ends at the level of the id (*ça*), which doesn't go very far. Stated differently, the point is that love is impossible and the sexual relationship drops into the abyss of nonsense, which doesn't in any way diminish the interest we must have in the Other (*S20*, 87).

Despite the rather off-hand dismissal of the 'poor idiot' (a term that ought to be carefully distinguished from *la bêtise* Lacan was address- ing at the beginning of his seminar, since such *idiocy* sends us back to the absolute particularity and insularity of a person, thus to Sade's forced masturbatory isolation), I would like to try to assess Sade's impact on Lacan – isn't he *too* eager to dissociate himself from the 'idiot'? Couldn't this calculated aloofness be read as a trace of Lacan's *bêtise* (his 'silliness' or merely his own blind spots)?

Following a writer and thinker Lacan appreciated and quoted (only to end up rejecting his main contention, implied by his title at least) – Pierre Klossowski – we might try to characterise Sade as 'our neigh- bor'.[29] It should be stressed that Lacan's central thesis about the underlying presence of an evil God in Sade, even under the pretence of atheism, was already to be found in Pierre Klossowski's *Sade My Neighbor*. In a chapter entitled 'Under the Mask of Atheism', Klossowski shows how Sade seems to be looking for purity in a cruel nature dissociated from a creating God. Sade therefore keeps praising a perverse virginity (avoiding 'normal' heterosexuality and promoting anal intercourse between all) and finally speaks the language of a 'latent Jansenism'.[30] We might have to reexamine Lacan's rather prudent qualification: 'But that Sade, himself, refuses to be my neigh- bor, is what needs to be recalled, not in order to refuse it to him in return, but in order to recognize the meaning of this refusal.'[31] Klossowski also stresses a point that tends to vanish a little from Lacan's essay – that Sade was not merely a 'pervert' or a monster, but above all a writer. A boring and repetitive writer, to be sure, but one whose writings allow us to understand the crucial link between fantasy, the perverse imagination and the law, understood as the *jouissance* of the Other. It is the very excess of Sade's language and imagination that deludes the reader into taking fiction for what it is not. Sade himself always stressed this (with perhaps a good dose of hypocrisy). Here is what he said to a critic named Villeterque who thought that the theses of Sade's *Crimes of Love* could be attributed to the author: 'Loathsome ignoramus: have you not yet learned that every actor in any dramatic work must employ a language in keeping with his character, and that, when he does, 'tis the fictional personage who is speaking and not he author? ... Ah, Monsieur Villeterque, what a fool you are!'[32]

This point has not been lost on Klossowki, himself a novelist of distinction. He writes that:

> The parallelism between the apathetic reiteration of acts and Sade's descriptive reiteration again establishes that the image of the act to be done is re-presented each time not only as though it had never been performed but also as though it had never been described. This reversibility of the same process inscribes the presence of *non-language* in language; it inscribes a foreclosure of language by language.[33]

Sade's symptom is therefore not an etiological category such as 'sadism' – it is his writing, a writing that hesitates between the repetitive fantasy of outrage against a Mother Nature he abhors and a literal questioning of the function of the big Other's *jouissance*. One should not, however, take Klossowski's concept of foreclosure as identical to Lacan's translation of Freud's *Verwerfung*; Sade is not a psychotic, he is not Schreber, although like Schreber, he is above all a *Schreiber*.

In his seminar on ethics, Lacan concludes a little too hastily that Sade's case proves that Freud's theory of sublimation is quite wrong:

> If we consider sublimation in its most developed form, indeed in the fiercest and most cynical form in which Freud took pleasure in representing it, namely as the transformation of the sexual instinct into a

work which everyone will recognize his own dreams and impulses, and will reward the artist for having given him that satisfaction by granting the latter a fuller and happier life ... if we seek to grasp the work of Sade from this perspective, then it's something of a failure (*S7*, 200).

Indeed Sade's life was not a happy one: he was jailed for debauchery under the Old Regime from 1777–90, imprisoned for a short time at the height of Terror in 1793–94, which allowed him to see the mass-slaughters just before being freed as a consequence of Robespierre's downfall, then jailed again for his pornographic writings under the Consulate and the Empire (under direct orders from the puritanical Napoléon, it is said) between 1801 and 1814, when he died. Altogether some twenty-seven years in prison, quite a record, at the time, for someone who had never killed anyone!

However Sade was aware that this attempt to repress his passions had not in fact restrained them, on the contrary it had heightened their violence. The following is what he wrote to his wife in 1783, addressed less to her than to all those who had tried to suppress his writings: 'For example, you fancied you were sure to work wonders, I'll wager, by reducing me to an atrocious abstinence in the article of *carnal sin.* Well, you were wrong: you have produced a ferment in my brain, owing to you phantoms have arisen in me which I shall have to render real.'[32] This is a theme that recurs in Sade's letters: '*You* forced me to create phantoms!' These spectres become real in the sense that they have been written, despite all types of censorship. Is this sublimation then? Yes and no. Sade's very excesses, his scandalous reiterations of perverse fantasies that break all limits, explode even the relatively staid category of sublimation. Lacan seems closer to the truth when he compares Sade with Georges Bataille (who of course would put Sade at the pinnacle of the 'literature of evil') and quotes Maurice Blanchot, as we have seen.

> The real problem is something else. It is nothing else but the response of a being, whether reader or writer, at the approach to a center of incandescence or an absolute zero that is physically unbearable. The fact that the book falls from one's hands no doubt proves that it is bad, but literary badness here is perhaps the guarantee of the very badness ... that is the object of our investigation. As a consequence, Sade's work belongs to the order of what I call experimental

literature. The work of art in this case is an experiment that through its action cuts the subject loose from his psychosocial moorings – or to be more precise, from all psychosocial appreciation of the sublimation involved (S7, 201).

If, therefore, the existence (and the intransigence) of Sade proves Freud wrong about sublimation, one might say that by insisting upon writing Sade brought a coherence to his life that any serial killer will fail to achieve, and also forces the reader to acknowledge that writing can explore its limits – and thus question the very possibility of its own foreclosure.

The foreclosed language of Sade's fiction introduces the reader to a thinking of the 'outside' as if literature was ancillary to a curious and ironical pragmatism of fantasy. Sade's well-known irony, so evident in his letters from the Bastille to his wife, or better, his savage and disturbing humour, would thus ultimately question the position of the super-ego in any type of value system. His writings cannot be reduced to mere fantasies since they examine the way fantasy is determined from the outside by the law. And his sarcastic humour testifies to the division of the subject in the name of the super-ego (as Freud pointed out very clearly in his book on *Witz*).

More recently Monique David-Ménard has reexamined Lacan's confrontation of Kant and Sade in a new light, showing how Lacan misreads certain key elements of Kant's philosophy, erasing for instance the difference between knowledge and thought that is central to his critiques.[35] Lacan appears indeed as too Hegelian when he conflates Kant's notion of the thing-in-itself (equals X) with the respect for the law: both become unthinkable entities. David-Ménard also points out Lacan's difficulties when he postulates the same law of desire for Antigone and for the psychoanalyst. Like Klossowski, she suggests that Sade's works are not just a blueprint for male fantasy (the neurotic imagining of himself as a pervert). Sade cunningly points out the dark side of humanitarian ethics when he posits the issue of man's universality in his relation to the unconditionality of the law (even through a caricature of the law). Respect and blasphemy both address the same underpinning of fantasy by the law of desire, seen negatively as just the obscene *jouissance* of the Other.

I would like to suggest that one paradoxical consequence of Sade's subversion of the subject is that it ultimately opens up a new realm that can be identified with the domain of ethics – at least in the sense given to the term by Levinas. When Levinas discusses the thought of Martin Buber, he provides us with a short-hand recapitulation of the main themes with which he has been associated. He stresses the need for an ethical leap out of metaphysics.

> In my own analyses, the approach to others is not originally in my speaking out to the other, but in my responsibility for him or her. That is the ethical relation. That responsibility is elicited, brought about by the face of the other person, described as a breaking of the plastic forms of the phenomenality of appearance; straightforward-ness of the exposure to death, and an order issued to me not to abandon the other.... Responsibility for the other person, a responsi-bility neither conditioned nor measured by any free acts of which it would be the consequence. Gratuitous responsibility resembling that of a hostage, and going as far as taking the other's place, without requiring reciprocity. Foundation of the idea of fraternity and expia-tion for the other man. Here, then, contrary to Buber's I-Thou, there is no initial equality.... Ethical inequality: subordination to the other, original diacony: the 'first person accusative' and not 'nominative'. Hence the profound truth of Dostoyevsky's *Brothers Karamazov*, often quoted: 'We are all guilty of everything and everyone, towards everyone, and I more than all the others.'[36]

Levinas had already spoken of such an 'original diacony' – in the sense of 'being the servant of the other' – in *En découvrant l'existence avec Husserl et Heidegger*.[37] We may note that the Greek term Διακονος means 'servant' 'attendant', but also 'messenger', 'ambas-sador' or anyone who 'serves' a public function. Like Sade, but with a radically ethical emphasis, Levinas teaches us that we are all 'Hostages of the Other'.

Levinas's non-metaphysical system of ethics stresses the primacy of the Other – a capitalised Other that appears in any 'face' I happen to see and address. Is not this congruent with the ambiguity in Seminar XX between the Other and the other, in the name of what the other's body can symbolise of the big Other? If Lacan is indeed collapsing the distinction between the other (as my neighbour) and the big Other (as Levinas does all the time), what repercussions will this have on the issue of the body on the one hand and ethics on the other?

Sade could allow us to criticise a certain type of ethical innocence in Levinas; after all a face can be dissociated into teeth and a tongue that can be pulled out, a nose and ears that can be cut away, eyes that can be pierced, and so on! The Levinassian face cannot blissfully ignore the ever prersent threat of dismemberment or disfiguration. On the other hand Levinas could help us retrieve Adorno's point and expose in sadism the perverted epistemophilia it hides. The Sadean libertine wishes to reach impassibility, a detachment beyond horror because the subject believes he or she knows the truth about *jouissance*. However as Levinas would suggest, the issue is not to know but to desire, and any knowledge of *jouissance* merely reproduces the illusions of the 'non-dupes' who nevertheless err: *Les non-dupes errent*.... In spite of our vaunted knowledge of *jouissance*, we can now see the libertine as just another hostage of the Other.

The perverse subject has to give up him or herself completely in the name of the Other's *jouissance*, and is thus all the more the slave of this absolute *jouissance* – ironically, just as the moment he or she thinks he or she is the absolute master. Desire seems to provide the only way out by preferring the darker (or more obscure) path of ethical un-knowing, as Levinas's *Totality and Infinity* shows through its 'Phenomenology of Eros' and its detailed and compelling analyses of *jouissance* and representation. These finally lead to the formula: 'No knowledge, no power' (*Ni savoir, ni pouvoir*).[38] Is absolute passivity the best means of access to a truth of desire?

Lacan seems to develop this insight in a later seminar ('The Reverse of Psychoanalysis'). He explains that the big Other is this paradoxical being that 'has a body but does not exist' and only posits itself by saying 'I am who I am'.[39] Sade is important in the sense that he deploys all his efforts in order to try to placate this big Other. Sade ultimately shows himself to be the slave or hostage of divine *jouissance*. Lacan adds that this is why Sade remains a theoretician (*S17*, 75) because he is 'in love with truth' (*S17*, 76). His excessive love for truth precipitates him into purely symptomatic repetition. Truth thus appears as 'the sister of forbidden *jouissance*'. Or, to be more precise, truth is the 'sister-in-law' of *jouissance*; just as Sade seemed to be really in love not with his wife but with his sister-in-law Anne-Prospère de Launay de Montreuil, with whom he fled to the south in 1772 (as Lacan suggests, this is not unlike Freud's attachment for his sister-in-law, Mina Bernays). Perhaps Sade was in love with truth because of his sister-in-law, who embodied for him the old law of courtly love: there is no love in marriage (*S17*, 77).

Sade who was quoted in Seminar X as a key to understanding the 'reverse of the subject', is seen in Seminar XVII as a symptomatic hostage to truth and *jouissance*. Lacan (probably influenced by Deleuze's reading of Sacher-Masoch) therefore opposes Sade's lack of humour – his exhausting but ultimately deluded efforts to accumulate murders and transgression, so as to approach this absolute *jouissance* to which he will always feel inferior – to Sacher-Masoch's humour: a masochist will not need God, he will be happy with God's servant (*S17*, 75). Ultimately, if Sade is so boring it is because he remains a theoretician: the novels are stuck in the groove of an all-too theoretical demonstration. His love of truth forces him to become, in his lifetime, a martyr: which is why he attracts the passionate hagiography of Sadean specialists.

It looks as if the only way to overcome the theoretical dead-end is through Kant, provided Kant's humour is seen and appreciated. The precondition for a provisional way out might be found in Kant's articulation of his three *Critiques*. It was Freud who identified a rare moment of humour in Kant. In his discussion of the Schreber case, Freud reminds us that Kant remains the best model for any theoretical elaboration. He asserts that only a 'genetic' approach to understanding Schreber's 'feminine attitude towards God' can make sense of Schreber's belief that he has to become a woman, who will then be sexually abused by God and become the slave of God's *jouissance*. Before beginning his 'Attempts at Interpretation', Freud concludes his first chapter by quoting Kant's famous Irish bull (a Viennese goat, in fact): 'Or else our attempts at elucidating Schreber's delusions will leave us in the absurd position described in Kant's famous simile in the *Critique of Pure Reason*: – we shall be like a man holding a sieve under a he-goat [*Bock*] while some one else milks it.'[40]

Here Freud is referring to Kant's 'On the Division of General Logic into Analytic and Dialectic' – a section that opens with the momentous question: 'What is truth?' As Kant shows, such a question is absurd, since it presupposes the universality of the criteria of knowledge by which one could answer it. He adds:

> For if the question is in itself absurd and demands answers that are unnecessary, then it not only embarrasses the person raising it, but sometimes has the further disadvantage of misleading the incautious listener: it may prompt him to give absurd answers and to provide us with the ridiculous spectacle where (as the ancients said) one person milks the ram while the other holds a sieve underneath.[41]

This reference tends to show that if Lacan was right to try to make the 'fun' appear in Kant's writings through the use of Sade, he was definitely on the wrong track when he asserted that both Kant and Sade lacked humour: 'Already Kant would for next to nothing make us lose our seriousness, for lack of the least sense of the comic (the proof is what he says of it in its place). But someone who lacks it, himself, totally and absolutely, if you've remarked, is Sade' (*KS*, 69). I hope to have conveyed, with the help of Freud, that this is not exactly the case. Another detour is necessary. In Seminar IX on identification, Lacan tells his audience that he owns a very clever dog – a bitch, to be precise – who can almost talk (session of 29 November 1961). The dog is almost human, since she has always lived in human society. And this bitch was baptised Justine by Lacan, in a tongue-in-cheek homage to Sade's heroine! The two little vignettes about Surrealist animals (a milked ram, a talking bitch named Justine) become, in this context, emblematic. They figure the limit of human desire when confronted with what one imagines to be the *jouissance* of the Other, while allowing at the same time for some human and non-human humour to permeate purely theoretical issues.

If Freud has indeed succeeded where the paranoiac failed, by rewriting Schreber's system in a more coherent way, he may have failed where Kant's and Sade's systems have partly succeeded – in their absurd and irrational praise of rationality. Like Sade, Lacan 'loves truth' and intends to subvert the Law of morality. While it might be tempting to overvalue Sade's testimony as that of a scapegoat of *jouissance*, the ancient simile used by Kant could also suggest that we too – post-Freudian readers of Lacan, and grown all too wise to the universal function of phallic symbols – have milked the same ram or he-goat, while someone else, God, or maybe just our next-door neighbour, has been copulating with him – but through a different sieve!

8 *Ravishing* Duras, or the Gift of Love

Whereas the reference to Sade recurs in Lacan's texts, his engagement with Marguerite Duras has all the features of a sudden infatuation, of a brief but devouring passion. One may wonder why Lacan decided not to include his brilliant essay on Marguerite Duras in the *Ecrits* volume that was published a year later. Is it because, as he knew personally the writer whose production had increased dramatically in the mid-sixties, he felt that his short 1965 article was not definitive enough? Did he see it as a purely occasional piece, a personal 'homage' to a writer he admired, or a more tentative approach to the issue of femininity, an important stepping stone to be kept in reserve for later developments? Whatever the answer is, Duras's book had made a major impact on Lacan's circle, since it was widely discussed when it was published in 1964. Michèle Montrelay gave a long and powerful presentation on it in Lacan's Seminar[1]. It is clear that the new novel made a deep impact on Lacan himself. Following his usual method, Lacan read Duras's works extensively, and then arranged a meeting with the already famous writer. This is how Duras describes their interview: 'He gave me an appointment one day, at midnight, in a bar. He scared me. In a basement it was. To talk about *Lol V. Stein*. He told me that it was a *clinically* perfect delirium. He started questioning me. For two hours. I was reeling when I left.'[2]

Their encounter has been glossed by a few commentators and has given rise to numerous legends. One of them has been distilled by Jean Allouch in his rich collection of Lacanian anecdotes:

> *Le Ravissement de Lol V. Stein* had just been published. It is well-known that Marguerite Duras, who had operated a radical change of style with this novel, was afraid that it might not find any readers. It was in the subjective position of a solitude she had accepted but found difficult that she received one day a telephone call from Lacan.

He was suggesting a meeting that same day, at a very late hour, in a bar.

She accepts and arrives first. Soon after, she sees Lacan threading his way through the tables toward her. In a warm and affectionate tone, as he is now very close to her now, he blurts out: 'You don't know what you are saying!'[3]

This account, even if partly apocryphal, may give a hint as to Lacan's subsequent prudence, and to his decision to leave Montrelay, a brilliant disciple, use the novel for one of the first accounts of feminine writing and feminine sexuality that were then elaborated in Lacanian theory. Duras later felt that Lacan's astonishment at her prescience was more patronizing than humble, he was operating in a male phallocentric mode of appropriation of female truths reached directly by pure intuition, conforming to an old cliché: women guess without words truths that men are able to formulate in a consistent discourse.

What seems to have shocked readers was Lacan's genuine astonishment. How could Marguerite Duras, who made no allusion to psychoanalysis and did not seem to have read him, describe a feminine 'passion' that brings a woman close to psychosis in terms that are indeed so close to his own language? Lacan thus needed to ask Marguerite Duras where she had 'found' this character. She replied that she did not know. All this resurfaces in the essay itself, in which Lacan mentions Freud's homage to artists who always preceded him and alludes to the fact that he wanted the author's approval, but did not mind if he did not get it:

> I think that even if I were to hear it from Marguerite Duras herself that, in her entire *oeuvre*, she doesn't know where Lol has come from, and even if I could glean this from the next sentence she says to me, the only advantage that the psychoanalyst has the right to draw from his position, were this then to be recognized as such, is to recall with Freud that in his work the artist always precedes him, and that he does not have to play the psychologist where the artist paves the way for him.
>
> This is precisely what I acknowledge to be the case in the ravishing of Lol V. Stein, where it turns out that Marguerite Duras knows, without me, what I teach.[4]

There is indeed a striking coincidence between Duras's new themes (Lol V. Stein and the attendant characters will return in other novels and films, all circling around the study of an excessive passion that can lead to despair, madness or death) and a type of sensibility and discourse brought about by Lacan. It looks now as if Duras had written the French equivalent of what Djuna Barnes had managed to portray with more gothic gusto in *Nightwood*: an almost 'clinical' study of perversion as the effect of erotic passion coupled with aban-donment. Without calling upon the *Zeitgeist* or a historical turn in French culture just before the explosion of May 1968, one can speak of a surprisingly auspicious convergence of themes. Duras's new novel was soon heralded as the best example of what Hélène Cixous and other critics would be calling '*écriture féminine*'. However, a biog-rapher and historian like Elisabeth Roudinesco, for instance, takes a very critical attitude when documenting the short-lived infatuation for Duras that Lacan seems to have experienced in the mid-sixties. For her, Lacan's short essay is a mistake and a misfire:

> The article was not in the best taste: Lacan was content to formulate a number of glaring commonplaces. He first recalled that artists had preceded Freud in the discovery of the unconscious, and that Duras had similarly preceded Lacan in the Lola business. He then empha-sized that the figure *three* plays an important role in the story, affirm-ing finally that Lola was not a *voyeur*. She looks without seeing, being thus 'realized' through the circuit of the gaze. Lacan's text is studded with a multitude of compliments and pointless indulgences in flat-tery.[5]

Roudinesco defines what appears strikingly in this ornate and elabo-rate text: Lacan's self-conscious rhetorical presentation of a text that is a gift and an attempt at seducing the author.

In a similar vein, Leslie Hill, a good specialist of Duras's work, accuses Lacan of distortions and important misreadings, and stresses that Jacques Lacan's blindness derives from the fact that he identified with another 'Jacques' in Duras's novel, Jacques Hold, the narrator.[6] Without wishing simply to counter-balance these negative appraisals, I will try to do justice to Lacan's essay, a text that I consider crucial not only for its literary insights but also because it documents very exten-sively how Lacan intends to approach feminine difference and femi-nine *jouissance*. In fact, it looks as if the main defect of this 'Homage' lies in its brevity: Lacan tries to tackle all at once the issues of the Borromean knot, artistic sublimation, a 'grammar of the subject' discovered in graphs of desire and fantasy, the gaze as opposed to seeing, feminine otherness, the links between Marguerite Duras's work and the *Heptameron* – all this in eight pages. On top of this he also attempts to sum up a complex novelistic plot! His intention is also polemical. Even if he had called the novel 'a clinical' study in his conversation with Duras, he explains that he refuses to 'psycho-analyse' the characters. This is a motive we have already encountered, expressed here with particular pungency:

> A subject is a scientific *term*, something perfectly calculable, and this reminder of its status should terminate what can only be called by its name, boorishness: let us say the pedantry of a certain kind of psychoanalysis. This frivolous aspect of psychoanalysis, to remain sensitive, one hopes, to those who immerse themselves in it, ought to indicate to them that they are sliding towards stupidity; for example by attributing an author's avowed technique to some neurosis: boor-ishness. Or again, by showing it to be an explicit adoption of certain mechanisms which would thereby make an unconscious edifice of it: stupidity (*HMD*, 122).

What is this novel that seems to have attracted so many diverging and enthusiastic responses? It is amusing to see that the American presen-tation in the current edition accumulates distortions that are far worse than those attributed to Lacan. The cover states that:

> *The Ravishing of Lol Stein* is a haunting early novel [NB. In 1965, Duras had already published more than ten novels and as many plays since 1943 when her career began] by the author of *The Lover*. Lol Stein is a beautiful young woman, securely married, settled in a comfortable life – and a voyeur. Returning with her husband and chil-dren to the town where, years before, her fiancé had abandoned her for another woman, she is drawn inexorably to recreate that long-past tragedy. She arranges a rendez-vous for her friend Tatiana and Tatianas' s lover. [NB. In fact she just happens to come on the scene] She arranges to spy on them. And then she goes one step further...[7]

One expects some gory conclusion, something closer to *Psycho* than to a tale of bereavement and struggle with insanity. The moot issue is precisely the idea that Lol is a voyeur, a point that Lacan denies, whereas Leslie Hill claims it back for Lol, whom he wishes to see as actively engaged in some form of perversion.

What the blurb does not say is that there is no progressive revelation of the past, as would be the case in a Harlequin fiction. The novel opens with the first scene of the 'ravishing' and consists in a number of successive rewritings of this primal abandonment. The opening scandal is disclosed from the start. At a ball given for her engagement, Lola who is barely seventeen, sees her fiancé, Michael Richardson, inexplicably attracted by Anne-Marie Stretter. He falls under the spell of this older woman, who has come with her daughter to the casino, and they dance together all the night, oblivious of any one else. Anne-Marie Stretter, the wife of a vice-consul, leaves with Michael. They experience a brief passion that lasts only a few months, leaving Lol prostrate and half-demented. She says she did not experience pain and that she stopped loving Michael the minute he looked at Anne-Marie Stretter. Michael Richardson and Anne-Marie Stretter never return to the town of South Tahla where the event took place. Lol becomes a recluse until one day, still very fragile, she meets a total stranger whom on an impulse she marries. They move to another town and have children. She lives a strict and orderly life, under the suspicion from her husband, a famous violinist, that she is not completely cured. Ten years later, Lol and her husband go back to South Thala, and this is where Lol first meets Jacques Hold who is the lover of her old school-friend Tatiana Karl, now married to a doctor. She spies from a field of rye on the two lovers as they meet for their trysts in the Forest Hotel and obsesses about the beauty of Tatiana, 'naked under her black hair'. When Jacques Hold starts falling in love with Lol, she insists that the two lovers continue their meetings. He obeys, knowing all the time that she is there watching, leaving Tatiana unaware and offering their love-making to Lol. Finally, Lol remembers more and more of her first ravishment. She and Jacques go together to the Casino to reenact the primal scene and the momentous night of dancing. Lol can at last experience pain and freely talk about the past. At the end, however, she returns to the field to spy on the two lovers. The novel finishes on an inconclusive note: 'Lol had arrived there ahead of us. She was asleep in the field of rye, worn out, worn out by our trip.'[8]

Lacan writes that he heard from Marguerite Duras herself (as I heard her say this, too) that, for her, Lol Stein becomes incurably mad at the end. No happy ending for her therefore, no cathartic reenactment or replay that would help her out of a trauma! This is how Lacan puts it with some prudence:

And it is because the 'thought' of Jacques Hold comes to haunt Lol too insistently at the end of the novel, when he accompanies her on a pilgrimage to the scene of the event, that Lol goes mad. (The episode in fact contains signs of this, but I would point out that I heard this from Marguerite Duras.) The last sentence of the novel, which brings Lol back to the rye field, seems to me to bring about a much less decisive end than my remark would suggest. One suspects from it a caution against the pathos of understanding. Lol is not to be understood, she is not to be saved from her ravishment (*HMD*, 127).

Lacan, it seems, is here more cautious than the author of the novel in giving a diagnosis. It is because he is aware that interpretation itself is problematized by the novel – since Jacques Hold knows that any attempt at getting closer to her will only 'pervert' the truth: 'Now, I alone of these perverters of the truth know this: that I know nothing. That was my initial discovery about her: to know nothing about Lol Stein was already to know her.' (*RLS*, 72)

Lacan's 'homage' is thus addressed both to Marguerite Duras and to her novel *The Ravishing of Lol Stein* (let us note that it appeared in 1964 under the title of *Le Ravissement de Lol V. Stein*) – thanks to a curious syntax: his original title is 'Hommage fait à Marguerite Duras du *Ravissement de Lol V. Stein*' – literally 'Homage *to* Marguerite Duras *of The Ravishing of Lol Stein*' which immediately suggests a reversal of some theft or ravishing, since Lacan seems to be giving back to Duras her own novel in a gesture of loving homage. Without ado, the essay immediately focuses on the problem posed by the interpretation of the title. This is how it begins, letting one hear Lacan's voice and subjective position in its often tortured syntax:

> *Le ravissement* – this word is enigmatic. Does it have an objective or a subjective dimension – is it a ravishing or a being ravished – as determined by Lol V. Stein?
>
> Ravished. We think of the soul, and of the effect wrought by beauty. But we shall free ourselves, as best as we can, from this readily available meaning, by means of a symbol.
>
> A woman who ravishes is also the image imposed on us by this wounded figure, exiled from things, whom you dare not touch, but who makes you her prey.
>
> The two movements, however, are knotted together in a cipher that is revealed in a name skillfully crafted in the contour of writing: Lol V. Stein.

> Lol V. Stein: paper wings, V, scissors, Stein, stone, in love's guessing games you lose yourself.
>
> One replies: O, open your mouth, why do I take three leaps on the water, out of the game of love, where do I plunge?
>
> Such artistry suggests that the ravisher is Marguerite Duras, and we are the ravished. But if, to quicken our steps behind Lol's steps, which resonate through the novel, we were to hear them behind us without having run into anyone, it is then that her creature moves within a space which is doubled; or it is rather that one of us has passed thought the other, and which of us, in that case, has let himself be traversed?
>
> Or do we now realize that the cipher is to be calculated in some other way: for to figure it out, one must count *oneself* three.[9]

Lacan takes his point of departure from one important element that has disappeared – for no clear reason – from the English version: the decision by Lola to call herself simply 'Lol V. Stein' and not 'Lola Valérie Stein' after her fiancé has suddenly abandoned her. The amputation of her name embodies her 'theft', her clipped wings, and carries her through her catatonic depression. The scansion of her three names carries an emblematic weight, since every subject in this novel is not only dedoubled by pain of loss or love (Lacan later puns on the old French expression '*Je me deux*' meaning 'I am in pain' calling up something like 'I am two for myself') but also mediated by the detour of a third person. Reading the novel becomes indeed a 'counting oneself three', which is indissociable from the reiterated question, 'who is ravished?' To whom does this ravishing refer?

As Lacan continues, the novel's story consists less in the idea of a repetition of the traumatic event than in making a knot of all its elements:

> Thinking along the lines of some cliché, we might say she is repeating the event. But we should look more closely than this. ... This is not the event, but a knot retying itself here. And it is what this knot ties up that actually ravishes – but then again, whom? (*HMD*, 123).

'Counting to three' leads us indeed to see three triangles in the novel, in an analysis that is not far from that of Poe's 'Purloined Letter'. The first triangle posits Lol in one angle as the fascinated observer who cannot yet feel the enormity of her loss while Michael Richardson and Anne-Marie Stretter exchange a look of ravishment. They ravish each other to the point that they forget the rest of the world, as in a mystical or erotic trance. It is this trance that transfixes Lol's gaze and makes her an 'unseeing' subject. Precisely because she is no longer seen by her lover, she cannot see when gazing on the scene.

The second triangle seems to repeat the first but in fact subtly disrupts the parallelism. It posits Lol watching in the field while Jacques and Tatiana make love in the room. But first of all, she cannot see anything of the actual love-making from her position, only sees the lovers emerge at intervals when they come to the window. And then, only Jacques knows that she is there. It is in fact the presence of Lol in the field that makes him postpone a break-up with a mistress for whom he feels less and less attraction. The passionate words of love he whispers in her ear are in fact meant for Lol. We can say that in both triangles, there is a corner defined by an excessive *jouissance* that conjoins pain and desire while opening up to a space beyond. Lol occupies this place in the first triangle, whereas Jacques Hold occupies it in the second. It is in fact Tatiana who does not know what really takes place who has replaced Lol, and this is why she falls more and more desperately in love with Jacques. Meanwhile, Lol must believe in the fiction that Jacques Hold has a wonderful lover with Tatiana.

The apparent overlapping of two triangles that upon closer inspection do not repeat themselves has something to do with narratological uncertainty. Relatively early in the novel we discover a male character seen through the eyes of Lol. He then turns out to be not only Jacques Hold, Tatiana's lover, but also the narrator of the whole novel. By some twist of narratological plausibility, one has to assume that he mentions his presence in the story without saying who he is. When he finally admits of his presence, there is a shift from the third to the first person ('Arm in arm, they ascend the terrace steps. Tatiana introduces Peter Beugner, her husband, to Lol, and Jack Hold, a friend of theirs – the distance is covered – me.' *RLS*, 65), which is in no way definitive. There are a number of scenes in which the narrative hesitates between the two:

> He tells Lol Stein: 'Tatiana removes her clothes, and Jack Hold watches her, stares with interest at this woman who is not the woman he loves'...
> But Tatiana is speaking:
> 'But Tatiana is saying something,' Lol Stein murmurs.

> To make her happy, I would invent God if I had to.
> 'She utters your name'
> I did not invent that (*RLS*, 123).

Thus contrary to what Leslie Hill suggests,[10] Lacan never reduces the ambiguity in the narrative, he even points to its duplications. He begins by noting the privileged role of this character:

> The least we can say is that at this point the story puts one character in balance, and not only because Marguerite Duras has invested this character with the narrative voice: the other partner of the couple. His name is Jacques Hold.
> Nor is he what he appears to be when I say: the narrative voice. He is, rather, its anguish. Once again the ambiguity returns: it is his anguish, or that of the narrative? (*HMD*, 123).

Lacan then assumes that this 'anguish' is another trick performed by Duras to keep us both outside and inside this narrative. Of Jacques Hold, Lacan writes:

> He does not, in any case, simply display the machinery, but in fact one of its mainsprings, and he does not know how taken up in it he is.
> This allows me to introduce Marguerite Duras here, having moreover her consent to do so, as the third ternary, of which one of the terms remains the ravishment of Lol V. Stein caught as an object in her own knot, and in which I myself am the third to propose a ravishment, in my case, a decidedly subjective one (*HMD*, 123).

Literary critics tend to avoid this kind of direct intervention of the author in her narrative. Lacan does not hesitate to read Duras herself in the repeated mentions of 'I see' that punctuate the narrative: 'I see this...' (*RLS*, 45); 'This I invent, I see:....' (*RLS*, 46); 'I invent:....' (*RLS*, 46). Indeed Jacques Hold could be accountable for all these cases, since we understand at the end that he is – because of his love for Lol – reconstructing her whole story. But a number of characters point out to Jacques the limits of his own reconstruction – as for instance Tatiana does when she tries to understand what Lol meant when she said that 'her happiness' was close to her (she meant, of course, that Jacques Hold was not far away). Tatiana, enraged about not knowing something, exclaims:

'But what about this happiness, tell me about this happiness, please, just a word or two about it!'
I say:
'Lol Stein probably had it within her when she encountered it.'
With the same slow movement as before, Tatiana turns again to me. I pale. The curtain has just risen on the pain Tatiana is suffering. But strangely, her suspicions are not immediately directed at Lol.
'How do you know such things about Lol?'
She means: how do you know such things when a woman doesn't? (*RLS*, 139–40).

Therefore it looks a little disingenuous to reproach Lacan for echoing this question, since his own position is sketched there; in the third triangle, he is the fascinated 'voyeur' subjectively ravished by Marguerite Duras, who stands for the 'objective' agency by which the third angle is constructed – the novel itself. Anyone who has met Marguerite Duras, or seen films such as *Le Camion*, will remember her indubitable assertion: 'I see...' and a whole story follows, as when Gérard Depardieu is requested to visualise a blue truck, which soon after materialises out of nowhere.

The postulation of the third circle linking Lacan, Duras and *The Ravishing* is necessary to establish a new grammar of fantasy within which the subject is caught. This is not simply reducible to what René Girard has called 'triangular desire', in which a third person always mediates in the choice of the object. What these three triangles help Lacan calculate is the way in which any subject has to face her or his determination by the locus of the big Other. What happens to Lol – which is why Duras can state so precisely that she becomes mad at the end – is that she has been swallowed by this Other, be it called love, desire or *jouissance*. This void into which she falls at the end is circled by a letter, the love letter that the novel slowly describes. Or to quote Duras's lyrical evocation of it:

What she does believe is that she must enter it [this unknown], that that was what she had to do, that it would always have meant, for her mind as well as her body, both their greatest pain and their greatest joy, so comingled as to be undefinable, a single entity but unnamable for lack of a word. I like to believe – since I love her – that if Lol is silent in her daily life it is because, for a split second, she believed that this word might exist. Since it does not, she remains silent. It would have been an absence-word, a hole-word, whose center would have been hollowed out in a hole, the kind of hole in which all other words would have been buried.... By its absence, this word ruins all the others, it contaminates them, it is also the dead dog on the beach at high noon, this hole of flesh (*RLS*, 38).

The hole-word would be the linguistic condensation of the catastrophe she experiences in one second during the ball: an absolute dereliction that shatters whatever imaginary certainty she had entertained until then, or, to quote Blanchot, a 'writing of the disaster'. This word is thus impossible to utter, to write or to read in any language, since it obscures a frozen vision:

> What Lol would have liked would have been to have the ball immured, to make of it this ship of light upon which, each afternoon, she embarks, but which remains there, in this impossible port, forever anchored and yet ready to sail away with its three passengers from this entire future in which Lol Stein now takes her place. There are times when it has, in Lol's eyes, the same momentum as on the first day, the same fabulous force.
>
> But Lol is not yet God, nor anyone (*RLS*, 39).

And indeed she becomes 'God', but only at the end, if we admit that this is the moment at which she turns completely psychotic.

We can now understand why Lol, after the 'primal scene' of the ball, has focused all her attention on just one wish: the desire to see Anne-Marie Stretter undressed by her fiancé, Michael Richardson. This defines the grammar of her fantasy, as glossed by Lacan.

> But what exactly is this vacuity? It begins to take on a meaning: you were, yes, for one night until dawn, when something in that place gave way, the center of attention.
>
> What lies concealed in this locution? A center is not the same on all surfaces. Singular on a flat surface, everywhere on a sphere, on a more complex surface it can produce an odd knot. This last knot is ours.
>
> Because you sense that all this has to do with an envelope having neither an inside nor an outside, and in the seam of its center every gaze turns back into our own, that these gazes are your own, which your own saturates and which, Lol, you will forever crave from every passerby. Let us follow Lol as she passes from one to the other, seizing from them this talisman which everyone is so eager to cast off: the gaze.

> Every gaze will be yours, Lol, as the fascinated Jacques Hold will say to himself, for himself, ready to love 'all of Lol'.
>
> There is in fact a grammar of the subject which has taken note of this stroke of genius (*HMD*, 125).

As Freud does in his analysis of a fantasmatic scenario in 'A child is being beaten', here Lacan connects the grammar of a subject that can quickly turn into an object, of an active verb that becomes passive ('I am beating' becoming 'I am beaten') with his theory of the gaze as opposed to the eye – a theory he developed in Seminar XI (*The Four Fundamental Concepts of Pyschoanalysis*), as we have seen. A brief detour through the theory of the gaze is necessary – the story of the tin can by which Lacan was 'not seen' but 'gazed at' (or 'regarded') is a good analogy with Lol's vacant stare. The anamorphic stain or blot that was revealed to be a death mask or an oblique skull in the paint-ing the 'Ambassadors' offers another analogy. The following is a condensed version of his theory that Lacan then offers:

> You can verify it, this gaze is everywhere in the novel. And the woman of the event is easy to recognize, since Marguerite Duras has depicted her as non-gaze.
>
> I teach that vision splits itself between the image and the gaze, that the first model for the gaze is the stain, from which is derived the radar that the splitting of the eye offers up to the scopic field.
>
> The gaze spreads itself as a stroke on the canvas, making you lower your own gaze before the work of the painter.
>
> Of that which requires your attention one says, '*ça vous regarde*': this looks at you (*HMD*, 125–6).

Lacan returns to the central episode, the voyeuristic scenes linking Lol, Jacques and Tatiana in the second part of the novel. He comments at length on Jacques' anxiety, on Tatiana's deception, both of whom are dominated by 'the law of Lol' – that is, that they should go on to please her. Can one say that Lol is a Peeping Tom? Lacan believes that this is not the case: her absent stare is closer to the function of a gaze that does not see you than to an eye wishing to capture a vision. The fasci-nation that emanates from the whole novel thus hinges on the division between eye and gaze, love and desire, image and stain:

> Above all, do not be deceived about the locus of the gaze here. It is not Lol who looks, if only because she sees nothing. She is not a

voyeur. She is realized only in what happens.

Only when Lol, with the appropriate words, elevates the gaze to the status of a pure object for the still innocent Jacques Hold is its place revealed.

'Naked, naked under her black hair', these words from the lips of Lol mark the passage of Tatiana's beauty into a function of the intolerable stain which pertains to the object.

This function is no longer compatible with the narcissistic image in which the lovers try to contain their love, and Jacques Hold immediately feels the effects of this.

From that moment on, in their dedication to realizing Lol's phantasm, they will be less and less themselves (*HMD*, 126–7).

When Lacan says that Lol 'elevates the gaze to the status of a pure object for Jacques Hold', he implies that what Lol accomplishes is less the realization of a perverse fantasy that would repeat her fixation to another naked body fondled by another lover, than the very sublimation of this fantasy. Following Lacan's formulas in Seminar VII, one can say that she raises the gaze to the dignity of the Thing, an expression that, in the original French, is never far from the suggestion of refuse, excrement, waste ('... the most general formula that I can give you of sublimation is the following: it raises an object – and I don't mind the suggestion of a play on words in the terms I use – to the dignity of the Thing' (*S7*, 112). In fact Lacan seems to be revisiting the seminar on ethics when he writes his homage to Duras. As in this seminar, he points to the way the Horror concealed in the Thing provides a way of avoiding the body's base nature while keeping desire alive. Later, Lacan would say that this structure is aimed at contravening the principle that 'there is no sexual rapport'. This is the whole structure of what was called 'courtly love' in the Middle Ages, a structure in which a lady would parade herself as an object in order to tempt a lover even though she was married, while the lover would raise her 'to the dignity of the Thing', either by paying 'homage' to her through high deeds, bravery and valour, or, if the lover was a troubadour, through songs of praise. One now begins to understand the elaborate rhetorical flourishes that Lacan 'offers' to Marguerite Duras: he reinscribes her – and himself – in the ancient tradition of courtly love marked by passionate though chaste homage. This is how Lacan calls up this curious type of sublimation:

> The object involved, the feminine object, is introduced oddly enough
> through the door of privation or of inaccessibility. Whatever the
> social position of him who functions in the role, the inaccessibility of
> the object is posited as a point of departure.... Here we see function-
> ing in the pure state the authority of that place the instinct aims for in
> sublimation. That is to say, that what man demands, what he cannot
> help but demand, is to be deprived of something real. And one of you,
> in explaining to me what I am trying to show in *das Ding*, referred to
> it neatly as the vacuole (*S7*, 149–50).

We can now see Lol's madness in the light of another type of
madness, that of a desire that had to be posited as impossible. The
vacuole would be contained by the 'word' she hopes to find, a word
that signals that the catastrophe has already happened, but that has
been translated to a vision of nothing, in the pure memory of a blank
stare, of a fascinated expectation of what will have to remain off-
limits, outside the frame.

In the seminar on the ethics of psychoanalysis, Lacan connects this
structure of desire with what critics such as Denis de Rougemont
analysed as the Tristan myth, or what Lucien Febvre interpreted as a
moment of loss in religious belief that has to be replaced by erotic
mysticism. Thus in a vertiginous series of connections, Lacan moves
from the problem of unbelief in the sixteenth century and to the issue
of sublimation through book by Febvre on Marguerite de Navarre's
The Heptameron:

> She [Marguerite de Navarre] is not just a libertine author, but turns
> out to have written a treatise that is mystical in kind. But that is not
> something that excites the astonishment of the historian.
>
> He tries to show us what the collection of the tales that go under the
> title of the *Heptameron* might mean in the context of the time and of
> the psychology of their author.... Lucien Febvre teaches us how to read
> the *Heptameron*. Yet if we knew how to read, we wouldn't need him.
>
> As far as unbelief is concerned, it is from our point of view a place
> in discourse that is to be conceived precisely in relation to the Thing –
> the Thing is repudiated or foreclosed in the proper sense of
> *Verwerfung* (*S7*, 131).

Thus it is hardly a surprise to see Lacan pouncing on the coincidence
that gives two extraordinary female writers the same first name –
Marguerite. Lacan confesses that during his seminar on ethics he had

been inspired by the work of Marguerite de Navarre (whom he calls here Marguerite d'Angoulême, since she was indeed the daughter of Charles d'Angoulême). Marguerite was equally the author of the *Mirror of the Sinful Soul* – a mystical treatise that had the good fortune to be translated into English by an eleven-year old girl, Elizabeth, who later became Queen of England. Quoting his earlier disquisition on ethics and the thing, Lacan develops at some length the association he establishes, thereby sketching a whole theory of the evolution of the novel as a genre:

> This leads us to the ethics of psychoanalysis, a topic which, in my seminar, produced a schism within the unsteady ranks of the audience.
>
> In front of everyone, however, I confessed one day that throughout the entire year my hand had been held by some invisible place by another Marguerite, Marguerite of the *Heptameron*. It is not without consequence that I find here this coincidence of names.
>
> It seems quite natural to me to find in Marguerite Duras that severe and militant charity that animates the stories of Marguerite d'Angoulême, when they can be read free from the prejudices which are intended solely to screen us off from their locus of truth.
>
> This is the idea of the 'gallant' story. In a masterful work, Lucien Febvre has tried to expose the trap its sets.
>
> I would draw attention to the fact that Marguerite Duras has received from her readers a striking and unanimous affirmation of this strange way of loving: of that particular way of loving which the character – whom I placed not in the role of narrator but of subject – brings as an offering to Lol, the third person indeed, but far from being the excluded third.
>
> I am delighted to see this proof that the serious still have some rights after four centuries in which the novel feigned sentimentality, firstly to pervert the technique of the convention of courtly love into a mere fictional account, and then to cover up the losses incurred – losses parried by the convention of courtly love – as it developed into the novel of marital promiscuity.
>
> And the style you adopt, Marguerite Duras, throughout your Heptameron, might well have paved the way for the great historian I mentioned earlier to attempt to understand some of these stories for what they really are: true stories.
>
> But sociological reflections on the many changing moods of life's pain are little when compared to the relationship that the structure of desire, which is always of the Other, had with the object that causes it (*HMD*, 128).

Going back to the associations he developed in Seminar VII (p. 131) about the superior 'truth' embodied in the *Heptameron*'s tales, Lacan implies here that the novel has lost a world of passion and desire, romanticised in the name of 'sentiment' – only to be trivialised in the nineteenth century as the novel of adultery. His thesis again calls up Girard's title, 'Romantic Lie and Novelistic truth', the original French title of which was later translated into English as *Deceit, Desire and the Novel*[11] – a critical essay that was, by the way, much in debt to Lacan himself. In the long passage just quoted, Jacques Hold is called the 'subject' and not just the narrator, which means not only that Duras is the real narrator, Hold's puppet-master, but that above all she provides as in a diagram the very structure of the desiring subject caught up between the Other (O) and the small a, or the object of desire in fantasy.

To illustrate the comparison, Lacan sends us to one of the tales in Marguerite de Navarre's *Heptameron*, the story of Amador and Florida, a text that we must engage with a little more deeply. This story, the tenth of the stories narrated on the first day, tells how Amador, a beautiful and valiant nobleman without an inheritance, decides one day to fall in love with Florida (then only twelve), the daughter of the count of a region in Aragon. To remain close to this lady he marries a woman who belongs to the court and offers a good pretext to see his lady often: Aventurade, a rich woman who is Florida's confidante and provides an ideal cover for his real passion. Amador spends a few years away fighting in war, but he returns often and finds that he cannot sufficiently hide the passion he feels for Florida, who still has no inkling of this attraction. In order better to conceal his passion, he tries to take a mistress, an attractive lady named Paulina who guesses that she is only needed as a cover. Then Amador confesses his love to Florida, adding that he does not expect anything from her in return for his steady devotion. Florida replies that she does not understand: 'If you already have what you desire, what can it be that now makes you tell me about it in such an emotional manner?'[12] Amador replies that she should not fear an evil design, that he simply discovered that he could not hide from Paulina his love for Florida. This has an important effect on Florida: 'At these words Florida was filled with delight beyond bounds. Deep within her heart she began to feel stirrings that she had never felt before.'[13] However Florida then marries the king to whom she has been promised, while Amador is taken prisoner by the King of Tunis and spends two years in captivity. Upon his return, Florida is ready to take him as a 'friend'. Later she is ready to accept him as a lover too, but, unhappily, he is ordered to leave again and Aventurade, already sick, has a bad fall and dies. On the night before Amador's departure Florida comes to see him in his room, where he is lying distraught in bed. Amador takes this as an opportunity to make a wild attempt on her virtue. Florida scolds him severely, reminding him of all his speeches about her honour. Still struggling within, she resolves to love him without giving in to his sexual demand.

Four or five years elapse, during which Amador is in mourning, not so much for his dead wife, as everyone believes, as for Florida's lost love. His reputation as a warrior grows. He decides to stake everything on a final attempt on Florida, with the help of her mother, who has become his ally. Sensing this and fearing another assault, Florida tries to disfigure herself by hitting her mouth and eyes with a stone. This does not deter Amador. Amador and Florida find themselves again alone in a room, and he exhibits all the violence of his love. This is a second 'rape' and it fails like the first. Florida cries out for her mother, who is surprised at her daughter's stubborn resistance and stops talking to her. Amador goes back to combat, and surrounded by enemies kills himself rather than be taken prisoner again. Subsequently Florida enters the Convent of Jesus.

It looks as if this was not just the blueprint for *La Princesse de Clèves* a century later, with an important change in the mother's function, but also a condensation of all the tales of inaccessibility Lacan has mentioned, with a realistic study of the male rage this can trigger. This cautionary tale from the feminine point of view (at least this is the 'lesson' Marguerite draws at the end of the first day) becomes exemplary for Lucien Febvre, who takes it as a point of departure to study the structure of courtly love. In his *Autour de l'Heptameron*[14] he devotes several chapters to this single story. In Chapter 5, entitled 'From courtesy to Rape', he explains Amador's sudden reversals (professing a pure and chaste love but twice attempting to rape his lady) not only according to the customs of the times but also through biographical factors. For Febvre, there is no doubt that this tale alludes to real events, and barely disguises Marguerite herself in the role of Florida (she was the sister of the king) while Amador was actually Bonnivet, a handsome and well-known courtier who had married Bonaventure du Puy du Fou, whose name clearly returns as Aventurade.[15] The story of how Marguerite was almost raped by

Bonnivet was narrated by Brantôme in his *Dames Galantes*. Moreover Febvre suggests that to understand the collection of stories well, one would need to write a whole history of subjectivity in connection with sexuality – 'For our self has a whole history'[16] – a project something like Foucault's last essays on the history of sexuality.

Hence what Febvre – followed with great interest by Lacan – stresses in his commentary on *The Heptameron*, is the 'real' nature of these stories. They are not 'inventions', because the social background is never elided and they are all based on particular cases of love understood as passion, almost 'rage'. When Amador first falls in love with Florida it is a deliberate rather than an emotional act. He does it on purpose, *se délibéra de l'aimer*, as the French text clearly says, underlining the rational choice of being irrational. The apparent clash between Platonic love and sexual love (seen here as rape) covers up a more perverse disposition, the lover's decision to become a slave in a masochism that will at one point explode and claim its due. There is no idealism in this story of frustrated passion, a tale that persistently calculates dowries and ransom money. Febvre identifies the emergence in about 1520–60 of a new type of writing – linked with a new genre, the novel, and not far from that of the free 'essay', introduced by Montaigne. This writing constructs a new type of subjectivity that appears unstable, fluctuating, a locus of mediation between almost incompatible urges and drives. This also presupposes a disjunction between love and marriage, between a real desire that has to be kept hidden at any cost, and a series of deceptive manoeuvres that are compatible with advancement and promotion in the social world. The final irony of the tale is that Amador's courtship of Florida succeeds only in seducing Florida's mother! Both Marguerite de Navarre and Montaigne seem to rail against the illusions of those who would wish to link love and marriage – an illusion denounced by Montaigne as a sort of 'incest'.[17]

Amador's story shows that sublimation never works as a peaceful process: there is always an intractable remainder, a point linked by Lacan with his dissatisfaction with the Freudian concept ('This is the meaning of sublimation, something that still confounds psychoanalysts because, in handing down the term to them, Freud's mouth remained sewn shut', (*HMD*, 127). At the end of his homage, in a long rhetorical flourish, Lacan makes the connection between Amador and Lol more explicit, while implying that he believes Duras's story to be somewhat autobiographical:

Take the exemplary tale in Book X of Amador, who is not a choir boy. Devoted even unto death to a love which, for all its impossibility, is in no way Platonic, he sees his own enigma all the more clearly by not viewing it in terms of the ideal of the Victorian happy ending.

For the point at which the gaze turns back into beauty, as I have described it, is the threshold between-two-deaths, a place I have defined, and which is not merely what those who are far removed from it might think: it is the place of misery.

It seems to me, Marguerite Duras, from what I know of your work, that your characters are to be found gravitating around this place, and you have situated them in a world familiar to us in order to show that the noble women and gentlemen of ancient pageantry are every-where, and they are just as valiant in their quests; and should they be caught in the thorns of uncontrollable love, towards that stain, celes-tial nocturne, of a being offered up to the mercy of all..., at half past ten on a summer's evening.

You probably couldn't come to the aid of your creations, new Marguerite, bearing a myth of the personal soul. But does not the rather hopeless charity with which you animate them proceed from the faith which you have in such abundance, as you celebrate the taciturn wedding of an empty life with an indescribable object (*HMD*, 129).

The final metamorphosis of Marguerite Duras into an allegory of the three theological virtues – hope, faith and charity – is surprising. When suggesting that all these stories were based on reality, Lacan was probably disappointed, like Amador himself, by Marguerite's coyness (or at least her refusal to disclose anything that would confirm his hypothesis). As Leslie Hill and other commentators have noted, it is not just two but three Marguerites that Lacan seems to call up when he superimposes Lol Stein and *The Heptameron* ; how could one forget Marguerite Anzieu, alias 'Aimée' – a pen-name that could have come straight from Marguerite de Navarre's pen – as the first feminine initiator of the circuitous paths of 'mad love', criminal jeal-ousy, erotomania and psychosis?

As Roudinesco, Jean Allouch and Leslie Hill have pointed out, the coincidences do not stop with the first name – Marguerite. Lacan's famous patient, upon whose case he had built his thesis and written on paranoid psychosis – and who, by a curious quirk of fate, became his father's cook after the war – was not only named Marguerite but owed the name to her maternal grandmother, Marguerite

Donnadieu.[18] And Marguerite Duras's real name was Marguerite Donnadieu! As is well-known, Lacan did not recognise Didier Anzieu, Marguerite's only son, when he started psychoanalysis with him in 1952. And it was only later that the famous French writer and psychoanalyst realised that his mother had preceded him in Lacan's interests. Alerted by the troubling superimposition of names, Lacan cannot have missed this in 1964 when he read Duras's new novel. Was not Lol V. Stein's name like an anagram of LOVe? Was she another Aimée, resurrected by Duras's praised 'artistry'? What Roudinesco describes as Lacan's only 'novel' – 'A Novel of his Youth'[19] – contains a detailed exegesis of two novels written by Aimée. According to Lacan, her style is unlike that of most paranoiacs and bears a resemblance to Duras's later style: 'It is a succession of very short sentences; they generate each other speedily and easily, with a tone of great verve.'[20] It would be too far-fetched to juxtapose the story of Aimée's youth, her 'projective jealousy'[21] and her beautiful texts interspersed with poems, with Duras's novel.

What finally matters is that there was indeed a real basis for Lacan's seduction by Marguerite Duras's tale of quasi-psychosis. Lacan shows himself to be motivated not only by admiration but also by a consistent scientific interest: Duras teaches him how to use a literary text to 'calculate the subject' and not remain caught up in fascination. Since the process of 'ravishing' is another name for this fascination, one can now better understand why Lacan wants to 'give back' to Duras her own text by a carefully calculated rhetorical homage. He plays the role of the analyst by letting her own mesage be sent back to her, but in an inverted form. This homage initiates another circle in the 'calculus' of the subject's knots, since it links different levels of subjective and objective articulation in a more complex grid that Lacan will later develop with Joyce. Duras remains a very important stage in his confrontation with the riddle of femininity: in this case the letter of literature has been able to let Lacan and his readers see how female desire confronts itself with *jouissance* while calling up the ancient fiction of love, always hesitating between comedy and tragedy.

9 Tragedies and Comedies of Love: from Plato to Claudel and Genet

Our reading of Duras has brought us to the enigma of a divine love experienced in a feminine key and proposed as a gateway to a different sexuality: God would be a name for the *jouissance* of a barred woman, as Seminar XX states. Lacan evokes his fascination for a philosophical topic that he calls a 'literary' theme: woman's enjoyment. 'That too is a theme, a literary theme. And it's worth dwelling on for a moment. I've been doing nothing but that since I was twenty, exploring the philosophers on the subject of love.'[1] To develop this insight, I take as my point of departure a series of remarks by French philosopher Alain Badiou on Lacan's theory of love. These remarks come from a lecture given at the 1990 Paris conference on 'Lacan and Philosophy', during which a number of critics and writers fought bitterly over Lacan's heritage.[2]

Badiou belonged to the group of *normaliens* who had worked with Althusser on science and Marxism when Lacan came onto the scene in the mid-1960s. When asked by the students to define his ontology, Lacan replied that his theory had nothing to do with usual philosophies of the subject. He then accused all philosophical systems of wrongfully relying on a kind of phenomenology that always posited the primacy of a perceiving or thinking subject. Psychoanalysis, on the contrary, begins with the recognition that, because its subject is determined by unconscious desire, the subject is split, multiple, shattered. This has remained Badiou's starting point; recognition of an 'anti-philosophy', coupled with a theory of love, was crucial to Lacan's original intervention in culture.

This was news to the philosophy students, who in February 1966 asked a series of rather naive questions to Lacan. This is how they started:

> You have spoken of the mirage generated by a confusion between consciousness and the subject, an illusion denounced by the psychoanalytic experience. Now, philosophy talks about consciousness (Cartesian cogito, transcendental consciousness, Hegelian self-consciousness, Husserl's apodictic consciousness, Sartre's pre-reflexive cogito ...). How can psychoanalytic experience account for the misrecognition produced when a subject identifies with his own consciousness?[3]

Lacan answered by identifying the source of the students' question in an obituary homage to Merleau-Ponty, a text in which he attempted to distinguish his position from that of one of the best representatives of French phenomenology. In this text, Lacan denounces the idea of reducing subjective agency to 'I think'; for him, the confusion between the subject and consciousness is an original sin of philosophy. He does not deny that there can be a Cartesian moment when the subject and consciousness coincide: it can be found in the deduction of a 'cogito' such as has been performed by Descartes in his *Meditations*. Here is what Lacan says:

> It is at this moment of coincidence itself as seized by reflection that I wish to mark the place of the entrance of psychoanalytic experience. If it is only beheld in time, the subject of the 'I think' reveals what it is: a being determined by a fall. I am he who thinks: 'Therefore I am', have I commented elsewhere, to underscore that the 'therefore', denoting causality, begets an inaugural division that separates the 'I am' of existence from the 'I am' of meaning.
>
> This splitting [refente] is precisely what is brought to us every day in psychoanalytic experience. I am anguished by castration while at the same time I consider it impossible. Such is the crude example given by Freud to illustrate this splitting, that functions at all the levels of any subjective structure. I say that it has to be taken as fundamental and as the first hint of originary repression.
>
> I say that all the 'consciousnesses' that you have spread out in such a neat row, to culminate with Sartre's, have no other function than to bridge, suture this gap in the subject, and that a psychoanalyst recognises its stakes, namely the attempt to lock up truth (for which the perfect instrument would of course be the ideal promised by Hegel under the guise of absolute knowledge).[4]

Lacan dismisses two parallel and fundamental mistakes, one made by psychology (defined by a discourse of the total and unsplittable 'self'), the other by philosophy – a discourse that claims to base the utterance of truth on a universal consciousness. The two major delusions, that of a 'science of the self' and that of a 'discourse of the absolute', rest on parallel misprisions about the relation of subjects to desire. In this discussion Lacan adds typically that he was struck by the fact that, for all their questions, the students did not ask him from where he was speaking, as if his enunciative position did not matter and could be taken for granted. They were guilty of the same category mistake as the discourses of philosophy and psychology: having collapsed the 'subject' and the 'ego' they misunderstand the way enunciation structures or punctures any enounced statement.

In spite of his double critique, Lacan's project entails a constant confrontation with modern phenomenology, a discourse that is often seen as linked to a theory of consciousness, from Husserl's *Cartesian Meditations* to Sartre's *Transcendence of the Ego* and Merleau-Ponty's *Phenomenology of Perception*. Although he prefers quoting Heidegger on an a subjective notion of 'existence' (*Dasein*), Lacan's notion of the ego, defined as an imaginary projection, could lead to a refutation of the Cartesian subject. The position of the Unconscious as the locus of desire and therefore of all last-instance subjective determinations seems to decentre the rule of the *ego cogito* posited by Descartes. Yet Lacan claims for his own discourse a concept of the subject (as a subject of science) that can nevertheless be derived from the Cartesian *cogito*. What changes with Lacan, is that if desire is the main concept, there is no full subject of desire; desire is always desire of the Other, and psychoanalysis works with the subject of a given fantasy. This fantasy enacts a specific division of the subject, a division caused by an object. This object, called by Lacan *objet petit a*, is the main concept of psychoanalysis, as we have seen. It is interesting to note that this concept gradually emerged from Lacan's 1960–61 seminar on transference. We shall pay closer attention to this soon.

When Badiou tries to make sense of Lacan's antiphilosophical position he is careful to distinguish it from another type of antiphilosophy that could be identified with the Sophists.[5] Lacan is not a philosopher because he insists that all his thinking derives from his experience as a psychoanalyst, but he is not a Sophist either, primarily because he posits a truth. Does this qualify him as a Platonist? Badiou would say yes, in a sense. He sums up Lacan's theses thus:

1. There is a truth and it is articulated in language.
2. This truth, however, can never be fully articulated, it can at best be 'half-said'.
3. This truth cannot be determined by logical or other absolute criteria, since it is less a judgment than an operation: it cannot be disentangled from the performative gesture by which a subject can understand how she or he is 'caused', that is, determined by desire and the object of desire.

This sends us back to a number of arguments we have already surveyed. The main point of interest at this juncture is the fact that Badiou derives from these axioms the need to leave a central role to love. Love is the site of a crossing between the law of desire and the law of truth. As he explains, love aims at pure being, at the surprise of an event, be it provided by a sudden passion or a renewed daily occurrence. In a similar fashion Beckett speaks of the 'short-circuit' of requited passion:

> 'Love requited,' said Neary, 'is a short circuit,' a ball that gave rise to a sparkling rally.
> 'The love that lifts up its eyes,' said Neary, 'being in torments; that craves for the tip of her little finger, dipped in lacquer, to cool its tongue – is foreign to you, Murphy, I take it.'
> 'Greek,' said Murphy.'[6]

Murphy's irregular heartbeats and seizures can be explained by his inability to love, and by the attendant fact, of Cartesian descent, that his 'conarium' (pineal gland) has 'shrunk to nothing'. When he confesses that love remains Greek to him, this modern Cartesian and 'seedy solipsist' dismisses a theory of love deriving from Plato and about which he wishes to know nothing. However Descartes's famous pineal gland, our 'third eye', would thus be not only the seat of the link between the body and the soul, but also the organ of love. As Badious states, 'love aims at Being', creating a short circuit that conjoins a truth defined by the surprise of a sudden revelation and the reality of desire acting out its effects along the chain of signifiers. Hence can one say that, for Lacan, one has to speak (or think) in Greek in order to believe in love?

As Badiou suggests, Lacan's theory aims primarily at subverting the usual philosophical opposition between being and nothingness, because he understands the unconscious as the effect of a lack-in-being (*manque à être*). This effect takes the logical and libidinal form of transference; love is not reducible to the 'transference love' that is such a technical tool in the process of psychoanalysis, but transference love works so well because it exploits the preexisting structure of love in any subject. Like Hegel, Lacan attempts to bridge the gap between materialism and idealism by exploiting the resources of a negativity he inscribes in the subject. His confrontation with Plato will therefore become all the more revealing, since all 'antiphilosophers' have had either to kill or to refute Plato (Nietzsche, Heidegger, logical positivists and Derrida all confirm the rule). According to Badiou, who refuses to reduce Plato to a simplistic formula of idealism and stresses the complexity of the later dialogues revolving around the idea of 'participation', if it not entirely sure that Lacan is a straight Platonist, it is clearly Plato who is Lacanian!

Plato often occupies the position of master in Lacan's texts. In Seminar VIII Lacan compares Plato and Sade in a very idiosyncratic manner: 'Plato is a master, a true master, a master of the times when the city starts decomposing, swept away by the democratic wave that announces the great imperial convergences – a sort of Sade, but funnier.'[7] A little later Lacan praises Plato's 'infernal humor' (*S8*, 105). Following Nietzsche's main insight, Lacan often opposes Socrates, who seems to provide a blueprint for psychoanalytic maieutics a few centuries in advance, and Plato, a high master of philosophy, who has retained all his political ambitions (this portrayal of Plato cannot but call up Kojève, who remained a 'real master' for Lacan). Besides, Lacan agrees with Nietzsche's main thesis in the *Birth of Tragedy*: Socrates has no feeling, no sympathy for tragedy, a genre that he clearly cannot understand (*S8*, 102).

Socrates, who only spoke and never wrote, can be seen as the first psychoanalyst: does he not insist upon the link between truth and individual discourse, forcing individuals to renounce the security of generalisations to disclose where they stand in person facing truth? And if he flaunts his ignorance as a preliminary move in discussion and dialectics, he admits that the only thing he knows anything about is love: his severely limited knowledge bears on Eros and *erotika*. In *Symposium*, Socrates announces to his friends: 'love is the only thing in the world I understand'.[8] This is confirmed in the first half of *Phaedrus*, where Socrates affirms his mastery in 'matters of love' (*erotika*). Socrates precedes Freud in this knowledge. Lacan goes as far to say in his own seminars that the *Symposium* can be compared to a recording of an analysand's session (*S8*, 38) and that psychoanalysis has to deal with 'love' as a major issue. In Seminar XX for instance, when Lacan returns to the question of love motivated by the 'One', his language is decidedly Platonist: 'Then what is involved in love? Is love – as psychoanalysis claims with an audacity that is all the more incredible as all of its experience runs counter to that very notion, and as it demonstrates the contrary – is love about making one? Is Eros a tension toward the One?' (*S20*, 5). Before unpacking a little more the central thesis of 'There is the One', which in later years pushes Lacan away from his earlier stress on the Other, let us follow his reading of the *Symposium* to see what he finds there.

Both Freud and Lacan posit a similar 'Greek' notion of love when they refer either to Empedocles, who saw the two conflicting principles of love and hate as underpinning the whole universe, thus suggesting the twin principles of Eros and Thanatos to Freud, or to Plato, whose *Symposium* is quoted at length by Freud in *Beyond the Pleasure Principle*. Freud praises Aristophanes's image of these divided giants who spend their lives pining for the other half, seeing it as a confirmation that only mythical elaboration can do justice to theories of love. Like many readers, Freud attributes Aristophanes's tale of the halved creatures to Plato himself, and obviously Lacan agrees, since he says that 'in the *Symposium*, the only orator who speaks of love as befits it ... is a clown'. (*S8*, 106). The fantastic idea of original giants who are cut into two by Zeus, come either from the Sun (and are thus made up of two male halves), from the Earth (two female halves) or from the Moon (one male half, one female half) cannot simply be attributed to Plato. According to a renowned specialist of Plato, the 'whole tale of the bi-sexual creatures is a piece of gracious Pantagruelism.... Plato's serious purpose must be looked for elsewhere.'[9] Besides, as is well-known, Aristophanes is precisely the worst enemy of Socrates. His derision of the philosopher in *The Clouds* was an important factor leading to the trial and subsequent condemnation to death of Socrates. Since *The Symposium* begins by celebrating the victory of an actor, the beautiful and effete Agathon (who, by the way, is described as an 'effeminated fop' in *Thesmophoriae*) we cannot bracket off the 'dramatic context' of the dialogue: is it a comedy or a tragedy? This question has some important repercussions for Lacan's theory of love.

When Lacan starts reading *The Symposium* he stresses the centrality of the issue of love in psychoanalytic practice. Psychoanalysis
presupposes a bracketing off of the body, an *époché* concerning libidinal drives, since nothing but speech can take place between the
analysand and the psychoanalyst (*S8*, 24). And echoing Freud's
famous remark, Lacan also believes that the aim of a psychoanalysis
is not to 'cure' the patient, or to bring him or her some 'good' – it is
not for the patient's good that all this is taking place – but to help the
patient to love. Lacan merely asks: 'Does it mean finally that I have to
teach the patient how to love?' (*S8*, 25). Socrates would answer yes,
but against a background of indecision regarding all other abstract
concepts, including the *philia* or love that is implied in *philosophy*
(love for wisdom). Lacan then explores the context of the dialogue,
stressing the political role of Alcibiades – a historical figure that he
describes as half-way between Kennedy and James Dean! (*S8*, 34) –
and his privileged link to Socrates. He returns to the links between
'courtly love' (quoting *The Heptameron* once more) and 'Greek love'
(defined here quite prosaically as 'love for beautiful boys'). Both
types of love imply some measure of sublimation – a sublimation
that does not rule out perversion (*S8*, 43). Lacan reverts to his analysis of *Hamlet* and *Antigone* to suggest that love is close to a perversion of sublimation, and remains fascinated by beauty. Agathon's
definition of love is very modern since it announces what has not
dominated the star system. The cinema, as Lacan suggest, would
have pleased Plato: it fulfills all of Plato's ideas about the model, the
ideal as bright shapes whose commodified copies are shades
endlessly reproduced (*S8*, 45). Hollywood is also a good example in
that it shows how love is a 'comic feeling' (*S8*, 46). From Plato to
Hollywood, a single structure has seized love in its network of signifiers: there is always the lover as the subject of love, the *erastes*, and
the loved one (the *erôménos*) as the object of love, someone who has
this little something that the subject lacks. The whole issue is to
determine whether what the object has is identical to the object that
causes desire. And this is what Plato shows very clearly in *The
Symposium*.

According to the formula outlined above, love is structured like a
metaphor, since it tends to raise some object to the dignity of the
precious part or symbol replacing the lacking object of desire. There is
an essential substitution at work here, and it is often either poetry or
theology that can systematise such a sublimation. This is why the

successive speakers in *The Symposium* often invoke poems, myths
and tales of the gods. Lacan does not hesitate in this context to
provide his own allegory in order to define love – in a rare effusion of
lyricism:

> See a hand stretching toward the fruit, the rose, the log that suddenly
> flares in the fire: its gesture of reaching out, attracting, fanning, is
> closely linked with the maturation of the fruit, the beauty of the
> flower, the sparkling of the fire. But if in this reaching movement the
> hand has gone far enough, if from the fruit, the flower, the log,
> another hand comes out and reaches out to the hand that is yours, at
> that moment your hand freezes in the open or closed fullness of the
> fruit or flower, in the explosion of a flaming hand – and what happens
> then at this moment is love (*S8*, 67).

He then reviews the first speakers in the banquet of *The
Symposium*, opposing Pausanias' sociology of love to Phaedrus' initial
mystagogy of love. Both speeches are lofty and deep, calling up all the
resources of mythology and comparative anthropology current in
Plato's times (for instance in 182c Pausanias links oriental despotism
and the repression of any type of love). Lacan explains that he
consulted Kojève about *The Symposium* but the only hint Kojève
agreed to give him about this dialogue was 'You will never interpret
The Symposium if you do not understand why Aristophanes hiccups'
(*S8*, 78)! Lacan had already pointed out the pun on Pausanias in
539c–d:

> When Pausanias had paused' [you see the kind of tricks we catch
> from our philologists, with their punning derivations] the next
> speaker, so Aristodemus went on to tell me, should have been
> Aristophanes; only as it happened, whether he'd been overeating I
> don't know, but he had got the hiccups so badly that he really wasn't
> fit to make a speech.[10]

The Symposium had stipulated that each speaker should follow the
order of their seating arrangement; with this hiccup, Aristophanes
skips his turn and the next speaker is Eryximachus, the doctor, who
before delivering his speech tells the playwright how to stop his
disturbing hiccup. Then he delivers his brilliant extemporisation on
the primitive giants sawn in two.

Reading the text closely in Greek, Lacan notices that the passage introducing Aristophanes is full of other repetitions, creating a sort of echolalia, as if the language was mimicking this hiccuping fit. Lacan concludes that Aristophanes has been convulsed with laughter during Pausanias' sententious discourse, so as to suggest that Plato himself found it ridiculous (S8, 78). Indeed even Eryximachus reproaches Pausanias for not having properly finished his speech (186a). If we reread this passage using these 'glasses' (as Lacan suggests – S8, 81), it becomes clear that the long and involved discussion of whether youths yielding to older men are right only when they think they will profit morally and not financially, to conclude with the maxim repeated several times; 'it is right to have the lover have his way in the interest of virtue' (185b) becomes highly parodic and even hilarious. Eryximachus then puts the matter more scientifically and less hypocritically when he declares that 'medicine is the science of the erotics of the body' (in Lacan's retranslation of 186a, in S8, 89). He adds that this is a very good definition of the aims of psychoanalysis.

Lacan's reading of Aristophanes' speech is highly idiosyncratic, mixing irreverence with more traditional philological speculations. He warns his audience that his method will not be historical or scholarly: what counts for him is what any given text 'makes us hear' (S8, 98) – even though it is vital to visualise the specific universe of discourse that produced it. This world of discourse is vectorised by a thinking of the One; it is only against this background that we can understand the scene of 'castration' achieved by Zeus. Let us not forget that Lacan has already defined the gods as belonging to the domain of the Real: 'The gods are the mode of revelation of the Real' (S8, 58). Aristophanes' speech is thus crucial for Lacan, although not at all Plato's last word in The Symposium.

Aristophanes' discourse stresses the One at the beginning. It prepares for the scene of castration, symbolised by Zeus cutting the bodies of the giants. The discourse is uttered by a clown, a Shakespearian fool, a stage jester. Truth is uttered by a speaker who breaks with the decorum of preestablished verities. Aristophanes demonstrates through his body the power of the body: he hiccups, laughs, disrupts the formal order of speeches. He announces the way in which a drunk Alcibiades will disrupt the entire procedure of exchanges. This type of Bakhtinian derision attacks the entire epistemology of the times, since it applies to the figure of perfection (namely the sphere), an irony that can threaten even Plato's system, or at least what is exposed in *Timaeus* about the sphere. Thus the dialogue comes dangerously close to self-parody, even more pointedly as we readers know what the outcome of the confrontation between Socrates and his judges, prodded by Aristophanes' taunts, will be.

Lacan is attentive to the comic element in Aristophanes' speech, and the wealth of images that hover between the trivial (the original double creatures being halved like an egg are sliced with a hair) and the theoretical (since the concept of the sphere was taken very seriously as an archetype by the Greeks). After a long discussion of the sphere in Greek philosophy, he compares Aristophanes' theory with infantile theories (such as that of Little Hans, who believed that his 'weeweemaker' could be removed), but with the aim of stressing that in spite of his general tone of banter it is only Aristophanes who manages to convey something of the pathos and urgency of love. This is no doubt linked to a very realistic evocation of physical castration, and to the notion of a passion that forces us to find our 'second halves' and then to unite with them so indisslubly that we feel ourselves to be 'one' again. The urgency of this new tone is confirmed in the following speech by Agathon: as a professional tragic actor he displays all the resources of sophistry and rhetoric, dazzling his audience with conceits and comparisons, but only to produce a trivialised image of love as 'the father of delicacy, daintiness, elegance and grace' (197e).[11] 'It is probably for us a rich lesson to see how Agathon, the tragedian has turned love into a comic *romancero*, whereas it is Aristophanes the comedian who talks of love with an accent of passion that is almost modern' (*S8*, 138). This chiasmic structure forces us to pay more attention to the setting and the narratological construction of the dialogue.

When it is Socrates' turn to praise love, he too uses myth to convey his meaning, and quotes a woman, Diotima, who taught him everything he knows about love, especially its genesis. Love is famously described as the child of *Poros* and *Penia*, that is, of 'Resource' and 'Need' or 'Misery' (203b–c). Lacan sees in Socrates' dialogue with Diotima another way of bypassing the 'aporia' created by love, while anticipating his definition of love as 'giving what one does not have' (*S8*, 148). Those who love lack something, Diotima says. And she suggests that it is with beauty that lovers find a primordial object. Lacan does not stress the content of the myth as much as the way it is delivered. Love is conceived in the night, without its mother being aware of anything. Diotima's mythical genesis is a knowledge that points to Socrates' lack of knowledge.

Things start speeding up with Alcibiades' arrival. Being already drunk, he goes straight to Agathon, sits next to him, separating him without knowing it from Socrates, who has designs on him. Everything changes at this point because we are not just at a 'meeting of old queers' (*S8*, 161), as Lacan says, rather we see love in action – not merely speeches about love. *The Symposium* discloses its dramatic nature in that it stages itself. Alcibiades' praise of Socrates provides a crucial term for Lacan – *agalmata* (the gold effigies of gods that are enclosed in figures called sileni.) The following is what Alcibiades says about the older philosopher, his master, who has so far rejected all his sexual advances:

> I don't know whether anybody else has ever opened him up when he's been being serious, and seen the little images [ἀγαλματα] inside, but I saw them once, and they looked so godlike, so golden, so beautiful, and so utterly amazing that there was nothing for it but to do exactly what he told me (216e–217a).[12]

The *agalma* becomes the main term that Lacan extracts from the dialogue. It encompasses elements from the fetish (it is a glittering object that fascinates), is compared to Melanie Klein's 'part object', and then turns into Lacan's own concept of the *objet petit a*. As metonymy of unconscious desire, this object is what we find within someone whom we really love.

If, as Lacan alleges, love keeps ties with the roots of 'gallant' – a word that derives from *gal*, the Old French word for shine – love allows us to see the *objet a* when it both opens and seals a gap within the subject. The object images the division of the subject, the break in the image, and the cut of castration. It is a piece of the body, detachable as an organ would be. It can in fact be embodied by almost anything, by any margin or border in the libidinal body – lips, the rim of the anus, the tip of the penis, the vagina, the eyelids and the eye they contain, the aperture of the ear. The partial object causes desire, and Alcibiades' declaration that he discovered it in Socrates is no doubt linked to the fact that Socrates refused himself to him, in spite of his interlocutor's beauty and fame. In a later development in the same seminar Lacan presents the formula of the hysteric's desire as follows (S8, 289, 295):

$$\frac{a}{(-\varphi)} \diamondsuit A$$

while the obsessional fantasy is symbolised as (S8, 295):

$$\cancel{A} \diamondsuit \varphi \, (a, a', a'', a''',...)$$

This algebra is merely a way of visualising the role played by *objet a* in fantasy: for the hysteric, the desire of the Other is underpinned by an impossible or refused object that hides the minus phi of imaginary castration. The obsessional allows his or her position to be replaced by the barred Other, who in a way desires the subject. This desire passes through the phallus as a 'measure' for the series of substitutive objects. What matters at this point is simply that Lacan has found in Socrates' *agalma* a language with which he can formalise love, transference and their objects.

We have seen how Socrates would gently turn Alcibiades down, how he could continue speaking despite the passionate embrace of their bodies. Lacan concludes that 'it is because Socrates knows what love really is that he does not love' (*S8*, 184), a formula later expanded into 'Socrates, because he knows, substitutes one thing for the other. It is not beauty, nor askesis, not identification with God that Alcibiades desires, but this unique object, this something he saw in Socrates, and from which Socrates pushes him, because he knows that he does not have it' (*S8*, 190). Socrates in fact desires, but he does not love: he does not believe in the lure of the *agalma*, he does not believe in the object. Since he knows what love is, he can transfer Alcibiades' love towards its real object – Agathon.

The upshot of Alcibiades' speech is that he warns Agathon not to be seduced by Socrates in the way he has been, which has brought only frustration. Socrates has therefore acted like a good psychoanalyst, he has used the agency of transference love in Alcibiades to turn him away from himself and send him back to the real object of his desire, Agathon. Lacan can thus take up his allegory of the stretched hand:

> For desire in its root and essence is desire of the Other, and this is properly speaking here that one find the mainspring of love's birth, if love is what happens in the object toward which we extend a hand pushed by desire, and just when desire lets its fires rage, the object

lets us glimpse a response, another hand extended toward us as the object's desire (*S8*, 212).

This desire entails a moment of blindness, of un-knowing. A psycho-analyst will be strong enough to stay in this position, letting his or her desire be stronger than any love captivated by the beauty of the object. Like Socrates, she or he lives by a paradox: one *knows* that desire implies a subjective position in which knowledge is lacking.

Another lesson of the famous Platonician dialogue is that the father of all philosophers appears obliged to renounce his metalanguage, he is forced to let us see the dialectics of transference in action. 'We have been able to seize in the very scenario opposing Socrates and Alcibiades the last word of what Plato has to say concerning the nature of love. This supposes that in the presentation of what may be called his thought, Plato deliberately left room for enigmas ... ' (*S8*, 200). For Lacan, Plato is as much as a playwright as a philosopher. In the last part of his Seminar on transference, he talks about 'The Oedipus Myth Today' and gives us an analysis of modern tragedy. The lack of a metalanguage for Plato implies that transference can only be enacted on a stage ultimately dominated by the agency of the Other. Eros, the god of love, is finally seen in the moveable scene of *Eteros*, the other as big Other, a locus from which one can deduce the One. What Freud had called the 'means of representation' and the 'consid-erations of representability' in his chapter on the dream-work[13] now stands out as an active 'presentation' driven by transference and underpinned by desire for the Other.

Rather than closing our examination of Lacan's reading of *The Symposium* with a reiteration of his definition of love – 'love is to give what one doesn't have', whose implications were recently teased out of by Derrida[14] – it seems more rewarding and productive to follow the dynamics of his commentary. Seminar VIII moves from one block – the reading of Plato – to another block, a detailed commentary on Claudel's historical trilogy: *The Hostage, Stale Bread* and *The Humiliated Father*. The two blocks of text – the one a philosophical extravaganza with various speeches about love, showing us the acme of culture in classical Greece, the other an early twentieth-century dramatic saga about one family, followed through three generations – seem to have very little in common. Yet for Lacan both texts are essen-tial components of a systematic demonstration of the *montage* of desire and love and their dramatic 'considerations of representability'.

What attracts Lacan to Claudel's plays is once more a particular agency of the signifier. He explains that he had been reading the correspondence of Claudel and Gide, and had seen the difficulties Claudel had had to surmount because of the strange name he had invented for the family in his chronicle. Claudel's first heroine is called Sygne de Coûfontaine, her first name calling up 'sign' in French (with a curious y) and her last name posing a redoubtable problem to typesetters because of the circumflex over the u. In stage directions, the custom is to write all names in upper case letters, but French type-faces do not allow for a circumflex over a capital. As the publishers he approached were unwilling or unable to produce the plays because of this typographical hurdle, Claudel decided to publish them himself at his own expense. With this name, and another name in the second section ('Lumîr', which is supposed to be Polish but is actually a pun on 'lumière'), Claudel confirms Lacan's theory of the letter elaborated after Gide's example: *cou*, without a circumflex, means 'neck' – an unfortunate prefix since apart from the two main protagonists in *The Hostage*, the whole family has fallen victim to the revolutionary guillo-tine. The circumflexed *coû*, on the other hand, pushes the meaning towards 'cost' ('*coût*'). Not only is this proof that something is missing from the symbolic system of typography, it also signals the trace of a particular *jouissance* – the *jouissance* of a family name, of characters who have been forced to pay the cost (*coût*) requested by Fate in order to enjoy the possibility of desires that would become transgressive given contrary historical circumstances.

Since these the plays have not been translated and are not well known, a brief summary of the plot is necessary.[15] The setting of the first play, *The Hostage*, is post-revolutionary France at the culmina-tion of Napoléon's power, just as he is about to lose the unfortunate Russian campaign. The main characters are two cousins, Georges and Sygne, who have only just survived the turmoil of revolutionary terror. Napoléon is in Moscow, and Georges, who is back from exile in England and has lost everything, is both declaring his love to Sygne – who has saved as much as she can of the family domain – and hiding the Pope in the cellar of the convent that is now the Coûfontaine home. However the Pope's hiding place is known by Turelure, the arch-villain, who agrees not to denounce them if Sygne consents to marry him. She refuses, but is then subtly pushed into strategic acqui-escence by her confessor, who believes that the Pope's safety is more important than her happiness. She marries him and subsequently gives birth to a son. Georges later tries to shoot Turelure but Sygne shields him with her body, thus receiving the fatal bullet. As she lies dying, despite Turelure's entreaties she refuses to see her child or pardon her husband. This refusal, clearly presented as anti-Christian, marks an important ethical step in the retrieval of Sygne's own desire, but will result in the equivalent of Antigone's *Atè* for her descendants.

Lacan admires Claudel's stroke of genius at having Turelure utter the proud motto of the family – *Coûfontaine, adsum!* (Coûfontaine, here I am) – in a last attempt to get Sygne to forgive and bless him as she dies. Claudel changed his mind about the conclusion of *The Hostage*: in the first version Sygne does forgive, but in the version that was actually performed she refuses to the end. And in spite of Claudel's Catholicism (it must be added that it was a particular Catholicism, since he was converted at the age of eighteen after reading Rimbaud's poems) there is a scathing critique of the Pope (old, weak, ineffectual, too compromised by the *realpolitik* of the times) and the confessor, a shady type who uses moral blackmail to force Sygne to renounce her love and life. The 'Hostage' of the first play is not the Pope, as the plot seems at first to suggest, but Sygne, forced by her confessor to betray her own desire, to renounce all her hopes for the continuation of her true family heritage.[16]

Stale Bread begins twenty years after Sygne's death. Her son Louis, now an adult, kills his senile father in a ploy organised by his lover, Lumîr whose only desire is to help Poland, and Sichel, the father's mistress, presented as a cunning Jewess. Louis does not actually shoot his father, rather Turelure dies of fear. Louis then marries not his own mistress but his father's, Sichel, thus recreating a classical Oedipal plot. The play ends on a note of betrayal of Christian values and on the domination of the most sordid calculations. The final play, *The Humiliated Father*, again takes place twenty years later (1869–71), but this time in Rome. It focuses on Pensée, Sichel's daughter, who takes after her mother and is extremely beautiful, but is blind. She also possesses uncanny insight, and is portrayed as a sort of Jewish Antigone. However unlike Antigone she does not give up everything for her father. She falls in love with a man named Orian de Homodarmes, a soldier who is related to the Pope, his uncle and spiritual counsellor. He seems to be very ambivalent about love, but he does return Pensée's love and they conceive a child together. He soon dies in battle against the Germans, sending a last message (together with his heart, buried in a flower pot) through his brother, telling

Pensée that she should live no matter what and marry Orso, who is more handsome and has been in love with her. She decides to live for the sake of her child but refuses to marry Orso immediately. The play ends with the promise of reunion for the two brothers, one living, the other dead, and Pensée who has felt her child stir in her womb when smelling the flowers springing from Orian's heart.

What makes it possible for Pensée to recapture her own desire? She looks back to her grandmother, Sygne, who has sacrificed everything for other concerns – or for the concerns of the Other. Stressing how this knowledge seems to be lacking in Sophocles' characters, Lacan uses Claudel's trilogy to emphasise the importance of understanding how any symptom is produced by three generations, and how the myth of Oedipus can still structure the theatre. *Stale Bread* is clearly Claudel's modern variation of Sophocles' pattern: Louis 'kills' (without really killing, a little like the hero of *Playboy of the Western World*) a father who is already a caricature of himself, and he thereby puts himself in the hands of a 'Jewish' desire defined by Lacan as the wish to share *jouissance* by all (*S8*, 343). It is all the more ironical to see the same character reappear in the third part of the trilogy as the French ambassador to Rome, engaged in dealings with the Pope. Claudel's main focus however, is not so much the diminished or 'humiliated' paternal function as the praise of feminine desire, a desire that establishes itself through a complex transgenerational history, caught up between a set of 'signs' (here again the allegorical function of Sygne's name is crucial) and the 'thought' of desire (Pensée means thought). As Lacan repeats in his seminar, Pensée is the thought of desire (*S8*, 352, 364). The 'thought of desire' can be opposed to the 'utopia of *jouissance*' shared by Sichel and Lumîr, and both together constitute the family's *Atè*. What follows, then, is a systematic fluctuation between the comedy of paternal pretensions, ruses, struggles and usurpations, and the tragedy of female renunciation of *jouissance* (*S8*, 346).

The male equivalent of this feminine position is the saint. Lacan sees Orso as a sort of saint, and to make his point he cites a conversation between Orso and Pensée in which Orso claims that he is pushed by 'another desire' that needs continuously to exceed its bounds:

> Then I knew another desire.
>   Without images or any action of intelligence, but all of one's being that purely and simply

Pulls and demands towards another, and the boredom with oneself, the whole soul breaks free horribly, and not this continuous burning alone, but a series of great efforts one after the other, comparable to death throes that exhaust the whole soul each time and leave me at the door of Nothingness! ...

I knew only too well that what I asked from you, you could not give me, and that what is called love,

Is always the same banal pun, the same cup too soon emptied, the matter of a few nights in a hotel, and again

Crowds, the amazing struggle, this horrible fun fair of life, from which no one can escape ...[17]

Refraining from any direct psychologisation of the author, Lacan simply notes that one can see repression at work in Claudel, and he stresses the fact that the saint, like Claudel, is obsessed by the category of having: he dispossesses himself of everything in order to own everything (*S8*, 417). What will Orso then own? His answer is simple: a 'joy' that cannot be reduced to a one- or three-night stand. However, although blind and Jewish – because blind and Jewish – Pensée manages to make him confess his love for her and conceive a child. Here is what Pensée answers, calling up the infinite sacrifice made by her grandmother, who saved the Pope:

And now in my veins the greatest sacrifice is united with the greatest unhappiness, and the greatest pride,

The greatest pride united to the greatest degradation and deprivation of honor, the Frank in one person with the Jew.

You are Christian, and I, the blood that runs in my veins is the very blood of Jesus, this blood out of which a God was made, now disdained.

For you to see, I had to be blind probably.

For you to have joy, I needed to have this eternal and speechless night that my fate is to devour![18]

Pensée's pathetic rhetoric points out what makes the saint's *jouissance* horrible and monstrous (S8, 417). The saint can only love God, but what he calls 'god' is another name for his or her *jouissance*. In a general conclusion linking Claudel and Plato, Lacan shows that his definition of love ('To give what one does not have') is enriched by Diotima's myth of love's genesis in Poros and Penia, and by Claudel's neo-Catholic praise of an absolute desire that finds loopholes for

feminine love. Both elaborations, the feminine myth and the masculine tragedy of humiliation, finally end up praising life – in the figure
of the child to be born at the end of the third play – and rebirth which
also suggest that the demand of love triumphs over the dialectics of
renunciation and sacrifice.

Love is therefore inseparable from a precise delimitation of what
Lacan calls the *objet petit a*, this *agalma* that Alcibiades sees in
Socrates, but which Socrates knows he does not have. 'We will have to
deal with the little *a* all along the structure, for it is never relayed in its
libidinal attraction' (*S8*, 452). As a final demonstration of the role of
this *objet a* Lacan turns to another play – this time a comedy. In the
very last session of Seminar VIII he alludes to Jean Genet's play *The
Balcony*, upon which he had commented at length (as he had done
with Claudel) in Seminar V three years earlier. At the time of Seminar
V Lacan was above all interested in exploring the genre of comedy, as
we saw in his analysis of Gide's almost comical whining when his wife
burnt his letters. Lacan explores Genet's play – after first giving a long
summary of its plot – to suggest that the phallus is always a thing of
comedy. The scene that interests him most is the first act, where we
slowly discover that the various 'figures' engaged in diverse sexual
acts are all performing roles: they are customers of a brothel in which
all sexual fantasies can be bought and staged. Thus the Bishop, the
Judge and the General are performative identities that explore the
various aspects of the symbolic order and are here exploited for their
perverse side, moving constantly from sadism to masochism, and
from masochism to fetishism, in a scene that glorifies images, mirror-
ing and illusion, as Genet writes.[19]

In Seminar VIII Lacan emphasises the idea, expressed by the
whores – actors in the brothel, that there should always be a feature
that shows the illusion to be just such. Irma, the brothel owner,
explains to her friend Carmen (one of the whores) that she pays great
attention to blending authentic details with fake details in the scenar-
ios she creates for her customers: for instance her 'Saint Theresa' has
a 'real' wedding ring, but is adorned with black frills that show under
the nun's habit.[20] As Lacan comments, 'in the execution of the
fantasy, one needs to keep a trait that shows it is not true, otherwise, if
it was completely true, one would not know where one is' (*S8*, 454).
He sees this as the function of the 'barred signifier': a signifier that
indicates that the signifier is only ever a signifier. This is what applies
to the phallic function as such: it can never fulfil its function as *objet*

petit a to the end. The phallus is more often than not a barred signifier telling us that it is 'not there' – or more precisely, that it is a figure of comedy (a point that should never be forgotten, especially if we are tempted to see it in a tragic mode, as the gaping lack giving access to desire). The tyranny of the repetitive fantasy (we see how the three roles in *The Balcony* must respect as much verisimilitude as possible, which entails a lot of fetishistic details and garments, without going too far and subverting the boundaries of the Real, the Imaginary and the Symbolic) is always overcome by excess of desire, with its metonymic displacements, and by the absoluteness of love as a total and unconditional demand. All this seems to prepare Lacan's later elaboration of another place for feminine enjoyment – a place that both Duras and Joyce describe compellingly.

10 Joyce's *Jouissance*, or a New Literary Symptom

Before systematically engaging with the last writer to be commented upon at some length by Lacan – Joyce – it might be useful by way of introduction to return briefly to Gide – an author for whom Lacan had a peculiar fondness and tended to see as Joyce's French counterpart. In April 1975, at a time when he was immersed in a spate of critical work on Joyce following an invitation to open the June 1975 International James Joyce Symposium in Paris, Lacan quoted Gide's ironical novel, *Paludes*:

> It is worth giving all its due to the proverb translated and glossed by André Gide in *Paludes* – *Numero deus impare gaudet*, which he translates as 'Number two is happy being odd' (*'Le numéro deux se réjouit d'être impair'*). As I have said for some time, this is quite right, since nothing would realize the two if there was not the odd, the odd that begins with three – which is not obvious immediately and makes the Borromean knot necessary.[1]

To understand this old schoolboy joke one needs only to imagine the usual mistranslation of the Latin tag (meaning roughly: 'God likes odd numbers') which, by a French literalisation, turns into a pleasant Lacanian paradox: an odd number two! The passage Lacan quotes from Gide's novel suggests that freedom derives from odd numbers, which no doubt has some link with the sexual 'oddity' I have already mentioned.[2] *Paludes* is the most postmodern of Gide's novels – indeed it could be signed Donald Barthelme – and it opens with an ironical preface that leaves the reader free to make sense of an 'open' text:

> Before explaining my book to others, I wait for others to explain it to me. To want to explain first of all means immediately restricting the meaning; for if we know what we have meant, we do not know that

we meant only that. – One always says more than THAT. – And above all, what interest me is what I have put there without knowing it, – that part of Unconscious that I would like to call God's part. – A book is always a collaboration, and whatever it is worth, the more the scribe's part is small, the more God's welcome will be great. – Let us wait for the revelation of things from everywhere; from the audience, the revelation of our works.[3]

Of course, with such a parodic *'sotie'* (this is the name Gide gave to *Paludes*, a word suggesting 'a satirical farce', since indeed the novel provides an infectious caricature of French intellectuals and esthetes at the turn of the century), one cannot be sure that even this statement is to be taken seriously – especially in view of its suspicious pseudoreligious overtones. However the motto could well be taken up by Joyce, who declared more than once that he had not written *Finnegans Wake* alone but had used countless 'collaborators' (or as the *Wake* puts, 'anticollaborators'): the great Letter of the Wake is described as a 'chaosmos of Alle' in which everything changes all the time, partly because of the 'continually more or less intermisunderstanding minds of the anticollaborators'.[4]

The reference to Joyce in a context heavily determined by curious speculations on what looks like numerology is not fortuitous. Indeed when Lacan begins his seminar on Joyce he explains that he is about to take a departure or a new 'step', because he has at last managed to go beyond the Trinitarian scheme that underpins the logic of Borromean knots he has elaborated so far. He had, up to his *R, S, I* seminar of 1974–75, toyed with the possibility of organising the three 'registers' of the Real, the Symbolic and the Imaginary – we have seen how their chronological order should entail another list, starting with the Imaginary, moving on to the Symbolic and finishing with the Real – in such a way that they are, on the one hand, well 'knotted together' and can, on the other hand, call up the signifier of 'heresy' (the capitals R, S, I, pronounced in French, sound roughly like *hérésie* – the nearest American equivalent would be something like IRS). At the very end of this seminar Lacan reveals the key to his central intuition:

I have been taking a look at Joyce because I have been solicited to open a conference. Well, if Joyce is completely caught up in the sphere and the cross, it is not only because he read a lot of Aquinas thanks to his education with the Jesuits. You are all as caught in the sphere and the cross. Here is a circle, the section of a sphere, and within the cross. Moreover, this also provides the plus sign.... But no-one has perceived that this is already a Borromean knot.[5]

He then shows how one can move from Figure 1 to Figure 4 by animating the cross and making it result from two curves that are also sections of two interlocking circles:[6]

Figure 1   Figure 2   Figure 3   Figure 4

What Clive Hart has skilfully and convincingly described as the basis of Joyce's world-view in *Finnegans Wake* – a grid made up of an inter-locked sphere and cross – is a structure that accounts for a linguistic universe that seems to be circular (as everyone knows, the first words of the book, 'riverrun, past Eve's and Adam's', follow up from the last words of the last page: ' ... along the') and yet keeps generating new versions in an attempt to provide a solution to the old paradox of the quadrate circle, or in terms of the *Wake*, the notion of 'squaring the circle' and 'circling the square'. It seems that Lacan has fully accepted Hart's thesis in *Structure and Motif in Finnegans Wake*[7] and that his numerology accounts for this. Besides, at the time he was working on a new structure for his school, having launched an original form of collective work: 'cartels' – small reading groups for the psychoanalysts of the school, with the number of active participants fluctuating between a minimum four and a maximum of six. This pragmatic issue was present in Lacan's mind when he decided to tackle the formida-ble figure of Joyce.

In a seminar he admits to being haunted and obsessed by or even 'the prey of the knot'[8] – a Borromean knot he has not looked for but just 'found', thanks to a lucky coincidence (as Roudinesco explains, it was Valérie Marchand, a young mathematician who participated to Guilbaud's seminar on topology who gave Lacan the concept of Borromean knot, that is, a way of interlocking three rings in such a way that if you take out one, the other two fall apart).[9] His unexpected meeting with Joyce represents another happy coincidence. One should note that like Lacan, Joyce always claimed that the main ideas in his works were due to 'coincidences', lucky discoveries of something he did not know he was looking for.[10] At the start of the following year's Seminar Lacan recalls his promise to look into 4, 5, and 6 and explains how Joyce came at the right time and place to stop him:

> The solicitation of Jacques Aubert, here present and no less pressing, had led me to usher in Joyce as the title of a Symposium. This is how I have allowed myself to be drawn away from my project, which was, I had announced last year, to entitle this Seminar 4,5,6. I was content with the 4, and I am glad of this, since with 4, 5, 6, I would surely have succumbed.[11]

What Roudinesco has called Lacan's exploration of 'the Borromean planet',[12] in an ironical and mock-heroic account of the mid-1970s can look at times like a last-ditch struggle against approaching senility, hiding under exercises in practical topology, neo-Dadaist punning or sterile numerology. Having fallen under the sway of mathematicians such as Thomé and Soury, Lacan spends a lot of time in these seminars drawing complex knots and circles on the blackboard, pointing at them and then getting lost. His insistence that there is something to be read directly, in a 'real' that can be shown or merely calculated, described by mathematical topology, comes also from his customary reluctance to admit that these figures just modelise his theory. Someone once asked him whether the knot was a mere model, and he replied negatively: 'It does not constitute a model in as much as it keeps trace of something next to which the imagination fails [défaille]. And its mathematical approach in topology is insufficient.'[13] How, in fact, can one say that these Borromean knots resist the imagination, since they are highly visible and provide endlessly funny topological games? They may indeed embody a riddle, or a writing similar to the Name-of-the-Father, a point to which we shall return. However my personal view is on the whole less negative than Roudinesco's (for her the Joyce seminar belongs to the opaque public mumblings of Lacan's final years, when he was not himself any more). While acknowledging that Lacan at times seems to lapse into a private idiom made up of jumbled reminiscences from his previous seminars and writings, I believe that the *Sinthome* seminar is rife with exciting discoveries and new theoretical avenues. At the very least, one cannot but admire the theoretical courage of a thinker who is ready to destroy the possible systematisation of his insights by boldly exploring a *terra incognita* – Joyce's writings.

Whereas in the *R, S, I* seminar Lacan still considered that the three letters would make up the knot of the Name-of-the-Father, in the Joyce seminar he moves towards the concept of a more active nomination that in the end becomes almost identical to writing. With the concept of the '*Sinthome*', as we shall see, he adds a crucial fourth circle – the 'symptom' – to his triple knot. This has the important effect of both untying the earlier knot and suggesting a more dynamic process of naming as writing, or writing as naming. It is therefore obvious that his rediscovery of Joyce provided Lacan with his *felix culpa* – his happy sin, similar to Adam's expulsion from Paradise. It was Joyce who allowed him to overcome the all-too static figure of Trinitarian resolution (even if it took the signifier of 'heresy') so as to bring it closer to a more radical heretic, Joyce, and to achieve a final 'imbalancing' of the structure. Joyce's transformation into the Symptom becomes an allegory of the 'plus-one'; Joyce's name, his writing, his 'art' represent at the same time what does *not* work in the Trinitarian structure and what works too well – their artful link can repair an initial mistake in symbolic paternity.

As realised by a growing number of Joyce scholars – among whom Jacques Aubert's marvellous edition of *Ulysses* for the prestigious French Pléiade[14] stands as a crowning monument of erudition and scholarship laced with Lacanian ingredients – Lacan's concepts can provide a strong frame of reference for a general reassessment of Joyce's works. Many new readers have discovered the pleasure and hardships of a textual battle with the intricacies of *Finnegans Wake*, spurred by the influential readings provided by Lacan's seminar in the mid-1970s. Let us go back to the curious coincidence of the real and symbolical meeting between the two writers.

When the French Joyce scholar Jacques Aubert decided to invite Lacan to give the keynote address at the 1975 International Joyce Symposium he was organising in Paris, he could not guess that he would be luring Lacan into a relatively untrodden domain that would durably and radically change his theory. Lacan gave his talk, entitled 'Joyce the Symbol', at the Sorbonne on 16 June 1975, hinting that his chance encounter with James Joyce at Adrienne Monnier's bookstore and his being present at the *Ulysses* reading when he was twenty[15] were promising coincidences. One should not forget that Lacan was seventy-four when he systematically tackled the dense works of Joyce. It is also quite interesting to see that he reminisces a lot, creating an image of himself as a young man meeting the older Irish writer, already quite a celebrity, in Paris. We shall see how in this seminar he plays on the equivalence in French of *je nomme* and *jeune homme*: it is as if the imposed detour that makes him retrace the steps of Stephen Dedalus presented first as a young man and only later as an artist, provides Lacan with a rejuvenation cure! His encounter with Joyce in 1921 was seen as an omen, a fateful coincidence that was reawakened some fifty years later by Jacques Aubert. This living connection is essential: it looks indeed as if Lacan's work had been preparing itself, building up to this re-encounter with Joyce. Almost all the new elements he introduced into his theory in the early 1970s – the Borromean knot of the Real, the Symbolic, the Imaginary, the emergence of the Symptom in the real, the new importance given to *jouissance* in its connection with writing, the idea of writing as making a hole in reality, the theory of the lack of sexual rapport, the new figure of the father as a perverse father – all forcibly recur in the Joyce seminar, a seminar in which they find an elegant and final replotting: a reknotting, in fact.

I was present when Lacan gave his memorable speech at the Sorbonne,[16] and could not help feeling some unease in the face of Lacan's mixture of brilliant insights and trite biographical explanations. It took me a few years to disentangle the remarkably original readings from a groping and fumbling approach that owed its tentative character to the fact that Lacan had, after all, tried to do his homework honestly, and could not digest at once the enormous Joyce scholarship – a whole library from which Jacques Aubert was lending him new volumes almost weekly. Aubert has recounted how Lacan, following his usual pattern when he became interested in a new field, would often call him at his home around midnight and keep him busy for an hour with fresh queries about Joycean riddles or punning associations he wanted to check with an indisputable specialist. One can say on the whole that Lacan decided early on to play the role of the uninitiated reader, distinguishing his approach as that of a psychoanalyst from that of all the specialists who thrive on Joyce in the universities. More than once he remarks that Joyce had cleverly said that the best way to ensure immortality was to keep professors busy for centuries. Lacan does not aim at being just another commentator, his intervention is placed firmly within the discourse of the Analyst, and not that of the University.

Lacan situates the *objet a* as the Joycean text he wishes to engage with so as to produce a divided subject in the place of the reader, and not start from the presupposition of knowledge at S2, which will then determine the literary object.

$$\frac{a}{S2} \longrightarrow \frac{\$}{S1} \qquad\qquad \frac{S2}{S1} \longrightarrow \frac{a}{\$}$$

Discourse of the Analyst   Discourse of the University

And when he alludes to the 'Professor' in *Finnegans Wake*, he links this 'Jones' with Freud's rather conservative biographer (someone who would not allow his unconscious to interfere with his writing).[17]

Lacan began his talk on 'Joyce le symptôme' in a low key, mentioning his being in poor health, making fun of the newspapers that had announced 'Joyce the Symbol' rather than 'Joyce the Symptom'. This provided the opportunity for a first diatribe that allowed him to introduce his 'nomination':

> Why should they print *Joyce the Symptom*? Jacques Aubert relays this to them, and they throw in *Jacques the Symbol*. All of this, of course, is for them just the same stuff.
>
> From the *sym* that boles, what can it matter in the bosom of Abraham, where the all-rotten [*tout-pourri*, punning on 'Tout Paris'] will find itself in its nature of rags-to-riches for eternitall [*en sa nature de bonneriche pour l'étournité*]?
>
> Go to the *Bloch et von Warburg*, an etymological dictionary that is very solid, and you will read that 'symptom' was originally written *sinthome*.
>
> Joyce the *sinthome* is an homonymy with sainthood, about which I talked on television as some of you will remember (*JAL*, 21–2).

Lacan's starting point is simple and monolithic: Joyce *embodies* the 'symptom', a symptom that has to be written '*sinthome*' to call up an older form of the word used by Rabelais – a writer who can be seen as Joyce's predecessor in verbal experimentation. Note that the two words – *symptôme* and *sinthome* – can be pronounced almost in the same way, since in certain French pronunciations one skips the 'p' in the first word. Thus it is above all an archaic spelling that subtly changes a common term: this is a first hint of the crucial dimension of writing in naming.

Joyce's new name, the *Sinthome*, allows Lacan to see the Irish writer as a literary saint (through the rigorous homophony in French of '*sinthome*' and '*saint homme*') – a depiction that in fact accords quite well with the way Joyce wanted to present himself to his contemporaries and for posterity – while releasing all sorts of punning associations, with allusions to Aquinas (most commonly referred to in French as '*saint Thom*-as d'Aquin'), to 'sin' and to literature ('tomes'). Lacan sends his audience back to the disquisition on sainthood in *Television* – a passage that merits being quoted since it throws a lot of light on his view of Joyce, and his identification of Joyce with the letter as waste or refuse:

> A saint's business, to put it clearly, is not *caritas*. Rather, he acts as trash; his business being *trashitas*. So as to embody what the structure entails, namely allowing the subject, the subject of the unconscious, to take him as the cause of the subject's desire.
>
> In fact it is through the abjection of this cause that the subject in question has a chance to be aware of his position, at least within the structure....
>
> That is really the most amazing thing in the whole business. Amazing for those who approach it without illusions: that saint is the refuse of *jouissance*.[18]

Joyce is thus seen as the 'saint and martyr' of literature – the symptom of literature embodied by one man who has knowingly allowed himself to be devoured by letters, so as to be one with literature. This main intuition can only be supported by a parallel creative gesture by Lacan, or indeed a gesture of nomination: 'What matters for me is not to pastiche *Finnegans Wake* –one will always be inferior to the task– but to say how, by producing this title, *Joyce the Symptom*, I give Joyce nothing less than his proper name, a name in which, I believe, he would have recognized himself in the dimension of nomination' (*JAL*, 22). Lacan testifies to his fascination with the endless punning process of the *Wake*, and even though he admits that he cannot hope to emulate it he creates a number of puns and portmanteau words such as '*pourspère*' (*JAL*, 21) which combines '*pourriture*' (rot), '*prospère*' (prosper) and '*espère*' (hope). Lacan self-consciously founds his own critical discourse on a nomination: he calls Joyce the '*sinthome*', giving an active sense and function to a proper name when this symptom/*sinthome* will be seen to contain *jouissance* – a very particular type of *jouissance*. One can say that Lacan has managed to restore to Joyce's name the meaning of enjoyment as a verb. Lacan shares with Joyce a fundamental belief the word creates the world, but in a sinful nomination that suggests the pleasure of a prohibited act. Or to quote *Finnegans Wake*: 'This exists that isits after having been said we know. And dabal take dabnal!' (*FW*, 186.08–9). The creation of the world by the *logos* is closer to the Devil's influence than to a righteous Adam. Joyce's 'And the Devil take Dublin' is over-laid with richly stratified allusions using Sanskrit and Hebrew over-tones to testify to a crucial textualisation of a Biblical *dabar* (speech). Likewise Lacan's fundamental tenet that the Unconscious is 'struc-tured like a language' implies that our bodies and souls are deter-mined by collective cultural formations that shape the signifier. As we shall see later, when dealing with Joyce, Lacan goes one step further and shows that the ego (*moi*) and the word (*Verbe*) are made to coalesce in a dynamic and polysemic name: the name of Joyce, or Joyce-the-Name.

A striking feature in this inaugural lecture is that Joyce appears not primarily as the author of *Ulysses* – Lacan mentions the novel twice, but more or less in passing, with the idea of letting the Freudian Unconscious emerge from Stephen Dedalus's phrase 'agenbite of inwit', and then to dispel the notion that it might based on Homer's *Odyssey* (*JAL*, 22, 27) – but fundamentally as the writer of *Finnegans Wake,* a text described as his 'major and final work' (*JAL*, 26). Lacan's reservations are nevertheless numerous and forceful: when Joyce plays with so many languages, the dimension of truth risks being lost. *Finnegans Wake* remains fundamentally a very masculine symptom overdetermined by the 'Name-of-the-Father'; Joyce is seen as franti-cally erecting a literary monument in place of his father's real-life shortcomings; his writing compensates for failings that he excuses, negates and sublimates at the same time; if Joyce becomes the Symptom, he produces a text that can in no way deeply captivate its readers, since there is no clear reason why anyone should be inter-ested in Joyce's own symptom. Joyce appears 'unstuck', out of touch with the real unconscious process that he nevertheless tries to copy or imitate. This is why he flirts with Jung and is so in love with the spuri-ous spiritualism of a Mrs Blavatsky. And finally, one can detect a streak of literary megalomania when he uses *Finnegans Wake* as a 'stool' (*escabeau*) to reach immortality – an immortality that he owes to the toil of thousands of university scholars who labour under the delusion that they will crack the code and translate the riddle (even if these ultimately boil down to nothing more than interlocking crosses and spheres).

The *jouissance* Joyce ends up bequeathing his readers aims at the glorification of his name, a name that becomes a common noun when it translates that of Freud (in German, Freud is close to *Freude* meaning happiness or enjoyment) into English (*joy* contained in Joyce), and also into French as *jouissance*. Joyce not only missed Freud's theory of the Unconscious but stopped short of the final truth when he was on the point of discovering the key to his writing system, his theory of knots. Lacan is being strategically naive when he wonders aloud why Joyce published *Finnegans Wake* – a text whose puns seem random and rely on chance to catch the reader's Unconscious. Finally, Lacan's position is summed up by a surprising phrase: Joyce merely plays with the unconscious but appears 'unregistered to the Unconscious' (*désabonné à l'inconscient*, *JAL*, 24), as if he had achieved the aim of becoming the master of languages by bypassing any determination of his own language by a social and collective discourse of the Other. His mastery is tautological and finally masturbatory, when he attempts to suture his own knot with the name he leaves to our adoration.[19]

Thus in a baffling and fascinating talk, Lacan not only sketches what will become the theme of the seminar of the following year (1975–76), a seminar accordingly entitled 'The *Sinthome*', but also the theoretical task that kept him busy in his final years: the forceful confrontation with Joyce obliged him to go beyond the three interlocking circles of the Real, the Imaginary and the Symbolic – the three concepts that had been the mainstay of his theoretical elaboration for twenty years – to show that their knotting depends upon the function of a fourth circle, often called Σ (Sigma, for the Symptom).

What does Lacan, fundamentally, contribute to Joyce's scholarship? It looks as if his reading was based upon a biographical approach (he has obviously read Ellmann's famous biography with care). As Roudinesco has noted,[20] Lacan seems first to read *A Portrait of the Artist as a Young Man* and *Ulysses* as straight autobiography, often missing or erasing the important distinction between Stephen Dedalus and James Joyce, or even projecting a lot of himself into Joyce (this begins when he accounts for their similar Catholic backgrounds and educations). Very embarrassingly for a literary critic, Lacan systematically alludes to 'Joyce' when he speaks of Stephen

Dedalus. And, for instance, he explains Joyce's pursuit of an artistic career as a wish to compensate for a lack on the part of his own father, John Joyce. The father is understood to be absent, lacking, failing, and his son's writing aims at supplementing this fundamental deficiency. Writing operates in the place of paternity, as it were. By becoming a writer, Joyce burdens himself with a paternity his father seems to have rejected or belittled. Thus it looks as though there had been a sin, a mistake in the very writing of the Joyce family, where the three circles of the Real, the Imaginary and the Symbolic have not been properly tied together. Writing proceeds to a *raboutage*, that is, a sewing together, a splicing of these partially loose strings. '*Rabouter*' is used in parallel with *renouer*: to rejoin, reknot, reseam, refasten, retie. This suggests the very French image of the traditional 'rebouteux', the village bone-setter, who is often credited with the magical power to relieve a family of a curse, and also provides basic medical help. Even if one resists this approach – and we have seen that Lacan himself could resist an all too biographical approach with other writers – it is clear that Joyce is a writer who forces his life upon his reader.

What, therefore, is this original sin? According to Lacan, James Joyce remains caught up in his father's symptoms, all marked by a central 'perversity', even when rejecting him: both father and son are spend-thrifts and heavy drinkers, and seem unable to protect their families from disaster. While John Joyce could indeed imagine that he had 'killed' his exhausted wife (who died of cancer at an early age), Joyce's own cross was his daughter, Lucia, who started showing signs of derangement in the late 1920s, behaved more and more erratically and was institutionalised in 1934. Lucia's sad fate appears as a confirmation of Joyce's dangerous flirtation with psychosis. Lacan's reading is thus not so far from Jung's in his introduction to *Ulysses* in German. Like Jung, Lacan stresses Joyce's wish to defend Lucia against psycho-analysis so as to ward off any suggestion that his own writing is schizo-phrenic or psychotic, and like Jung he admits that Lucia drowns in the black waters of the Unconscious where a more experienced swimmer manages to return to the surface.[21] However Lacan denounces Joyce's tendency to fall into the trap of Jungism when he writes about univer-sal history in the *Wake*. The main consequence of these remarks was that the study of Joyce's works became the ineluctable foundation of any psychoanalytical investigation of the structure of psychosis: among psychoanalytic circles, Joyce's writings seemed to offer the key to Lacan's latest conceptualisation of psychosis.

The Joyce seminar was broken off by Lacan's third and final trip to the United States, during which he scandalised not only Bostonian high society (when he refused to wear a tie in an expensive restaurant) but also Noam Chomsky (when he told the linguist that he personally did not think with his mind but with his feet or his skull). These talks and open seminars provide a very revealing glimpse of what was going on in Lacan's mind at the time. At Yale he made his audience laugh as he opened a presentation with the assertion that he had been brushing up his English by reading Joyce in the original.[22] He showed an awareness of Chomsky's theory when he noted that Joyce had respected the grammatical structure of English in the dazzling portmanteau words and puns of *Finnegans Wake*. When asked about literature, Lacan opposed the letter to literature, saying he was not sure what the latter consisted of, throwing into the bargain the idea that Freud needed literature to grasp the Unconscious. Alluding to Freud's psychoanalytic reading of Jensen's *Gradiva*, he said:

> There is a new inflection of literature. Today, it does not mean what it meant in Jensen's time. Everything is literature. I too, produce literature, since it sells: take my *Ecrits*, this is literature to which I have imagined I could give a status which was different from what Freud imagined.... I don't think I am making science when I am making literature. Nevertheless, this is literature because it has been written and it sells. And this is also literature because it has effects, even effects on literature.[23]

It is clear from these cynical and cryptic remarks that Lacan was becoming aware of the impact of his theories on contemporary avant-garde writers, especially Philippe Sollers and his friends from *Tel Quel*.

Lacan develops his conception of the symptom by explaining that a symptom is what any patient will start by disclosing, often asking to be rid of it. But for his part, he will never promise that they can be ridden of the symptom.[24] By that time Lacan had identified the symptom with 'the most proper element of the human dimension'[25] and defined the psychoanalytic cure as the exploitation of puns and linguistic equivocation – without missing the sense of 'fun' (Lacan used the English word) provided by the Unconscious – in order to reconnect the symptom with the symbolic order.[26] In this sense psychoanalysts were invited to become Joyceans if they wanted to understand the right type of cure! Like psychoanalytic language, art can reach the real by performing the function of a hole. When the famous logician Quine asked Lacan whether the aim of psychoanalysis was to untie the knot, he answered negatively: 'No, it holds fast. One could state that if Freud demonstrates something, it is that sexuality makes a hole, but human beings have no idea of what it is. A woman is made present for a man by a symptom; a woman is man's symptom.'[27] This insight played an important role in the final development of Lacan's teachings, and had important repercussion on theoreticians such as Zizek.

The conceit according to which a woman is a man's symptom recurs in new elaborations on Joyce in the subsequent seminar. Lacan points to Joyce's only play, *Exiles*, as being emblematic of Joyce's main symptom:

> I have said of Joyce that he was the Symptom. All his works testify to this. *Exiles* is his way of approaching what was for him a central symptom, the symptom constituted by the lack [*carence*] proper to sexual relations.
>
> This lack or deficiency will not take any shape, but has to take one – which is for Joyce what ties him to his wife, the so-called Nora, during whose reign he imagines *Exiles*. One translates as if it was 'The Exiled Ones' whereas it can also mean a plural 'Exiles' as such. *Exile*, there can be no better term to express the non-rapport. The non-rapport means that there is absolutely no reason why he should take one woman among all women for his woman or for his wife.[28]

As I have already developed this insight in a few texts,[29] I shall only sum up the central argument here.

At one level, Richard Rowan can be described as Joyce's alterego, and the play's main dilemma is the way Richard deals with his common-law wife's seduction by an old friend of his, Robert Hand, who has been instrumental in bringing them and their son back from exile in Italy. Having returned to Dublin after many years, Richard is offered a post at the university, and seems pleased to be in touch with Beatrice, Robert's cousin, with whom he has corresponded for years. Beatrice is the sort of '*anima inspiratrix*' that an all too earthly and sensual Bertha cannot be. When Bertha tells Richard of the seduction scheme and begs him to intervene, he refuses, letting her choose freely. He nevertheless appears in the house to which Bertha has been invited, but soon leaves, preferring not to know what will take place that night. Masochism plays an important role in this play, and Richard is clearly on the side of Sacher-Masoch. At the end of the play, still not knowing whether Bertha has slept with Robert, Richard and she renew their vows and decide to found their love not on the bourgeois sense of security provided by marriage but on doubt, perceived as a 'living wound'. It is certain that Lacan's formula makes a lot sense in this play: Richard and Bertha can revise and redefine their love not as a relationship between two complementary male and female partners, but as incommensurably divided subjects who can accept an irreducible difference. That this acceptance creates pain – is even based on pain – is nothing compared with the ethical sense of freedom and empowerment they experience at the end. Bertha can then really embody Richard's 'symptom', while she remains an enigmatically free agent who testifies to an ever-renewed desire.

Ulysses can be shown to be similarly illuminated by Lacan's insights – the best example is provided by the careful annotations and solid preface to the French edition of the novel mentioned earlier.[30] As we have seen with previous Lacanian readings, there is a direct conflict with current psychoanalytical approaches. Thus in his seminar of 13 January 1976 Lacan heaps scorn on most neo-Freudian interpretations of Joyce. He selects Mark Shechner's *Joyce in Nighttown: A Psychoanalytic Inquiry*[31] as an egregious counter-model:

> Well, *Ulysses*, let's approach it. A certain Shechner, who imagines that he is a psychoanalyst because he has read many psycho-analytic books – this is a rather widespread illusion, especially among analysts – wanted to analyze *Ulysses*. This gives you an absolutely terrifying impression, suggesting that the imagination of the novelist, I mean the imagination that constructed *Ulysses* is entirely to be discarded. Unlike *Surface and Symbol*, this analysis of *Ulysses* wishes of course to exhaustive, because one cannot stop when one psychoanalyzes a book.[32]

Lacan does not go any further than this reproach of trivialisation, but he manifests once more his ire for those who decide to submit novels to wholesale psychoanalytic readings – and he does not spare Freud himself, who at least had the merit of 'restraining himself' since he never analysed long novels fully.[33] By staying at a greater distance from the novel, Lacan refrains from reading the 'Unconscious' of Stephen or Bloom.

On the other hand he shows the greatest respect for more classical books; he quotes Hugh Kenner and Clive Hart, and has been struck by the relevance of Robert M. Adams' *Surface and Symbol: The Consistency of Ulysses*.[34] Lacan is thus not averse to literary criticism when it throws new light on the textual process. He claims that Adams has well perceived the distinction between the Imaginary and the Symbolic, and has usefully pointed to the distinction between 'existence' and 'consistency' that had attracted Lacan's interest in other seminars. The notion that it is the surface of the text and not its symbols that endow it with consistency, and the definition of 'consistency' as 'what holds things together', seem to pave the way to the Lacanian concept of strings tied together in a knot. Is the knot something that 'ex-sists' to the strings, or is it just the locus where the four strings 'consist'? The consistency of Joyce's writing is made up of the many strands that are intertwined by a writing that posits an enigma. Because this enigma creates a 'hole', a textual gap or break that arrests the imagination, it manages to create beauty at the same time: 'Finally, only writing could be called beautiful – why not?'[35]

Lacan's main thesis with respect to *Ulysses* revolves around the issue of paternity: '*Ulysses* is the testimony of how Joyce remains trapped in his father, while disavowing him, which is exactly his symptom.'[36] Here we meet Joyce's second main symptom, after the lack of sexual relations. The more he denies his father, like Peter with Christ, the more he tightens the noose around his neck – a noose made up of the string of the fourfold knot. Thus Lacan does not believe that Bloom is a likely father for Stephen, nor that Stephen makes a believable Telemachus (*JAL*, 27). His aim is to stress the function of paternity while disentangling it from the Homeric structure. I have had the opportunity to echo this impression in Joycean circles, and I can verify that it still triggers very blunt or aggressive rejection. One would have to go back to the long and complex history of Joyce's reception, beginning with Ezra Pound, who voiced a similar skepticism about the 'father-and-son' idea and the Homeric parallels in *Ulysses*. Suffice it to say that this is still a contentious point among Joycean scholars, and that Lacan's insight is quite bracing and probably true. Besides, the idea cannot be reduced to a mere psychological projection, since Lacan adds that it is precisely this absence of real or symbolic fathers in the novel that shows how paternity is reduced to a pure name. For him, Joyce shows, *a contrario*, as it were, that the 'Symptom depends upon a structure in which the Name-of-the-Father is an unconditioned element' (*JAL*, 27). A full discussion of this issue would entail a systematic examination of the theological substratum of the links between Shakespeare, God and the artist – especially as it is developed by Stephen Dedalus in Chapter 9 of *Ulysses* 'Scylla and Charybdis'.

Moving between an excellent reading of the conclusion of *A Portrait of the Artist as a Young Man* and *Ulysses*, Lacan asserts the central role of the Father in Joyce. In the Seminar of 13 January 1976 he quotes the famous invocation to the 'old Father' at the end of the *Portrait* and describes Stephen as 'Joyce in so far as he deciphers his own enigma'.[37] He sees the continuity between the two texts in those terms. Stephen is a character who would say something like: 'After the father I have had, thank you, no more fathers. I'm fed up with fathers.'[38] He then investigates a literary problem that has been exposed by Adams: there is a curious duplication in that a remark made by Stephen in the library about Shakespeare that finds its way into Bloom's soliloquy at the end of the 'Sirens' episode. Whereas it is clear that Stephen knows all the particulars of Shakespeare's life, how could Bloom muse about the Bard in these terms: 'In Gerard's rosery of Fetter Lane he walks, greyedauburn'? Is this meant to be a quotation from Stephen's interior monologue? Joyce seems to be deliberately putting in question the limits between the Unconscious of his two male characters, which is literalised when they end up as 'Blephen and Stoom'. Lacan refers to this debate so as to suggest that even if Bloom and Stephen cannot be credible as 'symbolic father and symbolic son', they unite in the last episodes as a single male textual substance, as a pure writing that turns more and more auto-referential, which ultimately asserts the domination of the Name-of-the-Father.

The last weeks of the Joyce seminar were devoted to more knots and meditations on Joycean *jouissance* as opposed to feminine *jouissance* (he alludes to the Japanese film 'The Empire of the Senses' to return to the ground covered in Seminar XX on 'God', identified with 'the *jouissance* of a not-all Woman').[39] Lacan also discovered the crucial term 'epiphany' quite late (January 1976) and then used it to show Joyce's way of reaching the Real – an insight that was later very convincingly developed by Catherine Millot.[40]. On 16 March 1976, Lacan announced some new reflections on the function of the ego, while noting disapprovingly Joyce's tendency to move towards a Jungian version of the collective unconscious: the collective unconscious is itself a symptom.[41] Then in the very last seminar, almost as an afterthought, it is Joyce's ego that occupies the fourth circle, where Lacan had previously put the sigma of the symptom. Joyce's ego is an effect of his writing and is thus identified with his symptom. There had been a 'mistake' (*faute*) in the knotting of the three circles of the Real, the Imaginary and the Symbolic, and to compensate for the error the Ego – in Lacan's drawing this not even a circle, but it is represented by double square brackets – plays the role of a clamp to keep the circles together. 'Why is Joyce so unreadable? Perhaps because he triggers no sympathy in us. What I am suggesting is that with Joyce, the ego comes to correct the missing relation. By such an artifice of writing, the Borromean knot is reconstituted.'[42] Joyce's ego can become the symptom; it exploits the ruses of a literary enigma, it is a creative artifice, a 'supplement' by which the spoken riddle turns into writing while reattaching all its components.

Why is this belated recognition of the centrality of the ego so surprising and paradoxical? In order to appreciate it we have to remember that Lacan's entire system is built as a war machine against 'ego psychology.' Since the 1950s his main polemical thrust had been directed at Anna Freud's legacy, in a wholesale critique of the 'Americanization of the Unconscious' that occurred when the first generation of Freud's disciples fled to the United States and elaborated a therapy whose main objective was to increase ego defences. Typically, Lacan's first publication in English was 'Some reflections on the Ego', a text first given as a lecture in London in 1951 and published two years later in *The International Journal of Psychoanalysis*[43] – ironically, just at the time he was being expelled from the International Psychoanalytic Association for his unconventional handling of therapy and his acerbic criticism of the institution. In this text Lacan stresses the dimension of language as constitutive of the ego, and the fact that Freud situates the ego in the dimension of hallucination, therefore of delusion or 'misrecognition'. The ego is a mystifying image of the body that lends a spurious totality to a fundamentally split speaking subject. In consequence, any attempt at bolstering the ego leads to a reinforcement of the neuroses one wants to destroy. Such is the most basic Lacanian tenet; it was therefore a completely unexpected move to have the old ego resurface with Joyce, even if it was to present the ego as knot, writing and symptom.

Let us note that Lacan speaks of the signifier *ego* – conforming to the English usage, and not to the French *moi*, to translate Freud's *Ich*.[44] This suggests a renewed confrontation with British and American ego-psychology. The idea of the lability and supplementarity of the Joycean ego is confirmed by a passage in *A Portrait of the Artist as a Young Man*, when Stephen remembers that a number of schoolboys had tormented him because he had stubbornly claimed Byron to be the greatest poet. After his 'friends' had viciously lashed out at him he had been overcome by anger, and sobbing and clenching his fists he had madly run after them. Then he had felt this anger falling from him, in a curious moment of dispossession: 'even that night as he stumbled homewards along Jones's road he had felt that some power was divesting him of that suddenwoven anger as easily as a fruit is divested of its soft ripe peel'.[45] Lacan remarks that this transformation of anger into disgust is suspect for a psychoanalyst, and sees in this emblematic scene the model of what might be called the Joycean body: a body that can fall from one's self, a mere envelope that by itself cannot really 'hold' the subject. While the critical evaluation of this particular scene may look like a case of overinterpretation, one can point to a few other similar scenes in the novel: for instance when Stephen accompanies his father in a trip to Cork he experiences a moment of subjective dispossession and needs the power of writing (he has been fascinated both by his father's initials carved in a desk, and also, more importantly, by the word *Foetus* carved in wood) and of naming to keep himself together:

> Victoria and Stephen and Simon? Simon and Stephen and Victoria. Names.... He had not died but he had faded out like a film in the sun. He had been lost or had wandered out of existence for he no longer existed.... It was strange to see his small body appear again for a moment: a little boy in a grey belted suit.[46]

The entire scene should be analysed at some length, and one could show how the Lacanian terms of the Real, the Imaginary, the Symbolic and the Symptom structure its logic.

Joyce's ego would constitute a 'peel', a mere covering that is loosely captured by the Imaginary. It is labile, porous, artificial and can be dropped just like that. For Joyce, then, as a consequence, the Real is not knotted to the Unconscious: it appears in symptoms that are metonymically linked to a place (Cork, Dublin). The knot performed by a writing that passes through paternity will therefore assume an even more essential function. 'What I am suggesting is that, for Joyce, the ego intervenes to correct a missing link. Through this artifice in writing, the Borromean knot can be reconstituted.'[47] The concept of the ego that is proposed is not therefore a 'natural' one: on the contrary it is even more artificial than before, but it cannot be reduced to the register of the imaginary. The new Lacanian *ego* is indeed, as Ezra Pound wrote in his *Cantos*, an 'ego scriptor'.[48]

However when Lacan was asked by Jacques Aubert to provide a written version of his talk for publication in the symposium proceedings in 1979,[49] he did not clearly put forward the concept of the ego, although its submerged influence was noticeable. The version Lacan sent Aubert is a completely different text from the oral presentation, it has become an *écrit* in which one recognises here and there certain traces of the original text. Its distinctive feature is that it now looks above all like a pastiche of Joyce's Wakean idiolect. Lacan's style in this text – published in 1979 and therefore one of the last, if not the last, 'authentic texts' written by him – is at its most obscure and punning. It jump-starts with a covert reappearance of the ego as *moi*: '*Joyce le Symptôme à entendre comme Jésus la caille: c'est son nom. Pouvait-on s'attendre à autre chose d'emmoi: je nomme*' (*JAL*, 31). ('Joyce the Symptom to be heard as *Jésus la caille*: this is his name. Could one expect anything less from me: I name'). The ironical reference to Francis Carco's novel, *Jésus-la-caille*, which portrays Parisian pimps and prostitutes, not only situates Joyce's name in the French literary tradition of the 1920s (precisely when Lacan met and heard Joyce) but also adds to his new nickname a populist twist, something like a *java* flavour. In the startling opening the pun '*emmoi*' links *de moi*, ('of me') with Emma Bovary and a submerged echo of Flaubert's famous phrase, '*Madame Bovary, c'est moi*'. After this, Lacan stresses that in French '*je nomme*' (I name) sounds exactly like *jeune homme* – the young man of Joyce's *Portrait*. From the beginning Lacan follows in the demiurgic steps of a young man Joyce, with whom he shares many characteristics – both having been marked by Jesuits and Catholicism, a revolt against the bourgeois order of their youth, an encyclopedic culture that culminates in a few schematic diagrams (Lacan's 'schemes' and 'knots' seem like exact counterparts of Joyce's 'schemes' and 'sigla', these little symbols representing the main characters) and the creation of a radically new language that allows them to think and write.

After a reiteration of the idea that 'Joyce the symptom' gives access to Joyce's name – that Joyce's real name is 'the Symptom' – Lacan directly tackles the issue of phonetics and multiple puns, and when returning to the theme of the 'stool' of the 'beautiful' (*escabeau*) he produces something that reads more and more like *Finnegans Wake*: '*Hissecroibeau à écrire comme l'hessecabeau sans lequel hihanappat qui soit ding! d'nom d'hom. LOM se lomellise à qui mieux mieux. Mouille, lui dit-on, faut le faire: car sans mouiller pas d'hessecabeau.*' (*JAL*, 31). To paraphrase: 'He believes himself beautiful, to be written like the stool he uses as ladder, without which nobody would be worthy of the name of man. MAN's lamella humanises itself as well and fast as it can. Sweat, he's told to wet it a bit, for without sweat no stool.' This dense passage condenses several pages of the actual seminar (18 November 1975), which follow Aubert's essay on the aesthetics of Joyce and criticise Joyce's conception of beauty. To deflate Joyce's notion of 'claritas', Lacan then offers the uncharitable hypothesis that Joyce became a writer above all because he was not virile enough: 'One believes one is a male because one has a little dick. Naturally, I beg you to excuse me here, one needs a little more than that. But since his dick was a little flabby, if I may say so, it had to be his art that supplemented it and compensated his phallic assertion' (*JAL*, 40). The phallus is described as the conjunction of the 'parasite', the male sexual organ, and speech. If all art occupies a phallic function, Joyce's artistic heresy provides a counterbalance to his illusion that he could be a 'male'. But he has understood that the main function of language is not the revelation of the full truth but equivocation – thus showing psychoanalysts the way: 'Finally, we have only this one weapon against the symptom – equivocation.... It is only through equivocation that interpretation works' (*JAL*, 42).

It seems that in 1979 Lacan had read *Finnegans Wake* and *Ulysses* much more closely and he quotes several passages such as the transformation of the title of Verdi's opera *La Forza del Destino* into the 'farce of dustiny' (*FW*, 162, 2–3), and manages to sum up the whole argument of *Ulysses* in one breathtaking paragraph (*JAL*, 34). He closes with a forceful link between Joyce's mastery on his own; '*Je suis assez maître de lalangue, celle dite française, pour y être parvenu moi-même ce qui fascine de témoigner de la jouissance propre au symptôme. Jouissance opaque d'exclure le sens*' (*JAL*, 36, roughly, 'I am enough of a master of the babble so-called French language to have reached that point which fascinates by testifying to the *jouissance* proper to the symptom. An opaque *jouissance* in that it excludes meaning'). Lacan sends us back to the concept of *lalangue*, which he had invented a little earlier to describe a child's 'babble' (he often said that the word was meant to call up 'lallation', archaic babytalk). As Nestor Braunstein has suggested,[50] we can safely surmise that Joyce acts not only as Lacan's double, but also as a literary *Doppelgänger* who allows him to make sense of his own opaque and baroque style, while permitting the return of the repressed 'ego'. It is indeed quite tempting to conclude that Lacan himself embodies the 'Ego-Symptom' presented as the fourth circle:[51]

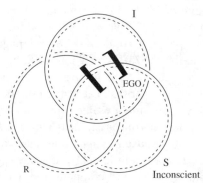

If we go back to the last insights in the *Sinthome* seminar we can see the function of a sort of rhyming slang that is created on the spot, especially when he abbreviates '*Noeud Borroméen*' as '*Noeud-Bo*', which then leads to 'Nebo', the sacred mount of which Pisgah is the summit, where God gave Moses the tablets of stone (Deuteronomy 34). 'Nebo', in which one can hear the French word for 'beautiful', '*le beau*', rhymes with an ego that migrates from Joyce to Lacan, and from Lacan to Joyce. Joyce, who consistently refused to be psychoanalysed and whose name ominously repeats and translates Freud's name, would seem to act as Lacan's wild psychoanalyst, unearthing in him the most stubborn ego-narcissism.

It looks as if the only way to avoid a regressive return to this position is to consider exactly what Lacan says about the function and site of the Symptom, caught up as it is between the signifier and the letter, or perhaps strategically wedged between speech and writing. I have stressed Lacan's sense of wonder about Joyce's use of puns and his recognition that he and Joyce are working on similar effects with language. This convergence was acknowledged as early as Seminar

XX, when Lacan revealed that he had already meditated on *Finnegans Wake*. In the crucial 1973 seminar '*Encore*', Lacan refers to *Finnegans Wake* just after an allusion to Philippe Sollers, the avant-garde writer who edited *Tel Quel*, in which a similar fascination for Joyce was shared by all contributors:

> I agree that Joyce's work is not readable – it is certainly not translatable into Chinese. What happens in Joyce's work? The signifier stuffs [*vient truffer*] the signified. It is because the signifiers collapse into each other, are recomposed and mixed up – read *Finnegans Wake* – that something is produced that, as a signified, may seem enigmatic, but is clearly what is closest to what we analysts, thanks to analytic discourse, have to read: the slip of the tongue. It is as slips that they signify something, in other words, that they can be read in an infinite number of different ways. But it is precisely for that reason that they are difficult to read, are read awry, or not read at all. But doesn't this dimension of 'being read' suffice to show that we are in the register of analytic discourse?
>
> What is at stake in analytic discourse is always this: you give a different reading to what is enunciated as a signifier than what it signifies.[52]

One might argue against his assertion that *Finnegans Wake* is not translatable into Chinese – at any rate a Chinese version has recently been completed. Joyce is presented here as a writer who can teach psychoanalysts how to use language and its numerous accidents. Precisely because the signifiers in his text are always elsewhere, always mean something else in another idiom, they slip not only between languages but also between speech and writing. This recurs in the first example Lacan quotes and analyses. A female voice is heard uttering: 'Who ails tongue coddeau, aspace of dumbillsilly?' (*FW*, 15.18) in a context of sexual wars, strong courtship leading to Viconian marriages. Lacan explains that he would never have recognised the French sentence '*Où est ton cadeau, espèce d'imbécile!*' hidden beneath what seem on the surface of the text to be purely English words:

> What is unbelievable, is that this homophony, here of a translinguistic kind, is only borne by letters that conform to English spelling.... There is something ambiguous in this phonetic usage, I am tempted to write faunic: the faunesque of the thing derives entirely from

letters, that is, something that is not essential to language, that has
been woven by the accidents of history. That someone may use this
in such a prodigious manner forces us to question the very nature of
language (*JAL*, 26).

Lacan wonders how Joyce can use writing to produce puns and equivocations, which betrays a 'metaphysical' or pre-Derridian mode of
investigation, a mode that is well summed up when he remarks that
the letter is 'not essential to language'. As Derrida noted as early as his
1962 thesis on Edmund Husserl's *Origin of Geometry*, Joyce's project
in *Finnegans Wake* was the exact opposite of Husserl's wish to reduce
equivocity to univocity, since he wished to 'take responsibility for all
equivocation, utilizing a language that could equalize the greatest
possible synchrony with the greatest potential for the buried, accu-
mulated, and interwoven intentions within each linguistic atom, each
vocable, each word, each simple proposition, in all wordly cultures
and their most ingenious forms'.[53] While Derrida admits that Joyce
only mimes radical historicism and needs to maintain a minimum of
univocity in order to be readable, his strategy is based on 'the general-
ized equivocation of a writing ... that circulates through all languages
at once'.[54] In a similar fashion Lacan stresses the process of equivocation in writing, while claiming precedence in this theoretical debate:

> A writing is thus a practice that supports thought. Only, the *Noeud-bo*
> changes completely the meaning of writing. It grants an autonomy to
> the said writing.
>   There is indeed another writing, which results from what we might
> call a precipitation of the signifier. Jacques Derrida insisted on this,
> after I showed him the way, by simply pointing to the signifier by
> writing it as S. It remains that the signifier, or what is modulated in
> the voice, has nothing to do with writing, which is perfectly demon-
> strated by my *Noeud-bo*.[55]

Lacan remains deaf to Derrida's suggestion that writing can be shown
to inhabit the most intimate phenomenological link between our
thinking and the inner language by which we believe we can hear
ourselves talk. Since he sticks to an essential difference between the
vocal linguistic substance he calls the signifier and the written effects
on language, one can understand why Lacan continues to be baffled
by Joyce, who presents a real riddle for him, whereas Joyce can be said

to be on exactly the same wave-length as Derrida's critique of logo-centrism.

At the same time Joyce's use of equivocation has practical uses for therapy: is Joyce 'the symptom, the pure symptom of what is our relation to language, when it is reduced to symptoms – i.e. to what effect it has when this effect is not analyzed – I would even add when one forbids oneself to play with any equivocation that might move the unconscious of anybody' (*JAL*, 27). Later this theory becomes more subtle. Lacan thinks that writing can 'catch' signifiers through letters that precipitate them. Without labouring the point that Lacan has not really understood Derrida's critique of logocentrism, one can say that he struggles to reach the same insight about a writing that plays on the hinge between sound effects and written effects. The example of 'Who ails tongue coddeau?' should suffice to prove that Joyce writes something that is meant to sound like something else – in a different language. Lacan therefore assumes that, for Joyce, 'something different from the rest of mortals' took place (whereas for Derrida, Joyce would merely exhibit a very general effect deriving from an essential property of language): for Joyce only, writing is essential to his being, to his ego. 'For Joyce, the ego has played a different role from that of the common mortals. And writing is essential to his ego.'[56] To illustrate this Lacan quotes the well-known anecdote about Joyce, who kept a view of Cork framed in cork: for him the framing device must have a structural link with the content. There is no form that could not be part and parcel of the writing process – this is why in Joyce the maximum of artifice is equivalent to the maximum of 'consistent' truth. Joyce's ego can absorb all of culture, it can encompass the entire orb, a world reduced to language – as was the case with the only two rivals he would acknowledge: Dante and Shakespeare. Whether or not one likes Joyce does not matter: unlike Marguerite Duras, who needed to be loved by her readers (and generally succeeded), Joyce does not care. The writing process he has set in motion is autonomous and can work for ever, it will always constitute and reconstitute his monstrous and fascinating ego – an ego that grows to the dimensions of the universe.

As we have seen, Lacan's reservations about Joyce are real, but his grudging admiration is immense and contains a fair share of mimetic fascination. Without going as far as Nestor Braunstein and suggesting that one can observe a subjective identification with Joyce, one can surely conclude that Joyce has become Lacan's symptom. There can be no identification without some degree of sympathy, as was obvi-

ously the case with Duras and the character of Antigone, for instance.
Joyce generates no real human interest in Lacan beyond a certain
number of biographical determinations that both violently reject, and
triggers no personal sympathy in him, but he is nevertheless a towering model. Joyce has indeed precipitated Lacan's symptom: he is literally a *sym-ptom*, something that precipitates, falls together, curiously,
enigmatically, unaccountably, at the same time.

This is why the question of Joyce's madness acquires a more crucial
importance. If he was mad, was Lacan mad? He thus asks in February
1976:

> After which point is one mad? Was Joyce mad? The fact that I will not
> solve the question today will not prevent me from working with my
> distinction between Truth and the Real.... I began by writing *Inspired
> Writings* , this is why it is no surprise that I find myself facing Joyce;
> this is why I can now ask: Was he mad? What was it that inspired his
> writings?[57]

Lacan then turns to Jacques Aubert, and tries to make him confirm
that Joyce tended to identify himself, mythically at least, with a
Redeemer. Aubert cautiously admits to finding only traces of this.[58]
After a few speculative remarks about Joyce's relationship with Nora
(who was like a glove to him), Lacan explains that the fantasy of taking
oneself for a redeemer defines exactly what he calls '*père*-version'.[59]
In a later development he returns to this ultimate transformation of
the Name-of-the-Father:

> The hypothesis of the Unconscious, Freud underlines it, can only
> hold if one supposes the Name-of-the-Father. To suppose the Name-
> of-the-Father, this is God. This is how, psychoanalysis, when it
> succeeds, proves that one can do without the Name of the father
> under the condition that one uses it.[60]

The reference to his 'Ecrits Inspirés' (1931) in *Annales Médicales* sends
us back to the earliest works of a Lacan who was trying to understand
the logic of psychotic discourse – which proves that the *Sinthome*
seminar has a testamentary quality and offers a rapid revision of all
previous theses and concepts. In his essay 'Inspired Writings', Lacan
had revealed his refusal of a purely medical approach to the language
of psychotics by referring to some experiments by Surrealist writers.

These texts cannot be reduced to the degraded verbal formulation of affective tendencies. They evince an actively ludic aspect whose intentional part, as its automatic part, ought not to be missed. The experiences made by certain writers on a mode of writing they have called Surrealist and whose method they have described very scientifically show the extraordinary degree of autonomy that graphic automatisms can reach, outside any hypnosis.[61]

In a bold move, Lacan refuses to distinguish the artful simulation of psychotic delirium, such as can be found in *The Immaculate Conception*[62] by Breton and Eluard, from the 'authentic' verbal productions of institutionalised patients: all these texts show the same structure, they are determined by preinscribed rhythmic formulas that are then subverted and filled with other meanings. Puns and homophonic patterns allow both poets and 'mad' patients to use language as a chain of signifiers, allowing desire to move along with the chain, while metaphors manage to break through and pass through the Saussurean bar, to use Lacan's later terminology.

What is interesting to note is that at more or less the same time as 'Inspired Writings' Joyce's friends, working with Eugene and Maria Jolas and Stuart Gilbert on the magazine *transition*, were also busy collecting and publishing such 'inspired writings'. For instance in *transition* no. 18 (November 1929), there is a text in French by Roger Vitrac on '*Le Langage à part*' which extensively quotes a medical treatise by Dr Seglas on 'Language trouble in alienated subjects' before alluding to poetic texts by Prevert and Desnos as illustrations of the same linguistic process[63]. All this, of course, is given in the context of the linguistic experiments of the 'revolution of the word' launched by Joyce. In a later issue of *transition* an essay by Stuart Gilbert, 'The Subliminal Tongue', starts with Joyce and then examines a few cases of psychotic language, including the psychical research on dissociation of personality by Morton Prince, who is also quoted in *Finnegans Wake*. At one point Gilbert quotes Gide's *Paludes* (with which we began this chapter) with an allusion to 'that part of Unconscious that I would like to call God's part'.[64]

The question of Joyce's potentially psychotic structure remained a haunting one for Lacan, and he never managed to provide an answer. His caution was of little use, since Joyce would subsequently be used by Lacanian psychoanalysts as an important 'case', an inevitable stepping stone by which to approach psychotic knotting and unknotting. Lacan once noted that Joyce would not have been analysable, not just because he was too much of a perverted Catholic, but also because he loved his symptom too much[65] – an insight taken up by Jacques-Alain Miller in his Preface to *Joyce avec Lacan* to suggest that Joyce forced Lacan to question the very foundations of psychoanalysis:

> Whence the reference to the egregious Joyce, who manipulates the letter outside effects of the signified, aiming at a pure *jouissance*. To call up psychosis was not simply applied psychoanalysis, it was, on the contrary, *with* the Joyce-symptom supposed to be unanalyzable, to question the discourse of the analyst, in so far as a subject who identifies with the symptom excludes himself or herself from analytic artifice. And perhaps a psychoanalysis cannot find a better end (*JAL*, 12).

In the 'end', however, we cannot avoid a reminiscence of Lucia Joyce, who figures as the trace, the remainder of the symptomatic formation: she was clearly psychotic, and, as most critics of *Finnegans Wake* agree, Joyce's main character (as Issy) and the main addressee of his last book. In that sense it is quite revealing to compare Lacan's trajectory with that of Joyce. Joyce's last years were darkened by his daughter's schizophrenia and his awareness that the eruption of political crises into world-wide conflagration would prevent people from becoming interested in the obscure linguistic experiments of *Finnegans Wake*. Lacan had also lost a daughter he adored, and if his last years were more fulfilled and rewarding than Joyce's, they were similarly darkened by political strife among disciples fighting for control of the school and the edition of his seminars. Like Joyce he never stopped experimenting, with new mathemes, knots, braids, bits of spliced string, puns and formulas.

As Miller has also noted in his Preface to *Joyce and Lacan*, one important effect of the encounter with Joyce was to force Lacan to revise his main concepts a last time (*JAL*, 11). Thus *Jouissance* has acquired a more positive meaning, closer to *sens* (meaning) or halfway between *sens* and *non-sens* – meaning and the absence of meaning. This excessive enjoyment is no longer systematically opposed to desire, but marks the written counterpart of a spoken desire. The concept of the symptom seen as *sinthome* provides a fine cusp between psychosis and normality: it becomes this extra-linguistic manifestation that nevertheless needs a writing to be produced, understood or responded to. This writing is not limited to literary writing, but engages with the fundamental constitution of the subject. Finally, it is the very late reintroduction of the ego as symptom that strikes the reader. The ego is not accused of being an ideological or metaphysical illusion, as in the 1950s, but has become a useful artifice, a writing effect. The ego intervenes as a subtle art of braiding, as the last knotting of the four circles. This suggests that in psychoses one can still find traces of an ego. In consequence it is the whole theory of the foreclosure of the Name-of-the-Father that has to be articulated in an original fashion: with Joyce, one moves between the 'original sin of the father' (Joyce wrote to his brother Stanislaus that *Finnegans Wake* was all about original sin) and writing as an overcoming of the sin, not a sublimation but a transmutation to the level of the symptom. Lacan seems to go back to Joyce's earliest insight when he described the Dublin he wished to portray in *Dubliners* – strangely enough, a text that Lacan never seems to quote – as a 'hemiplegia', a paralysis, and would declare he saw symptoms everywhere.[66]

The following table summarises the main displacements and re-alignments I have sketched:

Main articulations in the 60s:	*New accents in the 70s:*
• The Unconscious is based in the locus of the Other	• What matters is the stress on a barred or lacking Other (Ø, or S (Ⱥ)
• The Symbolic dominates until...	• The Real dominates until...
• R, S, I, become equivalent circles	• Σ appears as the fourth knot
• The barred subject of desire is the focus of literary analysis	• *Jouissance* of writing is the focus of literary analysis
• Foreclosure of the Name-of-the-Father	• Domination of *père-version*
• The Name in the Symbolic is the Key	• Naming is a creative gesture working with holes and knots in the Real.

Finally, in what could be described as a belated admission that Derrida was after all quite right, writing is seen as supplement and replacement. These terms now describe the function of art insofar as it strives to reach beauty. Speech keeps its pragmatic function, since it

works on *double entendre* and equivocation, the only weapon available to those who wish to fight against the lethal side of the Symptom.
There is not such a great danger of being caught up in the *jouissance*
of the signifier as such: what matters above all is allowing the *jouissance* of the signifier to be communicated from one Unconscious to
another. If Lacan is never very sure that Joyce succeeded in that effort,
he needed Joyce's strenuous literary efforts in order to write the
fourth knot of the *Sinthome*, and thus to make us aware of the lasting
riddle produced by enjoyment of the Symptom.

11 Conclusion

It is impossible really to conclude – as Flaubert said, silliness consists in wishing to conclude – but I would like briefly to recapitulate a number of major issues. Lacan, as we have seen, created a war machine against applied psychoanalysis, especially when applied to art and literature. Under the guise of a 'return to Freud', he was the first to criticise what passes as 'psychobiography' and 'deep psychology', even if this was the mode in which Freud himself worked. Can we say that 'Lacan' should sound like the name of a Trojan horse, of a virus that attaches itself to current psychoanalytic theory – so as to erase as much of it as possible, to let it devour itself until something radically new emerges? Is that how he wished to teach us to read?

Lacan's writerly 'return to Freud' nevertheless suggests a more positive programme: we can learn to read with Freud, if only we understand how to treat his theory not as a method but as a text. In fact the task that is proposed is simple: we must first revise our fundamental vocabulary and provide a sharper meaning to concepts that we take for granted, such as the letter, literature, writing, speech, image, symbol, metaphor, metonymy and so on. Then we need to elaborate a powerful model of the interactions between the barred subject of the Unconscious and the letter of literature, remember our sense of fun, and work with our favourite authors. This is a task for the future, upon which excellent critics have already embarked, and it has a great posterity.

Finally, if Joyce appears as Lacan's 'me altar's ego in miniature' (to quote *Finnegans Wake*, 463. 7), we may then wonder who read whom. Was Lacan just a reader, or is did he allow himself to be written in advance by Joyce? This hermeneutic circle can only be solved with Lacan's last word: a word that functions as a name, so as to let the proper name emerge within the symptom, or the symptom as a proper name. This describes a new type of circularity, catching up with Lacan's beginnings: he returned to his earliest investigations, his

'Ecrits Inspirés', in order to rediscover that writing had always been his symptom. In this theoretical loop one sees the lasting influence of a paranoic drift in Surrealism that no doubt played a great part for Lacan, and one can identify more precisely a 'paranoid style' in Lacan – and the encounter with Dalí was crucial – that never excluded an important element of infectious *fun* (he often used the English word in his seminars).

Thus Lacan's vaunted Gongorism offered an economy of writing that allowed him to negotiate between several traditions: the Renaissance courtier, whose domineering arrogance was tempered by a ready witticism and who met half-way the Surrealist admirer of feminine hysteria; while looking back to Viennese turn-of-the-century Jewish humour he never forgot the French tradition from which he derived, a tradition that was refined to an extreme in Mallarmé's sophisticated late prose style, where all the nuances of a prismatic thought blended with its unthought complements and components; and from there, he could dig for nuggets in a very ancient tradition he owed to his wide culture, going back to Greek and Latin authors and extending, an almost hubristic effort, to the most modern concepts derived from the hard sciences, including physics, mathematics, logics, linguistics and topology. Since Lacan placed the whole *Ecrits* under the heading of style by quoting Buffon's famous tag – 'Style is man himself' (*Le style c'est l'homme même*) – his varied readings tell us how much of our 'speaking being' (*parlêtre*) has been predetermined by style and how much can be seen as an agency productive of style. Style in that sense is not restricted to literature, but can define how one demonstrates a theorem or calculates a curve. Finally, he tells us that we have to invent our sense of style, borrowing and stealing as much as we can, especially from him, without ever forgetting that the result will only ring true if it is in some way connected with our symptom.

Finally could Lacan be seen as the symptom of our postmodern culture, of a more and more globalised web of traces? For readers such as Zizek, Lacan already belongs to popular culture, and the best place for him to address us is directly from the television set. Lacan may nevertheless remain a master, especially in his institutionalised dealings, where, like Mao, he launched a cultural revolution that partly failed. The new 'leap forward' should have brought us closer to an awareness of the truth of our desire. But, as we have seen, in May 68 Lacan had warned the students to be wary of any fascination for a master, especially when adorned with the seductive gear of revolutionary fervour aiming at the creation of a new identity. Was he, more than Mao, like Nietzsche's Zarathustra, who parodically subverts a structure of thought still dominated by religion? Lacan always refused to identify his 'big Other' with a *deus absconditus*, refusing with total intransigence any theoretical compromise with peers and friends such as Dolto and Vasse who expressed their own religious leanings. The cryptic formula he used in this context could be commented on at length: 'God is unconscious', which also meant 'God is the Unconscious'. It is precisely, through letters and literature that mystics have tried to express this wish to come as close to God as they could, even if they often felt and said that language stood in the way of their experience and had to voided, muted, emptied.

Finally, was avant-garde literature of the Joycean type the only writerly myth that Lacan acknowledged? The strategic place of myth should be addressed from the perspective of a new century looking back on another century. Beyond Lacan's deep affinities with Lévi-Strauss but also in the former's use of specific mythological constructions, we see the domination of literary and philosophical references. Lacan, like Freud, always bowed to the creators of systems and texts, and acknowledged the privileges of the *Dichter*. As we have seen, Lacan believed in a 'science of the subject' that would not be reduced to scientism or technological progress, and yet he also needed the 'voice of myth' to convey some of his ideas. Like Plato in the *Symposium* who needs Socrates to quote Diotima to tell the truth about love, Lacan often performs a similarly complex and daring gesture: 'I, the Truth, I am speaking ...', he wrote, multiplying the quotation marks, asserting at the same time that truth can never be fully disclosed, only 'half-said'. One should therefore not be blind to the role of self-mythification, even self-mystification, in Lacan's strategy. While becoming a 'name' for himself, which entailed quoting himself in the third person and agreeing (for a short period of time, it is true) to be the only author to sign articles in a theoretical journal such as *Scilicet*, he also provided us with the instruments of a radical critique aiming at demystification. And if 'Lacan' as a name condenses a whole myth, it might nevertheless be the only myth that psychoanalysis, now weak and wounded but emerging triumphant from the 'Freud wars', can leave us for the twenty-first century.

Notes and References

Unless English translations are given in reference, the translations from the French are the author's.

1 Jacques Lacan, from L to Z, or 'Against Interpretation'

1. See 'A Lacanian psychosis: Interview by Jacques Lacan' in *Returning to Freud: Clinical Psychoanalysis in the School of Lacan*, trans. and ed. Stuart Schneiderman (New Haven: Yale University Press, 1980), 19–41. A brief selection of Lacan's psychiatric case studies can be found in Jacques Lacan, *Travaux et Interventions* (Alençon: Arep Editions, 1977).
2. Ibid., 41.
3. Jacques Lacan, 'C'est à la lecture de Freud...', Preface in Robert Georgin, *Lacan* (Lausanne: L'Age d'Homme-Cistre, 1977), 15.
4. Ibid., 16.
5. Jacques Derrida, *The Postcard*, transl. Alan Bass (Chicago: University of Chicago Press, 1987), 425–6.
6. Philippe Lacoue-Labarthe and Jean-Luc Nancy, *The Title of the Letter*, transl. François Raffoul and David Pettigrew (Albany: State University of New York Press, 1992), 74.
7. Ibid., 90.
8. Ibid., 90.
9. Jacques Lacan, *Ecrits* (Paris: Seuil, 1966), back cover.

2 Lacan from A to L: Basic Lacanian Issues and Concepts

1. Jacques Lacan, 'Preface to the English edition' of *The Four Fundamental Concepts of Psycho-Analysis*, transl. Alan Sheridan (London: Penguin, 1979), viii.
2. Elisabeth Roudinesco, *Jacques Lacan*, transl. Barbara Bray (New York: Columbia, 1997).
3. Philippe Julien, *Jacques Lacan's Return to Freud: The Real, the Symbolic*

and the Imaginary, transl. D. Beck Simiu (New York: New York University Press, 1994).

4. See Mikkel Borch-Jacobsen, *The Freudian Subject*, transl. Catherine Porter (Stanford: Stanford University Press, 1988) and *Lacan: The Absolute Master*, transl. Douglas Brick (Stanford: Standford University Press, 1991).

5. Jacques Lacan, *Seminar XIII 'The Object of Psychoanalysis'* (1965–66), unpublished, transl. Cormac Gallagher, seminar of 15 December 1965.

6. Quoted by Roudinesco in *Jacques Lacan*, 376.

7. See Chapter 10, note 23.

8. Louis Althusser, 'Freud and Lacan' (1964–65) in *Writings on Psychoanalysis*, transl. Jeffrey Mehlman (New York: Columbia University Press, 1996), 21.

9. Ibid., 21.

10. Ibid., 91. This text was written in 1976.

11. I am quoting the most systematic presentation of the Four Discourses in *Seminar XVII: L'Envers de la Psychanalyse* (Paris: Seuil, 1991), 31. There are very useful discussions in Marc Bracher's *Lacan, Discourse and Social Change: A Psychoanalytical Cultural Criticism* (Ithaca: Cornell University Press, 1993), 53–80, and Bruce Fink, 'The Master Signifier and the Four Discourses', in Dany Nobus (ed.), *Key Concepts of Lacanian Psychoanalysis* (New York: Other Press, 1998), 29–47.

12. For a new series of schemes that at times come very close to psychoanalytic insights, see Algirdas J. Greimas and Jacques Fontanille, *Sémiotique des Passions* (Paris: Seuil, 1991).

13. Jacques Lacan, *Seminar XVII L'Envers de la Pyshcanalyse* (Paris: Seuil, 1991), 239.

14. Sigmund Freud, 'Analysis terminable and interminable', in Philip Rieff (ed.), *Therapy and Technique* (New York: Macmillan, 1963), 266.

15. Lacan, *Ecrits*, 193.

16. Jacques Lacan, *Seminar II*, 284.

17. Lacan, *Ecrits*, 303, 306, 313, 315.

18. Jacques Lacan, *Feminine Sexuality: Jacques Lacan and the école freudienne*, ed. Juliet Mitchell and Jacqueline Rose, transl. J. Rose (New York: Norton, 1985).

19. Nestor Braunstein, *La Jouissance: Un Concept lacanien* (Paris: Point Hors Ligne, 1992).

3   The Theory of the Letter: *Lituraterre* and Gide

1. Sigmund Freud, *The Origins of Psychoanalysis: Letters to Wilhelm Fliess,*

Drafts and Notes 1887–1902, ed. by M. Bonaparte, A. Freud and E. Kris (New York: Basic Books, 1954), 173. (Hereafter, *OP*.)

2. *OP*, 174.

3. *OP*, 360, 361.

4. Jacques Derrida, 'Freud and the scene of writing' in *Writing and Difference*, transl. Alan Bass (Chicago: University of Chicago Press, 1978), 196–231.

5. Jacques Lacan, 'Lituraterre', *Littérature* no3 (Paris: Larousse, 1971), 3.

6 Jacques Lacan, Seminar on 'The Purloined Letter', in John P. Muller and William J. Richardson, (eds), *The Purloined Poe*, 40. A footnote in Lacan's text sends his readers to *Our Exagmination Round His factification for Incamination of Work in Progress* – without any direct reference, but one may surmise that Lacan remembers the last 'letter' in the critical essays.

7. James Joyce, *Finnegans Wake* (London: Faber, 1939), 93.

8. Samuel Beckett and others, *Our Exagmination Round His factification for Incamination of Work in Progress* (Paris: Shakespeare and Co., 1929; London: Faber, 1972), 193–4.

9 Sigmund Freud, 'The Antithetical Sense of Primal Words', in *On Creativity and the Unconscious* (New York: Harper, 1958), 55–62.

10. Lacan, 'Lituraterre', 7.

11. Ibid., 5.

12. Jacques Lacan, *Seminar XX Encore*, 120.

13. Ibid.

14. Ibid., 122.

15. Jean Schlumberger, *Madeleine et André Gide* (Paris: Gallimard, 1956); Jean Delay, *La Jeunesse d'André Gide* (Paris: Gallimard, vol. 1, 1956, vol. 2, 1957).

16. Jacques Lacan, *Ecrits* (Paris: Seuil), 739. Emphasis in original.

17. André Gide, *Et nunc manet in te* (Paris and Neuchatel: Ides et Calendes, 1947).

18. Ibid., 80.

19. Ibid., 81.

20. Ibid., 84.

21. Jacques Lacan Seminaire V, *Les Formations de l'Inconscient* (Paris: Seuil 1998) 261.

22. Gide, *Et nunc manet in te*, 42.

23. Lacan, *Seminar V*, 257. (Hereafter, *S5*.)

24. Gide, *Et nunc manet in te*, 120.

25. Friedrich Nietzsche, *The Portable Nietzsche*, ed. and transl. Walter Kaufmann (New York: Penguin, 1976), 687. Nietzsche's statement was in Italian: (*Siamo contenti? Son dio ho fatto questa caricatura*). I have slightly modified Kaufmann's translation.

4   Poe's 'Purloined Letter'

1. *The Purloined Poe: Lacan, Derrida and Psychoanalytic Reading* (Baltimore: Johns Hopkins University Press, 1988). (Hereafter *PP*.)
2. Marie Bonaparte, *The Life and Works of Edgar Allan Poe: A Psycho-Analytic Interpretation* (1933), transl. John Rocker (London: Imago, 1949), xi.
3. Ibid., 689. I have retranslated Baudelaire's conclusion to 'Le mauvais vitrier' in *Petits Poèmes en Prose*.
4. Ibid., 483–4.
5. In the French version only, though cf. *Seminar II*, 240. The English translation has 27 April 1955 (p. 205 hereafter *S2*). I shall return to these dates later.
6. *PP*, 187–90.
7. See Slavoj Zizek, *Looking Awry*, (Cambridge, Mass.: MIT Press, 1991) (cf. p. 234 for a detailed presentation) 3–9, for a very useful discussion of Zeno in Lacanian terms.
8. Salvoj Zizek, *Enjoy your Symptom!* (New York: Routledge, 1992), 1–28. (Hereafter *EYS*.)
9. Lacan, *Ecrits*, 41–61.

5   *Hamlet* and the Desire of the Mother

1. Ella Freeman Sharpe, *Dream Analysis: a practical handbook for psycho-analysts* (London: Hogarth Press, 1951).
2. In this chapter I refer throughout to the the Hamlet section of the Seminar 'Le Désir et son Interpretation', reproduced in three consecutive issues of *Ornicar?* (numbers 24, 25 and 26, hereafter *O24* and *O25* – I do not quote the subsequent issue since it corresponds to the English translation of the seminar.
3. S. Freud, The Origins of Psycho-Analysis, Letter 71 (15 October 1897) 224.
4. See 'Le Temps Logique et l'assertion de certitude anticipée' (1945) in Lacan, *Ecrits*, 197–213.
5. S. Freud, *The Interpretation of Dreams*, transl. James Strachey (New York: Avon Books, 1965), 298.
6. S. Freud, 'Mourning and Melancholia', in *General Psychological Theory* (New York: Collier, 1963), 167–8.
7. S. Freud, *The Interpretation of Dreams*, 466.
8. Jacques Lacan, 'Desire and the Interpretation of Desire in Hamlet', transl. by James Hulbert, in Shoshana Felman (ed.), *Literature and*

Psychoanalysis. The Question of Reading: Otherwise (Baltimore: Johns Hopkins University Press, 1982), 20.

9. Ella Freeman Sharpe, 'The Impatience of Hamlet', *in Collected Papers on Psycho-Analysis* (London: Hogarth Press, 1950), 20.

10. The references throughout are to the edition of Shakespeare edited by Philip Edwards (Cambridge: Cambridge University Press, 1985). Here, p. 240.

11. Freeman Sharpe, 'The Impatience of Hamlet', 213.

12. T.S. Eliot, 'Hamlet and His Problems', in *The Sacred Wood* (London: Methuen, 1972), p. 98.

13. Ibid., 102–3.

14. Jacques Lacan, 'Desire and the Interpretation of Desire in Hamlet', in Felman, *Literature and Psychoanalysis*, 12.

15. Ibid., 11–52. (Hereafter *LP*).

16. Stéphane Mallarmé, *Oeuvres Complètes*, ed. H. Mondor and G. Jean-Aubry (Paris: Gallimard, Pléaide, 1945), 1564.

17. S. Freud, 'The Passing of the Oedipus-Complex', in *Sexuality and the Psychology of Love.*

18. Bruce Fink, 'Reading Hamlet with Lacan', in *Lacan, Politics, Aesthetics* Willy Apollon and Richard Feldstein (eds), (Albany: SUNY Press, 1996), 182. A very insightful reading is Stanley Cavell's 'Hamlet's Burden of Proof' in *Disowning Knowledge* (Cambridge: Cambridge University Press, 1987) p. 179–91. See also the very exciting Lacanian elaboration – with a bridge towards Benjamin's theory of the *Trauerspiel* – in Julia Reinhard Lupton and Kenneth Reinhard, *After Oedipus: Shakespeare in Psychoanalysis* (Ithaca: Cornell Uuniversity Press, 1993), especially on *Hamlet*, 60–118.

6   Antigone: Between the Beautiful and the Sublime

1. According to Alexandre Kojève's published notes on Hegel, Antigone is not a main 'character' or 'figure', which is surprising given his emphasis on death in the *Phenomenology of Spirit*. See for instance Kojève's essay 'The Idea of Death in Hegel's Philosophy', in *Introduction à la Lecture de Hegel* (Paris: Gallimard, 1947), 529–75. On the other hand, in his brief summary of the relevant section in the *Phenomenology* that analyses of the oppositon between the family and the state in the Greek world – Kojève never mentions the name Antigone and writes that 'the death of the brother does not change anything to the situation of the sister' (ibid., 101). He sees 'sublimation' or 'repression' at work in Hegel's analysis of the brother–sister link.

2. Sophocles, *Antigone*, in *The Theban Plays*, transl. B. F. Watling (Baltimore: Penguin, 1968), 140.
3. Ibid., 150.
4. This is Patrick Guyomard's central thesis in *La Jouissance Tragique* (Paris: Aubier, 1992), 59. 'Lacan's praise of Antigone is the application of a theory of desire in which death names the power and effect of the signifer, but at the same time it is a praise, although denied, of incest.'
5. G. W. F. Hegel, *The Phenomenology of Spirit*, transl. A. V. Miller (Oxford: Oxford University Press, 1977), 275.
6. Ibid., 288.
7. Ibid., 284; Sophocles, *Antigone*, I, 926.
8. I am quoting Martin L. D'Ooge's excellent annotated edition of Antigone: Sophocles, *Antigone* (Boston: Ginn and Co., 1887), 113.
9. See for instance Patricia Jagentowicz Mills, 'Hegel's *Antigone*' in Patricia Jagentowicz Mills (ed.), *Feminist Interpretations of Hegel* (University Park: Pennsylvania State University Press, 1996), esp 68–71.
10. Hegel, *The Phenomenolgy of Spirit*, 285.
11. *Seminar VII: The Ethics of Psychoanalysis*, 235–6. (Hereafter *S7*).
12. Sophocles,transl B. F. Watling (cf note no. 2) *Antigone*, 148.
13. Ibid., 147–8. .
14. Ibid., 149.
15. Patrick Guyomard suggest such an identification in *La Jouissance Tragique* (Paris: Aubier, 1992), 63.
16. Phillipe Van Haute, 'Death and Sublimation in Lacan's reading of Antigone', in Sarah Harasym (ed.), *Levinas and Lacan: The Missed Encounter* (Albany: SUNY Press, 1998), 102–20.
17. Sophocles, *Antigone*, 153.
18. Just as he has attributed by mistake to Oedipus the words spoken by the Chorus (the μη φυναι), Lacan imputes to Antigone the words 'not yielding', which are actually uttered by Creon. Guyomard, *La Jouissance Tragique*, 113, n. 28.
19. Jean Bolack, *La Mort d'Antigone: La Tragédie de Créon* (Paris: Presses Universitaires de France, 1999).
20. This is Guyomard's thesis in *La Jouissance Tragique*, 60–7.

7   Sade: Subverting the Law

1. D. A. F. de Sade, *Histoire de Juliette ou Les Prospérités du Vice*, in *Oeuvres Complètes*, vol. 24 (Paris: Pauvert, 1967), 337.
2. See Monique David-Ménard, *Les Constructions de l'universel* (Paris: Presses Universitaires de France, 1997), 10. She denounces Lacan's

misreading of Freud's theory of drives, which makes him believe that the pervert realises better than anyone else the detour needed by desire. See also Judith Feher-Gurevich, 'The Philanthropy of Perversion', in *Lacan in America*, (New York: The Other Press, 2000).

3. See Simone De Beauvoir, *Faut-il Brûler Sade?* (1955) (Paris: Gallimard, 1972), and Maurice Blanchot, *Lautéamont et Sade* (Paris: Minuit, 1949). See also 'Sade's reason' in *The Maurice Blanchot Reader*, edited Michael Holland, transl. B. Wall (Oxford, Blackwell, 1995) p. 74–99 and Pierre Klossowski, *Sade My Neighbour*, transl. A. Lingis (Evanston: North-western University Press, 1991)

4. Quoted by James Knowlson in *Damned to Fame* (New York: Simon and Schuster, 1996), 269.

5. Jacques Lacan, 'Kant with Sade', transl. James B. Swenson, *October*, no. 51, p. 55, first footnote.

6. Angelo Hesnard, *Les Psychoses et les Frontières de la Folie* (Paris: Flammarion, 1924).

7. De Sade, *Histoire de Juliette*, vol. 24, 210.

8. Marcel Hénaf, *Sade: The Invention of the Libertine Body*, transl. Xavier Callahan (Minneapolis: University of Minnesota Press, 1999), 27–40. Hénaf shows how the principle of a systematic logical saturation presupposes a Leibnitzian cosmology that aims at overthrowing the 'lyrical body'.

9. The French is of course stronger than this translation: '*Prêtez-moi la parttie de votre corps qui peut me satisfaire un instant, et jouissez, si cela vous plaît, de celle du mien qui peut vous être agréable.*' De Sade, *Histoire de Juliette ou Les Prospérités du Vice* in *Oeuvres Complètes*, vol. 19, 106–7.

10. De Sade, *Histoire de Juliette*, vol. 20, 181.

11. Marquis de Sade, *Justine, Philosophy in the Bedroom and Other Writings*, transl. Richard Seaver and Austryn Wainhouse (New York: Grove Weidenfeld, 1965), 157.

12. Jacques Lacan, 'Seminar X: Anxiety' (1962–63) unpublished translation by C. Gallagher from unedited French typescripts, 146.

13. Ibid., 147.

14. See David-Ménard, *Les Constructions de l'universel*.

15. Max Horkheimer and Theodor W. Adorno, *Dialectic of Enlightenment*, transl. J. Cumming (New York: Continuum, 1987).

16. Lacan, 'Kant with Sade', 55.

17. S. Freud, 'The Economic Problem in Masochism', in *General Psychological Theory* (New York: Collier, 1963), 197–8.

19. Ibid., p. 200–1.

20. G. W. F. Hegel, 'The Spirit of Christianity', in *Early Theological Writings*, transl. T. M. Knox and R. Kroner (Philadelphia: University of Pennsylvania Press, 1971), 188.
21. Ibid., 195.
22. Ibid., 213.
23. Ibid., 212.
24. Jacques Lacan, 'L'Etourdit', in *Scilicet*, no. 4 (Paris, 1973), 36.
25. Ibid., 37.
26. See Jean Hyppolite, *Genèse et Structure de la Phénoménologie de l'Esprit* (Paris: Aubier, 1945), 156–62, on the issue of' 'Alterity in Desire'.
27. Jacques Lacan, *Seminar XX On Feminine Sexuality. The limits of love and Knowledge 1972–1973*, transl. Bruce Fink (New York: Norton, 1998), 4. (Hereafter *S20*).
28. Nestor Braunstein, *La Jouissance: Un Concept lacanien* (Paris: Point Hors Ligne, 1992), 7–51.
29. Pierre Klossowski, *Sade My Neighbor*, transl. Alphonse Lingis (Evanston: Northwestern Uuniversity Press, 1991).
30. Ibid., 106.
31. Lacan, 'Kant with Sade', 74.
32. Quoted by Hénaf in *Sade*, 7.
33. Klossowski, *Sade MY Neighbour*, 41.
34. De Sade, *Justine*, 134.
35. Monique David-Ménard, *La Folie dans la Raison Pure* (Paris: Vrin, 1990), 179–245, and *Les Constructions de l'Universel* (Paris: PUF, 1997).
36. Emmanual Levinas, 'Apropos of Buber: Some Notes', in *Outside the Subject*, transl. Michael B. Smith (Stanford: Stanford University Press, 1993), 43–4.
37. Emmanuel Levinas, *En découvrant l'existence avec Husserl et Heidegger* (Paris: Vrin, 1988), 194–7.
38. Emmanuel Levinas, *Totalité et Infini* (La Haye: Martinus Nijhoff, 1965), 254.
39. Jacques Lacan, *Séminaire XVII, L'Envers de la Psychanalyse* (Paris, Seuil, 1991), 74. (Hereafter, *S17*).
40. Freud 'Psychoanalytic Notes upon an Autobiographical Account of a case of Paranoia (Schreber)', in *Three Case Histories* (New York: Colliers, 1963), 132. For a good philosophical reading of the question of madness in Kant's *Reason*, see David-Ménard, *La Folie dans la Raison Pure*. See also Slavoj Zizek, 'Kant and Sade: The Ideal Couple', in *Lacanina Ink*, no. 13 (1998), 12–25.
41. I. Kant, *Critique of Pure Reason*, transl. W. S. Pluhar (Indiannapolis/Cambridge: Hackett, 1996), 112. The usual reference to Kant's original editions is A58–B83.

8 *Ravishing* Duras, or the Gift of Love

1. Michèle Montrelay gave a presentation on *Le Ravissement de Lol V. Stein* in June 1965. The text was then rewritten and became the introduction to her *L'Ombre et le nom: Sur la féminité* (Paris: Minuit, 1977), 9–23. She begins by stressing her own experience of being 'ravished' by the reading: 'One cannot read this novel as another book. One is not the master of one's reading anymore. Either one cannot stand it, and one drops the book. Or one lets the Ravishing work, and one is swallowed up, annihilated. One reads, one reads without stopping, but as one reads, one forgets deeply.... This novel steals your thought from you. It carries you away into a sort of poverty in which love and memory become one.' *L'Ombre et le nom*, 9.

2. I have slightly modified the translation of the quote given by Leslie Hill in 'Lacan with Duras', reprinted in (ed.) John Lechte *Writing and Psychoanalysis: A Reader* (London: Arnold, 1996), 145.

3. Jean Allouch, *132 Bons Mots avec Jacques Lacan* (Paris: Eres, 1988), 166.

4. Jacques Lacan, 'Homage to Marguerite Duras, on *Le Ravissement de Lol V. Stein*', transl. Peter Connor, in *Duras by Duras* (San Francisco: City Lights, 1987), 124.

5. Elisabeth Roudinesco, *Jacques Lacan & Co.*, transl. Jeffrey Mehlman (Chicago: University of Chicago Press, 1990), 522.

6. Hill, 'Lacan with Duras', 160. Leslie Hill has written an excellent book on Marguerite Duras: *Marguerite Duras: Apocalyptic Desires* (London: Routledge, 1993).

7. The American translation by Richard Seaver was published in 1966: *The Ravishing of Lol Stein* (New York: Pantheon, 1966), back cover.

8. Ibid., 181.

9. Lacan, 'Homage to Marguerite Duras', 122. (Hereafter, *HMD*.)

10. Hill, 'Lacan with Duras', 156.

11. See René Girard, *Mensonge Romantique et Vérité Romanesque* (Paris: Grasset, 1961).

12. Marguerite de Navarre, *The Heptameron*, transl. P. A. Chilton (Harmondsworth: Penguin, 1985), 132.

13. Ibid., 133.

14. Lucien Febvre, *Autour de l'Heptaméron: Amour sacré, Amour profane* (Paris: Gallimard, 1944).

15. Ibid., 216–17.

16. Ibid., 224.

17. Montaigne, *Essais*, III, 5, 88, quoted by Febvre in, *Autour de l'Heptaméron*, 255.

18. See Jacques Lacan, *De la Psychose paranoiaque dans ses rapport avec la*

personnalité (Paris: Seuil, 1975); Roudinesco, *Jacques Lacan & Co*, 111–21. See also Leslie Hill's 'Lacan with Duras', 164, n. 7. The most extensive study of Lacan's famous case is Jean Allouch's excellent *Marguerite on L'Aimée de Lacan* (Paris: E.P.E.L., 1990). See p. 417 for interesting links between Duas's novle and the structure Lacan discovers in Marguerite Anzieu.

19. Elisabeth Roudinesco, *Jacques Lacan & Co*, p. 101. This is the title she gives to the whole chapter on Aimée and Loewenstein. The subtitle on page 109, 'Aimée or Rudolph', would sound even more Durassian if it quoted the full names: Aimée Anzieu-Donnadieu or Rudolph Loewenstein.
20. Lacan, *De la Psychose paranoïaque*, 179.
21. Ibid., 229. Lacan quotes Freud's essay on 'Certain Neurotic mechanisms in jealousy, paranoia and homosexuality' (1922).

9 Tragedies and Comedies of Love: from Plato to Claudel and Genet

1. Jacques Lacan, *Seminar XX*, 75.
2. M. Cardot, Y. Duroux, P. Guyomard, P. Lacoue-Labarthe and R. Major, (eds), *Lacan avec les Philosophes* (Paris: Albin Michel, 1991).
3. Jacques Lacan, 'Sur l'objet de la psychanalyse', *Cahiers pour l'Analyse*, no. 3 (1966) 5.
4. Ibid., p. 6.
5. Alain Badiou, 'Lacan et Platon: Le Mathème est-il une Idéee?', in Cardot *et al.*, *Lacan avec les philosophes*, 135–54.
6. Samuel Beckett, *Murphy* (New York : Grove Press, 1957), 5–6.
7. Jacques Lacan, *Séminaire VIII, Le Transfert* (Paris: Seuil, 1991), 104. (Hereafter *S8*).
8. Plato, *The Collected Dialogues*, ed. E. Hamilton and H. Cairns (Princeton: Bollingen Series, Princeton University Press, 1963), 532.
9. A. E. Taylor, *Plato, the man and his work* (London: Methuen, 1966), 209.
10. Plato, *The Collected Dialogues*, 539.
11. Ibid., 550.
12. Ibid., 568.
13. S. Freud, *The Interpretation of Dreams*, transl. J. Strachey, (New York: Avon, 1965), 344 , 374.
14. See Jacques Derrida, *Given Time: I. Counterfeit Money*, transl. Peggy Kamuf (Chicago: University of Chicago Press, 1992), 2–3, on Lacan, and 159–61, on Heidegger and a similar phrase – 'giving what one does not have' that Heidegger has discovered in Anaximander.

15. Paul Claudel, *L'Otage*, *Le Pain Dur* and *Le Père Humilié* (Paris: Gallimard, Folio, 1979).
16. See William Richardson, 'The Third Generation of Desire', in David Pettigrew and François Raffoul (eds), *Disseminating Lacan* (New York: SUNY, 1996), 182–7, for an excellent discussion of the contradictions between Claudel's theological position and Lacan's atheistic presuppositions.
17. Claudel, *Le Père Humilié*, III, 3, 396–7.
18. Ibid., 399.
19. Jean Genet, *Le Balcon* (Décines: Marc Barbezat, 1962), 10. Lacan's reading of Genet can be found in the 5 March, 1958 session of *Le Séminaire V. Les Formations de l'inconscient* (Paris: Seuil, 1998), 262–8.
20. Genet, *Le Balcon*, 74.

10   Joyce's *Jouissance*, or a New Literary Symptom

1. Jacques Lacan 'R.S.I. Séminaire 1974–75' ed. J. A. Miller, *Ornicar?* no. 5, (December–January 1975–1976), 49.
2. André Gide, *Paludes* (Paris: Gallimard, 1920), 70.
3. Ibid., 12.
4. James Joyce, *Finnegans Wake* (London: Faber, 1939), 118, lines 21, 25–6.
5. Lacan 'R.S.I. Séminaire', 37.
6. Ibid., 36.
7. Clive Hart, *Structure and Motif in Finnegans Wake* (London: Faber, 1962).
8. Ibid., 57.
9. Elisabeth Roudinesco, *Jacques Lacan*, already quoted 363.
10. For instance Joyce told his Swiss friend Mercanton: 'Why should I regret my talent? I haven't any. I write with such difficulty, so slowly. Chance furnishes me with what I need. I am like a man who stumbles along; my foot strikes something, I bend over, and it is exactly what I want.' Jacques Mercanton, in Willard Potts, eds, *Portraits of the Artist in Exile: Recollections of James Joyce by Europeans* (Seattle: Wolfhound Press, 1979), 213.
11. Jacques Lacan, 'Le Sinthome', Seminar of 18 November 1975, ed. J. A. Miller, in *Ornicar?* no. 6 (March–April 1976), 3.
12. See Roudinesco, *Jacques Lacan*, 359 ff.
13. Lacan, 'Le Sinthome', 19.
14. James Joyce, *Oeuvres II*, under the direction of Jacques Aubert (Paris: Gallimard, Bibliothèque de la Pléiade, 1996).
15. Lacan's memory is probably more accurate when he recalls being 20

as he attended the famous reading of sections of *Ulysses* that took place on 7 December 1921 (Lacan, born in 1901, was indeed 20 then) than of his meeting Joyce at La Maison des Amis des Livres when he was just 17. In 1918 Joyce had not yet moved to Paris, but it is quite possible that Lacan caught a glimpse of him in Monnier's bookstore late in 1920. See Jacques Aubert (ed.), *Joyce avec Lacan* (Paris: Navarin, 1987), p. 22.

16. Joyce le symptôme', in Aubert, *Joyce avec Lacan* (Henceforth *JAL*).

17. See the pointed remarks in *JAL*, 24.

18. Jacques Lacan, *Television*, transl. D. Hollier, R. Krauss and A. Michelson (New York: Norton, 1990), 15–16.

19. For useful close readings of these seminars see Roberto Harari, *Como se llama James Joyce? A partir de 'El Sinthoma' de Lacan* (Buenos Aires: Amorrortu editores, 1996). A very useful summary is provided by Ellie Ragland-Sullivan in 'Lacan's Seminars on James Joyce: Writing as Symptom and 'Singular Solution', in R. Feldstein and Henry Sussman, *Psychoanalysis and...* (New York: Routledge, 1990), 76–86.

20. Roudinesco, *Jacques Lacan*, p. 372.

21. See Jung's diagnosis of James Joyce and Lucia Joyce in Richard Ellmann, *James Joyce*, rev. edn (Oxford: Oxford University Press, 1983), 679–80.

22. Jacques Lacan, 'Conférences et Entretiens dans des Universités nord-américaines', in *Scilicet*, no. 6/7 (Paris: Seuil, 1976), 7.

23. Ibid., 34.

24. Ibid., 32.

25. Ibid., 56.

26. Ibid., 59.

27. Ibid., 60.

28. Lacan, 'Le Sinthome' in *Ornicar?* no. 7 (1976), 15.

29. In 'Note sur les ex-ils', in Aubert, *Joyce avec Lacan*, 97–106. An expanded version in English is *Joyce Upon the Void* (London: Macmillan, 1991), 21–42.

30. Aubert's Pléiade edition. See note 14.

31. Mark Shechner, *Joyce in Nighttown: A Psychoanalytic Inquiry* (Berkeley: University of California Press, 1974).

32. 'Le Sinthome' in *Ornicar?* no. 7 (1976), 15.

33. Ibid.

34. Robert M. Adams's *Surface and Symbol. The Consistency of Ulysses* (New York: Oxford University Press, 1962).

35. Le Sinthome' in *Ornicar?* (Paris) no. 7 (1976), p. 14.

36. Ibid., 15.

37. Ibid., 14.

38. Ibid., 14.

39. 'Le Sinthome', in *Ornicar?* no. 9 (1977), 38.

40. See her essay on 'Epiphanies' in *JAL*, p. 87–95.

41. 'Le Sinthome', in *Ornicar?* no. 9 (1977), 38.

42. 'Le Sinthome', in *Ornicar?* no. 11 (1977), 8.

43. Jacques Lacan, 'Some reflections on the Ego', *International Journal of Pyschoanalysis*, no. 34 (1953).

44. He acknowledges this in the 16 March 1976 seminar: 'I have produced some meditations on what the English call the *ego* and what the Germans call the *Ich.*' In 'Le Sinthome', *Ornicar?* no. 9, 34.

45. James Joyce, *A Portait of the Artist as a Young Man*, ed. S. Deane (New York: Penguin, 1992), 87.

46. Ibid., 98–9.

47. 'Le Sinthome' in *Ornicar?*, no. 11, (1977), 8.

48. Ezra Pound, *The Cantos* (London: Faber, 1986), 472.

49. *Joyce & Paris*, Jacques Aubert (eds), (Lille and Paris: CNRS, 1979).

50. Nestor Braunstein was the first Lacanian analyst to take the 'return of the ego' in Lacan's seminar with the theorteical seriousness it deserves. See his very lucid essays: 'La clínica en el nombre propio', in Helí Morales Ascencio (ed.), *El Laberinto de las Estructuras*, (Mexico: Siglo 21. 1997), 70–96 and 'El ego lacaniano', in Helí Morales and Daniel Gerber *En Las Suplencias del Nombre del Padre* (Mexico: Siglo 21, 1998), 53–74.

51. *Ornicar?* no. 11 (1977), 2.

52. Jacques Lacan, *Seminar XX*, 37 (translation modified) .

53. Jacques Derrida, *Edmund Husserl's Origin of Geometry: An Introduction*, transl. J. P. Leavey (Stony Brook: Nicholas Hays, 1978), 102.

54. Ibid., 102.

55. 'Le Sinthome' in *Ornicar?* no. 11, (1977), 3.

56. Ibid., 5.

57. 'Le Sinthome', in *Ornicar?* no. 8, (1976), 6.

58. Ibid., 9.

59. Ibid., 11.

60. 'Le Sinthome', in *Ornicar?*, no. 10, (1977), 10.

61. Jacques Lacan, '*Ecrits Inspirés*', in *De La Psychose paranoïaque dans ses rapports avec la personnalité, suivi de Premiers écrits sur la Paranoia* (Paris: Seuil, 1975), 379–80.

62. *transition* no. 18 (Paris, 1929), 176–90.

63. See Paul Eluard and André Breton, *The Immaculate Conception*, transl. J. Graham (London: Atlas Press, 1990).

64. Stuart Gilbert, 'The Subliminal Tongue', in *transition*, no. 26 (1937), 151.

65. 'Le Sinthome', in *Ornicar?* no. 9 (1977), 38. He quotes Jacques-Alain Miller who had pointed out that Lacan had said the same about the Japanese: consequently, there would be three categories of people who were not analysable, the Japanese, the Catholics, and Joyce.
66. James Joyce, *Selected Letters*, ed. R. Ellmann (London: Faber, 1975), 22. I have developed this point in *James Joyce, Authorized Reader* (Baltimore: Johns Hopkins University Press, 1991), 28–49.

Annotated Bibliography

1 • Lacan's main works

Here I shall refer only to the seminars that have been published in French by Editions du Seuil under Jacques Alain-Miller's editorial responsibility. Marcelle Marini's *Jacques Lacan, The French Context* (translated by Anne Tomiche, New Brunswick: Rutgers University Press, 1992) contains a very reliable and systematic description of all of Lacan's writings.

Ecrits: A Selection, transl. Alan Sheridan. New York: Norton, 1977; *Ecrits.* Paris: Seuil, 1966.

As this is Lacan's major anthology, it is crucial to begin with it. Note that the translation by Alan Sheridan only includes about one third of the French edition, and that it is frequently marred by severe misunderstandings that complicate an already tricky text. In a chapter entitled 'The Ecrits: Portrait of an editor', Elisabeth Roudinesco (*Jacques Lacan,* transl. Barbara Bray, New York: Columbia, 1997, 318–31) describes how François Wahl was instrumental in forcing a reluctant Lacan to publish this collection, and how it took them three years to bring the initial concept to completion. Lacan's major 'written' text will no doubt emerge more distinctly with the forthcoming translation of the complete *Ecrits* by Bruce Fink. As it is, the book contains two of Lacan's best-known essays, 'The function and field of speech and language in psychoanalysis' and 'The agency of the letter in the Unconscious or reason since Freud'. I recommend the commentary by John Muller and William Richardson (*Lacan and Language: A Reader's Guide to Ecrits,* Madison: International Universities Press, 1982); it is detailed, precise, informed and extremely helpful – it has even been translated into French, which is a sign that it fulfils a necessary function. In the current translation the architecture of the collection is upset by the absence of the essay on Poe that introduced the

French collection, the omission of all the philosophical pieces on Hegel, truth and negation, the absence of fundamental essays such as the 'Kant with Sade' piece, and above all, the omission of the highly dialogical introductions and transitions added by Lacan in 1966 when he revised his earlier texts, such as the important essay 'Logical Time'.

Seminar I, Freud's Papers on Technique (1953–54), transl. John Forrester. New York: Norton, 1998; Paris: Seuil, 1975.

The first public seminar at Sainte-Anne bristles with original insights and dialogues with important interlocutors: Hyppolite (on Hegel's theory of language) Anzieu, Mannoni, Granoff, Leclaire, Beirnaert. Rosine Lefort present a case study, calling up Freud's Wolfman case. Lacan introduces his own theory of Narcissism with a first optical scheme, engages in a protracted debate with Michael Balint and weighs the merits of Anna Freud versus Melanie Klein. The cover blurb alludes to the Zen master's unconventional (and antisystematic) pedagogy, thus launching the identification of Lacan with a Dadaist Zen master that later dominated the American reception of Lacanian ideas for a few years.

Seminar II, The Ego in Freud's Theory and in the technique of Psychoanalysis (1954–55), transl. S. Tomaselli and J. Forrester. New York: Norton, 1998; Paris: Seuil, 1978.

This seminar hinges on the notion, launched in the previous seminar, that the ego cannot be confused with the subject. After a series of discussions opposing Freud and Hegel, the seminar climaxes with a dazzling interpretation of Freud's 'Dream of Irma'. Lacan reads Poe's 'Purloined Letter' and then elaborates his 'L scheme' with the first articulation of the three registers: the Real, the Imaginary and the Symbolic. As if to stress the automatic dimension of the Symbolic, Lacan concludes with a surprising lecture on cybernetics. The numerous objections of his audience throughout force him to delineate more forcefully the limits of the three registers.

Seminar III, Psychoses (1955–56), transl. Russell Grigg. New York: Norton, 1993; Paris: Seuil, 1981.

Starting with the Schreber case, Lacan implicitly returns to his 1932 thesis and gives paranoia a more rigorous treatment. After a careful reading of Freud's case and of Schreber's *Memoirs*, he hits upon the concept he lacked in the 1930s: that of foreclosure (*Verwerfung*) coupled with the theory of an unconscious writing he discovers in Freud's Letter 52. The seminar then moves on to tackle the issue of hysteria and the question 'What is a woman?', before concluding with a discussion of the signifier (it does not 'mean' anything) and a fully elaborated opposition between metaphor and metonymy – in short, disclosing the whole rhetoric of the Unconscious. What had been foreclosed in Schreber, and had generated his psychosis, was the paternal metaphor. Jean Delay, the author of the Gide psychobiography, also invites Lacan to speak on 'Freud in the century' and Lacan, who starts by noting that Freud's name means 'joy', gives the students in psychiatry a good hint: they must always read as much Freud as all the other authors on their syllabus, the difference will be immediately obvious, and in this way they will learn to reject the usual egological distortions of psychoanalytic theory.

Seminar IV, Object Relations and Freudian Structures (1956–57). Paris: Seuil, 1994.

One of the most detailed and productive seminars for clinical issues. The phallus and castration are the main concepts, especially when Lacan defines the 'imaginary triad' as composed of the mother, the phallus and the child' and distinguishes castration as the lack of an imaginary object, frustration as the lack of a real object, and deprivation as the lack of a symbolic object. He devotes illuminating pages to Freud on fetishism, phobia, feminine homosexuality and perverse fantasies in 'A Child is being Beaten'. Finally, an almost exhaustive analysis of 'Little Hans' takes up two hundred pages before concluding a very rich seminar with Leonardo's case. We see all the implications of the logic of the phallus as a concept with which Lacan starts to reread Freud's major works with increased impetus and sophistication.

Seminar V, The Formations of the Unconscious (1957–58). Paris: Seuil, 1998.

Lacan goes on reading Freud and starts from the *Witz* book to provide a structure of jokes that allows him to build stage by stage the complex scheme of desire that will resurface in 'Subversion of the subject and dialectics of desire' (1966). From the restoration of the paternal metaphor to the father's prohibition of the mother's body, the child has to learn the dialectics of the phallus: it hinges either on the question 'to be or not to be (the phallus)', or on 'to have or not have (the phallus)'. Molière's comedies (especially *L'Ecole des Femmes*), Jean Genet's *Balcony* and Gide's personal case meet on the ground of the comic appearance of the phallic object when it has replaced desire, or when it has embodied a fetishistic desire (as may be the case for a mother facing her son). This seminar, full of clever technical insights on the treatment of children, is also quite problematic in its new developments, looking at times like a phallocentric, conservative, almost Catholic repositioning of psychoanalysis.

Seminar VII, The Ethics of Psychoanalysis (1959–60), transl. Dennis Porter. New York: Norton, 1992; Paris: Seuil, 1986.

Probably Lacan's richest and most 'seminal' seminar, it is a seminar whose publication Lacan contemplated early on and then refused, for political as well as theoretical reasons, as he explains in Seminar XX (pp. 1 and 52–3). After introducing the concept of the Thing following a patient reading of Freud's *Entwurf*, Lacan then discusses sublimation, opposes Kant and Sade, returns to Klein's object, points out the limits of the moral law, and then launches into a brilliant discussion of *Antigone*, essentially characterised by a blinding beauty that can arrest desire between two deaths. He also provides a theory of courtly love, so as to confirm the aporia of sublimation facing the Thing; an important literary genre, if not the whole of literature, is founded on such an impossibility. Lacan concludes with the paradoxes of ethics, condensed in the pithy formula: 'One should never yield (or give up) on one's Desire'.

Seminar VIII, On Transference (1960–61). Paris: Seuil, 1991.

Two main parts balance this seminar: a systematic reading of Plato's *Symposium*; and a very exhaustive interpretation of Claudel's historical trilogy. Plato's dialogue allows Lacan to define 'transference love' as the main technical tool of psychoanalysis: Socrates's hidden secret, his *agalma*, forbidden object of desire for Alcibiades, anticipates on the dialectics of *objet petit a* as cause of desire. Since love and desire are closely articulated in this elaborate discussion, Claudel's plays provide another sense of transference, closer to the idea of a 'transmission' of desire down several generations. While Plato leaves us the emblematic figure of a Socrates who does not write and knows that he knows nothing, except love and *erotika*, thus perhaps 'inventing' psychoanalysis, Claudel's religious angle on the history of modernity accompanies this insight with another perspective: it is through the 'humiliation' of a perverse and 'real' father that one is forced to take symbolic paternity into consideration, even if this jars with a desire (both erotic and sublimated) that remains alive on the side of femininity.

Seminar XI, The Four Fundamental Concepts of Psychoanalysis (1964), transl. Alan Sheridan. New York: Norton, 1978; Paris: Seuil, 1973.

Best known for the discussion of the eye and the gaze, a detour and unexpected addition triggered by the publication of Merleau-Ponty's *The Visible and the Invisible* while Lacan was presenting other main concepts: the Unconscious, repetition, transference, the drive. This was the first open seminar at the Ecole Normale Supérieure, and it was logically the first seminar to be published, proving its centrality among the seminars and reaching a foundational status. Here Lacan's style becomes more difficult, even opaque at times, as he engages with complex notions: the gap opened by the Freudian unconscious for the 'subject of certainty'; the gods who belong to the Real; the *tuché* found in propitious repetition; the split between the eye and the gaze and the identification of the gaze with the *objet a*; the role of anamorphosis to show the Thing; the incompatibility between the subject of enunciation and the subject of the statement, generating one of the many serial rewordings of the Cartesian *ego cogito*; the construction of the circuit of the drive as always missing a vanishing object; alienation and aphanisis of the subject; the myth of the lamella and love; and the subject supposed to know, when knowledge is finally opposed to truth. In this multiplicity of new concepts and models, Lacan shows a renewed theoretical fecundity and begins to speak and think in his own idiom.

Seminar XVII, The Reverse of Psychoanalysis (1969–70). Paris: Seuil, 1991.

This is Lacan's most political seminar: it begins in the atmosphere of student unrest just after May 1968 ('contestation' was the current word, and did not spare Lacan, who reacted with customary aplomb and even savage wit in verbal skirmishes during the inauguration of the department of Psychoanalysis at Vincennes). Here one finds the most complete exposition of the theory of the four discourses and their various applications to culture, everyday life, psychoanalysis, gender and class. Knowledge and truth fight for supremacy in a seminar that is not completely under the shadow of Marx (strongly influenced by an always cynical Kojève), since among other things it contains a very stimulating discussion of Freud's sources for the murder of Moses. Thus Sellin's essay on Moses is presented in a fascinating critical review by Professor Caquot, a specialist of religious studies. The mythical murder of the father is still very much at the core of the four discourses.

Seminar XX, Encore (1972–73), translated as *On Feminine Sexuality, The Limits of Love and Knowledge 1972–73* by Bruce Fink. New York: Norton, 1998; Paris: Seuil, 1975.

This was the second seminar to be published, just two years after its completion, which was quite a record! After *Ecrits*, this is one of the most influential texts by Lacan. He clearly aims at taking a position on the crucial issue of gender in the face of growing feminist dissatisfaction with Freud and his own alleged phallocentrism. The Derridian camp is both acknowledged and rebuffed with an ambivalent praise for *The Title of the Letter* by Lacoue-Labarthe and Nancy. Lacan invents the concept of 'formulas of sexuation' in a spirited discussion of sexual difference, opposing the male side of sexuation to the female side in a little grid (p. 78):

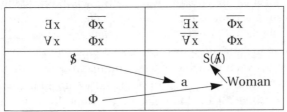

This means that the male side is inscribed under the heading 'castration' – the negation of the phallic function, while the barred Woman can choose to be the 'not whole' or 'not all', using a double negation to escape from a determination by castration. 'Her' side points to a barred Other with strong affinities with the mystical view of a *jouissance* of God. Universality is achieved through the phallic mode of negation (castration), while women are just plural and not universal.

Men can also decide to inscribe themselves under the feminine 'not all'. This is an often baffling seminar, full of wild puns and improvisations, very hard to translate. Lacan also meets the Borromean knot, and seems to find in it endless delights and the solution to the main riddles of writing.

Mitchell and Rose (eds), *Feminine Sexuality, Jacques Lacan and the école freudienne*, transl. J. Rose. New York: Norton, 1985.

Included in this excellent anthology is the central session of Seminar XX, presenting the formulas of sexuation, plus the main texts by Lacan that work with notions of sexual difference and the phallus. A very useful double introduction by the editors assesses Lacan's differences and convergences with feminist theory. The clearest exposition of Lacan's concept of the phallus.

Television; A Challenge to the Psychoanalytic Establishment edited by Joan Copjec, transl. D. Hollier, R. Krauss and A. Michelson. New York: Norton, 1990.

This wonderful little book puts together Lacan's *Television* (Paris: Seuil, 1974), the main pieces of the institutional debate that led to Lacan's struggle against the International Psychoanalytic Association and the foundation of his school, and a few well chosen texts, such as the introduction to the aborted 'Names-of-the-Father Seminar' during the 1963 crisis, the tense and hilarious discussion with leftist students at Vincennes, and the famous 'Letter of Dissolution' by which Lacan announced the end of the Ecole de Paris before launching the Ecole de la Cause Freudienne. *Television* (an actual television broadcast made and aired in 1973) is a stylistic *tour de force*, showing a dialogue between a visible master and his invisible disciple whose eager questions on all manner of broad topics (including What can I know? What ought I to do? What may I hope for?) determine the progression of the interview. Lacan decides not to compromise with a supposedly mainstream audience, and jumps from one brilliant paradox to the next. He begins famously and abruptly with: 'I always speak the truth. Not the whole truth, because there's no way, to say it all. Saying it all is literally impossible: words fail. Yet it's through this very impossibility that the truth holds onto the real' (p. 3), and ends with a cryptic riddle that sounds like a Joycean tongue-twister: '– between that which perdures through pure dross, and the hand that draws only from Dad to worse' (*De ce qui perdure de perte pure à ce qui ne parie que du père au pire*) (p. 46). But in between we have been warned to be patient: 'Ten years is enough for everything I write to become clear to everyone'. (p. 45). Jacques-Alain Miller's marginal annotations, bridging the gap between his initial questions and a rereading of the answers, either by way of mathemes or through quotes from Lacan's canon, not so much 'unpack' the text as make it rebound on itself, thus contributing to an atmosphere of dense self-referentiality.

2 • Critical approaches: a selection

Louis Althusser, *Writings on Psychoanalysis: Freud and Lacan*, transl. Jeffrey Mehlman. New York: Columbia University Press, 1996.

The best starting point to follow Lacan's flirtation with a Marxism that was relatively new and foreign to him, and the best collection of essays to assess the convergence and divergence with Althusser. Roudinesco's biography quotes Althusser as relishing the 'splendidly wicked wit' and 'intellectual terrorism' of a 'former Surrealist' master who would speak above the head of an audience that could not follow him (Roudinesco, *Jacques Lacan*, p. 304, see below). As she explains, this was precisely the situation that Althusser wished to change, and he was finally successful in this endeavour when Lacan moved onto the Ecole Normale Supérieure and had to adapt his discourse to an audience of young and brilliant philosophers who were reading not only Hegel and Heidegger but also Foucault, Frege, Gödel and Mao. If the correspondence with Lacan proves somewhat disappointing, or at least rather frustrating for Althusser, his personal involvement at the time of the dissolution of the school by Lacan is fascinating.

Mikkel Borch-Jacobsen, *Lacan, The Absolute Master*, transl. Douglas Brick. Stanford: Stanford University Press, 1991.

An excellent introduction to the main aspects of Lacan's earlier system, with stress on the Hegelian derivation in Lacan's thought. Borch-Jacobsen's astute philosophical sense and dialectical training make him reconstruct the logical steps leading from the mirror stage to the Symbolic and the linguistics of the signifier in the 1950s and 1960s. Besides exaggerating Lacan's affiliation with Kojève, the main limitation of the project is that it stops somewhat early in Lacan's conceptualisation, not really noticing the new departure implied by the stress on the Real, the Symptom, the Borromean knot and the *jouissance* of the Other.

Malcolm Bowie, *Freud, Proust and Lacan: Theory as Fiction.* Cambridge: Cambridge University Press, 1987.

This book is unrivalled in its analysis of Lacan's style, his literary models and his links with a very literary Freud. Bowie, who has since written an excellent short introduction to Lacan (*Jacques Lacan*, London: Fontana, 1991) shows all the literary talent and culture indispensable for such a task. He makes full sense of the hermeneutic and rhetorical strategies used by Lacan when rereading Freud. The comparison between Lacan's style and the French moralists, with hints at Pascal and Baltasar Gracian, are illuminating. Finally, an insightful parallel connects Proust, Freud and Lacan: all three are masters of language, and all three are possessed by the fiercest *libido sciendi* – an irrepressible compulsion to know, to forge or force theories on reality. Even if *Ecrits* does not exactly read like *Remembrance of Things Past*, its impact on literature and culture may prove as groundbreaking.

Joan Copjec, *Read my Desire: Jacques Lacan against the Historicists.* Cambridge, Mass.: MIT Press, 1994.

One of Copjec's best known books, this has the merit of squarely tackling the reproach of antihistoricism often voiced against Lacanian theory in the name of Foucault. Copjec uses a variety of strategies (she reads films noirs such as *Double Indemnity*, some vampire films, de Clérambault's photographs of exotically veiled and draped women and a few philosophical texts) to show the importance of Lacanian formulas in the field of sexuation and of cultural critique, and to stress Lacan's political relevance. She points out that a Foucauldian critique that remains blind to the effects of perverse enjoyment and the production of desire is not only reductive but also deceptive in its bandying around the master signifier of 'power'. Finally, Lacan's cultural critique appears to be capable not only of thinking history but also of historicising itself.

Robert Con Davis (ed), *Lacan and Narration. The Psychoanalytic Difference in Narrative Theory*. Baltimore: Johns Hopkins Press, 1983.

An early but extremely solid collection of articles dealing with the issue of narration, showing how narratology had to change so as to absorb the pressure exerted by the Lacanian probematisation of textual issues. Régis Durand makes sense of the important concept of 'aphanisis', borrowed from Jones by Lacan to point to subjective disappearance; Ronald Schleifer situates Lacan next to the work of Greimas; Jerry Aline Flieger provides an important assessment of the role of jokes; Shoshana Felman investigates 'Psychoanalysis at Colonus' and the Oedipian paradigms; and Beryl Schlossman, Juliet Flower MacCannell and Jeffrey Mehlman exploit Lacanian approaches to individual corpuses (mostly 'couples', with Montaigne and La Boétie, Stendhal and Girard, Proust and Benoist-Méchin). The book contains a very comprehensive bibliography.

Dylan Evans, *An Introductory Dictionary of Lacanian Psychoanalysis* . New York: Routledge, 1996.

As the author explains, rather than a real dictionary, this is an introductory reference book, modelled on the famous *Vocabulaire de la Psychanalyse* (1971), coauthored by Jean Laplanche and Jean-Baptiste Pontalis (*The Language of Psycho-Analysis*; transl. D. Nicholson Smith, London: Hogarth Press, 1973), a book that proved extremely influential in disseminating a fundamentally Lacanian reading of Freud's main concepts. Almost two hundred terms are listed, most of them Lacanian, some still quite Freudian, and they vary in degree of complexity, some being quite basic ('ego', 'subject', 'id') and others quite technical and complex ('*point de capiton*', '*sinthome*', 'Thing'). This is a very useful guide, clear, precise and above all historical: one can observe how Lacan continued to modify his concepts over the years, sometimes discarding a few, sometimes simply adding new layers of meaning without necessarily cancelling the older senses. '*Jouissance*' is a good example: first opposed to pleasure, then radically contradicted by desire, it has always maintained the suggestion of 'orgasm' but at first was mostly identified with phallic enjoyment, until the term later gave access to a purely feminine side of sexuation, while hinging on the *jouissance* of the Other. The systematic recapitulation of all the mathemes in the 'algebra' entry (pp. 7–9) is very useful.

Richard Feldstein and Henry Sussman (ed), *Psychoanalysis and...* New York: Routledge, 1990.

What is revealing in this fine collection of essay, is that by 1980 the name Lacan was more or less synonymous with the new in psycho-analysis. Samuel Weber focuses on the issue of authority and legacy in Lacan's archives and testament; Jane Gallop and Jerry Aline Flieger work towards a reconciliation of Lacan and feminist theory; and Ellie Ragland-Sullivan provides a very useful commentary on Lacan's Joyce seminar. Other literary applications include Henry James, Faulkner and Woolf (elaborated by Claire Kahane, Richard Feldstein and Charles Bernheimer). The high quality of these essays shows the fecundity of the intense debate in the late 1970s between Lacan and deconstruction on the one hand (evoked by Henry Sussman and Ruth Salvaggio) and Lacan and feminism on the other: Cixous and Irigaray loom large as post-Lacanian alternatives.

Shoshana Felman (ed.), *Literature and Psychoanalysis. The Question of Reading: Otherwise*. Baltimore: Johns Hopkins University Press, 1982.

This was one of the earliest (first published in 1977) anthologies in English on Lacanian approaches to literature and it has remained one of the most popular. It has the great merit of reproducing most of Lacan's *Hamlet* seminar, balanced by another neo-Lacanian approach (Daniel Sibony), and it includes Barbara Johnson's excellent piece 'The Frame of Reference: Poe, Lacan, Derrida'. Shoshana Felman's essay, 'Turning the Screw of Interpretation', is a book-length essay on James, Poe and other important issues. Finally, one rediscovers here a number of gifted writers (some of whom have since then abandoned the Lacanian field) who contributed to the introduction of these themes in English-speaking countries: Gayatri Spivak, Fredric Jameson and John Brenkman.

Sarah Harasym (ed.), *Levinas and Lacan: The Missed Encounter*. Albany: State University of New York Press, 1998.

A very challenging collection that tackles an original and delicate question: the 'missed' confrontation between two important thinkers who both use the 'big Other' as the foundation of their discourses, who both state that ethics is fundamental, and who both try to move between a 'phenomenology of Eros' bypassing Hegel's circular system and an openness to the absolute novelty of desire. To cite only a few of these exciting approaches, Tina Chanter examines the important role of Hegel for both Levinas and Lacan, Hans-Dieter Gondek analyses the role of the Cartesian *cogito* for Levinas and Lacan; Philippe Van Haute explores the concept of sublimation in a very original reading of Lacan on *Antigone*; and Drucilla Cornell tries to think the 'Beyond of the Real'. The assessment of irreducible differences between the two corpuses and approaches points to the 'wedge' role played by the Unconscious, a notion never fully acknowledged by the phenomenological tradition from which Levinas stems, while some of Lacan's philosophical short-comings or short-circuits are treated here with extreme clarity.

Philippe Lacoue-Labarthe and Jean-Luc Nancy, *The Title of the Letter: A Reading of Lacan*, transl. François Raffoul and David Pettigrew. Albany: State University of New York Press, 1992.

This wonderful short essay (perfectly translated) was written in 1973 but has not aged at all, perhaps preserved by the fascinating mixture of textual respect and philosophical suspicion evinced by the authors, a mixture well perceived by Lacan in his *Encore* seminar. Here is a very careful reading of Lacan's theory of the sign, documenting the various stages in the deconstructive process in which Lacan 'destroys the sign' so as to 'consolidate the science of the letter' (p. 39). Lacoue-Labarthe and Nancy view the algorithm signifer/signified as a diversion, almost a red herring. For them, Lacan does not so much use linguistics as rape and plunder Saussure in a creatively perverse way, disrupting the basic terms that form the basis of structuralist linguistics in order to erect his own conceptual edifice. His construction culminates on an unstable formation, caught up between a systematisation of the letter as circular agency but without a Derridian questioning of its foundation, and a Heideggerian mystique of language as word and truth, but without the implications of Heidegger's refusal to reduce truth to homologation. A very interesting introduction by the translators assesses the strong impact of this philosophical critique on Lacan himself.

James Mellard, *Using Lacan Reading Fiction*. Urbana: University of Illinois Press, 1991.

One of the most honest, straightforward and useful applications of Lacanian concepts to literature. Mellard has a disquieting tendency to rely on second-hand sources rather than on Lacan himself, but he is solid on the main theoretical points, and provides comprehensive and sharp critical reviews of immediate predecessors such as Stuart Schneiderman, Ellie Ragland-Sullivan and Peter Brooks. Mellard has the courage to express his doubts and disagreements (as early as the ironical dedication contradicting Lacan's motto that The Woman does not exist). His three literary examples – *The Scarlet Letter*, *The Beast in the Jungle* and *To the Lighthouse* – are well chosen and exploited with great gusto. Woolf's famous novel receives the most original interpretation in the name of *jouissance* and the *objet petit a*. Mellard does not avoid the danger of thematic or psychological read-ings (most of his insights are based upon character analysis), he gets lost at times in schemes that manage to become even more compli-cated than Lacan's own (p. 27), but the scholarship is sound, convinc-ing and highly relevant, as for instance when he engages, in the conclusion, with feminist critics such as Juliet Flower MacCannell and Christine Van Boheemen-Saaf.

Dany Nobus (ed.), *Key Concepts of Lacanian Psychoanalysis*. New York: Other Press, 1999.

A very competent presentation by excellent specialists in some of Lacan's trickiest concepts: *jouissance* (Dylan Evans), the four discourses (Bruce Fink), foreclosure (Russell Grigg), the desire of the analyst (Katrien Libbrecht), the mirror stage (Dany Nobus), the Borromean knot (Luke Thurston), the subject (Paul Verhaeghe) and fantasy (Slavoj Zizek). In these extremely well-documented and dense essays, packed with insights and bibliographical gems, all the authors have managed to avoid jargon, adopt a sound historical approach and remain clear and lucid: in short, this is an indispensable guide that can function as an introduction to Lacanian issues that really matter today.

David Pettigrew and François Raffoul (ed.), *Disseminating Lacan.* Albany: State University of New York Press, 1996.

A very comprehensive collection of recent essays on most of the current Lacanian issues: philosophy (with a brilliant contribution on Lacan and Merleau-Ponty by James Phillips), science (with good essays by Judith Feher-Gurewich on social theory and Joel Dor on the epistemological status of Lacan's mathematical paradigms') and literature (with William Richardson's useful summary of the issues at stake in Lacan's Claudel commentary, Pettigrew's definition of a generalised 'poetic unconscious', and Cora Monne on Lamartine's *Jocelyn*). This is a high-voltage collection that moves in many new directions and dimensions – including some interestingly critical remarks by Borch-Jacobsen on the Oedipus problems in Freud and Lacan: the author tries to show that when Lacan historicised the Oedipus pattern it was because he wanted to solve the problem by eliminating it altogether.

Ellie Ragland-Sullivan, *Jacques Lacan and the Philosophy of Psychoanalysis.* Urbana: University of Illinois Press, 1986.

A groundbreaking and massive synthesis on Lacan that indelibly marked the reception of Lacan in the United States. Lacan's thought is considered as a logically complete system but the wish to gloss over discrepancies and breaks leads at times to myopia and at times to theoretical overingenuity. The chapter on the 'I' versus the 'ego' is excellent – the four fundamental concepts are competently introduced and the three registers of the Real, the Symbolic and the Imaginary are well positioned. This book has the merit of treating Seminar XX seriously, leading to a good discussion of the formulas of sexuation in the last chapter. Paradoxically, nothing is said about the Borromean knot (one is reproduced on page 260 without being named) or the four discourses. It is rigorously contemporary and homologous with a book on Derrida that also oversystematises a way of thinking that seems more productive when approached through internal contradictions, jumps and hesitations: Rodolphe Gasché's *The Tain of the Mirror: Derrida and the Philosophy of Reflection* (Cambridge, Mass.: Harvard University Press, 1986).

Ellie Ragland-Sullivan and Mark Bracher (ed.), *Lacan and the Subject of Language*. New York: Routledge, 1991.

This is by far the best available selection in English on the topic, and I recommend very highly all the essays in the last section on literature. Colette Soler's 'Literature as Symptom' is worth quoting. She explains quite rightly that Lacan 'reverses Freud's position' on literature, insisting that it is not 'that the written text must be psychoanalyzed: rather, it is that the psychoanalyst must be well read' (pp. 213–14). There can be no 'applied psychoanalysis' because works of art are not direct emanations of the Unconscious. They resist interpretation as much as they lend themselves to it. However, for Lacan, literature yields a number of double names or conceptual couples: 'Hamlet, desire', 'Antigone, beauty', 'Poe, the letter', 'Joyce, the symptom'. Soler's remarks on the symptom that creates the singularity of the subject and the function of a *jouissance* outside meaning are excellent. Likewise the essays by Judith Miller on Lacan's concept of 'style', Stuart Schneiderman on Poe, Lila Kalinich on the Wolfman (the best Lacanian reply to Abraham and Torok about the Wolfman's vocabulary) and Slavoj Zizek on truth, the Real and the Symptom provide the best possible introduction to current issues in literature. Quite a breath of fresh air after so many dichotomies of signifier/signified coupled with metaphor/metonymy grinding slowly and systematically through canonical texts.

Julia Reinhard Lupton and Kenneth Reinhard, *After Oedipus: Shakespeare in Psychoanalysis*. Ithaca: Cornell University Press, 1993.

The title of this excellent book is a little misleading in that it aims at moving away from a purely Freudian interpretation of Shakespeare (it starts with 'The motif of the three caskets') to a Lacanian one. What is highly original is the confrontation between Lacan's main notions (not limited to the ethics seminar) and Walter Benjamin's *Trauerspiel*. The focus is almost exclusively on *Hamlet* and *King Lear*, which they approach both competently as literary scholars (using an abundant documentation, going back to Sophocles and Seneca, for instance) and with a real dialectical sense that makes Lacanian concepts come alive when they seize new textual problems. The authors make good use of Lacan's schemes, which they illuminate retroactively, and provide a lasting reappraisal of the Shakespearean intertext in Lacan.

Elisabeth Roudinesco, *Jacques Lacan*, transl. Barbara Bray. New York: Columbia University Press, 1997.

This biography by a renowned specialist in the history of psycho-analysis in France was greeted with passion when it was published, leading French reviewers to ask: 'Should one burn Lacan?' This book is indispensable if one wants to understand the cultural phenomenon of Lacanism in its local and universal dimensions. It is less a collec-tion of juicy anecdotes than a serious and historical approach to Lacan's cultural revolution, understood historically, as a type of new counter-power linked with an archive in the making. The elements likely to create controversy concern the Lacanian legacy, fraught as it is with political, institutional and personal problems. Roudinesco examines very critically the official version handed down by Lacan's son-in-law and literary executor and does not hesitate to show the darker side of Lacan (in his dealings with his first wife and their chil-dren, for instance). She also questions the authenticity of crucial texts such as the notorious open letter by which Lacan announced the 'dissolution' of his school. She has strong opinions on clinical issues, and reconstructs the personal and institutional logic that led Lacan to adopt the 'variable session' as a new tool (this led to his exclusion from the International Psychoanalytical Association), a bold but defensible practice later perverted when it resulted in sessions that lasted only five minutes or just a few seconds. Besides being a histo-rian, she is also a psychoanalyst and denounces what she sees as a travesty of psychoanalytic practice, attacking as much the excesses of Lacan's later years (although, by then, being analysed by him amounted to a status symbol) as the undiscriminating reverence of disciples who reproduced the worst aspects of their master's example. But she does justice to Lacan's genius: Lacan made history by a radical rethinking of psychoanalysis that can only be understood well when situated in the European intellectual climate of the times. The care with which Roudinesco follows the genesis of the 'Aimée' and the redaction of Lacan's groundbreaking thesis on paranoia, and the patience she shows when she unravels all the intricacies of Lacan's life-long flirtation with philosophy, from Spinoza to Hegel and then Heidegger, prove that it was indeed high time to assess Lacan's works and cultural impact critically, rigorously and historically.

Ben Stoltzfus, *Lacan and Literature: Purloined Pretexts*. Albany: State University of New York Press, 1996.

This is a very typical example of informed and astute Freudian criticism disguised as Lacanian discourse. The readings of D. H. Lawrence, Hemingway, Camus and Robbe-Grillet are solid, but they 'work' along very classical Freudian axes, with the usual problematics hinging on Oedipal desire, castration, bliss and fantasy, all based upon character analysis. Lacan serves a merely decorative function here, so as to update the critical discourse, and Derrida is invoked in the same way. Rare theoretical asides, alas, reveal a profound misreading of Lacan's most basic concepts. For instance the couple S1 and S2: in a reading of Hemingway's *The Garden of Eden*, a discussion of David's use of the French '*la mer*' produces a graph in which S1 is the first signifier: *la mer*, whose signified is 'the sea', and S2 is called the repressed 'referent': *la mère* (the mother) (pp. 97 and 99) – whereas it is quite obvious that for Lacan there would be only one signifier in this case, namely something like '*lamer,*' whose fundamental polysemy would then create effects along the signifying chain. The main thesis underlying all readings is that writing repeats past traumas, reenacting fantasies that may not have taken place at all (p. 95) – a notion that is indisputable but one hundred per cent Freudian! Much less Freudian is the remark that the dream is a purely 'iconic, masked mirror of the unconscious' and faces its 'linguistic reflector' provided by fiction (p. 2). There is also the very naive idea that as more and more canonical literature has been 'done' (that is, perhaps, been read to death) by psychoanalytic approaches, newcomers have been left with a shrinking field. For those who might worry, just check, the list (a conservative one, if I may say) is provided on page 5. However one should not be too severe: the subtitle has already excused itself and confessed to a 'purloined theory' playing a simple function of 'pretext'.

Slavoj Zizek, *Enjoy Your Symptom! Jacques Lacan in Hollywood and out*. New York: Routledge, 1992.

Slavoj Zizek is often referred to as a 'phenomenon', which may have something to do with his professional training as a philosopher, specialising in Kant, Hegel and the German Romantics. Or it may have to do with his style, which is fast, funny, infectious and dynamic: Lacan becomes an MTV star, the King (yes, capitalised, like Stephen of the same name) of the sexy sound-bite, a maniacal French rapper whose lilting aphorisms spread around like subway graffiti or a Gallic alphabet soup full of bad puns, and whose mathemes turn into as many sophisticated sleek tools, from electrical can openers to power drills and video games playing with popular culture. But let us not grudge our pleasure or mix our metaphors: Zizek seduces, but he also explains. He is at times, it is true, the Lacanian who explains too much (does this sound like a Hitchcock title?). But isn't there *always* an answer in Lacan? The real problem is not the answer, for there are too many answers, it is: what's the question?

Slavoj Zizek, *Looking Awry: An Introduction to Jacques Lacan through Popular Culture.* Cambridge, Mass.: MIT Press, 1991.

This is Zizek's most stylish book, the best written perhaps, and the fastest. It is a wonderful introduction to Lacan and often seduces students who would never dream of opening *Ecrits* or even glancing at ... (here, choose one of the previous items in the list). It has a rigorous progression, starting off *in medias res* with Zeno's paradox as an image of the unattainable *objet a*, moving into the domain of fantasy with discussions of the Real and the Thing through science-fiction stories and horror movies. The second section is devoted to Hitchcock and capitalises on a few Lacanian paradoxes: the 'non dupes' err, the gaze is a stain, anamorphosis provides the truth of painting and film, while *The Birds* embody more than allegories of the castrating mother – it is an issue of beaks versus eyes. The third part reaches new heights with considerations of modernism and post-modernism, obscenity and pornography, bureaucracy and enjoyment, the nation and the Other. The pages devoted to the *Sinthome* are brilliant. It is a brilliant book. And it contains much, much more.

3 • Further readings

This list is limited to important books on Lacan or on Lacanian approaches to literature available in English. The reader should also consult the incredibly exhaustive bibliography provided by Michael Clark in *Jacques Lacan: An Annotated Bibliography* (New York: Garland, 1998, 2 vols). This is critical bibliography at its best, and can be read for its own sake, especially if one wishes to follow Lacan's intellectual progression. The reader can also consult the standard bibliography by Joël Dor, *Bibliographie des Travaux de Jacques Lacan* (Paris: InterEditions, 1983), supplemented by Joël Dor, *Thésaurus Lacan: Nouvelle Bibliographie des Travaux de Jacques Lacan* (Paris: EPEL, 1994, 2 vols). There is also an excellent bibliography at the end of Dylan Evans' *An Introductory Dictionary of Lacanian Psychoanalysis* (New York: Routledge, pp. 225–36).

Benvenuto, Bice and Roger Kennedy, *The Works of Jacques Lacan: An Introduction*. London: Free Association Books, 1986.

Benvenuto, Bice, *Concerning the Rites of Psychoanalysis, or The Villa of the Mysteries*. Cambridge: Polity Press, 1994.

Boheemen-Saaf, Christine van, *The Novel as Family Romance*. Ithaca: Cornell University press, 1987.

Boheemen-Saaf, Christine van, *Joyce, Derrida, Lacan and the Trauma of History*. Cambridge: Cambridge University Press, 1999.

Bouveresse, Jacques, *Wittgenstein Reads Freud: The Myth of the Unconscious*, transl. C. Cosman. Princeton: Princeton University Press, 1995.

Bracher, Marc, *Lacan, Discourse and Social Change: A Psychoanalytical Cultural Criticism*. Ithaca: Cornell University Press, 1993.

Braunstein, Nestor, *La Jouissance: Un Concept lacanien*. Paris: Point Hors Ligne, 1992, forthcoming in English by Verso.

Brivic, Sheldon, *The Veil of Signs: Joyce, Lacan and Perception*. Urbana: University of Illinois Press, 1991.

Caudill, David S., *Lacan and the Subject of the Law: Toward a Psychoanalytic Critical Legal Theory*. New Jersey: Humanities Press, 1997.

Chaitin, Gilbert D., *Rhetoric and Culture in Lacan*. Cambridge: Cambridge University Press, 1996.

Clément, Catherine, *The Lives and Legends of Jacques Lacan*, transl. A. Goldhammer. New York: Columbia University Press, 1983.

Davis, Robert Con (ed.), *The Fictional Father: Lacanian Readings of the Text*. Amherst: University of Massachusetts Press, 1981.

Derrida, Jacques, *Writing and Difference*, transl. A. Bass. Chicago: University of Chicago Press, 1978.

Derrida, Jacques, *The Postcard*, transl. A. Bass. Chicago: University of Chicago Press, 1987.

Dor, Joel, *Introduction to the Reading of Lacan: The Unconscious Structured like a Language*, transl. S. Fairfield. New York: Other Press, 1999.

Dor, Joel, *The Clinical Lacan*, transl. S. Fairfield. New York: Other Press, 1999.

Ellmann, Maud (ed.), *Psychoanalytic Literary Criticism*. London: Longman, 1994.

Feher-Gurewich, Judith, and Michel Tort (eds), *The Subject and the Self: Lacan and American Psychoanalysis*. Northvale: Jason Aronson, 1996.

Feldstein, Richard, Bruce Fink and Maire Jaanus (eds), *Reading Seminar XI: Lacan's Four Fundamental Concepts of Psychoanalysis*. Albany: State University of New York Press, 1995.

Felman, Shoshana, *Jacques Lacan and the Adventure of Insight*. Cambridge, Mass.: Harvard University Press, 1987.

Fink, Bruce, *The Lacanian Subject: Between Language and Jouissance*. Princeton: Princeton University Press, 1995.

Fink, Bruce, *A Clinical Introduction to a Lacanian Psychoanalysis: Theory and Technique*. Cambridge, Mass.: Harvard University Press, 1997.

Freud, Sigmund, *The Origins of Psychoanalysis: Letters to Wilhelm Fliess, Drafts and Notes 1887–1902*, ed. Bonaparte, A. Freud and E. Kris. New York: Basic Books, 1954.

Freud, Sigmund, *Writings on Art and Literature*, ed. N. Hertz. Stanford: Stanford University Press, 1997.

Gallop, Jane, *Reading Lacan*. Ithaca: Cornell University Press, 1985.

Grosz, Elizabeth, *Jacques Lacan: A Feminist Introduction*. New York: Routledge, 1990.

Gunn, Daniel, *Psychoanalysis and Fiction*. Cambridge: Cambridge University Press, 1988.

Hartman, Geoffrey (ed.), *Psychoanalysis and the Question of the Text*. Baltimore: Johns Hopkins University Press, 1978.

Hogan, Patrick and Lalita Pandit (eds), *Criticism and Lacan: Essays and Dialogue on Language, Structure and the Unconscious*. Athens: University of Georgia Press, 1990.

Ingersoll, Earl G., *Engendered Trope in Joyce's Dubliners*. Carbondale: Southern Illinois University Press, 1996.

Julien, Philippe, *Jacques Lacan's Return to Freud: The Real, the Symbolic and the Imaginary*, transl. D. Beck Simiu. New York: New York University Press, 1994.

Leader, Darian and Judith Groves, *Lacan for Beginners*. Cambridge: Icon, 1995.

Leader, Darian, *Why Do Most Women Write More Letters Than They Post?* London: Faber, 1996.

Lechte, John (ed.), *Writing and Psychoanalysis: A Reader*. London: Arnold, 1996.

Lee, Jonathan Scott, *Jacques Lacan*. Amherst: University of Massachusetts Press, 1990.

Lemaire, Anika, *Jacques Lacan*, transl. D. Macey. London: Routledge, 1979.

Leonard, Garry M., *Reading Dubliners Again: A Lacanian Perspective*. Syracuse: Syracuse University Press, 1993.

MacCannell, Juliet Flower, *Figuring Lacan: Criticism and the Cultural Unconscious*. Lincoln: University of Nebraska Press, 1986.

Macey, David, *Lacan in Contexts*. London: Verso, 1988.

Marini, Marcelle, *Jacques Lacan, The French Context*, transl. A. Tomiche. New Brunswick: Rutgers University Press, 1992.

Muller, John P. and William J. Richardson, *Lacan and Language: A Reader's Guide to Ecrits*. New York: International Universities Press, 1982.

Muller, John P. and William J. Richardson (eds), *The Purloined Poe: Lacan, Derrida and Psychoanalytic Reading*. Baltimore: Johns Hopkins University Press, 1988.

Rabaté, Jean-Michel (ed.), *Lacan in America*. New York: Other Press, 2000.

Rose, Jacqueline, *Sexuality in the Field of Vision*. London: Verso, 1996.

Roustang, François, *The Lacanian Delusion*, transl. G. Sims. Oxford: Oxford University Press, 1990.

Samuels, Robert, *Between Philosophy and Psychoanalysis: Lacan's Reconstruction of Freud*. New York: Routledge, 1993.

Sarup, Madan, *Jacques Lacan*. Hemel Hempstead: Harvester, 1992.

Schneiderman, Stuart (ed.), *Returning to Freud: Clinical Psychoanalysis in the School of Lacan*. New Haven: Yale University Press, 1980.

Schneiderman, Stuart, *Jacques Lacan. The Death of an Intellectual Hero*. Cambridge, Mass.: Harvard University Press, 1983.

Shepherdson, Charles, *Vital Signs: Nature, Culture, Psychoanalysis*. New York: Routledge, 2000.

Smith, Joseph H. and William Kerrigan (eds), *Taking Chances:*

Derrida, Psychoanalysis and Literature. Baltimore: Johns Hopkins University Press, 1987.

Turkle, Sherry, *Psychoanalytic Politics: Freud's French Revolution.* New York: Basic Books, 1978.

Verhaeghe, Paul, *Does the Woman exist? From Freud's Hysteric to Lacan's Feminine,* transl. M. du Ry. New York: Other Press, 1999.

Weber, Samuel, *Return to Freud: Jacques Lacan's Dislocation of Psychoanalysis,* transl. M. Levine. Cambridge: Cambridge University Press, 1991.

Wilden, Anthony (ed.), *The Language of the Self: The Function of Language in Psychoanalysis.* Baltimore: Johns Hopkins University Press, 1968.

Williams, Linda Ruth, *Critical Desire: Psychoanalysis and the Literary Subject.* London: Edward Arnold, 1995.

Wright, Elizabeth, *Psychoanalytic Criticism: Theory to Practice.* New York: Routledge, 1985.

Wright, Elizabeth, *Psychoanalytic Criticism: A Reappraisal.* New York: Routledge, 1998).

Wyschogrod, Edith, David Crownfield and Carl A. Raschke (eds), *Lacan and Theological Discourse.* Albany: State University of New York Press, 1989.

Index

Abraham, N.   214
Adams, R.M.   168–9
Adorno, T.W.   93, 102–3, 105, 112, 192
Alcibiades   141, 143, 145–7, 152, 202
Allais, A.   56
Allouch, J.   115
Althusser, L.   14, 19–21, 28, 52, 135, 187, 207
Anzieu, D.   134, 201
Anzieu, M. ('Aimée')   2, 133–4
Aquinas   18, 155, 161
Aristophanes   13, 140, 142–4
Aristotle   5, 74, 77, 80
Artaud, A.   1
Aubert, J.   157–60, 172, 173, 178, 197

Badiou, A.   135, 137–9, 195
Balint, M.   201
Balzac, H. de   39
Barnes, D.   117
Barthelme, D.   154
Barthes, R.   12, 34
Bataille, G.   14, 15, 67, 109
Baudelaire, C.   43–4, 48
Beauvoir, S. de   85, 192
Beckett, S.   86, 138, 188
Beirnaert, L.   201
Benjamin, W.   190, 214
Benoist-Méchin, J.   209
Bernays, M.   113
Bernheimer, C.   210
Bion, W. R.   15
Blake, W.   37
Blanchot, M.   85, 109, 125, 192
Blavatsky, H. P.   162
Boehme, J.   97
Bolack, J.   83, 191

Bonaparte, M.   42–5, 48–9, 189
Borch-Jacobsen, M.   16,   187, 207–8, 213
Boswell, J.   36
Bourdieu, P.   23
Bowie, M.   1, 208
Bracher, M.   197
Brantôme, P. de   132
Braunstein, N.   27, 106, 174, 177, 187, 198
Brenkman, J.   210
Breton, A.   178, 198
Buffon, G. L. L.   184
Butler, J.   26

Camus, A.   59, 216
Caquot, A.   205
Carco, F.   172
Carpaccio, V.   93
Cavell, S.   190
Chanter, T.   211
Chomsky, N.   165
Cixous, H.   117, 210
Clark, M.   217
Claudel, P.   5, 12, 13, 17, 135, 147–51, 196, 203–4, 213
Clérambault, G. de   208
Coleridge, S. T.   59, 63
Copjec, J.   11, 206, 208
Cornell, D.   211
Crébillon, C. P. J. de   49, 53

Dali, S.   184
Dante, A.   2, 5, 177
David-Ménard, M.   85, 102, 110, 191–3
Davis, R. C.   209
Dean, J.   141
Delay, J.   35–8, 188, 202

Deleuze, G.   87
d'Eon, Chevalier   47
Depardieu, G.   124
Derrida, J.   6, 9, 13, 16, 21, 28, 31,
    44, 49–53, 139, 147, 176–7, 181,
    186, 188, 195, 205, 211, 213,
    216
Descartes, R.   136–8, 204
Desnos, R.   179
Dixon, V.   32
Dolto, F.   185
D'Ooge, M. L.   191
Dor, J.   218
Dora   18
Dostoyevsky, F.   43, 104, 111
Douglas, Lord A. 37
Durand, R.   209
Duras, M.   3, 5, 17, 26, 79, 115–34,
    135, 153, 177–8

Eckermann, J. P.   36
Eliot, T. S.   62, 63, 68, 190
Elizabeth I   129
Ellmann, R.   163, 197
Eluard, P.   179, 198
Empedocles   140
Evans, D.   209, 212

Faulkner, W.   210
Febvre, L.   128–9, 131–2, 194
Feher-Gurewich, J.   85, 192, 213
Feldstein, R.   210
Felman, S.   209, 210
Fink, B.   68, 106, 187, 190, 200,
    212
Foucault, M.   5, 16, 26, 87, 207–8
Flaubert, G.   172, 183
Flieger, J. A.   210
Fliess, W.   29, 30, 54
Frege, G.   2, 207
Freud, A.   170, 201
Freud, S.   1–3, 5, 8–9, 13–15,
    17–20, 29–31, 33, 42–3, 44–6,
    48, 54–9, 61, 67–8, 73, 74, 79,
    86, 89–90, 98, 103–4, 108, 110,
    113–14, 116, 126, 132, 136,
    139–41, 147, 160, 162–3, 165,
    170, 174, 183, 185, 192, 197,
    201, 202, 208, 209

Gallop, J.   210
Gasché, R.   213
Genet, J.   5, 13, 40, 135, 152–3,
    196, 203
Gide, A.   2, 5, 17, 27–9, 35–41, 45,
    51, 148, 152, 154–5, 179, 188,
    196, 202, 203
Gilbert, S.   179, 198
Girard, R.   124, 130, 194
Gödel, K.   207
Goethe, J. W. von   9, 36, 59, 63,
    70
Goncourt, de (brothers)   36
Gondek, H. D.   211
Gracian, B.   208
Granoff, W.   201
Greimas, J. A.   22, 187, 209
Grigg, R.   212
Guilbaud, P.   156
Guyomard, P.   82, 191

Harasym, S.   210
Hart, C.   156, 168, 196.
Hegel, G. W. F.   12, 15, 18, 20, 21,
    69–73, 104–5, 110, 136, 139,
    190, 193, 201, 207, 215, 216
Heidegger, M.   7, 14, 15, 20, 34, 52,
    81, 111, 137, 139, 207, 211, 215
Hemingway, E.   216
Hénaff, M.   91
Hesnard, A.   86, 192
Hill, L.   117, 118, 123, 133, 194, 195
Hitchcock, A.   9, 11, 118, 217
Homer   162, 168
Horkheimer, M.   93, 102–3, 105,
    192
Husserl, E.   111, 136, 137, 176
Hyppolite, J.   15, 105, 193, 201

Irigaray, L.   210

James, H.   210
Jameson, F.   210
Jakobson, R.   5–6, 14, 15
Jarry, A.   95
Jensen, W.   165
Johnson, B.   28, 49, 53
Johnson, S.   36
Jolas, E.   26, 59, 61, 160, 209

Joyce, James   2, 3, 5, 13, 18, 19, 25, 27, 28, 32, 153, 154–82, 183, 185, 196–7
Joyce, John   164
Joyce, Lucia   164, 180
Julien, P.   14, 186
Jung, C.-G.   32, 162, 164, 170, 197

Kafka, F.   9
Kahane, C.   210
Kahane, J.   86
Kalinich L.   214
Kant, I.   8, 15, 77, 78, 87–9, 91–9, 101–7, 110, 113–14, 193, 203, 216
Kauffmann, P.   80
Kennedy, J. F.   141
Kenner, H.   168
Klein, M.   145, 201, 203
Klossowski, P.   85, 107, 108, 110, 192, 193
Kojève, A.   14, 15, 105, 139, 142, 190, 205, 207

Lacoue-Labarthe, P.   7, 8, 15, 186, 205, 211
Lafayette, Madame de   131
Lamartine, A. de   213
Laplanche, J.   209
Lawrence, D. H.   216.
Leclaire, S.   201
Lefort, R.   201
Leonardo da V.   43, 202
Levinas, E.   111–12, 193, 210–11
Lévi-Strauss, C.   7, 14, 16
Libbrecht, K.   212
Locke, J.   15
Lupton, J. R.   190, 214

MacCannel, J. F.   209, 212
Mallarmé, S.   11, 66, 184, 190
Mannoni, M.   201
Mao, President   22, 184–5, 207
Marchand, V.   156
Marini, M.   200
Marx, K.   19, 21, 22, 205
McCormick, E.   196
Mehlman, J.   209
Mellard, J.   212

Mercanton, J.   196
Merleau-Ponty, M.   12, 14, 15, 136, 137, 204, 213
Michelangelo, B.   68
Miller, J.-A.   14, 180, 199, 200, 207, 215
Miller, Judith   214
Millot, C.   26, 169
Mitchell, J.   26, 187
Molière   13, 38, 203
Monne, C.   213
Monnier, A.   158
Montaigne, M. de   132, 194
Montrelay, M.   115–16, 194
Montreuil, A. P. de   112
Montreuil, Présidente de   99
Muller, J.   200
Mulvey, L.   11

Nancy, J.-L.   7, 8, 15, 186, 205, 211
Napoléon (Bonaparte)   109, 148
Navarre, Marguerite de   26, 118, 128–34, 141
Nietzsche, F.   1, 40–1, 76, 139, 188, 195
Nobus, D.   187, 212

Oedipus (complex)   13, 17, 32, 45, 54–6, 59, 60–1, 67, 68, 76, 78, 147, 149, 213

Pascal, B.   208
Paul (St)   101
Pauvert, J.-J.   90, 93
Pécheux, M.   52
Pettigrew, D.   213
Phillips, J.   213
Pius XII (Pope)   14
Plato   2, 5, 23, 135, 139–47, 151, 185, 195, 203–4
Poe, E. A.   4–6, 11, 17, 20, 24, 28, 32, 33, 42–53, 121
Pontalis, J. B.   209
Pound, E.   168, 172, 198
Prevert, J.   179
Prince, M.   179
Proust, M.   36, 208, 209

Quine, W. V. O.   166

Rabelais, F. 160
Racine, J. 4
Raffoul, F. 213
Ragland-Sullivan, E. 210, 212–14
Reinhard, K. 190, 214
Richardson, W. 196, 200, 213
Ricoeur, P. 15
Riviere, J. 26, 40
Robbe-Grillet, A. 216
Robertson, J. M. 62
Robespierre, M. 109
Rose, J. 26, 187, 206
Roudinesco, E. 14, 117, 156, 157, 163, 186, 194, 207, 215
Rougemont, D. de 128

Sacher-Masoch, L. von. 113, 167
Sade, D. A. de 5, 8, 12, 17, 27, 45, 78, 79, 84, 85–114, 115, 139, 191–2, 203
Sainte-Beuve, C.-A. 36
Salvaggio, R. 210
Sartre, J.-P. 4, 12, 59, 136–7
Saussure, F. de 15, 211
Schleifer, R. 209
Schlossman, B. 209.
Schlumberger, J. 35–9, 188
Schneiderman, S. 212, 214
Schreber, D. P. 18, 19, 108, 113, 201–2
Seglas, J. 179
Sellin, E. 205
Shakespeare, W. 2, 5, 9, 12, 13, 17, 24, 25, 54–68, 143, 169, 177, 210
Sharpe, E. 54–9, 61, 65, 189–90
Shechner, M. 167, 197

Sibony, D. 210
Silverman, K. 11
Socrates 139–41, 144–7, 152, 185, 203–4
Soler, C. 214
Sollers, P. 165, 175
Sophocles 2, 5, 12, 13, 17, 32, 55–6, 58, 60, 69–84, 150, 178, 191, 203
Soury, P. 157
Spinoza, B. de 15, 215
Spivak, G. 210
Stendhal (Henri Beyle) 209
Stolzfus, B. 216
Sussman, H. 210
Swedenborg, E. 97

Thomé, M. 157
Thurson, L. 212
Torok, M. 214

Valéry, P. 3
Van Boheemen-Saaf, C. 212
Van Haute, P. 78, 191, 211
Vasse, D. 185
Verdi, G. 173
Verhaege, P. 212
Vitrac, R. 179

Weber, S. 210
Wilde, O. 37
Wittgenstein, L. 20
Woolf, V. 210

Zeno 51
Zizek, S. 4, 8, 9, 11, 21, 52–3, 81, 166, 184, 189, 212, 214, 216–17

Jewish Meditation

A Practical Guide

ARYEH KAPLAN

SCHOCKEN BOOKS   NEW YORK

Originally published by Schocken Books in 1985.

Library of Congress Cataloging in Publication Data

Kaplan, Aryeh
Jewish meditation: a practical guide
1. Meditation(Judaism)
1.Title
BM723.K288 1985 2967'2 84-23589

ISBN 0-8052-1037-7

The publisher acknowledges with gratitude
the assistance of Mrs. Anita Lasry in the preparation of this book.

Manufactured in the United States of America
['95]   29

CONTENTS

Introduction vii
1. What Is Meditation? 3
2. Why Meditate? 8
3. Techniques 15
4. States of Consciousness 25
5. Jewish Meditation 40
6. Mantra Meditation 54
7. Contemplation 64
8. Visualization 77
9. Nothingness 83
10. Conversing with God 92
11. The Way of Prayer 99
12. Relating to God 107
13. Unification 122
14. The Ladder 132
15. In All Your Ways 141
16. The Commandments 147
17. Between Man and Woman 154
18. Remolding the Self 161

INTRODUCTION

Ｐeople are often surprised to hear the term "Jewish meditation." Otherwise knowledgeable Jews, including many rabbis
and scholars, are not aware that such a thing exists. When shown
texts that describe Jewish meditation, they respond that it belongs to esoteric or occult corners of Judaism and has little to do
with mainstream Judaism.

It is therefore not surprising that many current books on meditation give scant attention to Judaism. Although most writers
seem to be aware that mystical elements exist in Judaism, their
discussion is usually restricted to the Kabbalah or the Chasidic
masters. Most books on meditation emphasize Eastern practices,
and in some instances Christian meditation, but Jewish meditation is for all practical purposes ignored.

For students of meditation, this is a serious oversight. Judaism
produced one of the more important systems of meditation, and
ignoring it is bound to make any study incomplete. Furthermore,
since Judaism is an Eastern religion that migrated to the West,
its meditative practices may well be those most relevant to Western man. Without a knowledge of Jewish meditative practices, an
important link between East and West is lost. This omission is all
the more significant in light of considerable evidence that the
Jewish mystical masters had dialogue with the Sufi masters and
were also aware of the schools of India.

For the Jew, however, the lacuna is most serious. Jews are by nature a spiritual people, and many Jews actively seek spiritual meaning in life, often on a mystical level. Generations ago, large numbers of Jews were attracted to the mystical traditions of groups such as the Freemasons. Today, many American Jews have become involved in Eastern religions. It is estimated that as many as 75 percent of the devotees in some ashrams are Jewish, and large percentages follow disciplines such as Transcendental Meditation.

When I speak to these Jews and ask them why they are exploring other religions instead of their own, they answer that they know of nothing deep or spiritually satisfying in Judaism. When I tell them there is a strong tradition of meditation and mysticism, not only in Judaism, but in mainstream Judaism, they look at me askance. Until Jews become aware of the spiritual richness of their own tradition, it is understandable that they will search in other pastures.

A few years ago, I was invited to speak in a small synagogue in upstate New York. The weather was bad that evening, and only twenty people showed up, so instead of giving the lecture I had planned, I gathered everyone into a circle and just talked. Most of the people there had relatively little knowledge of Judaism. In the course of our talk, I began to discuss the Shema and how it can be used as a meditation (see chapter 3). One of the women present asked if I would do a demonstration, and I agreed.

The whole meditation could not have taken more than ten or fifteen minutes. Ordinarily, it would have taken longer, but in this situation I felt pressed for time. Still, at the end, everyone present, including me, was literally breathless. Collectively, we had experienced a significant spiritual high.

"Why can't we ever do anything like this at services?" asked one of the men. It was a question I could not answer. The discussion turned to how cold and spiritually sterile synagogue services can be, and how a technique like this, which works so well in a group, could make the service infinitely more meaningful. Together we questioned whether the synagogue service was initially meant to be a meditative experience.

If finding spiritual meaning is difficult for the uncommitted Jew, it is sometimes difficult for the Orthodox Jew as well. I have been approached by yeshiva students who are committed to observing the rituals of Judaism but fail to see how these practices can elevate them spiritually. Even more troubling is the number of Orthodox Jews who are involved in disciplines such as Transcendental Meditation. Most of them express uneasiness about these practices but feel that the benefits outweigh the dangers. When asked why they do not seek this type of experience in Judaism, they give the same answer as uncommitted Jews: they are not aware that such an experience can be found within Judaism.

When my first book on the subject, *Meditation and the Bible,* was published in 1978, it sparked a new interest in Jewish meditation in many circles. For most people, it was the first intimation that Jewish meditation existed. Although the work drew on a considerable amount of published material, most of the sources had never been translated from the Hebrew and were available only to experienced Hebraic scholars. Even then, much of the material was difficult to understand for someone who had not engaged in meditative practices. To make this material accessible, the keys to understanding had to be found, and many of these keys existed only in ancient, unpublished manuscripts.

It is significant that most of the important texts on Jewish meditation have never been published, even in their original Hebrew. The most important works exist only in manuscript, locked away in libraries and museums. To research this book, as well as a subsequent work, *Meditation and Kabbalah,* the manuscripts first had to be located; this involved searching through scholarly journals and library catalogues. Once the manuscripts were found, copies had to be obtained, and when they were located in places like the Lenin Library in Moscow, this was not an easy task. Many of the manuscripts were hundreds of years old, written in obsolete scripts that could be deciphered only with considerable effort. The effort was worth it, however, and many important keys to Jewish meditation were discovered.

Because so little on Jewish meditation was ever published,

many people argued that meditation was to be found only in the backwaters of Judaic literature—in works not even worthy of publication. Actually, many works dealing with Kabbalistic methods of meditation were not published because the practices were dangerous and were not meant for the masses. Still, even these works shed considerable light on obscure passages found in published mainstream works; they are an integral part of the puzzle, without which major areas of Judaism are difficult, if not impossible, to understand. Once the puzzle began to come together, it became clear to me that some of the most important mainstream Jewish leaders of the past relied on various meditative techniques.

With the publication of *Meditation and the Bible*, interest in Jewish meditation began to grow. Even the Lubavitcher Rebbe issued a directive that Jewish forms of meditation should be explored. Groups that taught and practiced Jewish meditation were formed in the United States and Israel. I felt privileged that my books formed the basis of many of these groups.

Unfortunately, a number of groups also involved in "Jewish meditation" were practicing something far from Judaism. Some of them attempted to adapt Eastern practices to Jewish audiences, or to Judaize Eastern teachings. Although these groups attracted a following of sorts, they were not teaching Jewish meditation.

Meanwhile, together with a group of committed Jewish psychiatrists and psychologists, I began to experiment with the techniques I had found in the literature. Together we explored the inner space of the meditative state. Among the participants were David Sheinkin (of blessed memory), Seymour Applebaum, and Paul (Pinchas) Bindler. Other members who made important contributions to the group were Arnie and Roz Gellman, Miriam Benhaim Circlin, Sylvia Katz, Jeff Goldberg, Gerald Epstein, Perle Epstein, and many others.

One important discovery we made was that most texts dealing with Jewish meditation assume that the reader is familiar with the general techniques, and intend only to provide additional detail. The details were fascinating, but when we tried to translate them into practice, we discovered that too much information was missing. It was like trying to use a book on advanced French cuisine without a rudimentary knowledge of cooking. The recipes were there, but a novice could not use them. In the case of Jewish meditation, the ingredients were there, but the means of mixing them together were omitted or glossed over.

To some degree, the puzzle was pieced together in my two previous meditation books. However, neither of these books was meant to be a practical guide. Many people expressed the need for a guide to Jewish meditation written in nontechnical terms for the layperson. It was out of these requests that the idea for this book was born.

This book presents the most basic forms of Jewish meditation, especially as discussed in mainstream sources. It assumes no special background on the part of the reader either in Judaism or in meditation. It is my hope that this book will at least begin to provide its readers with insight into the spiritual dimensions of the Jewish heritage.

Aryeh Kaplan
December 17, 1982

1

WHAT IS MEDITATION?

What is meditation? For someone who has been involved in the practice, the question need not be asked. For a person who has never had any contact with meditation, however, the subject is shrouded in mystery. To many people, the term "meditation" suggests an image of someone sitting in the lotus position with eyes closed in serene concentration. Others may associate meditation with holiness and spirituality. Individuals seeking spirituality might look into various disciplines of meditation without having any idea of what they are looking for.

In its most general sense, meditation consists of thinking in a controlled manner. It is deciding exactly how one wishes to direct the mind for a period of time, and then doing it.

In theory this may sound very easy, but in practice it is not. The human mind is not a domesticated animal, but rather seems to have a mind of its own beyond the will of the thinker. Anyone who has ever tried to concentrate on a subject, only to have his mind drift to other thoughts, is aware of this. Sometimes it seems that the more one tries to control one's thoughts, the more they refuse to be controlled.

It is strange that most people have never given a thought to their thoughts. Thoughts are so much part of our being that we take them for granted. One of the first steps in meditation is learning how not to take our thoughts for granted.

A simple exercise will demonstrate how difficult it is to control your thoughts. In theory this exercise seems ridiculously simple, but in practice it is tantalizingly difficult.

This is the exercise: Stop thinking.

Normally, when one is not otherwise occupied, there is a constant flow of thought passing through the mind. In this reverie, one thought flows into another, almost automatically. This flow of thought goes on and on, like an internal conversation with oneself. Usually, this reverie is so much part of our mental environment that we do not pay attention to it.

The first exercise is to become aware of your thoughts by trying to stop them. Try to blank out your mind for a few minutes and not think of anything at all. Sound easy? Stop reading now and try it.

All right. How long did it last? Unless you are very unusual, or have had meditative experience, you could not keep your mind blank for more than a few seconds. If nothing more, the period of mental silence was probably interrupted by the thought, "I'm not thinking," or "I'm trying not to think." In practice, it is extremely difficult to turn off thought. As we shall see, control over the thought process is one of the goals of some meditative disciplines.

There is another way in which you can try to control your mind. When you finish this paragraph, close your eyes. You will probably see lights or images flashing before your eyes. Give yourself a few moments to relax, and these flashing lights will subside and develop into a series of kaleidoscopic images in the mind's eye. These images will arise and change spontaneously with little or no direction by the conscious mind. One image flows into another as still another grows and develops. It is almost impossible to concentrate on these mind-begotten images, because when you try, they disappear.

Now, with your eyes closed, try to control these images. Try to depict the letter *A* in your mind's eye. Unless you have practiced this technique for some time, it is impossible to hold on to this image.

One of the techniques of meditation is "imaging," evoking an image in the mind's eye and holding it there. In Jewish meditation, this is known as "engraving." Here the image is fixed in the mind as if it were engraved, so that it can be held in the mind as long as one desires. This technique can be perfected only through extensive training.

Having tried these two exercises, you can see that the mind has a "mind of its own." There are thus two parts to the mind, one that is under the control of the conscious will and one that is not. That part of the mind under the control of the will is called the consciousness, while that which is not is called the unconscious or subconscious. Since the subconscious is not under the control of the will, one cannot control what it passes into the conscious mind.

One of the goals of meditation, then, is to gain control of the subconscious part of the mind. If one were to succeed, one would also gain a high degree of self-mastery. This, too, is a goal of meditation.

This explains why so many disciplines use breathing exercises as a meditative device. Breathing usually occurs automatically and is therefore normally under the control of the unconscious mind. Unless you are consciously controlling your breathing, it will mirror your unconscious mood. This is one reason why breathing is one of the indicators in a lie detector test.

Yet, if you wish, you can control your breath, and do so quite easily. Breathing therefore forms a link between the conscious mind and the unconscious. By learning how to concentrate on and control your breath you can go on to learn how to control the unconscious mind.

The thought process itself is also controlled to a large degree by the unconscious, but it can also be controlled by the conscious mind. This is most obvious in the case of the reverie. When one is relaxing and not paying particular attention to it, the reverie flows from one thought to another without conscious effort. Indeed, there are a number of psychological techniques that try to imitate this "free association," in order to gain an understanding of the unconscious mind. However, no matter how free the association may be when one is expressing it to a second party, it is never as free as in the case of pure reverie. The reverie thus can also be seen as a point of interface between the conscious and unconscious. By learning how to control the reverie, one can also learn how to control the unconscious.

The same is true of the visions that appear in the mind's eye. Since they are not under the control of the conscious mind, they are obviously coming from the unconscious. Controlling them is very difficult without practice; one can learn to control them, however, and doing so also serves to form a bridge between the conscious mind and the unconscious.

One of the most powerful benefits of meditation is control over the unconscious mind. One learns to use the conscious mind to control mental processes that are usually under the control of the unconscious. Gradually, more and more of the subconscious becomes accessible to the conscious mind, and one gains control of the entire thought process.

Sometimes, different parts of the mind appear to be acting independently. The conflict between two parts of the mind can be so strong that a person feels like two separate individuals. During such inner conflict, it seems that one part of the mind wants to do one thing, while the other part wants to do something else.

Thus, for example, a person may be drawn toward a sexual temptation. One part of the mind is thus saying yes very loudly. Yet, at the same time, another part of the mind may feel that the act is morally reprehensible. This second part of the mind may be saying no with equal loudness. The person may feel caught in the middle, between the two voices.

In classical Freudian psychology, this would be seen as a conflict between the id and the superego. In our example, the id would be saying yes to the temptation, while the superego would be saying no. Somehow, the ego (the "I") mediates between these two subconscious voices. Although Freud's schema ties it into a neat package, introspection shows that the conflict is actually more complex than the simple picture of the id and superego. Sometimes not two but three, four, or more voices seem to be giving different signals in the mind. If a person were to learn to control his subconscious, he could avoid much of this conflict.

There are many theories about the subconscious, and a full discussion is far beyond the scope of this book. However, if meditation is controlled thinking, it implies that the individual has the entire thought process under control, including input from the subconscious. The experienced meditator learns how to think what he wants to think, when he wants to think it. He can always be in control of the situation, resisting psychological pressures that work on the subconscious. He is also in control of himself, never doing something that he knows he really does not want to do. In many schools, this self-mastery is one of the most important goals of meditation.

2

WHY MEDITATE?

Meditation, which is thought directed by will, can bring many benefits. Most people learn how to think as very young children, and throughout their adult lives, they do not think any differently than they did as children. That is to say, most people use their minds in a manner not essentially different from the way they did when they were six years old. Through meditation, one can control the thought process and learn to think in new ways, thus gaining new and richer mind experiences.

It is significant that in Kabbalah, one's normal mode of thinking is referred to as the "mentality of childhood" (*mochin de-katnuth*). More advanced modes of thought and states of consciousness, on the other hand, are referred to as the "mentality of adulthood" (*mochin de-gadluth*). One learns these methods of "adult thought" through meditation, through which one develops the ability to transcend the ways of thinking one learned as a child.

In chapter 1, for example, we discussed how different parts of the mind act independently. Thus, a person might want to concentrate on a task at hand, but at the same time other concerns pop into his mind, disturbing his concentration. While one part of the mind is trying to focus on a problem, other parts may be drawing attention to different ideas. As long as this is true, concentration is not complete.

For this reason, a person usually uses only a small portion of the mind. As much as he might try to concentrate on a thought or task, parts of his mind are engaged in other activities. Sometimes the rest of the mind is merely passive. At other times however, other parts of the mind may actually be acting in opposition to one's concentration. Unless one is able to control the entire mind, one cannot develop full concentration.

People often think of concentration in terms of problem-solving. It can also involve the most basic of experiences. Suppose, for example, that you are trying to experience the beauty of a rose. At the same time, thoughts about your business may be pushing their way into your mind. Your attention does not stay focused on the rose and you cannot see the rose totally, in all its beauty.

But there is another factor that prevents you from experiencing the rose completely. Earlier, we discussed the spontaneous images that arise in the field of vision when the eyes are closed. Actually, you can also see these images with your eyes open in a darkened room. Once you are aware of these images, you can even see them with your eyes open in a well-lit room. The reason you are normally not aware of these images is that they are very faint compared with the images entering your mind from your open eyes. Nevertheless, they are constantly with you.

Now suppose you are trying to appreciate the beauty of a rose. No matter how hard you try to focus your mind on the rose, the image of the rose is competing with the self-generated images in the mind. It is as if there were a screen of extraneous imagery between you and the rose, preventing you from seeing it with total clarity.

In a meditative state, however, it is possible to turn off the interference and concentrate totally on the rose. As we shall see, with training, one can turn off the spontaneous self-generated images and thus remove the screen. The beauty of the flower when seen in these higher states of awareness is indescribable to someone who has never experienced it. The most I can say is that the rose actually appears to radiate beauty. This can be true of anything else in the world.

Another important goal of meditation is thus enhanced awareness and perception. The greater the portion of the mind focused on an experience, the more the experience will be enhanced. When every cell in your brain is tuned in to experiencing the rose, the experience is indescribably different from what you would see in your usual state of consciousness.

This works in one of two ways. The most simple way in which meditation works is to quiet down all parts of the mind not concentrating on the immediate experience. In this mode, the experience is not enhanced directly, but rather all interference with it is removed. Thus, you may be looking at the rose with no greater awareness than before, but without the mental static, it will appear much more vivid. It is somewhat like trying to tune in to a faint radio station; even if you cannot amplify the volume, you will hear the station more clearly if you can eliminate the static. This mode of meditation can be reached through most meditative techniques and is the state of consciousness most readily attainable in its lower levels.

The second way in which meditation can enhance an experience is by focusing more of the mind on it. Ultimately, as one becomes a more experienced meditator, one can learn to focus the entire mind on a single experience. This is analogous to turning up the volume of a radio or using a system of greater fidelity. This level is attained in the more advanced states of meditation, and one can use it to exert the total force of one's mind on anything one desires.

Of course, neither mode is generally attained without the other. When you quiet other areas of the mind, you also focus more of the mind on the experience. Conversely, focusing more of the mind on the experience almost always involves blocking out other experiences and thoughts.

This increased awareness can be used in many ways. Meditation can be used to gain a greater and clearer awareness of the world around us. Looking at something like a rose while in a meditative state of consciousness, one can see much more in it than one would otherwise see. It has been said that one can see the entire universe in a grain of sand. In a high meditative state, this is actually possible. As one's capacity for concentration increases, one can also become aware of subtle phenomena that are not otherwise detectable. Thus, the world of the meditator may become much richer than that of those who have never had the experience.

Here again, there is a language barrier. If one has never experienced these phenomena, then one cannot comprehend a description of them. The situation can be better understood through analogy.

For the average sighted person, a page of braille feels like bumpy paper and nothing more. A blind person, however, does not have his sense of sight competing with his sense of touch, and hence experiences less "static." Furthermore, since he uses his sense of touch more often, his tactile sense is enhanced. With practice, he learns to decipher the patterns of raised dots as letters and words. It is true that a sighted person can also learn to read braille, but those who have mastered it usually read with their eyes closed, so that their faculty of sight will not interfere with their sense of touch.

Reading braille is a good example of an experience that is meaningless to a nonsensitized person but has a world of meaning for a sensitized person. Many such experiences may exist in the world, and meditation can teach one to "read" these messages.

Another analogy may express this even more clearly. Many blind people learn to navigate by listening to the subliminal echoes given off by buildings and other large objects. This is why blind people often tap their canes constantly; they listen to the echoes produced by the tapping, and the echoes warn them of obstructions. The strange thing is that blind people claim that they do not actually hear these echoes, but sense them in a manner that they cannot describe. Rather than speak of this experience as hearing an echo, a blind person will describe it as sensing an obstruction. These echoes are not perceptible to a sighted person since the flood of information experienced through vision overwhelms them completely. Moreover, there is a learning period during which a blind person becomes sensitized to these echoes.

On a more esoteric level, in Tibetan medicine, as well as in Kabbalah, a number of illnesses can be diagnosed merely by feeling the pulse. The subtle differences in the feel and rhythm of the pulse can provide a skilled practitioner with a picture of the body's state of health with uncanny accuracy. Observing the Dalai Lama's personal physician make such a diagnosis, a famous doctor reported that he had witnessed something bordering on the supernatural.

The secret, however, is twofold. First, the practitioner must learn to enter a deep state of concentration in which the pulse beat fills his entire world of sensation and the subtlest variations in it stand out clearly and vividly. The practitioner is thus able to garner a great deal of information from the pulse beat. To him, every pulse beat is an encyclopedia of information about the body. Once he learns how to "read" the pulse beat in this manner, he can then learn what every variation means. People who have attempted to learn this technique report that it can take as much as fifteen years to master it well enough to make an accurate diagnosis.

A number of Judaic sources speak of meditation as a means of attaining extrasensory perception (ESP) in such areas as telepathy, mind-reading, clairvoyance, and predicting the future. These powers may also involve increased awareness. In the ordinary state of consciousness, ESP signals received by the mind may be overshadowed by the perceptual information entering the brain, as well as by the mind's natural "static" or "noise." As discussed earlier, this static consists of thoughts and images spontaneously produced by the mind which are not under the conscious mind's control. In the meditative state, when this noise or static is quieted, ESP phenomena may become more readily discernible. A number of ESP experiments appear to indicate that this is true, and that meditation enhances the effect. Unfortunately, as in the case of most ESP experiments, results depend on so many variables that unambiguous conclusions are difficult to obtain.

Another purpose of meditation is to attune the mind to certain truths (or Truths with a capital *T*). When a person tries to explore questions such as the meaning of existence, the true goal of life, or the ultimate nature of reality, the answers remain elusive, tickling the edge of the mind. Possible answers hover on the borderline of consciousness, but are so subtle that they cannot be discerned through the static of the mind.

One of the most elusive truths is knowledge of the self. Generally we see ourselves only through a thick veil of ego. For this reason, it is impossible to see ourselves as others see us. Through meditation, however, we can remove the veil of ego, and see ourselves with a degree of objectivity. In this manner, we can look at ourselves objectively as a third person. We are then able to see our own shortcomings and overcome them.

The self-awareness engendered by meditation can also strengthen the ego when needed. Thus, a person with a weak self-image and feelings of inadequacy can learn to be more self-assured. He can examine his motivations and learn to become more inner-directed, doing the things he desires, and not simply what others expect of him. He can look objectively at his relationships with others and learn to improve them.

One of the most powerful uses of meditation is to gain an awareness of the spiritual. Although we may be surrounded by a sea of spirituality, we are not usually aware of it. Spiritual sensations are quite faint and usually overshadowed by the world of the senses. Even in a state of sensory deprivation, the self-generated thoughts of the mind tend to obscure spiritual sensation. However, if a person can quiet down all extraneous thoughts, he can then "tune in" to the spiritual. This tuning-in is what is known as the mystical experience. In this sense, meditation is the most important technique of mystics all over the world.

The most vivid experiences were those attained by the prophets in the Bible. In the biblical sense, a prophet is more than a person who merely sees the future. Rather, he is one who has such a strong experience of the spiritual that he can use it to garner information. Sometimes this information includes knowledge of the future, hence the popular conception of a prophet as one who sees what has not yet occurred. Nevertheless, the true prophet has access to many other truths besides knowledge of the future. It is important to realize the important role that meditation played in the careers of the prophets of Israel.

On its highest level, meditation can provide a person with an experience of God. This is certainly the highest possible spiritual experience. Our perception of God is often clouded by ego and anthropomorphism, so that we tend to see God as a mirror image of ourselves. By freeing the mind of these encumbrances, meditation can help us to open our minds totally to the experience of God. In many religious traditions, including Judaism, this is the highest goal of meditation.

3

TECHNIQUES

At this point it would be useful to discuss and classify the various meditative techniques, both Jewish and non-Jewish. The techniques of almost all meditative systems can be classified in similar ways; this does not imply any special relationship between Jewish and non-Jewish meditation. Rather, since a general concept of meditation exists, all forms have characteristics in common, which in turn can be used to classify various techniques.

The situation is analogous to that of prayer, which is important in all religious traditions. Certain elements are characteristic of all prayer. This does not mean that one system of prayer is derived from another, or even that a relationship exists between the systems. Rather, the similarities stem from the fact that there are a limited number of basic ways of relating to God, and these will be found in prayer wherever it exists.

Thus, almost every prayer can fit into one of three categories: praise, petition, and thanksgiving. We can praise God and speak of His greatness. We can petition God and ask Him to provide us with the things we need and want. Finally, we can thank God for what He has given us. In Jewish prayer, these three divisions are formalized and follow a set sequence. Nevertheless, if we were to examine prayers of all the world's faiths, we would find that with few exceptions they would all fall into one of the three categories.

The same is true of meditation. There are a finite number of ways in which a person can interact with his own mind, and these form the categories of all meditation. Thus, when one understands meditation in general, one can then understand Jewish meditation in particular. Since meditation involves subtle experiences that may be unfamiliar to many readers, I shall begin with a mundane example.

I have defined meditation as a controlled manner of thinking. On the simplest level, you can decide to sit down for the next half hour and just think about one particular subject. Let's say you decide that for the next half hour you will think about rearranging your furniture. In your mind's eye, you might imagine how various arrangements would look and even plan how to move the heavier pieces. During that half hour, you will have been meditating on furniture arrangement. It is as simple as that. There need not be anything esoteric or mysterious about meditation. No special surroundings are required, nor must any particular body position be assumed. You could have meditated while walking around the block, while sitting back in your easy chair, or while relaxing in the tub. The very fact that for a specific time period you were thinking about a specific topic rather than letting your mind wander at random makes it a meditative experience.

Of course, it is not always that easy. What do you do when other thoughts begin to creep into the mind? Remember that the decision was to think about arranging furniture *and nothing else*. If this meditation is actually going to be a controlled thinking experience, then you will need a technique to rid yourself of undesired thoughts. You might gently push the extraneous thoughts out of your mind or otherwise pull your mind back to the desired subject. Whatever method you use to keep your mind on the subject, in doing so you will be developing the rudiments of a full-fledged meditative technique.

Meditation on rearranging your furniture may be a trivial example. But suppose you decided to spend a half hour meditating on how to rearrange your life. You might find yourself thinking about fundamental questions such as these:

What do I ultimately want out of life?
What gives my life meaning?
What is the meaning of life in general?
If I had my life to live over, what would I do with it?
What ideals, if any, would I be willing to die for?
What would bring me more happiness than anything else in
the world?

You have probably already thought about these questions at some time in your life. However, chances are that you thought of them only briefly. Unless you have been involved in a discipline that encourages it, you have probably never spent a full half hour, without interruption, thinking about any of these questions. If you have never done so before, the first time may be very shocking. You may discover that you have no idea of what you perceive as your purpose in life. You may have never thought about the meaning of life at all.

Indeed, after a half hour of pondering any of the above questions, you might decide that the question needs more than one session of meditation. You might decide to have a half-hour session once a week. To make sure that you continue, you may decide that at a certain time every week you will spend a half hour meditating on the purpose of life as well as your own personal goals. You will then be on your way to developing a discipline of meditation.

After several weeks of such meditation, you will probably begin to notice yourself growing in a number of areas. You might decide to reevaluate the direction of your life and make major changes in your life-style. You might find yourself more secure in your dealings with others, more confident about how you are spending your time. You may also find that you are constantly gaining new insight into your own personality and motivations.

At this point, you might feel that once a week is not enough. You may decide to increase the frequency of your meditation to two or three times a week or even once a day. You will then discover why many schools of meditation suggest or require that meditation be a daily exercise.

As you continue to explore what is most meaningful to you, you may come to a point where you feel that you are reaching a new threshold. You may find yourself pondering not only the meaning of your own life, but the very meaning of existence in general.

At this point, you will have discovered God.

Before discussing this further, it is important to define God. We often think of God as being "out there," far away from the world. But it is important to realize that God is also "in there"—in the deepest recesses of the soul.

Here are two ways in which a person can discover God.

First, a person can reflect on questions such as these: What is beyond space and time? How did the world come into existence? Why does the world exist? What came before time? By pondering such questions, a person can find God, but he will find God only in the sense that God is "out there."

The second way in which one can find God is by delving deeper and deeper into the self in the manner discussed earlier. Here also one finds God, but one is finding Him in the sense that He is "in there."

This twofold manner of discovering God is related to the Kabbalistic concept that God both encompasses and fills all creation. When we say that God is above all things and beyond all things, we are speaking of Him in the sense that He encompasses and defines all creation. This is the concept of God as being "out there." However, in another sense, God is very close to us—closer than the air we breathe, closer than our very souls—and in this sense He fills all creation, and is "in there."

Once a person discovers God in this manner, he might want to transform his meditation into a conversation with God. If one discovers God as the ultimate depth of one's being, then the way to relate to this depth would be to relate to God. At this point, one's meditation into the meaning of existence might become a silent conversation with God.

It is significant to note that according to the Midrash, this is exactly how Abraham's career began. First Abraham began to contemplate the meaning of life and existence, and it was in this manner that he discovered God. Abraham then began to have a dialogue with God. Abraham's experience can be seen as a paradigm of how to begin a relationship with the Divine.

Again, the problem of extraneous thoughts may arise. One way to help alleviate this problem is to speak to God out loud rather than just in the mind. One would then be speaking to God orally.

Using oral conversation as a meditative technique is an ancient Jewish practice, documented in a number of important texts. In particular, it was a technique stressed by Rabbi Nachman of Bratslav, as we shall see in chapter 10.

There are three important things that could be said about the above type of meditation:

1. It is a verbal type of meditation: it involves words in thought or speech, rather than images.

2. It is inner-directed: the entire form of the meditation comes from within the person rather than being determined by an external stimulus.

3. It is unstructured: when the person sits down to meditate, he has no preconceived notion of what direction the meditation will take.

Some people find an unstructured meditation too loose. In order to put structure into your meditation, you can write out an agenda. You may decide that every day for a given period of time, say a week, you will meditate on one subject; then you will go on to a second subject for the next week. Thus, if you are meditating on how to reorder your life, you might decide to spend one week meditating on your relationship with your spouse, a second week meditating on your relationship with your children, and then two weeks meditating on your career.

As soon as one sets up an agenda of meditation, it becomes a structured meditation. Of course, a meditation can be loosely structured or tightly structured, again depending on what one wishes to accomplish. Meditating with an agenda is a practice favored by the Musar schools in Judaism. This form of meditation is especially effective when one wants to perfect one's habits or one's way of life in general.

Another way to add structure to your meditation is to use a biblical verse as the object of meditation. You could take verses randomly from the Bible or seek out verses that apply to the subject of your meditative interest. It is possible to make the entire meditative session, for a day, a week, or a month, revolve around that verse. Your goal would still be to rearrange your life, but you would be trying to do so in the context of that biblical verse. The verse could also form the basis of a conversation with God.

The method of basing a meditation on a verse, known as *gerushin,* was used by the mystics of Safed in the sixteenth century. Although the method was used extensively, the texts provide few details. It appears that a number of ways are possible.

The simplest way to use a biblical verse as a meditation would be to read the verse before meditating, perhaps memorizing it, and then use it as a point of departure for unstructured meditation. The meditator begins by meditating on the verse and then goes on to direct his mind to the subject upon which he wants to meditate. The course of meditation could lead the meditator far from the original verse; the verse would serve merely as the initial focus of the meditation, not as its entire subject. This means of meditation is also discussed in Judaic literature.

Alternatively, you may write the verse on a piece of paper. During the course of meditation, you could then reread it, directing your mind back to the verse from time to time. This is particularly effective if you wish to apply the verse to a particular life problem; in this way, the verse becomes an integral part of the meditation.

Eventually, you may wish to make the verse the entire subject of meditation. In a sense, your meditation would become a conversation with the biblical verse. You would be thinking about the verse, looking at it in different ways, seeking different possible interpretations, and attempting to apply it to your particular life problems. If the verse has a specific lesson, you might use a series of meditative sessions to integrate the verse into your personality. Although we have used a biblical verse as an example, any saying or teaching could be used as the basis for such a meditation. To simplify our discussion, however, we will continue to speak of a biblical verse.

The verse can be used either visually or verbally.

If the verse is used visually as the basis for meditation, write the verse on a piece of paper and use it as a focus. Fix your gaze on the verse; do not take your eyes off it. The verse should become the center of your attention to the exclusion of everything else. It should be as if nothing else in the world exists other than the verse. You can then gaze at the verse and allow your thoughts to flow freely. On a more advanced level, you could use this method to clear the mind of all thought other than the verse.

This method is known as visual contemplation. Using a verse is just one means of accomplishing such meditation. The subject of your contemplation could also be a candle flame, a flower, a picture, a pebble, or any other object.

Since this practice entails using something external to the mind as the object of meditation, it is known as an externally directed meditation. This meditation can be either structured or unstructured.

The simplest way to do the meditation would be to gaze at the object and let your thoughts flow freely. This would be an unstructured meditation. However, if you used the method to fill the mind completely, banishing all other thoughts, then this in itself would impose structure on the meditation, and it would constitute a structured meditation.

When one contemplates an object, one looks at it, paying acute attention to every detail. As one continues to gaze, even the most minute details become significant. One can look deeper and deeper into the object, trying to see its inner essence and obliterating all other thought from the mind. Beyond the inner essence, one can strive to see the Divine in the object and use it as a springboard to reach God.

In lieu of gazing at the written verse, you could repeat the verse over and over for the entire period of meditation. This would be a verbal meditation as opposed to a visual contemplation. Here again, the meditation could be unstructured, where the mind is allowed to roam wherever the verse takes it. Alternatively, it could be structured, where all thought other than the words of the verse is removed from the mind.

Of course, here again, the subject of meditation need not be a biblical verse. Any sentence, word, or phrase can do. As we shall see, the great Chasidic leader Rabbi Nachman of Bratslav prescribed using the phrase "Lord of the Universe" as a meditative device.

In Eastern traditions, the repeated phrase is known as a mantra, and meditation using such a phrase is called mantra meditation. One of the best-known examples of a system based on mantra meditation is Transcendental Meditation. Since there is no equivalent English term for this type of meditation, I shall use the term "mantra" where necessary.

There are, then, three ways in which the above-mentioned meditations can be classified. They can be either visual or verbal, structured or unstructured, internally or externally directed.

Inner-directed, unstructured meditation is most valuable as a means of examining one's life or finding meaning in life. Externally directed, structured meditation is most often used to focus the mind and thought processes or to gain a transcendental experience.

Although most meditative methods are visual or verbal, other faculties can be the focus of meditation as well. Thus, instead of meditating on an object or verse, one could meditate on a sound, such as the chirping of a cricket, the rush of a waterfall, or a musical note played over and over. One would be using the sense of hearing to direct the meditation, although in these cases the meditation would be nonverbal.

In a similar manner, the meditation could involve the sense of smell. Indeed, there are Hebrew blessings said over fragrances, and in practice they can make the enjoyment of a fragrance into a meditative experience. The blessings over food can make a meditative experience out of tasting and eating. The sense of touch, too, can be the focus of a meditative experience.

It is also possible to use the kinesthetic sense as the object of meditation. This would consist of meditating on a body movement or a series of body movements. This is a method used by the Sufis in their dance meditations. Chasidim often use this form of meditation in dancing and in their slow swaying motions.

Any action meditation can be seen as using the kinesthetic sense, even if other senses are involved. The main thing is to concentrate on the act and elevate it to an expression of divine worship. This can include even mundane acts such as washing the dishes.

In Judaism, action meditation is most important when connected with the performance of the commandments and rituals. Many Jews and non-Jews think of the precepts as routine, ritualistic actions. Many Jewish sources, however, speak of the commandments as meditative devices, which can bring a person to a high level of God consciousness. When the commandments are seen in this light, they assume great spiritual significance.

A final focus of meditation can be one's own emotions. Thus, for example, one can focus on the emotion of love in exactly the same way that one can focus on a flower or a candle flame. One can ponder the love one feels for another person and enhance the emotion, experiencing it totally without any outside interference. One can also take this intensified love and direct it toward God or toward one's fellow man. Indeed, the commandments "Love God your Lord with all your heart, all your soul, and all your might" (Deut. 6:5) and "Love your neighbor like yourself" (Lev. 19:18) actually mandate such a meditation. When one directs one's mind to love God and one's fellow man, one provides one's life with an entirely new focus.

Control of the emotions is a very important element of self-control in general. Often the concept of self-control conjures up the image of an emotionless, dry, rigid way of life. If a person is in complete control of his emotions, however, he can call forth any emotion he desires and is free to enhance it as he wills. Rather than be controlled by emotions such as love, yearning, or awe, he can control them. One can evoke these emotions and blend them together, painting every aspect of life with a rich palette of feelings. Control of the emotions can thus lead a person to experience a richer blend of feelings in his daily life than the average person generally experiences.

The final types of meditation do not make use of any device, but involve direct control of the thoughts. These are usually considered the most advanced forms of meditation.

One such technique involves the exercise mentioned in chapter 1, in which you were asked to try to stop thinking for a period of time. For most people this is impossible, and it is an excellent demonstration that the mind is not entirely under the control of the will. After a few seconds of trying not to think, thoughts begin to creep into the mind, and after a short period, they often return in a torrent.

Like many other disciplines, this, too, can be developed. If a person practices stopping his thought flow, he can learn to do so for longer and longer periods; eventually, he can learn to turn his thought processes on and off at will. This may sound easy, but in practice it takes years of intense practice to perfect this ability.

Since this type of meditation does not use anything as a focus, it is often called nondirected meditation. In its more advanced forms, it can actually focus on "nonthought" or on nothingness. This form of meditation can be dangerous and should not be attempted without a practiced guide or master.

Most of the methods that I shall discuss in this book, however, are fairly straightforward and safe if practiced properly. They can be readily learned and can bring the meditator to increased awareness and higher states of consciousness.

4

STATES OF

CONSCIOUSNESS

Most discussions of meditation speak of higher states of consciousness that can be attained through the practice. For the initiate these states of consciousness may be familiar, but for the outsider they are extremely difficult even to imagine. Much has been written about higher states of consciousness, but the discussion usually concludes with a statement that these states are indescribable and ineffable.

There is an important reason that such experiences are indescribable. In the case of objective, external phenomena, a group of people can agree on words to describe them. This is how language in general is constructed. Thus, two people can look at a rose and agree that it is red. Since they are both seeing the same rose, they both have a common experience of which they can speak.

However, when people try to discuss personal experiences in higher states of consciousness, the experiences are entirely internal. I have no way of knowing what is in your mind, so even if you try to describe it, I have no way of being sure of what you mean. Furthermore, since the experiences are internal and individual, it is difficult for people to find a common ground to develop a descriptive vocabulary. Vocabulary is based on shared experiences, and by definition, internal experiences are difficult if not impossible to share.

For example, let us assume that while in a meditative state, I saw in my mind a color that has no counterpart in the external world. Suppose it was totally different from any other color and impossible to describe in terms of other colors. How could I even begin to describe what the color looked like? There would be no words in human vocabulary to describe it. The same is true of many meditative experiences. This fact makes it extremely difficult to develop an epistemology of the meditative state. One ends up trying to describe experiences for which no language exists.

This may be true, but since one of the aims of meditation is to reach higher states of consciousness, we should at least have some idea what this means. The problem is that higher states of consciousness are not only difficult to describe, but also difficult to define. There appears to be no objective epistemology through which one can know for sure that one is in a state of consciousness different from the everyday waking state. Nevertheless, on the basis of subjective experiences and reports, it is possible to gain some understanding of these states of consiousness.

The two most familiar states of consciousness are the waking state and the sleeping state. These are two states of consciousness that are universally known and recognized.

Beyond that, we know that sometimes we may feel drowsy, while at other times we are particularly alert. This demonstrates that there are different levels in the waking state of consciousness. Experiments in which brain waves are measured also indicate that different states of brain activity exist in the waking state. Evidence from sleep laboratories indicates that there are also at least two states of consciousness involved in sleep, the first being the nondream state and the second being the dream state, in which rapid eye movement (REM) is observed.

Certain drugs have an effect on a person's state of consciousness. The best known is alcohol, which has the general effect of diminishing alertness, although since it removes inhibitions, it can also lead to increased awareness in some areas. Other, more potent drugs, such as LSD and mescaline, appear to increase the ability to focus on specific sensations, such as beauty, color, form, and the like. A full discussion of drug-induced states of consciousness is beyond the scope of this book. Instead, we shall explore states of consciousness that can be self-induced.

I recall that when I was in *yeshivah,* a few friends and I decided to have a contest to see who could memorize the most pages of Talmud. For me, it was an interesting experience. The first page took considerable effort and time, perhaps several hours. As I continued, each page became progressively easier. Eventually, after ten pages or so, I found that I could memorize a page after three or four readings. By the time I had gone through some twenty pages, I could memorize a page with a single reading. What had originally been extremely difficult had become relatively easy. My friends reported the same experience.

It is well known that memory is a faculty that can be trained. People who regularly memorize large quantities of information find themselves able to do so very readily. Professional actors, for example, can memorize the lines in a play or movie in one or two readings. Similarly, many professional musicians can memorize a score almost immediately.

What was interesting from a subjective viewpoint was that it did not seem to me that my memory had improved. Rather, it seemed that when I looked at a page, I was looking at it differently. It was as if my memory was wide open and the material was going directly into it. It felt as if there was normally a barrier between perception and memory and that this barrier had now been removed.

Logically, this would make sense. If we remembered everything we saw or learned, our memory would rapidly become cluttered with useless information. The mind therefore has a sort of filter that prevents unwanted information from being stored in the memory. The problem is that the filter is sometimes there when one does not want it—such as when one wishes to memorize something. With training, however, one can learn to remove this filter at will.

The point is that when a person has trained his mind to memorize, his awareness when reading material to be memorized is completely different. It could be said that he is in a different state of consciousness at the time.

Let me give another example. When I was a graduate student in nuclear physics, I was once working on an extremely difficult mathematical problem for a paper. I became totally involved in the problem and worked on it for almost seventy-two hours without interruption. In order to solve the problem, I had to invent a number of original mathematical techniques and procedures. But the strange thing was that when I read the final paper two years later, I found it almost impossible to understand the mathematics. It was difficult to believe that I had created this mathematical structure.

Anyone who has ever worked on a difficult problem, especially in mathematics or the sciences, knows that at a certain point the mind seems to "lock on" to the problem. At that point, solving the problem becomes the most important thing in the world, and every fiber of one's being is concentrated on finding a solution. Subjectively speaking, I know that I can accomplish things when in a "locked-on" state that I cannot accomplish otherwise.

In one of my advanced physics courses, I had a difficult mathematical problem on a test. I worked on the problem for a while and then, realizing that I was not making any progress, skipped to the next problem. Fortunately, this was a test in which one had to answer only three out of five questions. Several months later, I was working on another paper and in the course of my calculations found myself confronted with a similar problem. This time, however, I was "locked on" to the problem and totally involved in it. Much to my surprise, I was able to solve the same problem that had stumped me on the test, literally in seconds. It felt like the simplest thing in the world, and indeed it was, since in the course of my calculations I was routinely solving problems that were much more complex and difficult.

I use the term "locking on" since this is the subjective feeling that one has in the kind of problem-solving that I am describing. When one is locked on to a problem, there is tremendous, almost sensual joy in solving it. It is possible to go without food and sleep, to dismiss all fatigue, until the problem is solved. Beyond this, it appears that one can call forth intellectual resources of which one is usually totally unaware.

Being locked on to a problem also brings a person into a state of consciousness different from his normal state. A much greater portion of the mind seems to be involved in solving the problem than in a normal mental state. It could therefore be considered a "problem-solving" state of consciousness.

I also remember a period during which I was painting. I had just learned how to use acrylics and had found that I could produce a fairly decent piece of work. Whenever I got involved in a painting, it seemed that I was also "locked on" to the project; I would find it extremely difficult to leave it. Again, I was able to create paintings that were surprising even to me. It appeared that when I was creating, I was going into a higher state of consciousness. Subjectively, I did not simply feel a sense of greater awareness or alertness; rather, I felt as if I were thinking in an entirely different mode.

The difference between ordinary intelligence and genius may not be so much a matter of a person's innate ability as his ability to "lock on" to the work at hand and get into a higher state of consciousness. Ordinary people consider works of genius beyond their reach, but this might not be true, since the creator himself may be surprised at what he produces when in a "locked-on" state of consciousness. The degree of creativity that one has, whether in art or in problem-solving, may be several orders of magnitude greater when one is in a "locked-on" state than when one is in a normal state of consciousness. It may be that the secret of genius is the ability to lock on to problems or creative efforts on a much deeper level than most people ordinarily attain.

This locked-on state of consciousness appears to be associated with increased physical energy. The pulse is quicker, and one may perspire profusely. Sometimes, one even has the experience of trembling with creativity. It seems that while one is in such a state, the energy that one is utilizing is much greater than normal, and not only is the mind completely involved in the creative effort, but also the body.

There appears to be, however, another type of problem-solving consciousness. The first time I became aware of it was when, in the course of Kabbalistic research, I was trying to figure out the properties of a five-dimensional hypercube. The problem was extremely difficult, since it involved trying to visualize what would happen when the hypercube was rotated through five-dimensional space. I had spent several afternoons sweating over the problem, without even coming close to a solution.

Then, one evening, I was relaxing in the bathtub, and my mind wandered to the problem, almost offhandedly. Suddenly, every aspect of the problem seemed perfectly clear, and relationships that had been impossibly complex were now easy to visualize and understand. By the time I got out of the tub, I had worked out the problem completely.

Eventually, I began to realize that this was happening to me often. Sitting in the tub was an excellent time to solve the most difficult problems. But the experience was very different from being locked on to a problem. Quite to the contrary, the mind was free to wander wherever it wanted, but it seemed to hit upon the right answers with surprising clarity.

It seems that the mind has two modes in which it possesses abnormal ability to solve problems. One is the "locked-on" mode, in which the energy of both mind and body is increased. The other is when a person is completely relaxed and the mind drifts to the problem on its own.

I think of the "locked-on" mode as a "hot" mode of thought and the relaxed mode as a "cool" mode of thought. In both cases, one's problem-solving ability is tremendously expanded. In hot concentration, the entire body is brought into play and, as it were, the adrenaline is made to flow. In cool concentration, body and mind are quieted down as much as possible, so that the mind is able to focus on the problem like a laser beam.

These two examples may seem far removed from the usual discussion of the higher states of consciousness associated with meditation. However, there are important links.

First, there are intellectual modes of meditation. In some traditions, they are associated with "the way of the intellect." Some types of meditation appear to be designed to produce precisely the states of consciousness in which problem-solving ability is enhanced.

There is also a direct relationship to the better-known forms of meditation. Mantra meditation, which consists of repeating a word or phrase over and over, is said to elicit the "relaxation response." Many clinical psychologists use this type of meditation to induce relaxation in their patients. Indeed, a type of mantra meditation known as Standardized Clinical Meditation (SCM) has been devised as a therapeutic tool, devoid of all mystical elements.

While this technique appears to relax the body, it also increases the mind's activity. Mantra meditation can be used to relax the body and bring the mind into a state of "cool concentration." When a person is in such a state, his control of his mind processes seems to be increased. This can be demonstrated by a simple experiment:

Sit down in a straight-backed chair. Your back should be straight, since if you are in a hunched or slouched position, you will begin to feel cramped after a while. This experiment should be done at a time when you know that you will not be disturbed or interrupted.

Begin by relaxing completely. Then close your eyes. Initially, you will see lights and images flashing in the mind's eye. After a minute or two, these flashes will begin to coalesce and take the form of kaleidoscopically changing images, as discussed earlier. As you relax, the images will begin to change more and more slowly, and eventually they will remain in the mind's eye long enough for you to focus on them.

Just concentrate on the images. If other thoughts enter the mind, gently push them out. Try to maintain your concentration on the forms that arise in your mind's eye, and on nothing else. Gradually, you should find that you can hold on to an image for quite a while.

The first few times you do this, try to relax and concentrate on the images in your mind's eye without doing anything else. Each session should last for twenty to thirty minutes. Gradually, your ability to hold images and focus on them should increase.

Once you have reached this stage, you are ready to demonstrate to yourself the effects of mantra meditation. Since you are only experimenting, and not making a long-term discipline of it at this point, it does not matter what you use for a mantra. It can consist of a nonsense phrase, a favorite line of poetry, a phrase from the Bible, or any other group of words. Some people find the words "My name is ——" an easy phrase to begin with. If you wish to make a more spiritual experience of it, you can use Rabbi Nachman's mantra, "Lord of the Universe," or its Hebrew equivalent (see chapter 5).

Sitting comfortably, just repeat your experimental mantra over and over. At this point, it does not matter how you repeat it. You may wish to chant it slowly, whisper it, or silently mouth the words. The phrase should be said slowly, over and over again, for the entire session. After a while, you will begin to feel very relaxed and at the same time very alert.

Now, while repeating the mantra, pay attention to the images formed in your mind's eye. As the mind quiets down, these images should become more and more vivid, and you should be able to hold them in the mind for longer and longer periods. The images may become spectacular and beautiful, sometimes even breathtaking.

The images formed in the mind's eye constitute one of the few objective indicators of the meditative state. You know that you are in a meditative state when the imagery in the mind's eye begins to take on a more substantial and permanent form. While imaging is not the only manifestation of higher states of consciousness, it is an indicator that is important and easy to describe objectively. Other indicators are also manifestations of one's control over the mental process, just as visualization is.

Since this is being done as an experiment, it is not advisable to go too far in this direction without carefully planning out a course of meditation. But the experiment shows that in higher states of consciousness, one's ability to form images in the mind and concentrate on them is greatly enhanced.

After progressing in meditation and learning how to concentrate, a process that can take weeks or months, one can learn how to control the images seen in one's mind's eye. At this point, one can conjure up an image and hold it in the field of vision as long as one desires. As we shall see, this in itself can become a form of meditation.

Earlier, we discussed the random images that appear in the mind's eye and spoke of them as being a sort of static produced by the brain. Although this static is most easily seen with the eyes closed, it also exists when we are looking at things; at that time, it tends to dull our perception. Thus, if one is looking at a rose, the experience of the rose's beauty is diminished by this static.

When a person learns how to hold an image in the mind, however, he can also control the mind's static. He can then see things without being disturbed by the brain's self-generated images. This is especially significant in the appreciation of beauty. If a person "turns off" the mind's static and then looks at a rose, the image in his mind's eye will contain nothing other than the rose. Since at this point he can see the rose without any static, the beauty of the rose is enhanced manyfold. This is one reason that many people report an enhanced sense of beauty while in the meditative state. Indeed, many people learn meditation primarily to experience the new aesthetic experiences that can be encountered in such states of consciousness.

Once a person learns how to control the visions in the mind's eye, he can progress to increasingly more advanced visualizations. The simplest stages of visualization are straightforward; one conjures up images of figures, letters, objects, or scenes. What one sees is not much different from what one sees with normal vision. Nevertheless, to make the images in the mind's eye appear as solid and real as waking images requires considerable training. As one becomes more advanced, the images can appear even more real than what one sees with open eyes.

The more advanced one becomes in controlling one's mind, the more control one has over what one can see in the mind's eye. When a person becomes expert in visualization, he will be able to see things in the mind's eye that he could never see with his physical eyes. From descriptions in Kabbalistic and other mystical works, it appears that many experiences encountered in higher states of consciousness fall into this category.

Thus, for example, the Zohar speaks of the "lamp of darkness." This appears to denote a darkness that radiates. Similarly, in Talmudic sources, there are references to "black fire." There is a teaching that the primeval Torah was originally written "with black fire on white fire." This is something that we cannot see with ordinary vision, and indeed, it is impossible to imagine in a normal state of consciousness. Ordinarily, we see bright colors, not blackness or darkness, as radiant.

In the mind's eye, however, it is possible to visualize a lamp radiating darkness. It would be like the negative image of a lamp radiating light. Just as when one sees light, one is aware that energy is being radiated, when one sees the lamp of darkness, one would be aware of negative energy radiating. Visualizing "black fire" would be a very similar experience. When a person has learned to control his visualization experience, negative energy becomes a simple thing to visualize.

It is also possible for a person to intensify his perception of beauty in an image in his mind's eye. This is beyond the enhanced perception that we have discussed earlier, in which one removes the static and focuses the entire mind on a beautiful object. Rather, one would be turning up the "beauty" dial in the mind, to make the mind particularly sensitive and appreciative of beauty. The image that one then sees in the mind's eye may appear thousands of times more beautiful than an image seen with the physical eyes, since one is intentionally amplifying the sensation of beauty.

This is significant, since Beauty (*tifereth*) is one of the Ten Sefiroth discussed in Kabbalah. The Ten Sefiroth are Will (*keter*), Learning Ability (*chokhmah*), Understanding (*binah*), Love (*chesed*), Strength (*gevurah*), Beauty (*tifereth*), Dominance (*netzach*), Submissiveness (*hod*), Sexuality (*yesod*), and Receptivity (*malkhuth*). These Sefiroth may be looked upon as "dials" in the mind that can be used to amplify the experiences associated with them. Thus, since Beauty is one of the Ten Sefiroth, one can turn up the "dial" and amplify the sensation.

Another important phenomenon that can be experienced in a higher, controlled state of consciousness is panoscopic vision. Normally, when one looks at a solid object, one can see only one side of it at a time. Similarly, in the mind's eye, one usually visualizes something only one side at a time. Of course, in the case of a real object, one can rotate it to see the other side, and one can do the same in the mind's eye. In a higher state of consciousness, however, it is possible to attain panoscopic vision, whereby one can look at an object in the mind's eye from all sides at once.

Thus, for example, if one were looking at America on a globe, one would not be able to see Asia, since it is on the opposite side of the globe. However, in a higher state of consciousness, it would be possible to visualize the globe and see America and Asia simultaneously. It is impossible to describe this sensation to one who has never experienced it. A number of modern artists, such as Picasso, seem to have had such experiences and attempted to depict them on canvas.

The human mind can normally visualize an object only from one side because this is the way we see with our eyes. This is merely due to habit from the time of infanthood. When one learns how to control one's mental processes, one can break these habits and visualize things in totally different perspectives. Panoscopic vision is one example of this phenomenon.

There is evidence that the prophet Ezekiel had such an experience in his famous vision. He describes certain angels, known as *chayyoth*, as having four different faces on four different sides: the face of a man, the face of a lion, the face of an ox, and the face of an eagle. Yet he continually stresses that these figures "did not rotate as they moved." What he was saying was that although he saw the *chayyoth* from only one side and they did not rotate, he could see all four faces at once.

Even more spectacular is the fact that in an advanced state of consciousness, it is possible to visualize more than the usual three dimensions. Of course, with our physical eyes, we never see more than the three-dimensional world around us. However, in higher meditative states, it is possible to visualize four and sometimes even five dimensions. There is evidence that the *Sefer Yetzirah* (Book of Creation) contains meditative exercises that include such visualizations.

Synesthesia is another important phenomenon observed in higher states of consciousness. Human senses tend to be compartmentalized, so that different parts of the mind deal with different senses; one part of the mind may deal with sight, while another deals with hearing. In a normal state of consciousness, we do not see sounds or hear colors.

In higher states of consciousness, however, the barriers between the senses are lowered. In such states, one's sense of sight can be used to perceive sounds. Similarly, one is able to hear colors, see fragrances, and feel sights. This is the experience of synesthesia, which means "mixing of senses."

Even in a normal state of consciousness, on an ethereal level, one may have a vague feeling that a sound or melody has a particular texture or color. This is because the barriers between the senses are never totally absolute. In higher states of consciousness, however, the spillover can become quite vivid. For example, one may see a piece of music as a complex visual pattern. I am saying not that the music is *associated* with the pattern, but that the music *is* the pattern. It is a very strange sensation, which is impossible to describe to someone who has never experienced it.

There is Talmudic evidence that synesthesia was associated with the mystical state of revelation. When the Ten Commandments were given, the Torah describes the people's experience by stating, "All the people *saw* the sounds" (Exod. 20:18). An ancient Talmudic source states that "they saw that which would normally be heard, and heard that which would normally be seen." This is a clear example of synesthesia.

Another phenomenon that can be visualized in a higher meditative state is nothingness. When we think of nothingness, we often think of it as simple blackness, a vacuum, or the interplanetary void. None of this, however, is true nothingness. Blackness or space cannot be nothingness, since "blackness" and "space" are things themselves. Nothingness must be the absence of everything, even of blackness and empty space.

If you want to know what nothingness looks like, just focus on what you see behind your head. (In some systems, one focuses on what one sees *inside* the head.) Obviously, you cannot see anything behind your head. But this means precisely that what you see behind your head is nothingness. Therefore, if you want to know what nothing really looks like, concentrate on what you see behind your head.

If you wanted to visualize nothingness in a meditative state, you would have to take this perception of nothingness and bring it into your mind's eye. In a normal state of consciousness, this would be impossible, but in higher states of consciousness, with training and practice, it can be accomplished. Indeed, in a number of systems of meditation, it is an important practice.

For one thing, filling the mind with nothingness is a highly effective way of clearing it of all perception. There are some experiences that are so subtle that even the visualization of blackness or empty space could overshadow them. However, when the mind is filled with the experience of nothingness, it is open to the most subtle influences.

One of the influences that the mind can detect while visualizing nothingness is the spiritual. In such a state, the spiritual can appear very spectacular, since the nothingness in the mind can be filled with that which comes from the Without.

Of course, visualizing nothingness is a highly advanced technique. The spiritual, however, can be experienced on much simpler levels. Indeed, there appears to be an area of the mind that is particularly receptive to the spiritual experience. Sometimes, without warning, a person can have a spiritual experience that leaves him awestruck or exhilarated. A more intense spiritual experience can have a profound effect on a person's entire life.

Just as a person can amplify his sense of beauty through meditation, he can also amplify his sense of the spiritual. If part of the mind is particularly sensitive to the spiritual, then through meditation this sensitivity can voluntarily be enhanced and increased.

This results from the control of the mind that one has during the meditative experience.

Enhanced spiritual experiences are associated with the states of consciousness experienced by prophets and mystics. The senses are blocked out, and all sensation, both internal and external, is eliminated. In such states of consciousness, the feeling of the Divine is strengthened, and a person can experience an intense feeling of closeness to God. Meditations of this type can bring a person to the most profound and beautiful experiences imaginable.

A world of caution is in order at this point. The experiences that a person can have in these states of consciousness can be so beatific that he may not want to return to his normal state of consciousness. It is possible for a person to become completely lost in the mystic state, actually swallowed up by it. Therefore, before exploring these highest states, be sure that you have something to bring you down safely. It is very much like flying a plane. Taking off is exhilarating, but before you take off, you had better know how to land again.

For this reason, most texts on Jewish meditation stress that before embarking on the higher levels, a person should have a master. Then, if he goes "up" and does not know how to come down, or does not want to, the master will be able to talk him down.

Other sources indicate that mystics would actually take an oath to return to a normal state of consciousness at the end of their meditative sessions. Then, even if they were not inclined to return, they would be bound by their oath.

All texts on Jewish meditation stress that the person embarking on more advanced forms of meditation should first develop a strong internal discipline. This is very important, since higher states of consciousness are very enticing and it is possible to lose one's sense of reality. However, if a person is in control of his actions and emotions in general, he will also remain in control of his sense of reality. Rather than negate his life, his meditative experiences will enhance it.

It is in this context that a common folk saying states that people who study Kabbalah go mad. This obviously does not mean the academic study of Kabbalah; although Kabbalah is a difficult intellectual discipline, it is no more dangerous than any other study. However, involvement in the more esoteric forms of Kabbalistic meditation can be dangerous to mental health, especially if the meditator proceeds without adequate preparation.

In a sense, it is like climbing a mountain. Even for an experienced climber, there is always an element of danger. If a person had limited experience, he would not even think of climbing a difficult mountain without a guide; to do so would be to court disaster. The same is true of one who tries the more esoteric forms of meditation without proper training and discipline.

The forms of meditation presented in this book are not dangerous mountains. Rather, they are gentle hills, which are safe to climb, but from which one can see wide vistas.

5

JEWISH MEDITATION

In the previous chapters, we have discussed the discipline of meditation in general. Before we can understand Jewish meditation, we must first have a good idea of the nature of meditation in its broadest sense. The phenomenology and psychology of Jewish meditation are not particularly different from those of other systems. The goals and results, however, are often very different.

There is ample evidence that meditative practices were widespread among Jews throughout Jewish history. References to meditation are found in major Jewish texts in every period from the biblical to the premodern era. One reason that this has not been universally recognized is that the vocabulary of meditation has been lost to a large degree, especially during the last century.

Until the rise of the Jewish Enlightenment, mysticism and intellectualism had equal status within Judaism. The ostensible goal of the Enlightenment, however, was to raise the intellectual level of Judaism, and positive as this may have been, it was often done at the expense of other Jewish values. The first values to fall by the wayside were Jewish mysticism in general and meditation in particular. Anything that touched upon the mystical was denigrated as superstition and occultism and was deemed unworthy of serious study.

Even Kabbalah, which contains mysticism par excellence, was reduced to simply an intellectual exercise; its deeper meanings were totally lost. In earlier chapters we discussed how many phenomena experienced in a meditative state cannot be understood rationally. This premise was not recognized by the nineteenth-century rationalists, and even the ineffable became the subject of philosophical discussion.

For this and other reasons, all references to meditation vanished from mainstream Jewish literature about 150 years ago. This is true even in Chasidic literature, where meditation initially played a central role. Because of this antimystical trend, even Kabbalistic works published after around 1840 show a surprising lack of even the slightest mention of meditation. After a century of indifference, even the meanings of key words were forgotten.

In earlier literature, by contrast, references to meditation are abundant. This is true even in the Bible, although one has to resort to a kind of "verbal archaeology" to discover the true meaning of key words.

In any case, it appears from both biblical and postbiblical sources that meditation was central to the prophetic experience, and that this experience was attained in the meditative state. The Bible states explicitly that the prophets used chants and music to attain higher states of consciousness. Careful philological analysis of certain key words in the Bible suggests that they refer to specific meditative methods. This subject formed the basis of my first book on the subject, *Meditation and the Bible*. However, since the discussion consists largely of analysis of Hebrew words, it is beyond the scope of this book.

From the literature, it seems evident that a prophet would almost always experience his first prophetic experience while in a meditative state. Later, however, it would become possible for him to experience prophecy without meditation. Sometimes prophecy would come to a prophet unexpectedly and without warning. This probably involved a phenomenon sometimes referred to as "flashback." After a person has become adept at reaching higher levels of consciousness through meditation, he can occasionally reach such levels spontaneously as well. This seems to be evident in the experiences of a number of prophets.

There is also evidence that during the period when the Bible was written (until approximately 400 B.C.E.), meditation was practiced by a large proportion of the Israelite people. The Talmud and Midrash state explicitly that over a million people were involved in such disciplines. Regular schools of meditation existed, led by master prophets. The master prophets, in turn, were under the leadership of the primary prophets, the ones actually quoted in the Bible. In these schools, people were taught meditative methods in order to attain a closeness to God; as a side effect of such meditation, prophecy was also sometimes achieved.

Since nonprophets may have been practicing meditators, they would also experience spontaneous prophecy or visions, without actually meditating. This would explain the biblical accounts of individuals who had prophetic visions even though they were not meditating and had no prior prophetic experience. When a person engages in meditation on a regular basis, he can reach meditative states of consciousness spontaneously, without meditation, and these states can cause him to experience visions.

Everything found in later literature seems to indicate that these meditative schools required a strong discipline and faithful adherence to a strict regimen. The schools were extremely demanding, and were open only to those willing to devote themselves totally. Before even being admitted to one of these ancient meditative schools, a person had to be not only spiritually advanced but in complete control of all his emotions and feelings. Beyond that, the disciplines of the Torah and commandments were central to these schools, and these disciplines required a degree of self-mastery to which not everyone could aspire.

It appears that this was one of the attractions of ancient idolatry. While the Jewish meditative schools required extensive discipline and preparation, many idolatrous schools of mysticism and meditation were open to all. A person could at least think that he was having a transcendental experience, without adhering to the tight discipline of Torah and Judaism. It was very much like the situation today, when Eastern meditative groups seem easier to relate to than the strict discipline of Judaism.

For anyone who has ever had a taste of the transcendental, it can be an infinitely sweet experience, more pleasurable than love or sex. For many people, it was an experience after which they would actually lust. When the Talmud speaks of the "lust for idolatry," it could be speaking of the magnetic attraction that this spiritual experience had for people. If they could not get it from Israelite sources, they would seek it in idolatrous rites.

As long as the Israelites were in their homeland, the situation was more or less under control. Idolatry may have been a strong temptation, but the prophetic mystical schools were strong enough to unite the people and prevent them from assimilating. Even if individuals or groups backslid, they could always be drawn back into the fold. In sum, during the entire First Commonwealth, meditation and mysticism played a central role in Judaism; the spiritual leaders were the prophets, the individuals who were most advanced spiritually.

All this changed with the diaspora, which scattered Jews all over the world. It was realized that if the masses remained involved in prophetic mysticism, the temptations drawing them to idolatry would ultimately alienate them from the Torah. Isolated, widely scattered groups would be ready prey to false teachers and experiences. Therefore, around this time, the more advanced forms of meditation were hidden from the masses and made part of a secret teaching. Now only the most qualified individuals would be party to the secrets of advanced prophetic meditation.

One of the last of the great prophets was Ezekiel, who lived in Babylonia right at the beginning of the Exile. The first chapter of the Book of Ezekiel is one of the most mysterious parts of the entire Bible. In it, the prophet describes his visions of angels and the Divine Throne in extraordinary detail. According to one tradition, this vision contained the keys to prophetic meditation and, if understood, could serve as a guide to attaining prophecy. The study of this chapter became known as the "discipline of the chariot" (*maaseh merkavah*). The methodology was there, but without the key it could not be understood.

By the time of the rebuilding of the Second Temple, and the

establishment of the Second Commonwealth, the Jewish leadership was clearly aware of the dangers that chariot meditation posed if it were made available to the masses. First, without adequate teachers and masters, Jews living in the diaspora would pervert the methods or use them for the wrong ends. This in turn could lead to the splintering of Judaism into rival sects or to the establishment of religions alien to Judaism. The net result would be the disunification of the Jewish people.

Second, as discussed earlier, Jewish meditation was an extremely difficult discipline, which required years of preparation. If it were an accepted part of Judaism, it was feared that Jews would become frustrated by the difficulties of practicing it and be tempted to try non-Jewish forms of meditation. This, in turn, could lead them to idolatry and assimilation. Idolatry had been enough of a problem during the First Commonwealth, when all the Israelites were in their homeland; now, in the diaspora, there was a distinct danger that it would lead to the destruction of the entire nation.

Therefore, the Jewish leadership made a very difficult decision. The benefits of having the masses involved in the highest types of meditation were weighed against the dangers. Although the nation might lose a degree of spirituality as a result of the decision, it would at least survive. Henceforth, the discipline of the chariot had to be made into a secret doctrine, taught only to the most select individuals. The Great Assembly, which represented the first Jewish leadership in the Second Commonwealth, thus decreed: "The discipline of the chariot may be taught only to individual students (one at a time), and they must be wise, understanding with their own knowledge."

The Great Assembly also realized that the general populace would need a meditative discipline. But rather than have it be something loose and unstructured, they needed a discipline with a structure common to the entire Jewish nation, one that would serve as a means of uniting the people. It would have to contain the hopes and aspirations of the nation as a whole, to reinforce the unity of the Jewish people.

The meditative discipline that was composed by the Great

Assembly ended up as the Amidah, a "standing" prayer consisting of eighteen sections, which would be repeated silently, in an upright position, three times each day. It is true that nowadays the Amidah is thought of more as a prayer than a meditative device, but the most ancient sources regard it as a meditation. Indeed, the Talmud verifies that this was its original intention.

This also explains why the Great Assembly legislated that the same prayer be repeated three times each day. People often complain that saying the same prayer over and over is tedious and uninspiring. For anyone familiar with mantra meditation, however, the opposite is true. All types of mantra meditation involve repetition. In mantra meditation, the device repeated is a word or a phrase, and it can be repeated over and over for weeks, months, or even years on end.

The Amidah was meant to be repeated three times every day from childhood on, and essentially the same formula would be said for an entire lifetime. The Amidah could therefore be looked upon as one long mantra. In many ways, it has the same effects as a mantra, lifting the individual to a high meditative level of consciousness. As we shall, there is an entire literature that describes how the Amidah can be used in this manner. But most important, there is ample evidence that it was originally composed as the common form of meditation to be used by the entire Jewish nation.

From Talmudic times through the Middle Ages, an extensive literature dealing with Jewish meditation was written. Virtually every method found in general meditation can be found in ancient Jewish texts, as well as a number of methods that are found nowhere else. Indeed, a comparative study of meditative methods shows that the Jewish systems may have been among the most advanced in the world.

The Talmud speaks at length of meditation and meditative experiences, referring to it as the discipline of the chariot or "entering Paradise." There are numerous anecdotes about Talmudic sages, such as Rabban Yochanan ben Zakkai and Rabbi Akiva, engaging in these practices. The Talmud also says that the "original saints" (*chasidim rishonim*) spent an hour reciting the

Amidah; the context shows that it is speaking of a meditative rather than a worship experience. However, since meditation had become a secret doctrine within Judaism by Talmudic times, everything is couched in allusion and allegory. Only to one who is aware of the methods do the accounts even begin to make sense.

There were two major works on meditation that were most probably published during the Talmudic period (around 100–500 C.E.). The first is the *Sefer Yetzirah*, the Book of Creation. This is the most enigmatic text on Jewish mysticism. Over a hundred commentaries have been written on this text in an effort to unravel its mysteries, but they all tend to read their own systems into the text rather than extract its message. Careful analysis of the text, however, shows it to be an extremely advanced work on meditation.

Another important text from this period is *Heykhaloth Rabbatai* (Greater Book of the [Divine] Chambers). This is a primary text on *merkavah* mysticism, which describes some of the techniques used in the discipline of the chariot. This work is fairly explicit, but even here, unless one is familiar with meditative techniques, the text is largely opaque.

In the Middle Ages, meditation was a well-known technique and was discussed at length by the Jewish philosophers, especially in connection with prophecy. Such Jewish philosophers as Maimonides and Gersonides analyzed the meditative state in depth, contrasting the visions that one has in a meditative state with those in a dream state. The way it is discussed suggests that meditation was considered an integral part of Judaism.

Among Jewish mystics and Kabbalists, it was evident that meditation played a key role. A great deal was written during this period about experiences that one could have in the meditative state and how one's vision and state of conscious could be altered. Techniques were alluded to, but always in veiled hints, as if this teaching was bound to remain an oral tradition, never be put in writing. With one exception, we are left with tantalizing allusions, but no clear facts.

The one individual who broke the rule of secrecy was Abraham

Abulafia (1240–1296). He was a highly controversial figure for many reasons, not the least being the fact that he felt he was destined to be either a messianic figure or a harbinger of the Messiah. But, as he states explicitly in his works, he was the first to put the methods of Kabbalah meditation into writing. Although he was criticized in his time, later Kabbalists recognized that the methods he describes represent the true tradition of prophetic Kabbalism.

Soon after Abulafia's time an event was to occur that would eclipse meditation as the focus of Kabbalah. This was the publication of the Zohar in the 1290s. Although this mystical work contains many allusions to meditative methods, it does not speak explicitly about meditation. But the spiritual systems described by the Zohar are so complex that it would take a lifetime to understand them—and this is exactly what happened.

With the publication of the Zohar, Kabbalah entered a new era. Besides reaching mystical states and higher states of consciousness, Kabbalists now had a new goal, namely to understand the Zohar. This made Kabbalah into an academic discipline as well as a mystical one. One begins to find more and more books published on Kabbalah that regard it as a philosophy rather than as an experience. Indeed, by the fifteenth century, it was virtually impossible to write a book on Jewish philosophy without referring to the Kabbalah.

The mystical element, however, was still very important. Kabbalah study reached its zenith in the famed community of Safed, the city of saints and mystics. Foremost among the Safed Kabbalists was Rabbi Isaac Luria (1534–1572), usually referred to as the Ari. He was so spiritually sensitive that he became a legend in his own lifetime, but his main accomplishment was the vast body of Kabbalistic literature that he bequeathed to the world. The Ari unraveled the mystery of the Zohar, showing how its system could form the basis of a meditative discipline. Beyond that, he left a system of Kabbalah that is one of the most complex intellectual systems devised by man.

This, in turn, had the effect of further intellectualizing Kabbalah, making the mystical realm every bit as stimulating and fascinating as philosophy or Talmud. Thus, Kabbalah gained status as an intellectual discipline in its own right. The works of Kabbalists in the seventeenth and eighteenth centuries took their place as some of the most profound, complex, and challenging Judaic works ever written. But this phenomenon also had the effect of reducing the importance of meditation, even among Jewish mystics. For many, Jewish mysticism and Kabbalah had become an intellectual exercise and nothing more.

There was yet another influence that downgraded the importance of Kabbalah in this period. This was the reaction to the false messiah, Sabbatai Zvi (1626–1676). This charismatic individual twisted the teachings of Kabbalah and used it to support his warped messianic claims. His career ended when he was challenged by the Turkish sultan; he chose to convert to Islam rather than suffer martyrdom, leaving thousands of his followers totally disillusioned. The false messiah gave mysticism a bad name and brought about the eclipse of Jewish mysticism and meditation for almost a century.

A renaissance of Jewish mysticism occurred in the middle of the eighteenth century under the leadership of the famed Rabbi Israel, known as the Baal Shem Tov (1698–1760). The Chasidic movement, which he founded, was based on mysticism, and meditative exercises were central to the movement. An important early Chasidic technique involved using the daily service as a meditative exercise. Not only did the Chasidic movement bring meditation back into Judaism, but it infused the Jewish community with new energy and commitment as well.

Still, the established Jewish community saw the embryonic Chasidic movement as a threat. Since it had adopted unique and distinctive practices, many Jewish leaders felt that the movement could become a cult. It was also felt that the movement was too closely associated with a single personality, a trait reminiscent of the Sabbatai Zvi fiasco. A powerful opposition to Chasidism arose, going so far as to excommunicate the entire movement. Leading rabbinical sages throughout Europe were marshaled to express their opposition to the movement in the strongest terms.

This, in turn, had its effect on the Chasidic movement. Some elements of this movement took a road that had been traveled earlier, reducing all its mystical teachings to philosophy. Others chose to institutionalize the role of spiritual master, making allegiance to a master (or *rebbe*) the main distinguishing feature of Chasidism.

During the first three generations of Chasidism, there was hardly a published work on the subject that did not contain some mention of meditation and the mystical experience. In later works, however, mysticism is notably lacking. Indeed, in many areas, after 1850, the Chasidic movement developed a strong antimystical trend. Thus, one of the last bastions of Jewish meditation fell, and the entire practice was forgotten for over a century. Even the basic vocabulary of meditation seemed to have been lost. Scholars wrote about Jewish mysticism but ignored blatant references to meditation; key words for meditation were either mistranslated or misinterpreted. A situation arose in which meditation was virtually erased from the Jewish consciousness and obliterated from Jewish history.

At this point it would be useful to discuss the most common terms for meditation found in Jewish texts. Since all of these texts were written in Hebrew, the key words are also in that language. From their roots and form, considerable insight can be obtained into the types of meditation that they signify.

The most common word for meditation in Judaic literature is *kavanah*. This word is translated as "concentration" or "feeling" or "devotion." In context, the literature speaks of worshiping with *kavanah* or maintaining *kavanah* while performing a sacred act. However, looking at the origin of the word *kavanah*, we immediately see that it comes from the Hebrew root *kaven*, which means "to aim." Therefore, *kavanah* denotes "aiming" consciousness toward a certain goal. The most apt translation is "directed consciousness."

Earlier, we defined meditation as controlled thinking. In this sense, *kavanah* would be the most generic Hebrew term for meditation.

The word *kavanah* is most often used in relation to prayer or worship. In Judaism, as we shall see, the line between worship and meditation is often a very fine one. Many elements of the worship service are specifically designed to be used as meditations, to reach higher states of consciousness. We have discussed this usage with regard to the Amidah, but it is also true of a number of other prayers.

When one has *kavanah* in worship, one is allowing the words of the service to direct one's consciousness. The mind is brought to the state of consciousness defined by the prayer one is reciting. In this respect, the prayer is used to direct the consciousness.

The word *kavanah* is also associated with various actions, especially those involving fulfillment of the commandments or rituals. Here, too, *kavanah* denotes clearing the mind of extraneous thought and concentrating totally on the action at hand. The act itself becomes the means through which the person's consciousness is directed.

In addition to the general concept of *kavanah*, various Jewish devotional works, especially those of a Kabbalistic nature, contain collections of specific *kavanah* meditations, or *kavanoth*, for various rituals. These *kavanoth* are used to direct the mind along the inner paths defined by the esoteric meaning of the ritual.

Another important Hebrew term associated with meditation is *hitbonenuth*. Translated literally, this word means "self-understanding." It reflects a somewhat different type of meditation.

Normally, we look at things dispassionately and objectively. I may look at a leaf and even examine it very closely, but it does not affect me in any way. I am exactly the same person after as I was before. It does not change my state of consciousness at all. My mind is the same looking at the leaf as it would be otherwise.

However, I may also look at the leaf with the aim of using it to attain a higher level of consciousness or a greater degree of self-awareness. I would then be using the leaf as a means to achieve "self-understanding," or *hitbonenuth*.

The great Jewish philosopher Moses Maimonides (1135–1204) speaks about using *hitbonenuth* meditation while contemplating God's creation. One can achieve a profound love for God through such contemplation. This is effective precisely because it is not merely a simple contemplation of various aspects of God's creation, but is understanding oneself as part of this creation. When one sees God's creation, and understands one's own role as part of it, one can develop a deep and lasting love for God. Who has not gone out into the fields on a clear night and gazed at the stars, yearning to unlock their secret? One thinks about the vast, unfathomable reaches of the universe and stands in rapt awe. For many people, this in itself can be a "religious experience." It is an experience that can bring a person to feel a profound humility before the infinite vastness of the universe.

The next step is to go beyond the physical and contemplate the fact that this vast universe, with all its countless stars and galaxies, was all created by God. One ponders the fact that one ineffable Being created everything. We realize how different this Being must be from us, and yet we feel a certain closeness.

The final step is *hitbonenuth,* understanding oneself in the light of this vast creation. At this level, one asks the questions, "If God created this vast universe, then who am I? How do I fit into all of this?" At the same time, one may feel privileged that God allows us to have a direct relationship with Him. Imagine that the creator of all the stars and galaxies deigns to listen to me! Not only that, but He is concerned about me! Realizing God's greatness, and at the same time contemplating the closeness to Him that He allows us to enjoy, is precisely what can bring a person to profound love for God.

The Psalmist expressed this when he said, "I look at Your heavens, the work of Your fingers, the moon and stars that You have established. What is man that You remember him, a son of Adam that You even consider him? Yet, You have made him a little less than divine, You have adorned him with glory and honor. You made him master over all Your creatures and placed everything under his feet" (Ps. 8:4–6). We realize how insignificant we should be in God's eyes, and yet how significant we really are.

Hitbonenuth meditation can be focused on anything—a stone, a leaf, a flower, or an idea. One allows the subject to fill the mind and then uses it as a means to understand the self. It is a type of mirror in which one can see oneself in the light of true Reality. Using this mirror, one can see the Divine within oneself. Indeed, this may be the "mirror [*aspaklaria*] of prophecy" described in the Talmud. When one looks into this mirror and sees the Divine within oneself, one can also communicate with the Divine.

The final important Hebrew word for meditation is *hitbodeduth*. This is the most specific term for meditation and one that was used as early as the tenth century. Literally, the word means "self-isolation," and for this reason, the term escaped the notice of many students of Jewish mysticism. Many scholars have translated *hitbodeduth* simply as "seclusion" or "isolation," not realizing that it refers to meditation.

The key to this term is to be found in a text by Moses Maimonides' son, Abraham. He writes that there are two types of isolation, external self-isolation and internal self-isolation. External self-isolation simply involves being alone physically—going off to fields, woods, or caves, anywhere away from other people. This, however, is only the first step; external self-isolation is the doorway to internal self-isolation.

Internal self-isolation consists in isolating the mind from all outward sensation and then even from thought itself. From what one reads in most non-Jewish classical texts, this is what is usually defined as the meditative state. Therefore, *hitbodeduth* is the Hebrew term for any practice that brings a person into the meditative state. It is a state in which the mind is isolated, standing alone, without any sensation or thought.

It is known that sensory deprivation can help a person attain higher states of consciousness. Indeed, there are places in large cities where a person can buy time in a sensory deprivation chamber. In such a perfectly dark, soundproof chamber, one floats in a dense liquid at body temperature. Cut off completely from all outward stimuli, the mind can go off totally on its own and float toward higher states of consciousness.

True meditation, however, does not require a sensory deprivation chamber. Rather, by using a meditative practice, one can blank out all outside stimuli at will. At the same time, one also blanks out all extraneous thought, filling the mind with the subject of one's meditation. This is *hitbodeduth*, self-isolation in a meditative sense.

Vocabulary is very important, since without it one can read a Hebrew meditative text and not even be aware of the nature of the subject. One reason that people were unaware of the importance and influence of meditation in Judaism is that they were incorrectly translating key words in the most important texts.

The general impression one gains from studying these texts is not only that meditation was practiced by Jews, but that for quite a number of centuries it was a very important ingredient of Judaism. Clearly, Jewish meditation has been part and parcel of Judaism throughout the ages.

6

MANTRA MEDITATION

T he best-known form of meditation today is mantra meditation. The word "mantra" is an Eastern term denoting a word or phrase that is repeated over and over as a meditative exercise. In many types of Eastern meditation, mantra meditation is the central exercise, and it forms virtually the entire basis of Transcendental Meditation. Since there is no adequate generic Western term for this type of meditation, I shall use the Eastern term "mantra."

One immediate effect of mantra meditation is to relax the body. In this form of meditation, it seems that the more the body relaxes, the more active the mind becomes. It is as if energy is released by the body, which can be used by the mind.

In any case, meditation, especially using a mantra, is an excellent relaxation method. For this reason, a number of psychologists have developed religiously neutral forms of mantra meditation to elicit the "relaxation response." An entire system called Standardized Clinical Meditation (SCM) has been developed to utilize this form of meditation in a clinical context.

Mantra meditation most probably works largely through habituation. If a person is in a room all day with, say, a loudly ticking clock, his mind eventually turns off the sound of the ticking. Although he hears the ticking, it simply does not register. The person is said to have become habituated to the ticking sound, so that he no longer pays attention to it. This is an important mechanism through which the mind filters out the commonplace and allows the thinker to concentrate on what is important.

When one repeats a mantra over and over, the mind also becomes habituated to it. Eventually, one becomes able to say it without the words registering in the conscious mind. By this time, one has also formed the habit of erasing all thought from the mind while reciting the mantra. It is therefore a highly effective psychological means of removing all thought from the mind.

This may seem quite mundane and nonmystical. However, the mantra does not necessarily have to be the mystical element in the meditation. The mantra can serve as a means of clearing the mind of mundane thought, leaving it open to other, transcendental experiences. This can be true no matter how nonmystical the mantra is. Indeed, in certain types of clinical meditation, a nonsense word can be used as the mantra.

Nevertheless, if the mantra has spiritual power in its own right, it not only clears the mind of mundane thought, but also puts the meditator into a special spiritual space. The form of the mantra can be extremely important if one wishes to accomplish a specific spiritual goal in one's meditation.

Although mantra meditation is not the most typical Jewish form of meditation, it is one of the simplest. As in general meditation, it consists in repeating a word or a phrase over and over, usually for a period of half an hour each day. The most important element of the meditation is that it be done daily and that there be a commitment to continue the practice for a period of at least a month. It usually takes between thirty and forty days for the results of this type of meditation to become manifest.

There appear to be references to mantra meditation even in the Bible. On the basis of philological analysis, it seems that the Hebrew verb *hagah* denotes a kind of meditation in which a word or sound is repeated over and over. The great Hebrew linguist David Kimchi (1160–1235) writes that the word *hagah* denotes a sound or a thought that is repeated like the cooing of a dove or the growling of a lion. Nevertheless, the biblical references to this type of meditation are ambiguous and not clearly stated.

The earliest unambiguous reference to a mantra type of meditation is found in *Heykhaloth Rabbatai,* the primary text of Merkavah mysticism, dating from Talmudic times. The text presents a mystical "name" of God, which is actually a rather long phrase consisting of a number of mystical words or names. The instruction says that this phrase must be repeated 120 times, again and again. The technique is reminiscent of mantra meditation, especially in some Eastern systems in which the mantra is repeated for a set number of times.

It is significant that in the *Heykhaloth,* the mantra is seen not as an end in itself, but rather as the first step in the discipline of the chariot. The mantra was used to bring the initiate into a state of consciousness from which he could travel from chamber to chamber in the supernal worlds. Thus, rather than define the state of consciousness, the mantra brought the individual into the first stage of the meditative state, from which he could use other techniques to progress further.

In later Kabbalistic schools, it appears that biblical verses or selections from the Talmud or Zohar would be used as mantras. In sixteenth-century Safed, for example, there is mention of a technique known as *gerushin,* which appears to consist in repeating a biblical verse over and over as a sort of mantra. Besides bringing the meditator into a higher state of consciousness, the purpose of this technique was to provide him with deeper insight into the verse itself. As he repeated the verse, it would eventually appear as if the verse itself were telling the initiate its meaning. Rather than studying or analyzing the verse, the meditator would then be communing with it.

This concept is even more graphically illustrated in a technique used by Rabbi Joseph Caro (1488–1575) and his followers. Instead of using a biblical verse, this technique made use of a selection from the Mishnah, the earliest portion of the Talmud, completed around 200 C.E. A portion of the Mishnah (a particular paragraph or *mishnah*) would be repeated as a mantra, leading to a state of consciousness in which a *maggid,* an angelic being associated with the *mishnah,* would speak to the meditator. Again, the meditator would gain deep insights, not from studying or analyzing the *mishnah*, but by experiencing its spiritual essence.

It is significant that there may be an allusion to this technique in the Talmud itself. The Talmud speaks of reviewing a *mishnah* and says, "Repeating one's *mishnah* one hundred times is not the same as repeating it one hundred and one times." There may be an allusion in this teaching that even in Talmudic times, the Mishnah was used as a type of mantra.

There is also evidence that the Ari (Rabbi Isaac Luria) made use of a similar technique with the Zohar. Unlike other Kabbalists of his time, who analyzed the Zohar and tried to probe its mysteries intellectually, the Ari probed its depths by means of a meditative technique. Judging by the description of his technique, he seems to have used a short selection of the Zohar as a mantra, repeating it over and over until its meaning became clear. The Ari describes this experience by saying that the Zohar "spoke to him."

In relatively modern times, a practical form of mantra meditation was prescribed by the noted Chasidic leader Rabbi Nachman of Bratslav (1772–1811). Of all the Chasidic masters, none spoke of *hitbodeduth* meditation more often than he. As we shall see, his main technique consisted in engaging in conversations with God. Nevertheless, Rabbi Nachman said that if a person does not known what to say, he should simply repeat the phrase *Ribbono shel Olam*, which is Hebrew for "Master of the Universe." From the description of the technique, it seems obvious that Rabbi Nachman was prescribing the use of this phrase as a mantra to bring a person into a higher state of consciousness.

Here, too, Rabbi Nachman did not regard repeating the mantra as an end in itself. Rather, he saw it as a way of opening the mind in order to enter into conversation with God, a method that he maintained was the best way to get close to God. Still, he saw repetition as an important technique in its own right.

Since the phrase *Ribbono shel Olam* was prescribed as a mantralike device by Rabbi Nachman, some people refer to it as Rabbi Nachman's mantra. Some, for the sake of authenticity, prefer the Chasidic pronunciation, *Ribboinoi shel Oylawm*. In any case, it is an ideal phrase for anyone who wants to engage in an authentic Jewish mantra meditation. Not only was it prescribed by one of the great Chasidic masters, but the phrase itself was used as an introduction to prayer as far back as early Talmudic times. The expression *Ribbono shel Olam* was used as early as the first century B.C.E. by Simeon ben Shetach, and according to the Talmud, it was also in use in biblical times.

Mantra meditation is one of the simplest types of meditation. It is therefore a good place to begin if you wish to embark on a program of meditation. Rabbi Nachman's mantra, *Ribbono shel Olam*, is a good one with which to start. It also provides an excellent example of meditation in general.

You cannot begin a program of meditation without a certain degree of commitment. In order for it to have an effect, you must do it on a daily basis, spending at least twenty or thirty minutes repeating the mantra. If you do it every day, the effects become cumulative. However, when you miss or skip days, the cumulative effect is lost. Furthermore, it takes several weeks of discipline with a mantra to attain a full level of a higher state of consciousness. Some effects may be manifest immediately, but it takes a few weeks before you experience the full effects. If you have the commitment, the results can be striking.

At this point, a word of warning is in order. Mantra meditation is a fairly safe method for most people, but it can be dangerous for someone with a history of mental illness. If a person's connection to the real world is not strong to begin with, he may have difficulty reestablishing his connection with reality after a deep meditative experience. Just as certain forms of strenuous exercise must be avoided by people with a history of heart trouble, certain forms of mental exercise should be avoided by people with a history of mental illness. The Talmudic story of Ben Zoma, who lost his mind after a particularly intense meditative experience, serves as a warning. Any person with doubts about his mental stability should make sure that he has an expert guide before becoming involved with any type of intense meditation.

In general, the preparations for meditation are straightforward and simple. You should meditate in a time and place where you will not be interrupted or disturbed by people, phone calls, or noise. Rabbi Nachman said that it was best to have a special room for meditation if possible. Since this is a luxury that few can afford, you may choose a special corner of the house, a special chair, or a room where you can be alone at night when no one else is about. Rabbi Nachman also said that woods, hills, and fields are good places to meditate, especially when the weather is comfortable.

But the place is not important, as long as it is an environment where you will not be interrupted. You can even meditate under the covers in bed at night, if it is a place where you know you will not be disturbed, and Rabbi Nachman presents this as a viable alternative. An excellent place, if available, would also be the synagogue when no one is around to disturb the meditative session.

Many people associate meditation with the Eastern lotus position. However, we should remember that in the East it was common to sit on the floor or on a mat, so that the lotus position was close to the normal, comfortable sitting position for Eastern meditators. For Westerners, this position is difficult to learn and is initially quite uncomfortable. In practice, it is found that sitting in a comfortable straight-backed chair is just as effective.

In any case, this is of little relevance to Jewish meditation, since the systems do not prescribe any special position. It is true that there are references to sitting in a chair, but they are only meant as a suggestion. You may choose any position in which you can remain comfortable for a long period of time without moving the body or being subject to cramping.

During meditation, sit with the eyes lightly closed, totally relaxed. Your hands can rest comfortably on the table or on your lap. Your fingers should not be clasped or intertwined, as the Kabbalists teach that this should be avoided. Rather, if your hands are together, one should rest lightly on the other.

Before beginning a meditation, settle yourself in the place. This means sitting quietly in the place where you will be meditating, fitting into it and making yourself at ease. During this period, try to relax completely, clearing your mind of all extraneous concerns. Some people find it helpful to hum a relaxing melody during these preparatory moments. This period should last between five and ten minutes.

In this respect, the advantage of meditating in the same place every day becomes clear. You will come to associate that place with the serene mood developed during meditation, and after a few days, the calmness comes automatically as soon as you sit down in your meditation place. This tends to reinforce the process and make it easier to advance.

Let us assume that you are using Rabbi Nachman's mantra, *Ribbono shel Olam*. Repeat the phrase over and over, slowly, in a very soft voice. The meditative norm is that it should be said in the softest voice that you can comfortably pronounce. You can either whisper it or vocalize it softly, whichever is more comfortable to you.

There are no firm standards regarding this in Jewish meditation. Some people find it easier to whisper the mantra. It is also permissible to mouth it without voicing it at all. It is not recommended, however, that it merely be thought in the mind, at least for beginners. If the mantra is repeated mentally, without at least mouthing it, it can be interrupted by extraneous thoughts.

Therefore, one should not place too much emphasis on how the mantra is said, as long as it is said for the designated time. This usually consists of a period between twenty minutes and a half hour, as mentioned earlier. If you wish, you may use a silent timer to signal when the meditation period is over. This is preferable to looking at a clock, which takes the mind off the meditation. You can also have someone else signal you when the time is up. After a while, however, you will automatically know when the period of meditation is over.

At first, you may allow the mind to wander freely while reciting the mantra. As long as you have an inner awareness that the words *Ribbono shel Olam* denote "Master of the Universe," the words themselves will pull your thoughts in a meaningful direction. No matter where the thoughts lead, there is no cause for concern. A Chasidic teaching says that any thought that enters the mind during meditation does so for a purpose.

It is also instructive to pay attention to the visual images you see while meditating with the eyes closed. As you become more advanced, these images become clearer and more vivid, and it becomes much easier to focus on them. Beyond that, as days pass, your control over these images improves dramatically during the meditative state. The vividness of these images can also become spectacular.

One must be careful, however, not to take these images too seriously. As one advances, the images become more explicit and can take the form of visions. The neophyte meditator may be tempted to place great significance on these visions, and think that he is actually experiencing prophecy or the like. It is therefore important to realize that any visions one may experience are not important and that undue emphasis should not be placed on them. Unless a person is extremely advanced, it is assumed that any visions he experiences are creations of the mind and nothing more.

In the Kabbalah literature, there are warnings even to advanced meditators not to give credence to visions. Even the most impressive visions can be spurious and come from the Other Side. Indeed, acting on the basis of images seen while in a meditative state is considered to be extremely dangerous and detrimental to one's spiritual development. Therefore, when a person experiences images or visions, they should be taken as aesthetic experiences and nothing more. At most, they should be taken as the first hints of a spiritual experience.

In general, bodily motion destroys concentration during mantra meditation and should be avoided. Some people, however, report that a slight, very slow swaying, perhaps a half inch in each direction, helps ease tension during the initial stages. If you find this helpful, you may use it.

At first, during meditation, you may allow the mind to wander freely or concentrate on the images you see in your mind's eye. However, as you become more advanced, you should begin to allow the words of the mantra to fill the mind completely, blanking out all sensation. This involves keeping all other thoughts out of the consciousness. All of your attention should be focused on the words of the mantra, leaving no room for any other thought.

Of course, until you become proficient in this discipline, extraneous thoughts will constantly try to push their way into the mind. You must then gently push them out, forcing your concentration back to the words of the mantra. This can sometimes take considerable effort, but it is the means through which one gains control of one's thoughts.

Some people find it easier to banish extraneous thoughts if they recite the mantra very slowly. As we shall see, slowness is also used in other types of meditation. At other times, however, it may be preferable to recite the mantra rapidly, sometimes even racing through the words. Here again, each individual must find his own pace.

After the meditation is over, remain in place for approximately five minutes, allowing the mind to absorb the effects of the meditation. You also need some time to "come back down" before returning to your daily routine. Again, you may wish to hum a soft melody during this period. It should be a time of intimate closeness with the Divine.

You may wish to use the moments following a meditation to have a short conversation with God. As mentioned earlier, Rabbi Nachman saw mantra meditation primarily as a means of preparing for such a divine conversation, which he saw as a higher type of meditation. In any case, one can feel very close to God after a meditation, and it is a good time to express that closeness. Whereas Eastern schools see mantra meditation as an end in itself, Jewish sources seem to indicate that it is more of a preparation for a deeper spiritual experience.

Some sources state that after meditating, one should smell fragrant spices or perfumes, so as to reinvolve oneself in the physical world. It is also prescribed that some light food be eaten shortly afterward, since through the blessing, the food can elevate the entire body.

Of course, meditating on the phrase *Ribbono shel Olam*, "Master of the Universe," has great value in its own right, and some people may be content to make it a lifetime practice. Others, however, may want to use it as a way to learn meditative techniques and recognize higher states of consciousness, and then go on to what are considered more advanced methods.

7

CONTEMPLATION

A nother simple type of meditation is contemplation. I have discussed this form of meditation in a previous chapter, in the context of *hitbonenuth*, but here I shall discuss it in further detail and in practical terms.

Contemplation consists in sitting and concentrating on an object, word, or idea, letting it fill the entire mind. This is an excellent introductory meditation, insofar as it does not require any background in meditation or any advanced knowledge of Hebrew or Judaism. The techniques are the same as those of mantra meditation, except that the experience is visual rather than verbal.

Simple contemplation consists of gazing at an object for a fixed period of time. As in all forms of meditation, one should be as comfortable as possible. There is no need to avoid blinking the eyes, since this can lead to discomfort. Rather, one should sit and gaze at the object of contemplation in the most relaxed manner possible.

The object of contemplation can be almost anything—a pretty stone, a leaf, a flower, or written material. Pictures, images, and statues, however, are to be avoided, since contemplating them is dangerously close to idolatry.

As in the case of mantra meditation, one should sit quietly in the meditation place, adjusting to the space. The meditation itself should take between twenty and thirty minutes. After the meditation, one should remain still for five to ten minutes, absorbing the effects of the exercise.

Visual contemplation is valuable in many respects. I have spoken earlier of visualization, in which one creates images in the mind's eye. Contemplation is a very good introduction to this practice. Once a person has learned to look at an object correctly, he can also learn to control his vision. Contemplation engraves the image in the mind's eye, and this image can then be conjured up even when the object is not present.

You can begin by using the object of contemplation as a focus for unstructured meditation. This would mean gazing at the object while letting the mind drift off in any direction it desires. The contemplation focuses the mind, but thought is left unbridled. You can think about how to restructure your life, about the meaning of life, or about any other subject important to you. Rather than being the goal of meditation, contemplation is an adjunct to a meaningful unstructured meditation.

As one becomes more advanced, one gradually learns how to fill the mind with the visual image of the object of contemplation, banishing all other thought. This is very much like mantra meditation, except that instead of filling the mind with a word or phrase, it is filled with an image. Extraneous thoughts are also shunted aside in a similar manner; whenever a thought enters the mind, it is gently pushed aside, leaving the entire attention fixed on the object of contemplation.

At first one must make a conscious effort to rid the mind of extraneous thoughts. However, after a while, the object of contemplation becomes the total center of one's focus, and everything else seems to vanish. The experience of looking at the object becomes highly intensified. It is as if there were nothing else in the entire world besides the meditator and the object of contemplation.

When one reaches this state, every detail of the object assumes an importance of its own. Thus, for example, if one were contemplating a leaf, every line and vein on it take on major significance. One would see structure and patterns to which the mind would normally be oblivious. Every detail would become deeply engraved in one's consciousness.

There is great leeway in what can be used as an object of meditation. If desired, a different object can be used at each session. This is of necessity true if the object of contemplation is something perishable, such as a leaf or a flower. However, when a different object is used each time, the effects are not cumulative.

It is therefore best to use the same object for a relatively long period of time. If possible the object should remain the same for thirty to forty days, long enough to habituate to it. Then, the experience of each session is reinforced, and each day's experience builds on that of the previous days.

It is important, however, to realize that the object of contemplation is merely an aid and not an end in itself. One must be extremely careful not to make the object of contemplation into an object of devotion, since to do so would border on idolatry. Even when one becomes aware of the Divine in the object, it may not be made into a venerated object or an object of devotion. Since this is always a danger, it is best to limit oneself to types of contemplation actually mentioned in classical Judaic literature.

People sometimes ask, if one can only do one type of meditation, whether one should begin with mantra meditation or with contemplation. To a large degree, this is a matter of personal preference. Some people are more verbal, while others are more visually oriented. For one who is verbal, mantra meditation will work more effectively, while one who is more visually oriented may find it easier to fill the mind with visual contemplation. Of course, if a person has a spiritual master who knows his soul and psyche, then the master can help him to make the decision.

However, both mantra meditation and contemplation are meant to develop different areas of the mind and spirit. Therefore, both are important. There are also important meditations that involve the senses of the body. For beginners, however, mantra meditation usually seems the simplest.

Some people find it valuable to combine mantra meditation with contemplation. If a person has learned to focus his mind through mantra meditation, then he can also use this method to enhance his contemplation. It is very easy to fill the mind with a visual image when one is in a higher state of consciousness from mantra meditation. In this sense, mantra meditation can be seen as an excellent introduction to contemplation.

Furthermore, as we have seen, the most universal Jewish mantra is the expression *Ribbono shel Olam*, "Master of the Universe." This mantra does not negate physical reality but focuses our attention on the physical universe and makes us aware of its Master. Thus, this mantra is an excellent way of relating the visible world to its Creator.

There is a vast difference between the English concept of universe and the Hebrew concept. In English, the word "universe" comes from the Latin *unus*, meaning "one," and *versum*, meaning "to turn." Hence, "universe" denotes that which is turned into one, or that which is combined into an integral whole. Thus, in the secular sense, the universe is seen as the main unifying factor in creation.

The Hebrew word for universe, on the other hand, is *olam*, which is derived from the root *alam*, meaning "to conceal." Therefore, in a Hebrew sense, the universe is seen as that which conceals the Divine. Thus, when one says *Ribbono shel Olam*, denoting "Master of the Universe," one is saying that concealed behind the universe, there is a Master. Thus, in repeating this mantra, one is making oneself aware of the hidden reality behind the visible one.

When a person uses the mantra *Ribbono shel Olam* together with contemplation on a physical object, he can actually begin to see the Divine hidden in the object. He can make the object of contemplation into a link between himself and God. The object becomes a channel through which he can experience the Divine.

Although any physical object can be used as the focus of meditation, several are mentioned specifically in Judaic literature, especially in the Kabbalah. Each of these has an important significance in its own right.

One type of meditation mentioned in the Zohar (1:1b, 2:231b) involves contemplating the stars. The Zohar provides a biblical source for this type of meditation, from the verse, "Lift your eyes on high, and see who created these, the One who brings out their host by number, He calls them all by name . . ." (Isa. 40:26). The verse is seen by the Zohar as prescribing a contemplation meditation with the stars as its object.

The Zohar notes that in the verse, there are two key Hebrew words, *MI*, meaning "who," and *ELeH*, meaning "these." When these two words are combined, the Hebrew letters (capitalized here) spell out *ELoHIM*, the Hebrew name for God. Thus, when one looks at the "these"—things in the ordinary mundane world—and asks "who?"—who is the author and basis of these things?—one finds God. The Zohar presents this in the context of the stars, but it is true of any object of contemplation.

People often gaze at the stars and feel a sense of awe and smallness in the face of the Infinite. But if one does it as a specific meditation, contemplating the stars and removing all other thought from the mind, the sense of awe and the feeling of God's presence in creation are greatly enhanced. One's focus goes beyond the stars, seeking what is beyond them—the "who" behind the "these"—and one becomes aware of their Creator.

A beginner may find it difficult to contemplate the stars in this manner without becoming overwhelmed by extraneous thoughts. Therefore, a mantra such as *Ribbono shel Olam* can be extremely useful. As it were, one is looking at the stars as *concealing* a greater and deeper truth, and the mind and soul probe and search to penetrate this mystery. When saying *Ribbono shel Olam*—"Lord of the Universe"—one is, as it were, calling to God in the depths of the heavens, seeking to find Him beyond the stars, beyond the very limits of time and space. This can bring a person to an overwhelmingly deep spiritual experience.

There are other ways in which a mantralike device can be combined with contemplation. Thus, for example, one may contemplate a flower and wish to gain a greater awareness of its beauty. Contemplation itself, of course, will greatly enhance awareness, but a beginner may find it difficult to maintain concentration. However, the contemplation can be combined with an exercise in which one repeats the word "beauty" over and over while looking at the flower. This serves to amplify one's sensitivity and sense of beauty, so that the flower will actually appear to radiate beauty. The result can be an extremely powerful aesthetic experience. If one then realizes that the source of beauty is the Divine in the flower, then this beauty can also become a link with the Divine.

Similarly, one can gaze at one's own hand and repeat the word "strength" over and over. When one does this, one can become uniquely aware of the strength in one's own hand. It is true that strength is normally an abstract quality, which one can be aware of but cannot see. However, in a meditative state, the strength of one's hand becomes not merely something of which one is aware in an abstract sense, but something that one can actually see. It is impossible to describe what strength looks like, but it actually becomes visible. This is very much like a synesthesia experience, discussed earlier, in which one can see unseeable things such as sounds or fragrances. Here, one can see abstract concepts as well.

Another type of contemplation mentioned in the Zohar involves a candle or oil lamp. Many meditative systems make use of a candle, but Judaic sources indicate a preference for a small lamp using olive oil and a linen wick. This would be like the great *menorah* candelabrum that stood in the Jerusalem Temple, which may have also been used as the object of contemplation. Olive oil has a particularly pure white flame that draws the gazer into its depths. Of course, if such a lamp is not available, a candle may be used instead, since the main thing is the flame.

The Zoharic literature (*Tikkunay ha-Zohar* 21:50a) teaches that in contemplating a flame, one should be aware of its five colors: white, yellow, red, black, and sky-blue. These are the colors that one should see when deeply contemplating the flame of a candle or oil lamp.

On an intellectual level, this is impossible to understand. When you simply look at a flame, you may see white, yellow, and red, since these are the natural colors of fire. Even the black may not be that difficult to understand, since it can be seen as the darkness around the flame. As we have seen, darkness itself plays an important role in the meditative experience.

However, the sky-blue color appears to present difficulty. There is no evidence whatever of this color in the flame of a candle or lamp. Furthermore, from the context of the Zoharic teaching, it appears that this color appears outside and beyond the black, which is the darkness around the flame.

However, elsewhere, the Zohar (3:33a) provides a hint as to the nature of this sky-blue color. The Zohar says that the blue that one sees around the flame represents the Divine Presence, *Shekhinah* in Hebrew.

In order to understand this, however, one must actually do a candle or lamp meditation. It should be done in an otherwise dark room, with the candle far enough from the wall so that it casts no light on it. Again, one uses the standard contemplation technique, allowing the flame to fill the entire mind. One becomes aware of the colors in the flame, the white, the yellow, and the red; each color and gradation of color is extremely significant. One is aware of the heat and energy radiating from the candle, and, as in the case of the hand's strength mentioned above, one reaches a level at which one can actually see these abstract energies.

The next step would be to concentrate on the darkness around the flame. When one contemplates the darkness of the room, it becomes a very profound, palpable darkness. One sees it as a velvety blackness that appears to radiate darkness. This may be analogous to the "black fire" or "lamp of darkness" discussed in Talmudic and Zoharic literature. In this sense, experiencing the darkness can be more profound than experiencing the light.

However, when one gets deeper into the meditation, one will begin to see a sky-blue field around the darkness. The blackness will extend for a certain distance around the candle, but around this will be an experience of pure sky-blue. It will be the most beautiful sky-blue color imaginable, like that of a summer sky over the Holy Land. The color will have an almost awesome beauty.

Of course, the blue color is not a physical reality; it is entirely a creation of the mind. But according to the Zohar, the blue sensation is a revelation of the spiritual. In a sense, it denotes that one is seeing the spiritual essence of the light that is radiating from the candle.

There are sources that indicate that in more advanced meditative techniques, it is possible actually to see visions in this blue field (see *Sefer Yetzirah* 1:12). Furthermore, in conjunction with the revelation at Sinai, when the Israelites had a vision of the Divine, they saw "under His feet like a brickwork of sapphire" (Exod. 24:10). Similarly, when the prophet Ezekiel saw the Throne of Glory, he described it as being the color of the sapphire (Ezek. 1:26). Thus, blue is always a color associated with vision and prophecy.

This type of candle meditation is important for a number of reasons. First, it gives us an experience of "black fire" and "radiating darkness," both of which are important concepts in Kabbalistic sources. As we shall see, "black fire" plays an important role in other types of Jewish meditation.

Second, in learning how to see the blue aura around the candle, one can learn how to see auras in general. An aura is a bluish field that appears around people and other objects. To see such an aura, one can begin by gazing at one's hand against a blank white wall or a clear blue sky. One will eventually see something like an area of color that somehow "feels" different than either the object or the background. This blurred area of color appears to extend outward from an eighth to a quarter of an inch from the object. At first it may be difficult to see, but with practice the aura becomes highly evident. Contemplation dramatically increases one's ability to see it.

In Kabbalistic sources, this aura is known as the *tzelem*. There were some spiritual masters, such as the Ari, who could determine the state of a person's spiritual health on the basis of the aura. Of course, reading auras is a subject that is beyond the scope of this book.

The color blue is also associated with the spiritual in other ways. One of the important commandments involves the tassels that were once worn on the corners of all garments. This survives today in the *tallith*, the tassled garment worn for prayer. In ancient times, one thread of the tassels would be dyed a bright sky-blue, using a dye made from the purpura snail (see Num. 15:38). Although it is no longer used, the blue was seen as highly significant.

Thus, the Talmud provides us with a contemplation meditation on the blue thread of the tassel. It says:

The tassel is blue;
The blue is the color of the sea;
The sea is the color of the sky;
And the sky is the color of the Throne of Glory.

Therefore, one may use the blue thread as the subject of a contemplation meditation. It can then fill the mind with this sky-blue color, so that nothing else exists in the world besides this blue. One then meditates on the association and sees the blue as the sea. Of course, since the blue dye comes from an aquatic creature, one is reaching back in this meditation to the source of the blue. But one also experiences the cool calmness of the sea and the serenity of its depths.

The next stage is to associate the blue of the sea with that of the sky. Now one's thoughts soar up to the heavens, higher and higher, up to the farthest reaches of the sky. Then one's thoughts penetrate the sky, and one approaches the Throne of Glory. Thus, contemplating the color blue is seen as bringing a person into the spiritual on an entirely different level. What is very signficant, however, is the fact that this type of contemplation meditation is described explicitly in the Talmud.

It is also significant that, in Kabbalah sources, this sapphire-blue color is also associated with the "third eye." One reason is that this color is seen not with the physical eyes, but with a mental or spiritual eye. In this blue, one can see visions that are invisible to the physical eyes.

There is another type of contemplation that is fairly straightforward and simple. This consists in contemplating God's most sacred name, the four-letter Tetragrammaton, YHVH (יהוה). This contemplation has a number of important advantages, the most obvious being that since it is God's most sacred name, it provides one with a direct link to the Divine.

One must realize that it is forbidden to pronounce this name in any form whatsoever. This is because it is the holiest of God's names, and it is linked to every spiritual level. But for this very reason, this name can be used as a ladder through which a person can link himself to the highest spiritual levels.

To use this method of contemplation, this name of God can be written on a card or sheet and placed where it can be seen easily. Then it can be used as an object of contemplation in the usual manner.

One may wish to enhance this contemplation with mantra meditation. Here again, the mantra *Ribbono shel Olam* can be very useful. One is then relating to God directly both through the mantra and through the visual contemplation.

For this type of contemplation to be most meaningful, one must have some idea of the meaning of the four letters of God's name. As I have said, the Tetragrammaton is spelled YHVH (יהוה). It therefore consists of the four Hebrew letters *yod* (י), *heh* (ה), *vav*(ו), and *heh* (ה). These four letters have a very special significance.

This name can be understood on the basis of an ancient Kabbalistic teaching. The teaching states that the four letters contain the mystery of charity.

According to this teaching, the first letter, *yod*, denotes the coin. The letter *yod* (י)is small and simple like a coin.

The second letter, *heh* (ה), denotes the hand that gives the coin. Every letter in the Hebrew alphabet also represents a number. Since *heh* is the fifth letter of the alphabet, it has a numerical value of five. The "five" of *heh* alludes to the five fingers of the hand.

The third letter, *vav*(ו), denotes the arm reaching out to give. This letter has the form of an arm. Furthermore, in Hebrew the word *vav* denotes a hook, and thus *vav* has the connotation of connection. Indeed, in Hebrew, the word for the conjunction "and" is represented by the letter *vav* prefixed to a word.

Finally, the fourth letter, the final *heh* (ה), is the hand of the beggar who accepts the coin.

This is the essence of charity on a mundane level. However, "charity" can also be understood on a divine scale. The greatest possible act of charity is that act through which God gives to us. The greatest charity that God gives is existence itself. We have no claim to existence and cannot demand that God give it to us as our right. Therefore, when He gives us existence, it is an act of charity. Since this "charity" is denoted by the Tetragrammaton, the four letters represent the mystery of the creative link between God and man.

Here again, the *yod* represents the "coin." But this time, the coin is not a piece of copper or silver, but existence itself. As the tenth letter of the Hebrew alphabet, *yod* has a numerical value of ten. Hence, according to the Kabbalists, it alludes to the Ten Sayings of Creation. The concept of the Ten Sayings is found even in the Talmud and is not necessarily a mystical teaching. In the account of creation in Genesis, the expression "And God said" occurs ten times; these are the Ten Sayings. These sayings represent the entire act of creation, and therefore represent the "coin" of existence that God gives us.

The *heh* of the name is then God's hand, which holds the existence He wishes to give us. The *vav* is His arm reaching out to us, to give us existence. Finally, the last *heh* of the name is our hand, which accepts this existence. Of course, God must give us even this hand. Thus, in a sense, God gives us the "hand" through which we receive existence from Him.

As one gazes at the four letters of the Tetragrammaton, one can actually see this.

One begins by contemplating the *yod* (י), which is the smallest letter of the Hebrew alphabet, almost like a dot. One contemplates the *yod* and sees it as the initial point of creation, the Ten Sayings that brought creation into existence out of nothingness.

One then contemplates the first *heh* (ה) of the name. This is the level of the Divine at which a vessel comes into existence to hold the abstract power of creation. One sees God holding the power of creation, so as to give it to us. The opening at the top of the *heh* is the channel from God, while the opening at the bottom is the channel to us below. The *heh* is thus seen both as a five-fingered hand (based on its numerical value) and as a channel for the forces of creation.

One then contemplates the *vav* (ו). Here one sees God's power reaching out to us, wanting to give.

The most important letter is the final *heh* (ה). This is our hand, into which we receive what God is ready to give us. This represents our ability to receive from God.

The connection between the *vav* and the *heh* is extremely important. This is the connection between the Giver and the receiver. Unless this connection is made, we cannot receive anything from God.

In the Talmud and the Kabbalah, the letters of the Hebrew alphabet are seen as having tremendous spiritual power. Speaking of Bezalel, the architect of the Tabernacle that the Israelites built right after the Exodus, the Talmud says, "Bezalel knew how to combine the letters through which heaven and earth were created." Since the world was created with Ten Sayings, and the sayings consist of letters, the letters are seen as the primary ingredients of creation. Thus, when one contemplates the Tetragrammaton, the letters serve as the means through which a person connects himself to God and the creative process.

There is another way of looking at the four letters of the Tetragrammaton. The first two letters, *yod* (י) and *heh* (ה), are seen as representing the masculine forces of creation. The last two letters, *vav* (ו) and *heh* (ה), represent the masculine and feminine forces of divine providence.

This is very closely related to the previous discussion. The first *yod* of the Tetragrammaton is seen as the "coin," the Ten Sayings of Creation. This is the "seed" of creation, the masculine element. This "seed" must be placed into the womb of creation, which is the *heh*, before it can be brought into fruition. The *heh* thus represents both a hand and a womb. Both have the connotation of holding, although the symbolism is different.

The last two letters of the name, *vav* and *heh*, represent the masculine and feminine powers of divine providence. Providence denotes the power through which God directs the world. Here, the *vav* represents the "seed" of providence, the initial impetus that comes from God. In a sense, it is God's "arm" of creation reaching out to direct the world He created. The final *heh* of the name is the hand with which we accept God's providence. This can also be seen as the womb that holds the forces of providence. The small opening on the top of the *heh* (ה) is the opening through which the "seed" enters, while the large opening at the bottom is where the "child" emerges.

Of course, the forces of creation can never be separated, since if they were, the world would cease to exist. The forces of providence, on the other hand can be separated, as when God turns His face away from the world. When the masculine and feminine forces of providence are separated, the *vav* in the name is separated from the final *heh*.

In this meditation on the Tetragrammaton, one can unite the *vav* and the final *heh*. In Kabbalah texts, this is known as a unification, *yichud* in Hebrew. It serves to open the person to the forces of providence and make him aware of divine guidance in his life. Since the *heh* is the hand through which we receive from God, uniting it with the *vav* makes a person more aware of the Divine Presence.

As one gazes at the name of God written on the card or parchment, the black of the writing becomes blacker, while the white of the card becomes whiter. Eventually, one perceives the name as being written with "black fire on white fire." It is significant to note that according to the Midrash the primeval Torah was written in this manner, as "black fire on white fire."

After one has been involved in this form of meditation for a period of time, the "fire" begins to burn the name of God into one's mind so that one can easily visualize it, even without the card. This involves the method of visualization, another important technique of Jewish meditation, which is the subject of the next chapter.

8

VISUALIZATION

Earlier, I spoke about the images that one sees when the eyes are closed. An important discipline in meditation is learning how to control these images. When one has learned how to control them, one can also learn how to hold an image in the mind's eye. This technique is known as visualization.

A simple way to begin this discipline is to close your eyes and try to picture a letter of the alphabet, for example, the letter *A*. If you know the Hebrew alphabet, you can try to visualize the letter *alef* (א). Since there are Jewish meditations that use the letter *alef,* I shall use it as an example, although any other letter or figure could also be used.

To begin a visualization meditation, just close your eyes and relax, allowing the images in the mind's eye to settle down. If you have been practicing mantra meditation, you may want to use it as a relaxing mechanism. In any case, after a few minutes, the images in the visual field will become easier to control.

When the visual field is fairly calm, you can begin to try to visualize the *alef.* You may have an *alef* printed on a card and set the image of it in your mind. Then close your eyes and try to picture the *alef.* Try to see it with your eyes closed exactly as you saw it with your eyes open.

At first, this may be extremely difficult. The images that you see in your mind's eye are very difficult to control. If you have never done this before, it will be almost impossible the first time.

One important aid in visualization is the name of the object to be visualized. If you are trying to visualize the *alef*, you may repeat the word *alef* to yourself periodically. You may even wish to repeat the word over and over, as if it were a mantra. This not only relaxes the visual field, but locks the mind on to the *alef*. Repeating the word *alef* as a mantra will bring the letter into the mind's eye.

Another good aid is to initiate the visualization exercise with a contemplation meditation. If you wish to visualize the *alef*, first spend several days contemplating the letter written on a card approximately twenty minutes a day. This will serve to fix the image in the mind. It will then be much easier to fix the *alef* in the visual field with the eyes closed.

If you still encounter difficulty, the meditation session can be split between contemplation and visualization. Spend the first fifteen minutes of a half-hour session contemplating the *alef*, looking at it with your eyes open. Then, during the next fifteen minutes, you can try to visualize it with the eyes closed.

The ability to do this exercise varies from individual to individual. Some are able to do it the first time, while others have to work for weeks before they can visualize a letter. With patience and perseverance, however, it can be done by almost anyone.

Even after depicting the letter in the mind's eye, the average person will be able to hold the image only for several seconds. Then, like all such images, it will dissolve into other images. With time and practice, one eventually develops the ability to hold the image clearly and firmly in the mind's eye for extended periods. When this is accomplished, one has come a long way in gaining control over the mental processes.

The ability to hold an image in the mind's eye is discussed at length in the Kabbalah texts dealing with meditation. Thus, the *Sefer Yetzirah* refers to two processes in depicting the letters, "engraving" (*chakikah*) and "hewing" (*chatzivah*). Both processes are seen as important if one is going to depict the letters. As discussed in the previous chapter, the Hebrew letters are seen as channels of the forces of creation, and as such they can be used as a powerful means of drawing down spiritual energy. However, "engraving" and "hewing" are useful also for less esoteric forms of meditation.

The term "engraving" denotes fixing an image in the mind's eye so that it does not waver or move. No matter what other images may arise in the field of vision, the engraved image remains there, as if the image were actually engraved in the mind. Once a person has accomplished this, he can usually depict the desired image as soon as he begins his meditation, almost as a reflex.

However, even when the image is clear and steady—"engraved" in the mind, as it were—it is usually surrounded by other images. The next step is to isolate the image. Thus, for example, if one were visualizing the letter *alef*, one would attempt to isolate it and rid the mind's eye of all other imagery. This is known as "hewing," or *chatzivah*. The analogy is to hewing out a stone from the surrounding rock. The process consists in designating the desired stone and then hewing away the extraneous stone. One does the same thing in the mind, hewing away all extraneous imagery surrounding the desired form. All that is left is the image one desires.

There are a number of ways of "hewing" away surrounding imagery. One way is to replace all the mental images other than the *alef* with pure white. First focus on the *alef*, allowing it to fill the mind. Then gradually hew away the images around the *alef*, replacing them with white fire. Imagine the white fire burning away the other images. Begin with a small spot of white fire at the top of the *alef*, using it to burn away a small spot of imagery. Let the white fire expand, burning away larger and larger areas. As it moves around the *alef*, burning away images on all sides. Finally, one sees the *alef* alone, written in black fire on white fire.

In general, a visualization technique such as this is very valuable and can be used in other forms of Jewish meditation. Thus, many classical Kabbalah texts speak about *yichudim* or "unifications," which I discussed briefly in the previous chapter. For the most part, the meditational method of *yichudim* involves imaging various names of God and then manipulating the letters. In general, the method of *yichudim* is highly advanced and requires some knowledge of Kabbalah.*

A good introduction to the method of *yichudim* involves visualizing the Tetragrammaton, YHVH (יהוה). This is similar to the technique of contemplating the Tetragrammaton, described in the previous chapter, but here it is done without any external aid. Significantly, an exercise that entails visualizing the Tetragrammaton is mentioned in the *Shulchan Arukh*, the standard code of Jewish law. It is also an introduction to a number of other, more advanced techniques discussed in the Kabbalah.

By visualizing God's name, one can attain a tremendous feeling of closeness to God. One actually feels the presence of God and experiences a deep sense of awe in the presence. A number of classical Judaic sources find an allusion to such visualization in the verse "I have placed YHVH before me at all times" (Ps. 16:8). This type of visualization is also useful during worship and prayer.

Here, too, you can use contemplation as an introduction to visualization. If you find it difficult to visualize the Tetragrammaton, spend a number of days contemplating the name written on a sheet or card. You can spend the first half of a session contemplating the written name and the other half visualizing it with the eyes closed. Eventually, you will be able to visualize it without using the card at all.

Once you become adept at visualizing the name, you can use it for the simple *yichud* discussed in the last chapter. As discussed there, the *vav* (ו) and final *heh* (ה) of the name are the masculine and feminine forces of providence. When the *vav* and *heh* are separated, there is no connection between God and the world below other than His creative energy. Therefore, like a man and woman in love, the *vav* and *heh* yearn and long to be united, to bring God's power to the lower world. When the *vav* and *heh* are united, God's presence becomes palpable and one can have a very strong experience of the Divine.

---

*In my book *Meditation and Kabbalah*, a number of important *yichudim* are presented in their entirety.

One accomplishes this *yichud* by visualizing the divine name, YHVH (יהוה). One focuses on the *vav* and *heh*, making oneself aware of the longing and yearning of these two letters to unite. When the longing between the two letters becomes unbearable, they finally unite, and a spiritual flood is released. One feels this as a torrent of divine energy flowing through the body and mind. One is bathed in the spiritual experience and overwhelmed by it, totally opened up, like a vessel for the divine.

Once proficiency in visualization is achieved, there are more advanced methods that one can learn. One such method, mentioned in the Kabbalistic sources, is to imagine the sky opening up and to depict oneself ascending into the spiritual realm. One rises through the seven firmaments, one by one, until one reaches the highest heaven. On this level, one depicts in one's mind a huge white curtain, infinite in size, filling the entire mind. Written on this white curtain, one visualizes the Tetragrammaton.

The black of the letters and the white of the curtain become intensified, until the letters appear to be black fire on white fire. Gradually, the letters of the Tetragrammaton expand, until they appear to be huge mountains of black fire. When the four letters fill the mind completely, one is, as it were, swallowed up in God's name.

On a still more advanced level, the letters appear to be not merely written on the curtain, but solid objects, with both dimension and texture. One can see oneself actually entering into the letters, surrounded by their essence on all sides.

Finally, one can reach the level where one sees the letters as living entities, as if each letter were an angelic being. One becomes uniquely aware of the life force and spiritual energy in each letter, of the significance of the letters and of the flow of energy between one letter and the next. One becomes aware of the unification of the Giver with the receiver and of the ultimate male and female elements of creation.

These last methods can bring a person to very high spiritual levels and should not be taken lightly. The original sources state that before attempting any of these more advanced methods, one should spend the entire day in preparation, reciting the Psalms and studying Torah. Before beginning the meditation, one should immerse oneself in a *mikveh* (ritual bath) or any other natural body of water to cleanse oneself both physically and spiritually. Some sources also indicate that one should dress totally in white for these advanced meditations.

This type of visualization can be dangerous and should not be attempted without an experienced spiritual master or a meditation partner. The Baal Shem Tov recommends that one have a partner for any type of advanced meditation. Then, if necessary, one partner can bring the other back to the real world.

Visualization is valuable for another reason. In deeper forms of meditation, one often sees visions. As I discussed earlier, these visions should not be taken too seriously. Unless a person is very advanced and working under the tutelage of an experienced master, these visions are almost certain to be spurious. It is therefore recommended that when any visions appear, they be banished from the mind. If one learns to control one's visualization, then this is fairly easy. Some sources recommend that visions, when they occur, should be banished from the mind and replaced with the Tetragrammaton.

When one learns how to control the imagery in the mind's eye, there is much less danger that spurious visions will appear. One's meditation is then pure and undisturbed by low-level side effects.

9

NOTHINGNESS

Meditation on nothingness is a topic upon which I have touched briefly in an earlier chapter. Actually, this is a very advanced type of meditation and not for beginners. It is not recommended for practice without the guidance of a spiritual master and should never be practiced alone. I shall discuss it here because this technique is closely related to visualization methods and is important for understanding a number of other areas in Jewish meditation and mysticism.

Once proficiency has been achieved in visualization techniques, it is possible to attempt to visualize pure nothingness. Nothingness has no counterpart in the real world, so one must be able to create a perception of it in the mind. It is a useful technique to attain closeness to God and to achieve a realization of the self.

As in the case of other advanced techniques, this can be extremely dangerous. The reason why it should never be practiced alone is that one can get "swallowed up" in the nothingness of the meditation and not be able to return. Therefore, one should always have a partner or a spiritual master available to bring one back to objective reality.

Before we can begin to discuss this type of meditation, we must have an idea of what nothingness looks like. When one first thinks of nothingness, one may image it as being like the black-

ness of empty space. The interplanetary void may seem as close
to nothingness as a person can imagine. If one is expert in visualization, it is fairly easy to visualize empty space and pure empty
blackness. This indeed may be a first step toward visualizing
nothingness, but it is not nothingness. Space is space, and blackness is blackness—neither is nothingness.

A next step in attempting to visualize nothingness would be to
attempt to visualize pure, transparent, empty space, without any
background color. One can imagine oneself looking into a pure,
colorless, transparent crystal, with the transparency extending to
infinity. According to some commentaries, this is the connotation
of the "brickwork of sapphire" that the Israelites saw under God's
feet (Exod. 24:10). These commentaries translate the Hebrew
expression *livenath ha-sappir* as "transparency of crystal" rather
than "brickwork of sapphire." They say that it is related to the
meditation in which one images pure transparence without any
color. One images first the transparency of crystal and then the
transparency of pure colorless empty space.

One way to do this is to image the air in front of you. It is, of
course, perfectly transparent, and therefore you cannot see it.
Instead you see what is at the other end of the room. Using the
"hewing" technique described in the previous chapter, you
should be able to rid yourself of the image of the other end of the
room; then you will have a pure image of the transparent air
around you. It will be pure transparence, with no form or color.

Years ago, I found this to be a very helpful technique for
experiencing the presence of God. It is an important teaching of
Judaism that God is omnipresent, totally filling all creation. The
clearest statement of this is the verse "The whole world is filled
with His glory" (Isa. 6:3). God fills all creation and is even present in the air around us. I would therefore contemplate the air
around me and imagine it filled with God's presence. This would
bring a very great feeling of God's closeness.

Now, although this technique involves imaging the transparent
empty space, what is imaged is still space; it is not nothingness.

So what does nothingness look like?

It is taught that nothing is what you see behind your head. Of course, sight does not extend behind the head. Therefore, what you see behind the head is *nothing*. In other words, you see nothingness.

This teaching can be used as a contemplation. Attempt to contemplate what you see behind your head. You realize that it is nothing, but with practice, you will be able to make it into an object of contemplation. This is a powerful technique to gain a conception of pure nothingness.

In the Bible, it appears that this or a similar technique was used as a precursor of prophecy. There are a number of references to voices and prophecy seeming to come from behind. Thus, Ezekiel said, "I heard behind me a loud voice proclaiming, 'Blessed be God's glory from His place' " (Ezek. 3:12). Likewise, regarding a certain degree of revelation, the prophet said, "Your ears shall hear a voice behind you" (Isa. 30:21). This might indicate that by meditating on the nothingness seen behind the head, one opens oneself up to the experience of prophecy.

Other sources, however, indicate that instead of contemplating what one sees behind the head, one should contemplate what one sees inside the head. This is a method discussed by Rabbi Abraham Abulafia, one of the most important writers on Kabbalistic meditation. Of course, what one sees inside the head is also nothingness, so the experience is essentially the same.

To learn how to visualize nothingness properly can take years. It is not an easy discipline. However, once one has a good depiction of nothingness, one can use it as a powerful visualization technique. Of all the images one can visualize, the purest is a vision of nothingness.

Visualizing nothingness is also a technique used in the most advanced meditational exercises. If one visualizes nothingness and at the same time clears the mind of thought, the mind becomes a total blank. The mind is then at its most sensitive, open to even the most ethereal experiences. This is therefore an important technique for experiencing the spiritual.

This can sometimes be a traumatic experience. When one locks the mind on to a visualization of nothingness and clears the consciousness of all other thought, the mind becomes so sensitive that even the slightest sensation can be overwhelming. It is like turning up a radio to full volume, so that the softest voice becomes a roar. On the other hand, it is only at full volume that the weakest signals can be heard.

At this level, even the random thoughts that tug at the corner of the mind are felt as mental earthquakes. Before one can proceed, one must dampen all thought completely. Finally, when all thought is quieted, one can have an experience of the spiritual. This involves a deep feeling of awe, shame, and humility.

Some Kabbalists teach that this is the mystery of Ezekiel's vision. At the very beginning of his vision, the prophet says, "I looked, and saw a storm wind coming from the north, a great cloud, and flashing fire . . . " (Ezek. 1:4). The Zohar teaches that the wind, the cloud, and the fire are the three barriers through which a prophet must pass before he enters the realm of the Divine.

The first thing that Ezekiel experienced was "a storm wind." There is a double meaning here, however, since the Hebrew word for wind is *ruach,* which also means "spirit." Therefore, what Ezekiel saw can also be translated as "a stormy spirit." The stormy spirit relates to the first experience mentioned earlier. When there is literally nothing in the mind, all the natural agitations of the mind are greatly intensified. This is the barrier of the "storm wind" through which the prophet must pass.

The second barrier the prophet encounters is "a great cloud." This is the muffling and restriction of all thought, an opaqueness of the mind, in which nothing can be seen or experienced. It is a barrier that can easily discourage the prophet if he does not have the will to proceed further. As he is trying to ascend, he faces a cloud barrier beyond which he cannot see and which he must strive to overcome.

The final barrier is the "flashing fire." This is the sense of awe, shame, and dread that the prophet experiences when he first breaks into the spiritual realm. Throughout the Bible, fire is a metaphor for shame and dread. Fire burns and hence is an overabundance of sensation—a sensation so intense that it cannot be tolerated. Thus, while the cloud is the obliteration of sensation, the fire is the opposite, the overabundance of sensation. The cloud also shows the prophet that one who is unworthy will not see anything, while the fire demonstrates that such a person may be in danger as well.

This is the manner in which meditation on nothingness opens the door to prophecy. It can also be used to get in touch with the innermost self. This, of course, raises the question, What is the nature of the self?

Normally, when a person thinks of himself, the first thing he thinks of is his body. It is almost a reflex action. Ask a person to point to himself, and he will almost inevitably point to his chest. Perhaps, if he is more perceptive, he will point to his head, the seat of his brain, seeing the mind as being more representative of the self than the body.

The Kabbalists point out that the body is not the self. Since I can speak of "*my* body," the body cannot be "me." The body is "mine"—something associated with the me; but the ultimate me is something much more profound than the body. Using the same argument, I can also speak of "*my* mind." Indeed, I speak of "my mind" just as I speak of "my body." This would imply that just as the body is not the real me, the mind is also not the real me. Carrying the argument a step further, I can even speak of "*my* soul." This would imply that even the soul is not the real me.

This being the case, the question of selfhood becomes very difficult indeed. What is the real me? A hint to the answer can be found in the Hebrew word for "I," *ani* (אני). It is significant to note that if the letters of *ani* are rearranged, they spell the word *ayn* or *ayin* (אין), which denotes nothingness. This would seem to imply that the real "me" is the nothingness within me.

This can be understood in a fairly straightforward manner. The real me is my sense of volition. It is the intangible will that impels me to do whatever I decide to do. Even if I think, I must first will myself to think. In that sense, will is even higher than thought. It is obvious that it is the "I" that tells my mind to think.

However, the fact that I must will myself to think implies that the source of my will is on a level that is beyond thought. It is therefore impossible for me to imagine the source of my will, and there is no category in my conscious mind into which it will fit. Therefore, when I try to imagine the source of my will, the real "me," all I can depict is nothingness.

This can also be understood in another manner. Earlier I mentioned that there are three things that appear to be identifiable with the self: body, mind, and soul. As I noted, neither the body, the mind, nor the soul is the self. However, in another sense, the self is a combination of body, mind, and soul. The three together appear to define the self.

However, this has an important ramification. If body is not the self, and mind is not the self, and soul is not the self, but the combination of the three is, then the definition of the self is still an enigma. It would seem that it is possible to remove the body, remove the mind, and remove the soul, and still have some spark of the self. But when body, mind, and soul are removed, all that remains is nothingness. Again it appears that the self is nothingness.

It is not nothingness because of lack of existence. Rather, it is nothingness because of the lack of a category in the mind in which to place it. It is very much like the situation of what one sees behind one's head. One sees nothingness, not because there isn't anything there, but because one does not have eyes behind the head to see with. Where there is no sense organ, or no category in the mind, to grasp certain information, then that information is perceived as nothingness. If there is no other information competing with it, then it is an experience of pure nothingness.

This can also be understood in a deeper manner. If the most basic ingredient of self is will, then this must also be connected to the divine will. In this sense, a person's will comes from the spark of the Divine in the person. Therefore, when a person visualizes nothingness, he is, to some degree, in touch with the Divine within himself.

This can be understood on the basis of Kabbalistic teachings that the highest spiritual levels can be understood only in terms of nothingness. This may seem difficult to understand. To comprehend it, one must understand how Judaism in general, and the Kabbalists in particular, view God.

People often say that "God is spirit" or that "God is power" or that "God is love." But the fact is that none of these sentences is true. Actually, the sentence "God is . . ." is a statement that cannot be completed. To complete the sentence would be to place God in the same category as something else. If one understands the true nature of God, then this is impossible.

This truth is derived from the very basic Jewish teaching that God is the creator of *all things*. This has very important implications. For one, it means that even concepts as basic as will or mind are creations of God. Indeed, the Zohar explicitly states that God does not have will or mind in any anthropomorphic sense. Rather, in order to use will and mind to create the world, God first had to create these concepts. To say otherwise would be to imply that will and mind are coequal with God, which, again, is impossible.

Even logic itself must be seen as something created by God. Were this not so, and if we were to insist that God be bound by logic, then we would have to say that logic is higher than God, or more fundamental. Again, if we look at God as the creator of all things, then God must also be the creator of logic. This has important ramifications: if one discovers paradoxes in relation to God, it is not a problem. Paradoxes are merely ideas that transcend logic, and since God is the creator of logic, He can use it as He desires, but He is not bound by it. Of course, it is taught that God bound Himself by logic when He created the world, but this was a voluntary act, and not something intrinsic.

The fact that God created every category means that anything for which a word exists in the human language must of necessity denote something created by God. Even the word "God" itself denotes our conception of Him, and not His true essence. Since everything conceivable—including any category of thought that the mind can imagine—was created by God, there is nothing conceivable that can be associated with Him.

Let us say that I want to think about God. There is, however, no category in my mind in which I can place Him. Therefore, trying to depict God is like trying to see without eyes. When I try to see where there are no eyes, all I see is nothing. Similarly, when I try to think about God, all that my mind can depict is nothing.

The Zoharic literature expresses this by declaring to God, "No thought can grasp You at all." Rabbi Shneur Zalman of Lyady (1745–1813), one of the greatest Jewish mystics, notes that the Zohar uses the expression for "grasp" that is usually associated with a physical object. He explains, "Just as a hand cannot grasp thought, so the mind cannot grasp God." Our physical senses cannot grasp or detect thought and therefore experience it as nothing. The same is true of the way the mind experiences God.

Hence, the closest one can come to thinking about God is to depict nothingness and to realize that behind it is God. It is for this reason that nothingness meditation was seen as a means of drawing close to God.

This is not to say that we cannot speak about God at all. As the major Jewish philosophers point out, statements we make about God are either "attributes of action," stating what God *does*, or "negative attributes," saying what God *is not*. We may say that God is good, kind, loving, and omnipotent. However, these are all descriptions of what God does and how He acts, but not what He *is*.

It is important to realize that although we cannot speak *about* God, it is very easy to speak *to* God. Indeed, this is the subject of the following chapters.

When a person imagines nothingness, he should realize that this is the closest that it is possible to come to imagining God. Most certainly, this does not mean that God is nothingness. In every possible way, God is more real than anything else that exists. However, it means that since there is nothing in the human mind that can relate to God as He actually is, nothingness is the closest thing to a perception of God that we can obtain. When a person depicts nothingness, he must realize that behind the nothingness is God.

There is a method to image this. The technique consists in imaging the four letters of the Tetragrammaton as in chapter 8. However, when one "hews" away the surrounding imagery, instead of replacing it with "white fire," one replaces it with nothingness. One begins by imaging a small area of nothingness at the edge of the *yod*. This area of nothingness is expanded until it totally surrounds the four letters. The first few times that one attempts this, the letters may seem to be surrounded by transparent space. With practice, one can actually make the letters seem to be surrounded by nothingness.

If the letters are suspended in nothingness, there will appear to be nothing around them. In essence, the letters will fill the entire field of vision. Still, the letters are not warped or distorted in any way; rather, the space between them and around them is filled with nothingness. Of course, it is impossible to imagine this unless one has actually experienced it. Like panoscopic vision or synesthesia, it is something that cannot be described.

Another, even more advanced technique is to see the letters of the Tetragrammaton behind the nothingness. Then the letters are, as it were, hidden by nothingness, just as God Himself is. In a sense, this is similar to panoscopic vision. One "sees" nothingness, but one is simultaneously looking behind it, where one "sees" the letters of the Divine Name.

All of these techniques are described or alluded to in the Kabbalah literature. However, let me repeat that the techniques described in this chapter are all highly advanced and should not be attempted without expert guidance and considerable experience in meditational techniques.

10

CONVERSING WITH GOD

In the previous chapter, I discussed meditative techniques that are both highly advanced and potentially dangerous for a beginner. The technique that I shall discuss in this chapter, on the other hand, is very simple and is considered among the safest. Still, many people feel that it is one of the most powerful of all the Jewish meditative techniques.

Earlier, I spoke about how difficult it is to speak—or even to think—about God. God is totally ineffable, beyond the realms of thought and speech. Yet, as difficult as it is to speak *about* God, it is relatively easy to speak *to* Him. What person has not at some point in life prayed to God in his own words? If one is a believer, it is a natural reflex in times of trouble or distress to direct one's words toward God. When a loved one is ill or when one faces something unfaceable, one's thoughts and prayers automatically flow toward the Supreme Being. Prayer is a cry from the depths of the heart, from the ground of one's being, and communication is simple and direct.

Children naturally tend to pray to God. A child who is lonely or hurt will automatically call out to his Father in heaven. A child who has never been taught to pray may begin to do so on his own. It is as if there were a built-in instinct that leads us to call beyond the realm of the physical when we are in dire need.

It seems that, in general, Jews pray spontaneously less than non-Jews, at least nowadays. There seems to be a feeling that Jewish prayer must be in Hebrew, in a prescribed manner, with a predetermined wording. Many Jews are surprised to learn that there is an unbroken tradition of spontaneous prayer in the Jewish religion. If we look at the spectrum of Jewish literature, we find numerous references to spontaneous personal prayer. Many great Jewish leaders considered their own prayers to be very important to their spiritual development. And in Europe, it was the most natural thing in the world for Jews to cry out to God in their native Yiddish.

Although many sources discuss spontaneous prayer, one Jewish leader gave it a central role in his teachings: Rabbi Nachman of Bratslav. Rabbi Nachman was a great-grandson of the Baal Shem Tov, founder of the Chasidic movement. The Baal Shem taught that every individual could attain a strong personal relationship with God. Rabbi Nachman expanded this concept, teaching that the most powerful method to attain such a relationship with God is personal prayer in one's own native language.

This, of course, was not meant to downgrade the importance of the formal system of worship, which forms the Jew's daily order of devotion. The prescribed worship service is of paramount importance in Judaism. However, worship services can at times become dry and sterile. One's own personal prayers, on the other hand, are always connected to the wellsprings of the heart.

How does a person begin to speak to God? In times of crisis or trouble, it is almost automatic. There is a need to call out to someone, and one knows that God is always there. When our lives are on an even keel, on the other hand, it is not as easy. When everything is going our way, what is there to discuss with God? How does one begin a conversation? Sometimes, it is almost embarrassing.

It is very much like being away from a parent or a close friend for a long time. In times of crisis, it is easy to renew contact since the crisis itself serves as a point of departure. Similarly, when there are special occasions, it is easy to pick up the phone and say hello. This is why relatives often see one another only at weddings and funerals. Such occasions serve as an excuse to get together after prolonged absence.

To pick up the phone and, without any excuse, call a friend you have not spoken to in years is not a very easy thing to do. How does one justify the sudden, unexpected call? And perhaps most important of all, how does one justify not having made contact for the long period before the call?

For very much the same reason, it is difficult for some people to begin a conversation with God. How does one start such a conversation? And what does one say?

If you need an excuse, you can use this book. Tell God, "I just read this book about having conversations with God. I felt it was time I did it."

Another problem that people encounter when attempting to speak to God is that they feel inadequate. They are aware that God knows their shortcomings and sins, and they feel ashamed in His presence. Others may feel that their lives as Jews are not what they should be and that they cannot approach God as a Jew.

Even if one felt comfortable morally and religiously (and who really does?), there is a basic awe and feeling of inadequacy that everyone feels when trying to speak to God. It is told that the great Chasidic leader Rabbi Zusia of Hanipoli (c. 1720–1800) once came late to synagogue. When he was asked what happened, he replied that when he woke up in the morning, he began the usual prayer, "I give thanks before You . . ." (*Modeh ani lefanekha*). He said the first three words and could go no further. He explained, "I became suddenly aware of who the 'I' was, and who the 'You' was. I was struck speechless and could not continue."

All this adds up to the fact that many people consider it extremely difficult to initiate a conversation with God. Rabbi Nachman speaks about this at considerable length.

It is significant that Rabbi Nachman refers to this practice of speaking to God, not as prayer, but as meditation. It appears that the line between prayer and meditation here is a very fine one, but there is an important difference. When a person speaks to God spontaneously, whenever he feels impelled to do so, then it is prayer. When a person makes it a fixed practice and spends a definite time each day conversing with God, then it is meditation. As we have discussed earlier, meditation is thinking in a controlled manner. If this thinking consists in a conversation with God, it is no less a meditative experience.

In this context, Rabbi Nachman prescribes making a commitment to spending a fixed amount of time each day speaking to God. The amount of time he prescribes is approximately an hour every evening. In our fast-moving modern society, many find twenty to thirty minutes a more comfortable period for such conversation. The main thing is that it be for a fixed period of time and that it be practiced every day without fail.

The most difficult thing is to begin. Rabbi Nachman advises sitting down in the place where you meditate and saying to yourself, "For the next twenty mintes, I will be alone with God." This in itself is significant, since it is like the beginning of a "visit." Even if there is nothing to say, it is a valid experience since you are spending time alone with God, aware of His presence. If you sit long enough, says Rabbi Nachman, you will eventually find something to say.

If you have difficulty in beginning the conversation, Rabbi Nachman advises repeating the phrase "Master of the Universe" over and over. This can comprise the entire conversation. When you say these words, be aware that you are calling out to God. Eventually, your thoughts will open up, and you will find other ways of expressing yourself.

Of course, "Master of the Universe" is nothing other than *Ribbono shel Olam*, a phrase that I discussed earlier as a Jewish mantra. Here we see that it can also be used to call out to God in a most basic way, to establish communication.

If you still cannot begin speaking with God, Rabbi Nachman suggests making this difficulty itself the point of conversation. Tell God how much you would like to speak to Him. Explain to Him that it is hard for you to find something to say. Ask God to help you find words with which to address Him. Discuss the problem with Him as you would with a good friend. Once the conversation has begun, it is usually easy to continue.

Another point of departure can be the feeling of alienation and distance from God. You can initiate a conversation by asking God to bring you closer to Him. Tell him how far you feel from Him and how much closer you would like to be. Ask Him to help you find such closeness.

The conversation does not have to vary. One can speak to God about the same thing day after day, week after week. Obviously, it is impossible to bore God. Since this is a meditation, the regular habit of holding a conversation is as important as its content. If you are asking God to help you speak to Him, or to draw you closer, this exercise will help you develop your ability to hold more extensive conversations with God.

You can repeat the same sentence or phrase as often as you wish. Any significant sentence can be the point of the entire meditation. You can change the phrase or sentence that you are using at any time. Eventually, you will develop enough flexibility to express your thoughts to God freely.

In any case, just as with everything else, practice helps, and one can become proficient in holding conversations with the Infinite Being. Once you learn how to converse with God with ease, you can speak in a quiet, hushed voice, making yourself more and more aware of the One to whom you are speaking. As you converse, you will become increasingly aware of God's presence. At this point, the conversation with God becomes an awesome experience.

As the conversation becomes easier and more relaxed, the experience deepens. It becomes a powerful meditative technique, which can easily bring one to higher states of consciousness. In these states of consciousness, God's presence becomes almost palpable.

The question arises as to what advantage this method has over such other methods as mantra meditation or contemplation. Since this is an inner-directed meditation, it has some important advantages.

One of the purposes of meditation is to help banish the ego. This is often difficult in the modern world. Furthermore, in the high-pressure world of our everyday lives, a person must have a strong sense of self and purpose in order not to be trampled. For many people, a meditative regimen that weakens the ego and sense of self may be counterproductive. One may find one's goals in meditation diametrically opposed to one's ambitions and aspirations in the world.

The method of conversing with God does not have this drawback. It is true that, like other forms of meditation, this method can help a person overcome the ego. Nevertheless, this is a method that replaces the ego with something stronger. In speaking to God, a person can gain a view of himself from a different perspective and begin to see himself as a branch of the Divine. This type of meditation makes one, as it were, partners with the Divine. Thus, for example, if one has discussed future plans with God and still feels good about them, one's resolution and feeling of purpose are all the stronger.

Of course, this can have dangers in the opposite direction. If a person does not nullify his ego sufficiently, he can become so bullheaded and obstinate that people cannot deal with him. Nothing is so distasteful as a person who acts as if he has a direct line to God. Therefore, the goal is to attain and maintain a balance.

Besides strengthening one's resolve, conversing with God can also help one to find direction in life. I have discussed this earlier, when I spoke about a meditation concerned with rearranging one's life. Here again, by conversing with God, a person can see himself from a God's-eye view, as it were. He can then determine if the type of life he is leading is one that is worthy from God's point of view. If it is not, meditation will help him find ways of improving it.

It is significant that the Hebrew verb for praying is *hitpalel*. Hebrew linguists note that this is the reflexive of the word *palel*, meaning "to judge." Therefore, *hitpalel* means to judge oneself.

This is not difficult to understand in the context of our discussion. When a person speaks to God, he is able to see himself from a God's-eye view and he is judging himself in the deepest sense possible. He is looking at his most profound aspirations in the mirror of his prayer and judging whether or not they are worthy.

Little by little, the person can also purge himself of any encumbrances to prayer.

Actually, this is like a type of therapy. In many ways, speaking to God is like speaking to a therapist. What, then, is the difference between this method of prayer-meditation and psychotherapy?

First, it is true that both psychotherapy and meditation can help a person direct his life more effectively. In psychotherapy, however, the answer comes from without, while in prayer-meditation, the answer comes from within. If the person is basically healthy, his answers will reflect his own values and aspirations much more truly than if they are filtered through the eyes of a therapist who may have an entirely different value system. Prayer-meditation may also spur a person to learn more about life and its meaning from external sources, so that help can also come from without.

Furthermore, psychotherapy deals only with the mundane dimensions of man, and not with his spiritual dimensions. Prayer-meditation, on the other hand, deals primarily with the spiritual dimension. Psychotherapy is primarily a way of working out problems, while meditation is a method of enhancing the spiritual dimensions of life.

There are many ways in which prayer-meditation can be very much like self-therapy, and therefore, it has all the dangers inherent therein. As in therapy, a person can uncover deep, unresolved problems that can cause great pain and suffering if they are not worked out. In psychotherapy, one has the therapist to help if the situation becomes too difficult. If one is using meditation as self-therapy, on the other hand, one can get oneself into a psychological cul-de-sac and not be able to escape.

Therefore, if you find yourself using prayer-meditation as a form of self-therapy, it is very important that you have a guide who understands exactly what is happening. Without such a guide, the results can be more negative than positive. The guide should be someone who is well adjusted and psychologically strong, with extensive successful experience in guiding neophyte meditators. The guide's advice should help the meditator find a proper balance in his or her life.

11

THE WAY OF PRAYER

One of my students, a psychiatrist-healer, once told me that when he began his involvement in spiritual practices, he used to rush through the morning service so that he would have time to meditate. This went on for a few months. Then, in one of our classes, we discussed how the worship service itself was originally designed to be meditative exercise and how it could be used as such. After this, he told me, instead of rushing through the morning service, he used the service itself as his daily meditation.

Many Jews are still uncomfortable with meditation. They feel that it is something from another culture, tacked onto Judaism. Although many traditional sources discuss Jewish meditation, after a century of neglect, many Jews find the notion difficult to accept. Even the word "meditation" has an alien ring to it, as if it were something borrowed from another world.

On the other hand, the most accepted manner for a Jew to relate to God is through the daily services. An observant Jew worships (or *davens*) three times a day. In most communities, the synagogues hold daily services. Of course, in Orthodox circles, daily prayer is considered an important part of the daily regimen.

The three daily services are the morning service, known as *shacharith;* the afternoon service, known as *minchah;* and the evening service, known as *maariv* or *arevith.* The service on the Sabbath and festivals is essentially the same, except that a fourth additional, or *musaf*, service is added in the morning after the Torah is read.

The focus of each of these services is the Amidah, which literally means "that which involves standing." The Amidah is a silent prayer that must be said while one is standing. On weekdays, it originally consisted of eighteen prayers and petitions, and is therefore also referred to as the Shemoneh Esreh, which literally means "The Eighteen." In the first century, a nineteenth prayer was added, making this appellation not strictly accurate.

The Amidah can be found in any standard Jewish prayer book. Of the eighteen sections, the first three and last three are always essentially the same, both on weekdays and on the Sabbath and Holy Days. On the Sabbath and Holy Days, however, the middle twelve (or thirteen) prayers are replaced with a single section relating to the Sabbath or festival.

The most important part of the Amidah, especially from a meditative point of view, is the opening paragraph. This paragraph consists of a short prayer that establishes the worshiper's basic relationship to God. This paragraph always forms the beginning of the Amidah, whether on weekdays or on Sabbaths or festivals.

In order to use this section of the Amidah as a meditation, one must memorize it. It is best to do so in the original Hebrew, since the language itself has tremendous spiritual power. If one does not know Hebrew, it is permissible to recite the prayer in English or any other language. The words have power in any language, but not as much as they have in the original. In order to use the Amidah as a meditation, on the other hand, one should be able to recite it in the original and know its meaning.

The Amidah was authored just before the close of the prophetic period two and a half thousand years ago, during the early years of the Second Temple in Jerusalem. Ezra had returned from Babylonia to the Holy Land and was rallying the people to reestablish Judaism as a viable way of life. Jerusalem and the Holy Land had been reduced to ashes by the Babylonians under Nebuchadnezzar, and it was out of these ashes that Ezra and his followers built Judaism anew.

Toward this end, Ezra gathered together one hundred and twenty of the greatest sages of his time. This group, which also included the last of the biblical prophets, was known as the Great Assembly (*keneseth ha-gedolah*). The Great Assembly enacted a number of important rules in order to preserve Torah observance among Jews scattered all over the world. One of the major accomplishments of the Great Assembly was to canonize the text of the Bible.

It was the Great Assembly that first authored the Amidah. The prayer is therefore one of the most ancient in existence today. Among its authors were Haggai, Zechariah, and Malachi, who also composed books of the Bible. The same spiritual energy that went into writing the Bible also went into writing the Amidah. It was designated as a universal prayer and meditation for all Jews from that time on.

The power of the Amidah comes from the words themselves. The prayer was carefully composed by highly advanced spiritual individuals so as to enable a maximum relationship with God. As we shall see, in the first paragraph, a person is drawn closer and closer to God, until he feels the presence of God all around him, penetrating his very being.

Since the Amidah was composed as a meditation prayer, it is necessary to repeat it as often as possible. It is for this reason that it was required that the same prayer be said three times every day.

As discussed earlier, one of the reasons a mantra works is that when the words are said over and over, the mind develops a special resonance with them. The words can then be said automatically, without special effort or concentration. Since the mind is not concerned with *saying* the words, it can allow itself to be filled with their meaning.

The same is true of a prayer that is said every day. Eventually, one not only memorizes the words, but learns to say them automatically. After one has recited the Amidah three times daily for a few years, one can literally say the prayer without thinking. While this is a danger, it is also a great advantage. The danger is that the mind will drift away from the words and the prayer will become meaningless. Indeed, many people who worship every day find it very difficult to keep their mind on what they are saying. If the Amidah is treated simply as prayer, this is a problem. However, if it is treated as a mantra, then the automatic nature of the recital is a great boon. The words themselves become like a mantra, quieting the mind and removing from it all extraneous thought.

Of course, this does not mean that one should not think about the words of the Amidah, but the way one thinks of the words becomes very different. Instead of thinking of them in an intellectual sense, one allows the words to resonate through the mind. It feels as if the words were conveying their message in a nonverbal manner.

Thus, when one says in the first blessing that God is "great," one has an overpowering experience of God's greatness. Similarly, when one says that He is "mighty," one experiences His infinite strength. Like many experiences in the meditative state, however, these feelings are difficult to describe.

The Amidah is a single unit that should be said in its entirety without interruption. As a practical matter, however, the first paragraph is the most important part of the Amidah, and it is this section that sets the tone for the rest of the prayer.

For a person who has worshiped every day, making the transition to using the Amidah as a meditation may involve a change in orientation. Nevertheless, one who knows the words well and has learned the methods of meditation in general can make the transition. One may have recited the Amidah for years, even from early childhood; the only thing necessary to learn is to say it effectively.

However, a person who is not familiar with the Amidah will have to go through a preparatory period in order to memorize the words and become familiar with them. This period should take a minimum of thirty days. It may be difficult for the neophyte to learn the entire Amidah that perfectly in this short time. Nevertheless, the first paragraph consists of only forty-two words and therefore can be readily learned. This paragraph itself can be the meditation, while the rest of the Amidah is then read as a prayer.

If at all possible, learn this first blessing in the original Hebrew. If you can read Hebrew but do not understand the words, learn at least the translation of these forty-two words. If you cannot read Hebrew, try to get someone to transliterate them and learn to recite them in Hebrew. The spiritual benefits that can be gained from this method are so great that it would be worthwhile to learn Hebrew for no other reason than to be able to say the Amidah in its original language.

During the preparatory period, memorize the first paragraph. This is important because this paragraph should be said with the eyes closed. Some authorities say that the entire Amidah should be recited by heart. These authorities state that this was the reason why no prayer books were used during the Talmudic period. Since some people could not recite the Amidah by heart, it was ordained that a reader would repeat the prayer aloud for those who could not say it by themselves.

Once you have memorized the first blessing, recite it by heart as part of the three prescribed services for at least thirty days. After this preparatory period, you should be familiar enough with the paragraph to use it as a meditative device.

To use the Amidah as a meditation, one must be familiar with its basic rules. Indeed, a number of these rules make sense only if one looks at the Amidah as a meditation.

The first rule is that the Amidah must be said at the proper time. The morning *shacharith* Amidah can be said from dawn until the end of the first quarter of the day (approximately 10:00 A.M.) or, in an emergency, until noon. The afternoon *minchah* Amidah can be said from shortly after noon until sunset. The evening *maariv* Amidah can be said from nightfall until just before dawn.

Before any worship service, one must wash the hands. This is reminiscent of the *kohen* priests, who would wash their hands before performing the Divine Service in the Jerusalem Temple. Washing the hands is more than mere cleansing; it is a ritual purification that must be done in a prescribed manner. The washing is accomplished by pouring water from a cup or glass, first over the right hand and then over the left hand, washing the hands in this manner three times alternately.

One may not recite the Amidah unless one is properly dressed. In particular, men should cover their heads with a hat or a *yarmulke*. It also should not be said in the presence of other people who are not decently dressed, or where an unpleasant odor is present. Preferably it should not be said in a situation where there is anything that will disturb one's concentration.

By definition, the Amidah is said while standing. The feet should be together, which, as the Talmud states, is the stance of the angels. The head can be slightly bowed and the hands be placed over the heart.

Whenever possible, one should face Jerusalem when reciting the Amidah. If one is in Jerusalem, one should face the site of the Temple. The physical location of the Temple is a source of spiritual energy, and facing in this direction helps draw this energy from the site of the Holy of Holies. According to ancient tradition, this was the place that Jacob called "the gate of heaven" (Gen. 28:17), and as such, it is the primary source of spiritual energy.

When one says the word "blessed" (*barukh*) at the beginning and end of the first paragraph, one should bend the knees. When one says the next word, "are you" (*attah*), one should bow down from the waist. This bowing is repeated again at the beginning and end of the Modim, which is the next-to-last section of the Amidah.

Bowing is integral to getting oneself into the meditative state. According to the Talmud, one bows down fairly quickly but then comes up very slowly, "like a snake." The commentaries explain that this means raising first the head and then the rest of the body. When one comes up in this manner, it slows the body's tempo and puts the mind in a quieter framework. It thus has the effect of quieting the mind and making it more receptive for meditation.

With the exception of bowing, it is preferable to remain absolutely motionless during the Amidah. Some people have the habit of shaking and swaying during this prayer, but the codes of Jewish law regard this more as a nervous habit than as a means of improving one's concentration. Both the Kabbalists and many major codifiers state explicitly that all motion should be avoided in the Amidah.

If you find it impossible to remain absolutely still, you may sway very lightly, but excessive shaking or swaying tends to impair concentration in a meditative sense.

It is also important to close the eyes in the Amidah, especially during the first blessing, in order to get yourself into a meditative state. If you do not know the rest of the Amidah by heart, it can be said from a prayerbook.

The words of the Amidah should be said quietly, either in a very soft voice or in a quiet whisper. The voice should be directed inward rather than outward.

These methods will make the Amidah a more effective instrument of worship. If the Amidah is also to be a meditation, there is one more important condition, and this has to do with the pace at which the words are said. The Talmud relates that the "original saints" (*chasidim rishonim*) used to take one hour to recite the Amidah. From the context, as well as from a number of Kabbalistic sources, it is obvious that these original saints used the Amidah as a meditation. This teaching provides an important clue to the pace at which the Amidah is to be said if it is to be used as a meditative device. A simple count shows that the entire Amidah contains approximately 500 words. The original saints took an hour to say it, or some 3,600 seconds. Therefore, they said this prayer at a pace of approximately one word every seven seconds.

To say the entire Amidah at this pace is a highly advanced form of meditation. However, this pace is not difficult to maintain for the first paragraph, which is the most important. Since the first blessing contains forty-two words, to say it at the rate of a word every seven seconds would take just under five minutes. This is a reasonable time, yet long enough to put one into a deep meditative state.

This pace has the effect of quieting the mind in a most profound manner. It is a meditative state that appears subjectively to be very different than that obtained through ordinary mantra meditation or contemplation because the words one is saying define the meditation at every point.

There are two basic ways in which you can pace the recitation of the words. You can draw out each word as long as possible and then pause briefly to let the meaning sink in. Alternatively, you can recite the word and then wait for seven seconds before saying the next word. Each method is effective in its own way, and either can be used, depending on your preference.

While reciting a word, and for the period afterward, do not think of anything other than the simple meaning of the word. (The significance of the words of the first paragraph of the Amidah will be discussed in the next chapter.) Allow the words to penetrate your inner being, opening yourself to feel and see the meaning of each word. During the pause between words, the mind is hushed in anticipation of the next word and then cleared of all other thought.

Once you have said the first blessing in this manner, the rest of the Amidah flows easily. It is then a simple matter to recite the entire Amidah with a feeling of closeness to God and without any extraneous thoughts.

Some people find it beneficial to combine the Amidah with a visualization technique. Some sources indicate that while reciting the first paragraph, one should attempt to visualize pure white light. Other sources state that one should visualize the letters of the Tetragrammaton. Still another source teaches that it is beneficial to visualize nothingness while saying this paragraph. The person who is familiar with these techniques may find them beneficial in enhancing the meditative experience of the Amidah. Another alternative is to concentrate on the spontaneous images that arise in the mind's eye.

Eventually, however, one learns that the most powerful technique of all is to use the words of the Amidah and nothing else. When the words will the mind, one becomes oblivious to all other thought. The words draw the person to God, and the mind becomes completely filled with the Divine. In this manner, the Amidah can bring a person to some of the most profound spiritual experiences possible. Since it was composed for this purpose, this is by no means surprising.

12

RELATING TO GOD

A s we discussed in the previous chapter, the first paragraph of the Amidah is the most important element of the service for use as a meditation. Moreover, this blessing defines the I–Thou relationship between the worshiper and God. Let us explore this paragraph word by word.

The first blessing of the Amidah is:

Blessed are You, Adonoy,
  our God and God of our fathers,
God of Abraham, God of Isaac, and God of Jacob,
Great, mighty, and awesome God,
  Highest God,
Doer of good, kind deeds,
  Master of all,
Who remembers the love of the Patriarchs
  and brings a redeemer to their children's children
    for His name's sake,
      with love.
King, Helper, Rescuer, and Shield.
Blessed are You, Adonoy, Shield of Abraham.

The first word of the Amidah is "blessed," *barukh* in Hebrew. It is difficult to understand what the term "blessed" means when applied to God. A person can be blessed to have life, health, prosperity, children, and other benefits. But what does it mean when we say that God is blessed?

If we look at blessings in the Bible, we always find that God is giving the recipient of the blessing some good or benefit. For example, Isaac says to Jacob, "May God give you from the dew of heaven and from the fat of the earth . . ." (Gen. 27:28). The main point of this and other blessings in the Bible is that God will be granting the recipient a special providence and that He will have a special relationship and closeness to the one receiving the blessing.

A blessing is therefore an expression of God's immanence. When we say that God is "blessed," we are saying that His immanent presence is the source of all blessing. This implies that God is close—very close—to us. Many Jewish sources indicate that the word "blessed" specifically denotes God's immanence in the world.

When we recite the word "blessed" (*barukh*) in the Amidah, we should be aware that God is very close, permeating the very air around us. We should feel God in our bones, in our flesh, in our minds, in the deepest recesses of our souls. We should also be aware that God makes Himself available in order to enhance our closeness to Him.

The next word is "You," *attah* in Hebrew. This word refers to the I–Thou relationship that we have with God. Simply saying "You" to God makes us aware that we are speaking directly to Him. When we say this word, we should be aware of the Divine directly in front of us and feel all the love, strength, and awe that exist when we confront the Divine.

Then comes God's name, which in Hebrew is pronounced *Adonoy*. This name is actually written as the Tetragrammaton, YHVH, but since this most holy name may not be pronounced, the name Adonoy, which means "my Lord," is substituted. This substitution teaches us some very important lessons about the Divine.

The meaning of the Tetragrammaton on one level has been

discussed in chapter 7. However, there is another way of under-standing this name on an even deeper level.

The codes note that the Tetragrammaton, YHVH, appears to be related to the past, present, and future of the Hebrew verb "to be"; in Hebrew, "was" is *hayah*, "is" is *hoveh*, and "will be" is *yihyeh*. Therefore, the codes state, when one sees the Tetra-grammaton, one should have in mind that God "was, is, and will be"—all at once. This indicates that God is utterly transcenden-tal, higher even than the realm of time. God exists in a realm where time does not exist.

This also implies that God is totally different from anything else in creation. We cannot even begin to imagine a being exist-ing outside of space, for whom the very concept of space does not apply. It is even more difficult to imagine a being who exists outside of time, so much so that past, present, and future are all the same to Him. Our very thought processes are dependent on time and can function only within the framework of time. Yet none of this applies to God.

Of course, even to use the word "being" with relation to God is a misnomer and anthropomorphism. The only reason that we think of God as a "being" is so that we can speak to Him, and "being" is the only category into which we can fit that to which we can speak. Of course, the fact that "being" is the closest category into which we can place God does not mean that He is a being. As we have discussed earlier, there is no category into which we can place God.

There are two major supercategories in our minds into which all things can be placed: that of things and that of relationships or states. If we could place God in the category of things, then we would speak of Him as a being. However, if we placed Him in the category of relationships, we would speak of Him as a princi-ple. Thus, when we say that "God is the creator of the universe," we are speaking of Him as a being. On the other hand, when we say, "God is the creative force in the universe," we are speaking of Him as a principle.

The first time I used this concept in a class, one of my students asked a simple but very tricky question: "If God exists outside of space, how can we say that God is everywhere?" After a few moments of thought, the idea struck me. I asked the class, "Does the equation $1 + 1 = 2$ exist in space?"

The class's response was that this equation obviously does not exist in space. The equation $1 + 1 = 2$ is not a thing that can exist in space, but rather a mathematical relationship. It is a mathematical *principle*, and as such, it exists in the world of ideas, and not in space.

Then I asked another question: "Is there any place where $1 + 1 = 2$ does not exist?"

The obvious answer was no. Wherever one would go in the entire universe—and beyond—one would find that $1 + 1 = 2$. This simple equation is a good example of something that does not exist in space and yet, at the same time, exists everywhere. This is true of every universal principle. By nature, an abstract principle is not spatial and therefore exists outside of space. Yet, if we are speaking of a universal principle, such as any of the principles of mathematics, there is no place where it does not exist.

For many purposes, it would be useful to think of God as a principle rather than a being. For one thing, it would make it readily understandable how He exists outside of space and time, and yet fills all space and time. For another, an idea such as this breaks down the anthropomorphic ideas that people have about God.

One may be tempted to say, "God is a principle." However, as I discussed earlier, the sentence "God is . . ." is a statement that cannot be completed. God is the creator of all categories and therefore cannot fit into any of them. Both "principle" and "being" are approximations that we use because the mind has no category into which it can place God. It may be that a third, intermediate category might be a better approximation, but the mind has no example of it, and therefore, such a category cannot be imagined. Nevertheless, through meditation, one can gain a glimmer of the nature of this third category.

The Tetragrammaton appears to relate to God as a principle

rather than as a being. It denotes God's existence in the past, the present, and the future simultaneously, just like that of any other principle. Earlier, I discussed how the Tetragrammaton denotes the four steps in the process through which God gives existence to His creation (see chapter 8). In this respect, we are also seeing the Tetragrammaton as describing God as the creative principle.

Nevertheless, it is not easy to relate to a principle, which appears totally impersonal, and indeed is. In prayer and worship, it is much easier to relate to God as a being. Therefore, we do not pronounce the Tetragrammaton, but instead substitute *Adonoy*, "my Lord." This indicates that God is Lord and Master of all creation. In seeing God as Lord and Master, we are viewing Him as a being rather than as a principle. Mastery and dominance are anthropomorphic concepts that are most fitting to a sentient being.

As we reach the name of God that is written as the Tetragrammaton and pronounced *Adonoy*, we become aware that we are addressing a Being-Principle. We see God as the Principle that gives existence to all things. Yet, at the same time, we see God as a Being, and furthermore, as a Being to whom we can relate. When we speak to God, it is as if we are communing with existence itself, but at the same time speaking to it as if it were a person. At the same time, we realize that God is more than existence, actually the principle that allows existence to be.

When we pronounce God's name, *Adonoy*, we are aware that we are addressing the Infinite Being who is the absolute Other. The very next word, however, is *Elohenu*, which is translated as "our God." This shows the extent to which God allows us to relate to Him and draw close. As far above us as He is, He allows us to address Him as "our God"—as if, in a sense, He belonged to us. This is perhaps the greatest gift and miracle of all—that God allows us to call Him "ours."

The full expression in which we address God as ours is "our God and God of our fathers" (*Elohenu ve-Elohey avotenu*). The Baal Shem Tov explains this expression in the following manner:

There are two ways in which we can know God. First, we know about God because we have heard about Him from others. We have inherited a tradition about God from our fathers, from our ancestors, and from all the great people of the past.

This, however, is not enough. No matter how much a person may have heard about God, he must also have his own personal experience of God. Unless a person has experienced God for himself, he will never have any true idea of what God is. In a way, it is like love. If you have ever been in love, then you know what I mean when I speak about love. But if you have never been in love, the word is totally abstract. You may imagine that love is something very nice, but you have no experience of it. Even if you read what poets sing about love, you can understand it only on the most abstract level. However, if you have ever been in love, the word will have very powerful connotations for you.

The same is true of God. If you have experienced closeness to God even once in your life, then when I speak about God, you know exactly what I mean, and the concept has a very strong spiritual connotation. But if you have never had this experience, then God is something very abstract and can be described only on an intellectual level. We can speak about God, argue about Him, and even debate His existence. However, if you have ever experienced God, then there is nothing to talk about. As soon as I mention the word "God," you know exactly what I am speaking about, since God is as much part of your experience as He is of mine. One who has never been in love might argue that love does not exist. The same is true of one who has never experienced God. But for one who has had the experience, there is no question.

When one experiences God, however, there is always the danger that it is a false experience. That is, you may think that you are experiencing God, but you may actually be experiencing something very different.

It is for this reason that we say "and God of our fathers." The experience of God is not something that we are inventing, something that has no relation to our past. Rather, it is part of a tradition that goes back to our earliest ancestors. We affirm that we are not going off in our quest for God on our own, but doing so as part of an unbroken chain of tradition.

We then say, "God of Abraham, God of Isaac, and God of Jacob." We mention the Patriarchs because we see them as having attained the ultimate experience of God. For them the experience of God was so strong that they were willing to challenge their environment and change their lives because of it, becoming the spiritual trailblazers for millions that followed them. At this opening point in the Amidah, we attempt to direct our consciousness to the level of closeness to God that the Patriarchs had experienced.

It is taught that Abraham's primary experience of God was that of His greatness, whereas Isaac experienced God's strength and Jacob experienced His awesomeness. Thus, the peak experiences of the Patriarchs correspond to the next three expressions in the Amidah, "the great, mighty, and awesome God."

When one says that God is "great" (*ha-gadol*) in the Amidah, one should concentrate on greatness and immensity. Try to imagine how great God is. Think of the size of the largest thing you can imagine. Then go further and try to imagine the size of the planet Earth. Continue, and imagine the size of the sun, the solar system, the galaxy, and then the entire universe. Then realize how tiny this all is in comparison with the greatness of God. Compared with Him, the entire universe is less than a mote of dust.

This, of course, is contemplation on an intellectual level, and during the Amidah is not the time for such intellectualizing. When we say the expression "the great," we have to take the concept of greatness beyond the intellectual level. The mind expands with the concept of greatness and becomes aware of greatness and bigness in its purest and most abstract form. The concept of greatness reverberates through one's entire being, and one can then catch a glimpse of what it means in relation to God.

In Kabbalah, God's greatness is closely associated with His love (*chesed*). When we imagine an Infinite Being ready to listen to the voice of an infinitesimal creature, we realize that there can be no greater love. Thus, in the greatness, there is also love. This is another reason that Abraham is associated with God's attribute of greatness and love. It is taught that Abraham directed his life to emulate God's love. Abraham was an important personage in his time, with sufficient status to rub shoulders with kings and monarchs. Nevertheless, he would literally run to greet and serve even the lowliest of wayfarers (see Gen. 18:3,4).

The next word is "the mighty" (*ha-gibbor*). When one says this word, one should think of God's strength. Earlier, I mentioned how one can look at one's own hand and see the strength in it. When one says the word "the mighty," one should likewise concentrate on strength in its pure form. When one thinks about strength in terms of God, it expands until it overwhelms the mind. One then begins to have an inkling of strength as it applies to God.

Finally, we say, "and the awesome" (*ve-ha-norah*). This emulates the experience of Jacob at Bethel after he saw the vision of God and the ladder, when he said, "How awesome is this place!" (Gen. 28:17). When one is aware of God's greatness and strength, one is overcome with a feeling of awe. Rather than being a frightening experience, it is a sweet and beautiful awe, the awe that comes from standing in the presence of the Infinite.

The next phrase is "highest God" (*El Elyon*). This expression is designated to make us realize that when we say that God is "great, mighty, and awesome," these adjectives are not meant to limit Him in any way, but merely name the emotions and experiences that we have when we try to draw close to God. When one attempts to approach God, as we do in the Amidah, one first has a sensation of infinite greatness, then a feeling of infinite strength, and finally a feeling of overwhelming awe.

It is important to realize that God is above all these. The mind must therefore soar above greatness, above strength, above awe, and realize that God transcends any thought that we can possibly have. God is beyond the sky, beyond the stars, beyond the heavens, and even beyond the spiritual realm.

This last concept is important to reiterate. Often people speak of God as a Spirit or as being spiritual. However, God is above the spiritual just as He is above the physical. Just as He is the creator of the concept of the physical, He is also the creator of the concept of the spiritual. As creator of the spiritual, He cannot be encompassed by it. Therefore, as high as our concept of God may be, it cannot even begin to come close to His true essence. The Amidah puts this very succinctly when it refers to Him as "highest God."

Immediately after saying that God is the ineffable "highest God," we say that He is the "Doer of good, kind deeds." Although God is higher than any thought can conceive, He still does things that we can perceive as being kind and good. Therefore, when we say these words, we are aware of God's infinite goodness and kindness.

This is very closely related to a Talmudic teaching: "Wherever you find mention of God's greatness, you also find mention of His humility." What the Talmud is saying is that an Infinite Being is not limited by any human conception of greatness or smallness. God is so great that to Him a galaxy is no more significant than a bacterium. At the same time, He is great enough that a single human being can be as significant to Him as an entire universe.

After this, we speak of God as *koney ha-kol*, which has been translated as "Master of all," but which would be more literally translated as "Owner of all." Just as an owner can do as he pleases with his property, so God can do as He wills with all things. All creation is God's property, and He can do with it as He wills. Moreover, an owner takes possession of his property and associates it with his person. In a certain sense, anything a person owns is an extension of the self. In a similar manner, God associates Himself with His creation, and His essence permeates all existence.

The Amidah then links the past to the future, saying that God "remembers the love of the Patriarchs and brings a redeemer to their children's children. . . ." God thus shares our memory of the past, especially with regard to the Patriarchs, who were the first ones to bring God consciousness to the world. Just as we look to the Patriarchs for a paradigm of the God experience, God looks at their love for Him as a paradigm, and as a reason to remain close to their descendants no matter what happens.

We also see God as our hope in the future—no small thing in

this age over which hangs a Damocles' sword of nuclear destruction. We believe that God will bring a redeemer, who will make the world a safe and sane place to live. We have faith that there will come a time when all humanity will be brought back to the God consciousness that the Patriarchs enjoyed and that this will be a time of universal peace and good for all humankind. This is our ultimate hope in the future.

We conclude by saying that God remembers the Patriarchs and will bring a redeemer "for His name's sake." As we discussed earlier, God's name is much more than an arbitrary collection of sounds. Rather, it is a word that speaks of His essence and His relationship with creation. The name is an important focus of our God consciousness, as I have discussed in previous chapters.

God's name also figures both in the lives of the Patriarchs and in our hope in the future. The experience of the Patriarchs was always closely linked to God's name. The Torah tells that Abraham began his career by "calling in the name of God" (Gen. 12:8). The Patriarchs were thus the ones who initiated God consciousness to the world through His name. Not only did they link themselves to the Infinite, but they also identified It with a name.

The process begun by the Patriarchs will be completed by the promised redeemer, who will bring God's name to all humanity. One of the important prophecies regarding the messianic future is that "On that day, God will be One and His Name One" (Zech. 14:9). Not only will the entire world worship God, but everyone will call Him by the same name. This will indicate that the whole world will have the same God consciousness as the heirs of the Patriarchs. The Amidah expresses this by stating that the entire process will be "for His name's sake."

The initial portion ends with the expression "with love" (*be-ahavah*). It is love that bridges the gap between the past and future—even as love bridges the gap between man and woman. In a sense, the past and future can be looked upon as a male and a female. Just as the male impregnates the female, the past impregnates the future. The redemption in the future will come from the memory of the Patriarchs in the past. It is God's love spanning the chasm of time.

Moreover, God causes the processes of history to unfold, the goal being the perfection of humanity and society. This entire process is governed by love. We make ourselves aware of God's love at this point in the Amidah, and are totally saturated by it.

The first paragraph in the Amidah concludes with four words that are designated to bring God closer to the worshiper. These four words are "King, Helper, Rescuer, and Shield." Whereas in the first part of this paragraph we relate to God in a general manner, here we develop our personal relationship with Him.

These four words are the key to the entire Amidah. If one says them correctly, one is left in a perfect spiritual space for the rest of the service. Even if one has said the first parts of this paragraph without proper concentration, if these four words are said properly, they will bring the worshiper to such a closeness to God that the rest of the Amidah will be perfect. If one cannot say the entire first paragraph at the rate of seven seconds per word, as mentioned earlier, one should at least do so for these four words.

Let us look at these four words in detail.

The first word is "King" (*Melekh*). We begin by looking at God as our king and at our relationship to Him as that of a subject to a king. A king is far away, in his capital city, in his palace. If you want something from the king, you must send him a formal request, and it goes through his staff, his ministers, his secretary. Then, if you are lucky, after a few months you may get a reply. Therefore, when we address God as King, we see Him as majestic but distant. Help is available from him, but not closely available.

In the next word, we address God as "Helper" (*Ozer*). Now we see him as much closer than a king. A "helper" is someone whom we can readily approach. He is a friend whom we know we can always call on and who always will make himself available. Therefore, when we call God "Helper," we realize that we can call on Him at any time and He will be there for us. This is a relationship much closer than that to a king. In saying this word, we are beginning the process through which we draw closer to God.

Third, we address God as "Rescuer" (*Moshia*). Again, a rescuer is much closer than a helper. A rescuer is someone who is available to save you when you are drowning in a river; he is right there to jump in and pull you out. A helper may have the best intentions in the world, but if he is not close to you at all times, he cannot save you when you are in danger. Therefore, when we speak to God as our "Rescuer," we see Him as being available whenever we need Him, ready to rescue us in an instant. We recognize that God is always close enough to help us, even when we are in imminent danger. Thus, the relationship of Rescuer is much closer than that of Helper. This word brings us yet a step closer to God.

Finally, we speak to God as our "Shield" (*Magen*). A shield is even closer than a rescuer. A shield can help even when an arrow is flying at me and there is nothing else that can stop it. When the arrow is flying, there is no time for even the rescuer to intercept it. The shield must be there in place—right in front of me. Thus, when I address God as my "Shield," I can feel Him right in front of me. God is all around me, surrounding me like a suit of divine armor. I am totally aware of God's protective power, surrounding me on all sides. I feel that I am being protected by God, so that nothing in the world can harm me.

Thus, in the four words "King, Helper, Rescuer, and Shield," we become more and more aware of God's closeness. First we see Him as a benevolent but distant king, then as a willing helper, then as an nearby rescuer, and finally, as an immanent shield. In these four words, we make the transition from viewing God as a remote transcendental force to seeing Him as a protector who is closer than the air around us.

The one person who reached the level where he could constantly see God as his shield was Abraham. God had told him, "Do not fear, Abram, I am a shield to you" (Gen. 15:1). From that time on, Abraham had a constant perception of God as his shield. He was always aware of God being very close to him, surrounding him and protecting him on a most immanent and direct level.

It is for this reason that the first paragraph ends with the blessing "Blessed are You, Adonoy, Shield of Abraham." It makes us aware that such a level of God consciousness exists and that it can even be woven into a way of life, as in the case of Abraham. Of all the levels of relationship to God, the level of shield is the closest. Here we see God close enough to us to stop even a flying bullet. This was the level attained by Abraham, and at this point in the Amidah, we aspire to it.

The word "blessed" (*barukh*) occurs twice in this first paragraph. The paragraph begins with the word "blessed," and then it is repeated in the ending, "Blessed are You, Adonoy, Shield of Abraham." It is significant that it was ordained that we bow at each of these points.

As discussed earlier, the word "blessed" indicates God's immanence and His power of blessing, which permeates all creation. We bow when we say "blessed" to indicate that we are aware of this immanence. We feel that God is directly in front of us, and we are bowing to this Presence.

By the time we reach the end of the paragraph, we have raised our consciousness of God's immanence considerably. At the beginning of the blessing, we were aware of God's immanence, but only in an abstract sense. At the end, our consciousness of God's immanence is such that it is as tangible and palpable as a shield. To indicate our new awareness, we bow a second time.

There are two other places at which we also bow in the Amidah. These are at the beginning and end of the blessing of thanksgiving (Modim), which is the second-from-the-last section of the Amidah. To understand the reason for this, we must first understand the structure of the Amidah as a whole.

It is taught that the essential structure of any prayer should contain three elements—adoration, petition, and thanksgiving, in that order. This structure is maintained in the Amidah. The first three paragraphs consist of adoration, wherein we establish a degree of God consciousness in the mind. The first paragraph is the key to this process, as we have seen.

The second general part of the Amidah is that of petition, wherein we ask God for certain things. This part consists of the next fourteen blessings of the Amidah. It is significant to note that in Hebrew, the number fourteen is written out as *yod daleth*

(**ד'**), which also spells *yad*, the Hebrew word for "hand." As it were, we are asking that our petitions be answered through God's hand.

What we are doing essentially in the petition stage is using the spiritual energy developed in the first three blessings to bring about the things we want, both as individuals and as a nation. First we ask for our own personal needs, petitioning God for wisdom, closeness, atonement, healing, and blessing. Then we ask for the things that will affect the Israelite people as a whole. The latter part of the petition stage thus deals primarily with redemption.

According to this pattern, the Amidah should end with thanksgiving. In thanking God, we show awareness of the closeness and spiritual energy that He allows us to experience, and thus integrate it into our being. We would therefore expect the Amidah to end with the blessing of thanksgiving, or Modim, as it is called. Actually, however, this blessing is the second from the last.

There is an important reason for this, and that is so that the Amidah can end with a petition and blessing for peace. Once one has drawn down spiritual energy, one can find internal peace. This internal peace can be projected to enhance national and universal peace as well. When a person can fully thank God, in a mystical as well as a mundane sense, he is at perfect peace. In thanking God, we also draw in the energy that is developed in the service. The bowing acknowledges the power of God that we have drawn into our essence. Since this is the purpose of the blessing of thanksgiving, we bow once at its beginning and again at its end.

Bowing in the Amidah also has another important connotation. The Talmud states that one of the reasons why the Amidah has eighteen blessings is that they parallel the eighteen vertebrae of the spine and neck. The nineteenth blessing, which was added later, parallels the coccyx, the small bone at the base of the spine. This brings to mind the concept of *kundalini* energy that is discussed in Eastern teachings. This is not to suggest that there is any relationship between the Jewish teaching and that of the East, but merely to point out that the spine is universally recognized as an important conduit of energy. Moreover, whereas in *kundalini* meditation one strives to elevate energy from the base of the spine to the head, in the Amidah one brings energy from the mind to the rest of the body.

The Talmud also teaches that if one does not bow in the blessing of thanksgiving, one's spine turns into a snake. Obviously this is to be taken not in a physical sense, but in a spiritual meaning. One reason the Talmud gives for the number of blessings corresponding to the number of vertebrae is that one must bow low enough for each vertebra to be separated from the one next to it. The Talmud also teaches that when one bows, one should do so like a rod, but when one rises, one should do so like a serpent, raising the head first and then the body.

The *kundalini* energy is also seen as taking the form of a serpent. In Jewish tradition, however, the serpent is seen as the enemy of mankind. The serpent is the tempter, who tries to use sexual energy to draw humans away from God. The Talmud therefore teaches that if one does not bow during the Amidah, then one's spine turns into a snake. In contrast, the posture in *kundalini* meditation requires that the spine be kept perfectly straight and erect. If a person worships in this manner, without bowing, then his spine will become infused with the *kundalini* energy, which is the serpent.

Bowing may be a way of overcoming this energy of the serpent. The concept of *kundalini* is to bring energy up from the sexual area to the rest of the body. Bowing has the opposite connotation, namely that of bringing energy down from the head to the body. Therefore, when we bow, we lower the head toward the body. Only after we have bowed, and infused the body with spiritual energy, can we rise and lift energy from the spine to the head, "rising like a snake."

In this manner, the Amidah is designed to bring spiritual energy through the spine to the entire body. This is also a reason why this prayer is said with the feet together. As I have said, this is the stance in which angels are visualized. During the Amidah, one strives to bring oneself into an angelic mode, wherein the spiritual becomes dominant over the physical.

13

UNIFICATION

The most ancient and most important Jewish prayer is the Shema. This prayer consists of the words:

Shema Yisrael, Adonoy Elohenu, Adonoy Echad.
Listen, Israel, Adonoy, our God, Adonoy is One.

The words themselves are taken from the Torah (Deut. 6:4). In many ways this sentence can be looked upon as the most important verse in the Torah. First, the Torah designates that it be recited twice every day, in the morning and in the evening. It is also the key element in the parchment in the *tefillin* that are worn during daily worship, as well as in the *mezuzah* that is affixed to the doorpost.

The Shema is more than just a prayer. It is the basic declaration of faith for the Jew. It is one of the first things a Jew learns as a child, and the last words one is to say before dying. All through life, one is to say this sentence twice a day, without fail.

It would seem that the Shema would be perfect to use as a mantra. The Talmud, however, discourages this as a practice and says that one who repeats the Shema should be silenced. The concept of the Shema is that of unity, and therefore it is meant to be said only once at a time.

The Talmud notes that the Shema has the unique ability to

dispel the forces of evil. The Shema is said in bed, just before one goes to sleep at night. According to the Talmud, night is the time when the forces of evil are strongest, and the Shema has the power to protect us against them.

The reason for this should be obvious: evil has power only when it is seen as disconnected from God. If one thinks that there can be a force of evil apart from God, then one can be harmed by it. However, if a person recognizes that even evil is a creation of God, then it no longer has any power over him. God Himself said through His prophet, "I form light and create darkness, I make peace and create evil; I am God, I do all these things" (Isa. 45:7).

The Zohar explains the existence of evil with a parable. A king once wanted to test his son to see if he would be a worthy heir to the throne. He told his son to keep away from loose women and to remain virtuous. Then he hired a woman to entice his son, instructing her to use all her wiles with him. The Zohar then asks the rhetorical question: Is the woman not also a loyal servant of the king?

The purpose of evil is to tempt us and allow us to have free choice. Without the existence of evil, we would have no other choice but to do good and there would be no virtue in the good we do. But since God gave us free will and wants us to do good as a matter of our own free choice, evil plays a highly important role in His plan.

In the parable, as soon as the prince realizes that the woman is in the hire of his father, she is no longer a threat. The same is true of evil. Indeed, the Baal Shem Tov goes further in using this Zoharic teaching. He says, "Do not succumb to evil; emulate it." He explains that if evil is a loyal servant of the King, then you should be equally loyal. If evil does God's will, you should strive to do it equally well.

It is told that the great saint Rabbi Israel Meir ha-Kohen (1838–1933), better known as the Chafetz Chaim, related that he once woke up on a cold winter morning to say his prayers. The Evil Urge said to him, "How can you get up so early? You are already an old man, and it's so cold outside." The Chafetz Chaim replied to the Evil Urge, "You're a lot older than me, and you're up already." This also illustrates the concept of emulating evil rather than succumbing to it.

In any case, the Shema declares that God is One. If God is One, then His purpose must also be One. Since God's purpose in creation was to do good, then the only reason that evil exists is to enhance the world's ultimate good. If a person has a deep realization of this, then the forces of evil have no power over him.

A paradigm of this attitude can be found in the great Rabbi Akiva (c. 50–135 C.E.). Rabbi Akiva's watchword always was, "All that the Merciful One does is for the good." Rabbi Akiva faced his greatest test during the Hadrianic persecutions of the Jews around 135 C.E. The Romans had decreed that no one could teach Torah, under penalty of death, but Rabbi Akiva ignored them and carried on his vocation as Torah teacher. He was captured and sentenced to be killed by having his flesh torn away by curry combs, a most excruciating torture. Still, while he was being tortured to death in this manner, he told his students that he was happy, since he had been given the opportunity to suffer and die as an expression of his love for God. Death and torture held no terror for him, since he had a love that was more powerful than death.

Significantly, Rabbi Akiva's last words were the Shema. Even in the midst of his most terrible suffering, he was able to see God's unity and oneness, and therefore he could see God even in his suffering. Rabbi Akiva had been a student of Nachum Ish Gamzu for twenty-two years. Nachum was called Gamzu because, no matter what happened to him, he would say, "This too [*gam zu*] is for the good." Like his student, Nachum suffered terribly during his lifetime, but no matter what happened to him, he was able to see it as good.

The Shema is an integral part of the morning *shacharith* and evening *maariv* service. Together with a number of important prayers that surround it, it is said immediately before the Amidah. However, the Shema can also be said alone, as an important meditation in its own right.

From the wording itself, it is obvious that the Shema was

meant to be a meditation. If the only significance of the Shema were to declare that God is One, then the opening words, "Listen, Israel," would be redundant. But the Shema itself is telling us to *listen*—to listen and hear the message with every fiber of our being. It is telling us to open our perceptions completely, so as to experience God's unity.

It is also significant that the name Israel is used in the beginning of the declaration. This name was given to Jacob after he wrestled with the angel on his way home to Canaan. According to the Torah, the name Israel means "he who contends with the Divine" (Gen. 32:29).

In the Midrash and the Zohar, there is discussion about whether the angel with which Jacob wrestled was a good angel or an evil one. But the main point is that when a person contends with the spiritual, he is opening himself up to both good and evil, which means wrestling with the forces of good as well as those of evil.

A number of commentaries see Jacob's experience as having taken place in a meditative state. Jacob did not physically wrestle with an angel, but he perceived a spiritual being while meditating. The name Israel that Jacob received would then pertain to his entering into a spiritual state and contending with his experiences there.

It is precisely when one is in a meditative state that one has contact with the spiritual on an intimate level. The Shema addresses itself to such a seeker and calls him by the name Israel. The Shema is addressing the "Israel" in each one of us. This "Israel" is the part of us that yearns to transcend the boundaries of the physical and seeks out the spiritual. The Shema tells this "Israel" to listen—to quiet down the mind completely and open it up to a universal message of God's unity. However, the only time a person can listen perfectly, without any interference, is in the meditative state.

The Shema then says, "Adonoy, our God" (*Adonoy Elohenu*). This is the same expression encountered earlier in the previous chapter, in our discussion of the Amidah. As mentioned there, we recognize that God is a totally different entity Who exists outside even the realms of space and time. When we say "Ado-noy," we are speaking of that for which the mind does not even have a category. Yet, in the very next word, we call *Adonoy* "our God." We recognize that we can relate to God and experience His closeness to such an extent that we can call Him ours.

This is a very remarkable concept: we can think about the Infinite and still call It ours. The fact that God allows us to call Him "our God" is the greatest possible gift.

The Shema ends with "Adonoy is One" (*Adonoy Echad*). Here we are saying that no matter how many different ways we experience the Divine, they are all One and all have one source. We recognize that there is a basic Oneness in the universe and beyond, and in our search for the transcendental, it is precisely this Oneness that we are seeking. We see in God the most absolute Unity imaginable, the Oneness that unifies all creation.

The more we realize this, the more we begin to see that on an ultimate level there is no plurality. If there is no plurality, then we are also one with God. When saying the word "One" (*Echad*) in the Shema, one can realize this in a deep sense.

An objection might be raised here. If a person is one with God, how can he continue to exist? If he is one with God, then there is no room left for him to have an independent personality. How is it possible for a person to ever experience this oneness with God? The answer is that this situation is a paradox. To say that I exist and that God exists, and that I am one with God, is like saying $1 + 1 = 1$, which is, of course, logically impossible.

Nevertheless, we cannot say that logic is higher than God. Quite the contrary. Just as God created everything else, He also created logic. Logic is a tool of God's, but He is never bound by it. Therefore, if He wants one plus one to be one, it is no problem for Him. And if He wants a person to be one with Him, and still be able to experience it, it is also possible for Him.

This principle allows us to understand all theological para-doxes. To a large degree, in creating the world, God bound Himself by logic. Since He created man in "His image," man uses the same logic that went into creation and can therefore understand God's creation. However, when it suits God's purpose in creation to transcend logic, He can also do so, and this is what we perceive as paradox. Indeed, the concept of Divine will itself is a paradox. If God is the Creator of *all things*, then He must also be the Creator of the very concept of will. But how could God create will without this in itself being an act of will? In a sense, the creation of will is by its very nature paradoxical, like trying to pull yourself up by your own bootstraps.

The most powerful expression of will is love. This is also an integral part of the Shema. Every Hebrew letter has a numerical value corresponding to its position in the alphabet. The value of *echad* (אחד), the Hebrew word for "one," is thirteen (1 + 8 + 4). This, however, is the numerical value of *ahavah* (אהבה, 1 + 5 + 2 + 5), the Hebrew word for "love." Love is the power that breaks down barriers and unifies opposites. Two people who are deeply in love become one. The Torah says, "A man shall leave his father and mother, and attach himself to his wife, and they shall become *one* flesh" (Gen. 2:24). But the love and unity between God and man is greater than any possible between man and woman.

There are a number of prayers or "blessings" that surround the Shema when it is said as part of the morning service. The last words before the Shema itself are "Blessed are You, Adonoy, who chose His people Israel in love." Therefore, the word immediately before the Shema is the word "love," in the context of a blessing that speaks of the love that God has for His people.

Immediately after the Shema is the commandment "You shall love God your Lord with all your heart, with all your soul, and with all your might" (Deut. 6:5). This commandment speaks of the love that we must have for God. Therefore, the Shema is placed between two loves—God's love for us and our love for God. Both of these loves suggest the unity to be found in the Shema.

The Shema can be said as a prayer or a declaration of faith, and it is said as such by Jews all over the world. But if the words are said very slowly, and if a person prepares himself mentally, the Shema can be an extremely powerful meditation. Indeed, the Torah itself prescribes that the Shema be said twice daily, and it seems highly probable that this was originally prescribed as a short daily meditation for all Israel.

The technique consists in saying the words very slowly, in a manner very similar to that of using the Amidah for a meditation. In the Amidah, as noted in chapter 11, the prescribed rate was approximately one word every seven seconds. The Shema can be said even more slowly. You can dwell on each word for as long as fifteen or twenty seconds, or with experience, even longer. During the silences between words, let the meaning of each word penetrate your innermost being.

It is easier to use the Shema as a meditation than the Amidah, since the main portion of the Shema consists of only six words, which are easy to memorize. Before you can use these words as a meditation, you must know them well and by heart. You should be seated while saying the Shema and keep your eyes closed. Strive to be perfectly still, with no body motion whatsoever.

The Shema can be used as a meditation either as part of the regular services or alone. It is preferable to say it as part of the service, especially the morning service, which provides a proper setting and introduction to the Shema. In this service, the Shema is preceded by two prayers, or "blessings," as the Talmud calls them. The first blessing begins with a description of the astronomical world. The mind soars to the sun, the moon, the stars, and beyond, and contemplates the vast reaches of space, immense beyond comprehension. Yet, while one meditates on the vastness of the astronomical world, one sees it as all working to do God's will.

The mind then transcends the astronomical world and reaches up to the spiritual realm, to the world of the angels. We join the angels in their daily praise to God: "Holy, holy, holy, is the Lord of Hosts, the whole world is filled with His glory" (Isa. 6:3) and then, "Blessed be God's glory from His place" (Ezek. 3:12). One's mind reaches higher and higher, joining the highest angels in their quest for the Divine.

Then one enters the second blessing, which speaks of the "World of Love." Here we meditate on the love that God has shown us and how He drew us close to Him through the Torah and the commandments. We become aware of this love and meditate on it, drawing it into our innermost being. Then, we recite the Shema itself.

When the Shema is said as part of the morning service, one automatically goes through all these levels. However, even if one says the Shema alone as a meditation, one can go through all these levels as part of one's personal preparation. In either case, the Shema becomes not only a meditation, but a peak experience of love and closeness to God.

The words immediately following the Shema are usually translated in the imperative—"You *shall* love God, your Lord . . ."—implying that this is a commandment. However, the words can equally well be translated as "You *will* love God, your Lord," as a simple statement. The words imply that if we listen, and hear the message that God is ours and that He is One, then we will automatically love God. Love for God follows as a natural consequence to the experience of His essence and unity.

There is also another important element in the Shema as a meditation, and this concerns the actual spelling of the word. The first word, *shema* (שמע), is spelled *shin* (ש) *mem* (מ) *ayin* (ע). In the *Sefer Yetzirah*, the *shin* and *mem* are described as two of the three "mother letters."

It is easy to understand why the *shin* and *mem* are important. The *shin* has the sound of *s* or *sh*, and hence, of all the letters in the alphabet, it has the sound closest to white noise. White noise is sound that contains every possible wavelength, and is usually heard as a hissing sound. On an oscilloscope, the *s* sound would appear as a totally chaotic jumble with no structure whatsoever.

The opposite of white noise is pure harmonic sound. This is a hum, like the sound of a tuning fork. On an oscilloscope, this would appear as a perfect wavy line, the epitome of order and regularity. This is the sound of the *mem*.

The *shin* thus represents chaos, while the *mem* represents harmony. The *Sefer Yetzirah* says that the *shin* represents fire, while the *mem* represents water. The *shin* denotes a hot, chaotic state of consciousness, while the *mem* denotes a cool, harmonic state. This is significant, since in many meditative traditions, the *m* sound is seen as one that leads to tranquillity and inner peace. The sound itself seems to be conducive to the harmony that one seeks in the meditative state. The *s* or *sh* sound, on the other hand, is more closely associated with our normal, everyday level of consciousness. It is also interesting to note that the "still small voice" (1 Kings 19:12) in which Elijah heard God is translated by the *Sefer Yetzirah* as a "fine humming sound." It appears that the *m* sound was closely associated with prophecy.

Many of the Hebrew words that tend to focus the mind on a single object are made up of these two mother letters. Thus, the Hebrew word for "name" is *shem* (שֵׁם), which is spelled *shin mem*. Similarly, the word for "there" is *sham* (שָׁם). Both of these words have the connotation of the transition from the chaos of the general to the harmony of the particular. A name separates a single object from the chaos of all objects, while "there" separates a place from the chaos of all places. Both words therefore denote the transition from the concept of the *shin* to that of the *mem*.

An exercise discussed by the commentaries on the *Sefer Yetzirah* has been found effective for getting into the meditative state quickly and simply. It consists of alternating the sounds of the *shin* and the *mem*. First pronounce one sound for the period of normal exhalation, then inhale and pronounce the other for the same period of time. The pattern is: "ssssss," inhale, "mmmmmm," inhale, "sssss," inhale, "mmmmmm," inhale, and so on. The inhalation is silent and represents the third mother letter, the silent *alef* (א). This meditative method of alternating between the *s* and *m* sounds draws one deeper and deeper into the *m* sound. If one practices this exercise for a period of time, one can attain the ability to get into the meditative state merely by humming the *m* sound.

The fact that the first two letters of the Shema are *shin* and *mem* is highly significant. True listening involves a transition from normal "*shin*" consciousness to meditative "*mem*" consciousness. This can be accomplished in the very first word of the Shema.

Shema (שְׁמַע) is spelled *shin* (ש) *mem* (מ) *ayin* (ע). The Zohar states that the last letter, the *ayin,* is significant because it has a numerical value of seventy. In general, seventy is seen as representing plurality as it exists in the mundane world. Therefore, the *ayin* represents the seventy different forces of creation. These seventy forces are manifest in the seventy nations and seventy languages, as well as the seventy descendants who accompanied Jacob to Egypt. In listening to the message of unity in the Shema, one brings these seventy forces into the ear and mind, and unifies them with the Divine.

The Shema can be understood on many levels. However, as a meditation, the main thing is to allow the simple meaning of each word to penetrate the mind. One must understand the words, not with the intellect, but with the soul.

14

THE LADDER

One of the most vivid scenes in the Torah is that of Jacob's dream, in which he saw "a ladder standing on earth, with its top reaching heaven" (Gen. 28:12). There is a *midrash* that teaches that this ladder had four steps. According to the great Jewish mystics, they represent the fours steps one must climb to reach the highest level of the spiritual domain.

It is taught that these four steps represent the four levels of meditational involvement: action, speech, thought, and the level above thought. As we have discussed, the level above thought is experienced as nothingness.

These four levels also parallel the four letters of the Tetragrammaton, YHVH(י ה ו ה)(see chapter 7).

The first level is that of action, where we are still involved with our body. This parallels the final *heh*(ה) of the Tetragrammaton, which is the hand that receives. It is through the body that we receive all blessing from God. The "hand" that God gives us to receive His energy is the body, which He created in the Divine image. So the first and lowest level is involvement with the body and action.

The second level is that of speech. On the level of speech, we can be aware that we are communicating with the Divine. Speech is the angelic power in man, through which we can transcend our animal nature. Moreover, speech bridges the gap between the physical and the spiritual, and between man and God. Therefore, the level of speech parallels the *vav* (ו) of the Tetragrammaton, which is the arm with which God reaches out to us. *Vav* has the connotation of connection, and this parallels speech, which connects God and man.

The third level is that of thought. It is through the power of thought that we grasp what we can of the Divine. Thought therefore parallels the first *heh* (ה) of the Divine Name, which is God's "hand that holds." Thought is the "hand that holds" every experience of the Divine that we can experience.

Finally, there is the level above thought, which is experienced as nothingness. This is the ineffable experience of the Divine itself. This is the experience that we have only when all thought is turned off and we enter into the realm of pure experience, which is beyond thought.

The Kabbalists teach that the morning *shacharith* service is divided according to these four steps. The four divisions of the morning service are:

1. The Introductory Readings
2. The Verses of Praise
3. The Shema and its blessings
4. The Amidah

We have discussed the Shema and the Amidah in earlier chapters. Let us now see how they fit into the context of the rest of the service.

The Introductory Readings begin with blessings in which we thank God for our physical nature. They include thanksgiving blessings for our body functions, for our ability to stand, walk, and function in the physical world.

As discussed earlier, the word "blessed" when applied to God denotes His immanence in the world. When we recite the blessings for bodily functions, we are sensitizing ourselves to the Divine that is immanent in our own bodies. Thus, although on this level we may not yet be in touch with our spiritual nature, we become aware of our body as a receptacle for the spiritual. This is the level of the "hand that receives," discussed earlier.

The second half of the introductory section consists of readings dealing with the sacrificial system. These sacrifices consisted of both plants and animals. To understand the significance of these readings in the service, one must understand the place that sacrifice had in ancient Israel. The Hebrew word for sacrifice is *korban*, which literally means "that which is brought close." The animal sacrifices were thus seen as a means of drawing close to God.

The Talmud teaches that man is half animal and half angel. The body is the seat of man's animal nature, while the soul is the seat of his angelic nature. Since the body is the vessel of the soul, man's animal nature is the receptacle for his angelic nature.

There are times when man must elevate his animal nature and use it as a means of serving God. The Torah thus says, "You shall love God your Lord with all your heart and with all your soul" (Deut. 6:5). The Talmud interprets "your heart" to denote man's animal nature and "your soul" to denote his angelic nature. The verse therefore teaches that both must be devoted to the love of God.

When sacrifice was offered in ancient times, it was burned on the Great Altar in the Holy Temple in Jerusalem. The sacrifice symbolized that the animal in man also has a place in serving God. Since it is the body that is the receptacle of the Divine, the body and animal nature must also be "brought close" to God.

Therefore, the Sacrificial Readings in the Introductory Readings serve to make us aware that our bodies are vessels for the Divine. At this point in the service, we are still concerned with action and the physical body, but we are beginning to connect it with the spiritual.

The second part of the service is known as the Verses of Praise, and it consists of Psalms and other biblical praises of God. This part of the service parallels the level of speech. In reciting these biblical verses, we are using speech to connect ourselves to God. In this part of the service, we should also make ourselves keenly aware of the process through which we speak and pronounce the words. We should concentrate on our tongue and lips, and feel how they articulate each sound. This in itself can be a contemplation. We should also carefully listen to each sound and each word as we speak these praises of God.

This section is known in Hebrew as *pesukey de-zimra*, literally, "verses of *zimra*." The Hebrew word *zimra* has a double meaning: it can mean praise, but it also has the connotation of cutting. The Kabbalists therefore note that the verses of *zimra* serve to help us cut ourselves away from the physical. If man is half animal and half angel, then speech is uniquely associated with the angelic side of man. Indeed, where the Torah says, "God formed man from the dust of the earth, and blew in his nostrils a breath of life so that man became a living soul" (Gen. 2:7), the Targum (the authorized Aramaic translation) translates "living soul" as "speaking soul." Man's ability to speak is closely associated with his spiritual nature.

Therefore, during this second part of the service, we become aware of our own spirituality and the connection that we have with God. The praise we chant brings us into the space of this connection, where we can transcend our physical nature. All that exists for us is our speaking to God. The Jewish mystics therefore say that one is in the "World of Speech," since in this state, speech is one's entire world.

Thus, there is an important transition in the first two sections of the service. In the Introductory Readings, we are hovering over the physical world but still attached to it. In the Verses of Praise, we begin to transcend it.

The Verses of Praise conclude with the Song of the Red Sea (Exod. 15). After the Exodus from Egypt, the Israelites were pursued by the Egyptians. God rescued them by splitting the Red Sea and allowing them to cross. The Egyptians who chased them into the sea were drowned when the sea returned to normal. It was only after the crossing of the Red Sea that the Israelites gained total freedom.

The Kabbalists teach that the Egyptian Exile represents states of immature or constricted consciousness (*mochin de-katnuth*). At the end of the Verses of Praise we emerge from constricted consciousness to a state of expanded consciousness (*mochin de-gadluth*). This transition is made when we repeat the Song of the Red Sea.

After having completed the Verses of Praise, we are then ready to begin the third part of the service, which consists of the Shema and its blessings. This section of the service is said to correspond to the "World of Thought." The spiritual ascent that we make here is in pure thought. In the Verses of Praise, thought was secondary to speech; in the Shema and its blessings, speech is secondary to thought. Here, we are in a state of expanded consciousness, where thought is our entire world. The culmination of this section is the Shema itself, where all thought is filled with God's unity.

These first three sections of the service are also said to parallel the three lowest levels of the soul. In Hebrew, the lowest level of the soul is known as *nefesh*, the next is called *ruach*, and the highest is *neshamah*. The word *nefesh* comes from a root denoting "rest," and *ruach* means "wind," while *neshamah* is associated with breath.

The Kabbalists explain the significance of these three levels using a glassblower as an analogy. In this case, the glassblower is the Divine, while the vessel is the person. The glassblowing process begins with the blower's breath (*neshimah*) blowing into the tube that connects his mouth to the vessel he is blowing. This breath then travels through the glassblowing tube as a wind (*ruach*) until it reaches the vessel. Finally, the breath enters the vessel and forms it according to the blower's plan, and there it comes to rest (*nafash*).

In the case of the soul, the "blower" is the Divine. In describing the creation of man, the Torah thus says, "God formed man out of the dust of the earth, and He blew in his nostrils a soul [*neshamah*] of life" (Gen. 2:7). The highest level of the soul is thus the *neshamah*, which is, as it were, the "breath of God." This is the "vessel" that holds the spiritual nature that God wishes to give us. Hence, it can be said to parallel the "hand that gives," the first *heh* of the Tetragrammaton.

The second level is *ruach*, which is the "wind" blowing down to us from God's breath. This "wind" is seen as the connection between God's "mouth," as it were, and the person. Therefore, it parallels the *vav* of the Tetragrammaton and the angelic world, which also denote transition. It is significant that *ruach* is always associated with the spiritual experience, and the expression "Holy Spirit" (*ruach ha-kodesh*) is virtually synonymous with prophecy.

Finally, there is the level of *nefesh*, the lowest level of the soul, where it interfaces with the physical. This is the level where we are able to *accept* the spirituality that God desires to give us. Hence, it parallels the "hand that receives," the final *heh* of the Tetragrammaton. Since this part of the soul is essentially passive rather than active, it is called *nefesh*, which literally means the "resting soul." When the Torah speaks of punishment for certain serious sins, it says, "that soul [*nefesh*] shall be cut off." It speaks of the level of *nefesh*, the level of the soul through which one is able to receive spiritual sustenance from God. When this is cut off from *ruach*, a person is cut off from his spiritual source.

These three levels of the soul represent three levels of inner space. One travels through these three levels in the first three parts of the morning service. In the Introductory Readings, we gain an awareness of *nefesh*, the part of the soul that interfaces with the body. This is the level of action where the person gains an awareness of the body as a receptacle for the spiritual. On this level, one cannot feel the spiritual, but knows that the body is intimately attached to it.

In the Verses of Praise, a person becomes aware of the level of *ruach*, the divine wind-spirit. This is the inner space where one is totally aware of one's own spiritual nature and connection to God. This is also the level of speech. Just as speech traverses distance, so does wind. When you say the words of this section, try to feel the divine "wind" blowing through your being.

It is no accident that the word *ruach* means both "wind" and "spirit." We live in a sea of air that is so familiar to us that we remain totally oblivious to it. Similarly, we are oblivious to the sea of spirituality that surrounds us at all times. Nevertheless, when the air displays energy and moves, we feel it as a wind (*ruach*); when the spiritual displays energy and moves, we have an experience of spirit (*ruach*). The second section of the service is meant to elicit this experience.

In the third part of the service, which consists of the Shema and its blessings, we reach up to the World of Love and the realm of unity. Here, one is aware of *neshamah*, the Breath of God. There is a vast difference between the inner space feeling of *ruach* and that of *neshamah*. It is the difference between feeling a wind and a breath. A wind has energy and force, but it is impersonal. A breath is both personal and intimate. Feeling the breath of one's beloved is a most sensual experience.

Therefore, in the third section of the service, a person has a *neshamah* experience, in which he feels an intimacy with God, as if God were breathing on him, as it were. This is the level of divine love and unity.

After the Shema, one again recounts the story of the Exodus and repeats certain key phrases from the Song at the Sea. This is also a transition, but to a new, even more expanded level of consciousness that will lead to the Amidah. The third part of the service concludes with the blessing "Blessed are You, Adonoy, Redeemer of Israel." The "Israel" in the worshiper is here "redeemed" and allowed to enter the inner reaches of the divine realm.

This is attained in the fourth part of the service, the Amidah. Here, one enters into a realm that transcends thought. In the Amidah, we do not think about the words we are saying, but experience them. This does not mean that we are not aware of the words. Quite to the contrary: we are extremely aware, but on a level that goes beyond thought and penetrates every fiber of our being. It is as if the words are filling our entire consciousness and their innermost meaning is becoming one with the deepest reaches of our souls.

This level parallels the *yod* of the Tetragrammaton. This is not the level of the "hand" or "mind" that holds the divine essence, but the essence itself. Therefore, on this level, one is intimately aware of the essence in each word.

This level corresponds to a still higher level of the soul, even above *neshamah*. This fourth level of the soul is known as *chayyah*, which literally means "life force." If the level of *neshamah* involves an awareness of the breath of the Divine, then the level of *chayyah* is the awareness of the divine life force itself.

The Zohar states that a kiss is the merging of one breath with another. Love begins with physical attraction. Then, as lovers begin communication, they begin to speak. As they get closer, they stop speaking and are merely aware of each other's breath. Finally, they come still closer, and their communication becomes a kiss, at which point they are actually in physical contact. At this moment, in the kiss, they are aware of each other's life force. Kissing is thus a natural consequence of increased intimacy in speech. The two mouths come closer and closer and progress from speech, to breath, to the kiss. Thus, there are four levels in the intimacy of love: physical attraction, speech, breath, and the kiss. These same levels exist in the relationship of a person with the Divine.

The service is designed to bring a person through these four levels. In the Introductory Readings, one is attracted to God with one's physical being. In the Verses of Praise, one communicates with the Divine in speech. In the Shema and its blessings, one experiences intimacy with the Divine on the level of breath. Finally, the Amidah is the kiss, and the level of communication is with the life force itself. It is significant that the level of communication of the Amidah is life force, since the Hebrew word for "life" is *chai* (**ח י**), which has a numerical value of eighteen (8 + 10). Eighteen is also the basic number of blessings in the Amidah.

After the Amidah, there is a fifth section of the service, which is known as the "Descent of Influx" (*yeridath ha-shefa*). Here one strives to bring the spiritual levels that one has attained during the service into one's life. It is not enough to have the experience; one must also be able to hold on to it and keep it for the entire day.

We thus see that the daily service is much more than a mere

"order of prayer." It is, in fact, a spiritual pilgrimage in which one rises from one level of spirituality to the next, gaining ever-increasing intimacy with the Divine. It is a daily meditation experience that can have the most profound spiritual effects on a person.

15

IN ALL YOUR WAYS

One of the key teachings of Judaism is that one can experience a closeness to God in anything one does. The Talmud bases this teaching on the verse "In all your ways know him" (Prov. 3:6) and says that this short verse "contains the entire essence of the Torah." It teaches that no matter what a person does, he can dedicate it to God and make it into an act of worship. Even the most mundane act can serve as a link to the Divine.

Take a routine task, something that has to be done, like washing the dishes. It can be pure drudgery; however, if one elevates it to an act of worship, it can be an exalting experience through which one draws close to God. It all depends on one's intentions.

When washing dishes, one can think about the fact that the dishes will be clean for the next meal. The meal will be eaten so that the family will have the strength to go through another day, and perhaps gain a new and deeper awareness of God. People will recite blessings over food, making the act of eating into a sacrament. Thus, the washing of dishes, at least indirectly, can be seen as a means through which one will draw close to God in other ways.

The act itself can also be an elevating experience. Imagine that you are about to prepare a meal for the person you love more than anyone else in the world. Imagine that it is not just an ordinary meal, but one to celebrate an important milestone in your lives. All the love that you feel for this person is going into the preparation of this meal. It is to be a special meal, with everything just perfect.

Now imagine that you are washing the dishes that are going to be used for this meal. You would want every dish to be perfectly clean and shiny, without the slightest speck or spot. The act of washing dishes would then also be an act of love.

Think for a moment of the greatest love you ever had in your life. If you have ever been deeply in love, you know that there is a stage where the mind becomes almost obsessed with the one you love. No matter what you are doing—eating, sleeping, working—the person you love hovers at the edge of your consciousness. Everything else is unimportant—it is as if you are just marking time until you can see or speak to this person again. All other pleasures in the world are secondary to the pleasure of being in this person's presence.

It is possible to love God in this manner, and with even greater intensity. There is a level of love at which one constantly yearns and longs for a closeness to God. No matter what pleasures one enjoys, they are nothing compared with this feeling of closeness. True love for God can surpass even the greatest passion that can exist between man and woman.

When a person has such a love for God, then even an act as mundane as washing dishes becomes an expression of this love. Then, the more one concentrates on the act of washing a dish, the greater and more intense this love becomes. The act itself becomes an expression of love.

The more aware we become of God's love for us, the more open we become to loving God. If we concentrate on what we are doing, even an act as lowly as washing a dish can connect us to God. We may say to ourselves: Now I am washing a dish because I will be sharing a meal with God, and I love God more than anything else in the world.

Even a mundane act can thus become a vehicle to connect God's love for us to our love for Him. It is as if God's love is on one side, our love is on the other, and the act is in the middle.

This is reminiscent of our discussion of the Shema (see chapter

13). As noted there, the prayer right before the Shema ends with a statement of God's love for Israel; after the Shema, we say, "You shall love God, your Lord, with all your heart. . . ." We saw how the Shema, as the expression of God's unity, bridged these two loves. Therefore, when a person wishes to make an action represent the connection between the two loves, the action itself must be an expression of God's unity. This can be understood in the following manner:

If God is One, then He and His will must also be One. Since God is absolutely One, then He must be identical with His will.

On the other hand, things exist only because God wills them to exist. If God did not will an object to exist, it would simply stop existing. God gave each thing existence through His will, and it is only through His will that it can continue to exist.

This implies that God's will is in everything. However, if God is identical with His will, then God must also be in everything. Therefore, every action and every thing must be permeated with God's essence.

Now imagine that you are washing the dishes. You are concentrating on the act of washing, clearing the mind of all other thoughts. Any other thought that enters the mind is gently pushed aside, so that the task at hand totally fills the mind. You are totally aware of the act you are doing, and as far as you are concerned, nothing else exists in the universe.

Concentrate for a moment on a dish and realize that it is an expression of God's will and essence. Although it may be hidden, there is a spark of the Divine in the dish. There is also a spark of the Divine in the water with which you are washing the dish. When a person develops such an awareness, then even the most mundane act can become an intimate experience of the Divine.

This concept is manifestly more explicit in Jewish teachings regarding eating. It is taught that when a person eats, he should concentrate totally on the food and the experience of eating it, clearing the mind of all other thoughts. He should have in mind that the taste of the food is also an expression of the Divine in the food, and that by eating it, he is incorporating this spark of the Divine into his body. A person can also have in mind that he will dedicate the energy that he will obtain from this food to God's service. It is taught that when a person does this, it is counted as if the food he is eating is a sacrifice on the Great Altar in Jerusalem.

Therefore, eating itself can be a form of meditation as well as a means through which one can draw closer to God. It is for this reason that it was ordained that a blessing be recited before one begins eating. The blessing varies with each food, and a complete list can be found in most standard prayer books. Each general category of food has its own blessing. Thus, for example, the blessing over food that grows on a tree is:

> *Barukh Attah Adonoy, Elohenu Melekh ha-Olam,*
>   *Borey peri ha-etz.*
> Blessed are You, O God, our Lord, King of the Universe,
>   Who creates the fruit of the tree.

The first thing that one notices is that the blessing is in the present tense rather than in the past. The wording is, "Who *creates* the fruit," and not, "Who *created*." The blessing therefore immediately indicates that God's creative power is in the fruit right now, at the instant one is eating it. As soon as one has this awareness, the act of eating becomes an act of communing with the Divine.

I have already discussed the significance of the word "blessed" as it applies to God. Therefore, when we open the blessing with the words "Blessed are You . . . ," we are expressing our realization that God is immanent in all creation. When the blessing is said with deep concentration, as in the Amidah, the words themselves make us aware of this immanence.

Right after that, we refer to God as "our Lord" (*Elohenu*). As discussed before, this indicates that He makes Himself available to us and allows us to experience Him. It is because of God's immanence that He is accessible to us, and we can experience His closeness whenever we make a sincere attempt to do so.

Too much emphasis on God's immanence, however, might lead a person to minimize His greatness. One might even get too familiar with the Divine. Therefore, the very next expression in the blessing is "King of the Universe." We make ourselves aware that this Presence that we are addressing is the same Infinite Being that rules all creation, the same Presence that exists throughout the entire universe, in stars and galaxies beyond comprehension.

When we say that God is "King of the Universe," we avoid falling into the intellectual trap of pantheism. We are aware that God's presence permeates all things, but we realize that this does not mean that God is no more than the sum of all things. We therefore say that God is King of the Universe. A king's power may fill his entire kingdom, but this does not mean that the king and his kingdom are one and the same. Although God's essence permeates all creation, God Himself is infinitely higher than anything and everything He created.

We then conclude the blessing in the appropriate manner. In our example, the conclusion is, "Who creates the fruit of the tree." Other endings are, "Who creates the fruit of the ground," for most vegetables; "Who created the fruit of the vine," for wine; "Who brings forth bread from the earth," for bread; "Who creates various nourishing foods," for grain products; and "by Whose word all things exist," for any food not in one of the above categories. We designate the food and make ourselves aware of God's creative power and immanence in the food we eat.

The blessing should be said very slowly, with the mind cleared of all extraneous thought. When said in such a manner, the blessing before food can be a very powerful meditation.

People sometimes ask why Judaism does not have an eating discipline like many of the Eastern religions. Of course, Judaism does have one important eating discipline, namely keeping kosher. An animal must be slaughtered in a very specific manner before it can be eaten, and all the blood must be drained out completely. Certain species are absolutely forbidden.

The most important discipline of Judaism, however, involves the blessing. When a blessing is recited before eating, then the act itself becomes a spiritual undertaking. Through the blessing, the act of eating becomes a contemplative exercise. Just as one can contemplate a flower or a melody, one can contemplate the act of eating. One opens one's mind completely to the experience of masticating the food and fills the awareness with the taste and texture of the food. One then eats very slowly, aware of every nuance of taste.

When one eats with the proper state of consciousness, one can make do with a much smaller amount of food. The body's own wisdom determines how much food is required, and no more is desired, since one does not eat out of compulsion or out of nervous habit. Therefore, one eats exactly as much as one requires, no more and no less.

In general, then, Judaism sees even the most mundane acts as means of gaining God consciousness. Working, eating, dressing, all can be made into acts of worship. A person who does this can begin to see God in every facet of life.

16

THE COMMANDMENTS

In the previous chapter, I discussed how even mundane acts can be made into an act of worship through which one can experience the Divine. There are other actions, however, that are specifically designed to bring a person closer to God. These include the many commandments and rituals of Judaism.

It is taught that the Torah contains a total of 613 commandments. The idea of keeping 613 commandments may seem overwhelming. Indeed, one must be a scholar to even be able to find all 613 commandments in the Torah. However, there are a number of published lists of the commandments, and a study of these lists will show that most of the commandments pertain only to special cases, special people, or special places. Thus, for example, a large number of the commandments deal with the service in the Holy Temple in Jerusalem, which no longer exists, and even when it did exist, many of the rituals were the responsibility only of the *kohen* priests. Other commandments involve agriculture or criminal law and have little bearing on the day-to-day practice of Judaism.

Therefore, if one studies the commandments, it turns out that, for the most part, the practice of Judaism is defined by three or four dozen of them. These commandments define the structure of Judaism, and keeping them is what makes a person an observant Jew.

Besides the commandments found in the Torah itself, there are numerous rituals and customs that have become an integral part of Judaism. A number of these were legislated by the ancient sages because they saw that an additional spiritual aid or dimension was needed by the Jewish people. The additional rituals provided this dimension and allowed the person to have a full spiritual life, even where it was impossible to keep all the commandments.

Thus, for example, the Torah prescribes that all Jewish holidays be observed for one day. Later, when there was trouble fixing the calendar, it was legislated that festivals be kept for two days outside the Holy Land. On the surface, the reason was that there was a question as to which day the festival fell on. The Zohar, however, states that outside the Holy Land, it was impossible to accomplish spiritually in one day what must be accomplished on a festival. Therefore, a second day was added so that one would be able to complete the spiritual growth implied by the festival.

The same, to a large degree, is true of customs. The Talmud states that when the Jewish people adopt a custom, they are doing so on the basis of what is very close to prophetic inspiration. Witnessing the establishment of a custom, Hillel (first century B.C.E.) remarked, "Let the Israelites follow their own course. If they are not prophets, then they are apprentice prophets." This suggests that people have the power, collectively, to feel a spiritual need and fill it. Therefore, even customs can contain a powerful degree of spiritual energy.

It was also decreed that before performing many commandments and rituals, a blessing must be said. As discussed earlier, every blessing is a statement of God's immanence. However, since a commandment comes from God, it is also an expression of His will. As we have discussed earlier, God is identical with His will (at least on one level of understanding), and therefore God is uniquely present in His commandments. When a person performs a ritual mandated by a commandment, he or she has the opportunity to create a unique bond with God.

All the blessings said over commandments have a common beginning:

Barukh Attah Adonoy, Elohenu Melekh ha-Olam
asher kideshanu be-mitzvotav, ve-tzivanu . . .
Blessed are You, O God, our Lord, King of the Universe,
Who sanctified us with His precepts, and commanded
us . . .

In the blessing, we state that God "sanctified us with His commandments." In this statement, we recognize the commandments as a means through which God sanctifies our lives and raises us above the mundane. We see that the commandments are a special means that God gave us to experience the Divine. When keeping any ritual, we should see it as an expression of our desire to be close to God. Here again, love provides a pertinent example.

Imagine that you are in love. You are constantly trying to do things to please your beloved and draw closer to him or her. If the beloved makes a request, you may see it as a unique opportunity to express your love. There is no greater pleasure than doing something like that; the very fact that you are doing something that your beloved desires makes it a total act of love.

The same is true of God's commandments. These are not acts that one does on one's own to express one's love for God, but acts that God has asked us to do as an expression of this love. If one keeps God in mind when observing a commandment, the experience can be one of overwhelming love for and closeness to the Divine.

Furthermore, since these are God's commandments, they are closely and uniquely linked to God's will. This expression of the divine will is every bit as real as the will through which God created the universe. Therefore, a commandment is every bit as real as a physical object. If one meditates on this, one can see the observance as something real and palpable, filled with the Divine.

When you keep a commandment, try meditating on the fact that God's will is in the commandment. In a deep meditative state, you will actually be able to feel God's will in the action and the fact that God and His will are One.

Besides the blessing said before a commandment, there is another meditation that is recommended by the great Jewish mystics. It says:

I am doing this for the sake of the unification of the Holy One, blessed be He and His Divine Presence, with awe and love, in the name of all Israel.

The term "Holy One, Blessed be He" (*Kudesha berikh Hu*) is a common Aramaic term used to denote God, found in both the Talmud and the Zohar. To understand the meaning of this meditation, we must understand why this particular term is used.

I have explained that the word "blessed" when applied to God refers to His immanence. However, we must also understand what the word "holy" means when applied to God. Usually, when we say that something is holy, we mean that it is close to God or pertains to His worship. But what does the word mean when applied to God Himself?

When we use the word "holy" to describe a person or object, we are indicating not only that it is dedicated to God, but also that it is both separated and distinguished from the mundane. Therefore, when we say that God is "holy," we are saying that He is separated from the mundane to the greatest extent imaginable. Therefore, when we say that God is "holy," we are saying that He is utterly transcendent.

In Judaism, there is always a tension between God's immanence and His transcendence. When we say that God is "blessed" we recognize that He is holy, while when we say that He is "holy" we are aware that He is transcendent. God is, as it were, both very near and very far. The Kabbalists express it by saying that God both fills all creation and surrounds all creation. On the other hand, He is immanent and fills all creation; "no place is devoid of Him." On the other hand, He surrounds all creation and is totally Other than it.

When we speak of God as "the Holy One, blessed be He," we

are saying that He is "the transcendent One, Who is immanent."
We are declaring that God is utterly transcendent, but that we
can also experience Him as being immanent. The term "Holy
One, blessed be He" therefore bridges the gap between God's
transcendence and His immanence. It is as if God was very far
away but was stretching out His hand to enable us to grasp it.
This is represented by the *vav* (ו) of the Tetragrammaton, as I
have discussed earlier. Indeed, the Kabbalists explicitly state
that the expression "Holy One, blessed be He" denotes the Divine on the level of this *vav*.

Furthermore, the Zohar states that "the Holy One, blessed be
He, and the Torah are One." This is because the Torah is the
means through which God reaches out to us from His transcendence. Indeed, the Torah uses anthropomorphisms to describe
God primarily to make Him more understandable and "human"
to us and allow us to experience His immanence. The commandments in the Torah also serve as a link between God and human
beings.

The Kabbalistic meditation unifies "the Holy One, blessed be
He, with His Divine Presence." The Hebrew word for the Divine Presence is *Shekhinah,* which literally means "that which
dwells." The *Shekhinah* is a very important concept in Judaism in
general.

The *Shekhinah* is said to be wherever God's presence is manifest. Thus, it is taught that the *Shekhinah* was on Mount Sinai
when God gave the commandments and later in the Holy
Temple in Jerusalem. Furthermore, when an individual experienced prophecy, it was said that the *Shekhinah* rested on him.
Since the word *Shekhinah* comes from the root *shakhan,* meaning "to dwell," *Shekhinah* denotes that God appears to be
"dwelling" in a certain place.

But what does it mean when we say that God "dwells" in a
place? It cannot be taken literally, since God's essence fills all
creation. When we say that God "dwells" in a certain place, we
really mean that people can have an additional awareness of God
there. Wherever the *Shekhinah* rests, there is an enhanced ability to experience the Divine.

When God allows His *Shekhinah* to rest in a certain place or situation, it is as if He were giving us a hand with which to receive the experience of the Divine.

This is represented by the last *heh* (ה) of the Tetragrammaton. Here again, the Kabbalists teach that the *Shekhinah* represents the same level of the Divine as this final *heh*.

Therefore, when this meditation speaks of uniting "the Holy One, blessed be He, and His *Shekhinah*," it is speaking of uniting the levels of the *vav* and the *heh:* the arm reaching out to us, and the hand that God gives us so that we may receive. Indeed, some versions of this meditation state explicitly that the *vav* and the *heh* are being united. Observing a commandment allows us to unite the male and female aspects of God's presence in the world.

This is the essential purpose of keeping a commandment. God is always stretching out His arm to us, willing to give of His essence and spirituality. Before we can take it from Him, we must have a vessel with which to hold it, a "hand" with which to receive. The way we do this is by making ourselves receptacles for the Divine. God gives us the hand with which to receive the Divine, but we must bring it together with the outstretched arm. The goal of the commandments is to unite the *vav* and the *heh*.

When we say the above meditation, we should bear in mind that we are receptacles for the Divine. Try to feel the great hollow inside yourself that can be filled only by God's essence, and more than anything in the world, yearn that this hollow be filled.

At the same time, we should also be aware of God's presence all around us. We should contemplate the fact that God always wants to make Himself available, but needs an act on our part. The commandments serve as this medium, and through them God's essence is brought into our being. Therefore, when performing any commandment or ritual, we should be aware that we are drawing into ourselves the light of the Divine.

The meditation goes on to say that the commandment is being done with "love and awe." As we have seen, keeping a commandment can be a powerful expression of love. Love is the feeling that one wishes to unite with the Divine. There must be a boundary on this love, or one can become swallowed up by it completely. Therefore, love for the Divine must be balanced by awe. Love draws us closer to God, but awe keeps us from getting too close.

When we learn to look at the rituals and commandments in this light, all of Judaism takes on new significance. We can see the commandments as the path that God Himself gave for us to come close to Him and experience His presence.

17

BETWEEN

MAN AND WOMAN

In earlier chapters, I discussed how the last two letters of the Tetragrammaton, *vav* (ו) and *heh* (ה), represent the male and female forces of providence. The male force is that which acts upon the world, while the female force is that which allows the world to be receptive to God's power.

This is one reason that we refer to God in the male gender when we pray. Of course, although we usually refer to God as a male, in His true essence He is without gender. We refer to Him as a male, however, because we want Him to act upon the world through the male force of providence. We then leave ourselves open to God's providence, as a female is open to her mate.

The expression "the Holy One, blessed be He" is in the male gender and is therefore seen as denoting the male force of providence. It also relates to the *vav* of the Tetragrammaton.

The Hebrew word for "Divine Presence," on the other hand, is *Shekhinah*, which is a feminine noun. The *Shekhinah* denotes the final *heh* in the divine name as well as the female power of providence.

It is significant that the Torah presents man and woman together as comprising the image of the Divine. The Torah thus says, "God created man in His image, in the image of God He created him, male and female He created them" (Gen. 1:27). This clearly implies that male and female together form the "image of God."

The reason for this is obvious. A male and female have the power to do the most Godlike thing possible, namely, to create life. The power to conceive a child is so Godlike that the Talmud states that when man and woman create a child, God Himself is their third partner.

Therefore, a husband and wife should see each other as being a reflection of the Divine. When a woman looks at her husband, she should see him as a reflection of "the Holy One, blessed be He," the male aspect of the Divine. Similarly, when a husband looks at his wife, he should see her as the Divine Presence (*Shekhinah*), the feminine aspect of the Divine.

When a person attains this goal, he will fully appreciate his wife's beauty and see it as a reflection of the Divine. He will then also be aware of her inner beauty, which is a reflection of the beauty of the *Shekhinah*. When one can contemplate this, one is filled with a love toward one's spouse that parallels the supernal love between the masculine and feminine forces of the Divine.

The Torah tells about the love between Jacob and Rachel, and describes it as one of the greatest loves the world has ever seen. It tells how Jacob was willing to work as an indentured servant for seven years to win Rachel's hand, and how the seven years "passed like days, so much did he love her" (Gen. 29:20). The Jewish mystics explain that Jacob saw himself as the male aspect of the Divine and Rachel as the female aspect; he therefore had a love that was a counterpart of the love on high.

When one is looking for a spiritual master, the first thing to examine is the master's relationship with his wife. From the way a man treats his wife, one can know how he relates to the *Shekhinah*. No matter how deep the master's meditations seem to be, no matter how wise his words, if he does not have a good relationship with his wife, then there is something missing from his spirituality. Conversely, when a man has a good relationship with his wife, even in the face of temptation and adversity, it is a clear indication that he is on a high spiritual level.

I once knew a member of the Musar school of meditation who was married to a woman with a severe mental illness. But whereas she was filled with anger and abuse, he responded with love and devotion. No matter how mean she was to him, he constantly saw her as his link with the Divine, and gave love and respect accordingly. It would be nice to say that this love cured her, but in actuality it did not. However, when he was left a widower as an old man, this man would constantly say how much he appreciated and missed his wife.

It is also significant that there is no encouragement of celibacy in the Jewish tradition, mystical or otherwise. Moses, the greatest of all mystics and prophets, was married, as were all the prophets and sages. Sex is seen not as a weakness of the flesh or as a necessary evil, but as a means to drawing close to God on a most intimate level.

When man and wife see each other as personifications of the divine image, then the sexual act becomes something holy. It is nothing less than the coming together of the male and female forces of creation. On a physical level, this has the power to create a child, but these forces parallel those on high which brought all creation into existence.

The male and female forces of creation are represented by the *yod* (י) and the *heh* (ה) of the Tetragrammaton. This is very closely related to a fascinating Talmudic teaching: The Hebrew word for man is *iysh* (איש), while the word for woman is *ishah* (אשה). If one looks at the words, one sees that the word *iysh* contains a *yod* (י), while *ishah* contains a *heh* (ה). The Talmud says that these are the *yod* and *heh* of the Tetragrammaton.

If the *yod* and *heh* are removed from *iysh* and *ishah*, then the remaining letters of both words spell out *esh* (אש), the Hebrew word for "fire." The fires of passion that unite man and woman are seen as receptacles for the letters of the Divine Name, and hence, for the masculine and feminine elements of the Divine Essence. The passion that draws man and woman together stems from the fact that man and woman are counterparts of the male and female archetypes on high.

Therefore, when husband and wife are intimate, a man can see himself as being filled with the male aspect of the Divine, making an intimate connection with the female aspect. Similarly, a woman can see herself as the female aspect, receiving the male aspect. They can both realize that through their union, they are creating an "image of God."

For this to be accomplished, it is very important to avoid any extraneous thoughts during the sexual act. Partners should not think of any member of the opposite sex other than the sexual partner of the moment. As in any meditation involving action, concentration should be totally on the act itself, with all extraneous thoughts gently pushed aside.

There are several guidelines that are found in the Talmud and Kabbalah to enhance the meditative aspects of the act. First, the experience is meant to be primarily tactile, involving the sense of touch. Therefore, it should be performed in a room as dark as possible. Each party should have nothing distracting him or her from the experience.

It is also taught that there should be no clothing intervening between the two bodies. The Torah speaks of man and woman becoming "one flesh" (Gen. 2:24). This indicates that flesh should be in direct contact with flesh, so that the tactile experience is maximized.

The Kabbalah teaches that the sexual act should begin with words of endearment and then progress to kissing, hugging, and caressing, and finally to total intimacy. It is as if the process begins with the head and mind in speech and kissing. It then is drawn down to the hands and body in hugging and caressing. Finally, it is drawn to the reproductive organs, which are the seat of the greatest sexual pleasure. The sexual energy can be felt traveling down the spine and through the body, leading to the most sensitive areas.

God created the sexual act as one of the greatest pleasures that a human being can experience. For one thing, the act had to be pleasurable so that human beings would be drawn to it and thus perpetuate the species. But on a much deeper level, it is so great a pleasure because it allows man and woman together to emulate the Divine.

When a man and woman experience pleasure from each other, they can contemplate this pleasure as a meditative experience. This will have the immediate effect of enhancing the pleasure manyfold. If they see this pleasure as a gift of God, they will have great joy from it and, at the same time, experience a feeling of thanksgiving. On a deeper level, they can be aware of the spark of the Divine in the pleasure itself and elevate it to its source.

If a couple has such intentions, then the sexual act can be something holy. The Torah says that a married man may not "diminish his wife's conjugal rights" (Exod. 21:10). The Talmud interprets this to mean that it is one of the divine commandments that a husband and wife be intimate at regular intervals. Therefore, when being intimate, a husband and wife can also meditate on the fact that they are fulfilling one of God's commandments. Sex is not simply a mundane act that is being elevated, but a sacred act in its own right.

Very important in making sex a holy act is keeping the rules of family purity. This involves the woman's counting seven days after the end of her period and then immersing in a *mikveh* (ritual bath). The monthly menses are seen as a cleansing process, and immersion in the *mikveh* as a process of rebirth. (The philosophy of the *mikveh* is discussed at length in my book *The Waters of Eden*.) In many ways, immersion in the *mikveh* is more important to making sex a holy act than even marriage itself.

In general, using meditative techniques during intimacy can enhance the pleasure immeasurably. Such a practice focuses the minds of both partners exclusively on their mates and thus serves to strengthen the marriage bond. Couples who regularly use meditative techniques during intimacy have experienced important gains in their feelings toward each other. Couples who were experiencing marital difficulties found that when their sex life was sanctified, their love grew and other problems seemed to become inconsequential.

The type of meditation that a couple can do when they wish to conceive a child is somewhat different. This is because if they are on a certain level of consciousness, the thoughts that they have during intimacy can have a strong effect on the child conceived.

The Torah teaches that when Jacob wanted his sheep to conceive spotted, banded, or striped offspring, he cut rods with the appropriate markings, and set them out where the sheep mated (Gen. 30:37,38). It is taught that Jacob meditated on these rods, and when he was in a very high level of consciousness, he was able to project his thoughts on the the sheep being conceived and thus influence their markings. Deep meditation can have an effect on the genetic structure of one's offspring, as well as the child's spiritual makeup.

Therefore, when a couple wish to conceive, they should decide what traits they would consider most desirable in the child. They should agree on what they consider most important, and what they would most want their child to be. Then, using visualization techniques discussed in chapter 8, they should both visualize the child they want to conceive during intercourse. If this is done with total concentration, it can have a positive influence on the conceived child. While it is not a foolproof technique, especially if the members of the couple are not expert meditators, experience has shown it to have significant influence. Experience has also shown that couples who have difficulty in conceiving often have success when using such an imaging technique.

For many people, sex is associated with guilt and shame. But if we understand that God gave us sexual pleasure as a gift, we will realize that we can enjoy it to the fullest.

Of course, sex is also an area of great temptation. A person may have committed sexual acts, such as adultery, which are regarded as sinful. Here, too, one must realize that sins can be repented; as the Talmud states, "Nothing can stand before repentance." Even if one has fallen into temptation, one can ask, with all one's heart, for God's forgiveness. The fact that a person may have sinned or done wrong need not diminish or destroy his or her ability to experience the Divine.

Judaism views the sexual act as something very holy. It is a means through which a person can experience great intimacy with God. Judaism surrounds the sexual act with many rules and prohibitions, not because it views sex as something dirty or shameful, but because it views sex as something so holy that it must not be misused. Used correctly, with the right intentions and thoughts, sex can be the purest and holiest experience in the world, and meditation can enhance this aspect of the experience.

18

REMOLDING THE SELF

One of the most important meditative movements in Judaism is associated with the Musar school, founded by Rabbi Yisrael Salanter (1810–1883). *Musar*, self-perfection, was always an important element in Judaism; important texts on the subject were published as early as the tenth century. The Musar movement, however, made self-perfection its primary focus. The movement taught that a person should continually strive to grow spiritually, ethically, and morally throughout the course of his lifetime.

Interpersonal relationships were given a high priority in the Musar movement. It was not enough to be able to experience the Divine; one also had to be able to get along with others in the best possible manner. Anger, hatred, revenge, gossip, and jealousy were seen as bad habits that could stunt a person's spiritual growth. The premise was that if we grow in our relationship to God, we should also grow in our ability to relate in a positive way to our fellow human beings. The Musar school thus strove to make every individual into a saint in every sense of the word. People were taught to be sensitive to their own shortcomings and were encouraged to create personal programs to rectify them one by one.

To some extent, the Musar movement was a reaction to the Chasidic movement. Chasidism began as a mystical movement. In order to climb high spiritual mountains, experienced guides, or *rebbes,* were needed. In some Chasidic circles, however, the guide became more important than the mountain. Many Chasidim regarded their *rebbe* as the paradigm of the saintly man and lived the righteous life vicariously through him.

The Musar movement developed among the Mitnaggedim, opponents of the Chasidic movement. Musar schools taught that it was not enough to live the righteous life through a master. Every individual had an obligation to strive to live the righteous life in his own right. Beyond that, the Musar movement offered a program through which every person could gradually perfect himself.

There is an extensive Musar literature in Hebrew. Some of the most important Musar works, such as *Path of the Upright* (*Mesillath Yesharim*), by Moses Hayim Luzzatto, and *Ways of the Righteous* (*Orchoth Tzaddikim*), anon., have been translated into English.

The first part of the Musar program was to make a daily habit of reading a lesson from a classical Musar work. After reading the lesson, one was to spend a short period of time contemplating it and relating it to one's own life.

As the individual began to advance, this contemplation became a meditation. One would read a lesson from a classical Musar text on how to improve the ethical, moral, and religious quality of one's life, then meditate on this lesson for twenty to thirty minutes. This is a simple type of meditation, similar to the one described in chapter 3, where I discussed meditating on how to rearrange your life. It is a meditation in which one considers a particular aspect of one's life and thinks about ways to improve it.

In meditations such as these, extraneous thoughts are gently pushed out of the mind. Some authorities, such as the Baal Shem Tov, however, maintained that a person should pay attention to extraneous thoughts, since they could provide clues as to what direction to take. One may wish to make mental notes of these extraneous thoughts and then analyze them to see how to make use of them to help attain one's goals.

The program of self-improvement could include more than just moral issues. The Musar schools saw their method as a way of becoming a more effective human being. Problems such as shyness, indecision, lack of motivation, and the like could also be helped through Musar methods.

The second part of the Musar program consists of a mantralike repetition of the concept one is working on. For example, a person may have a tendency to gossip and want to break this habit. He may realize that gossip is harmful to others and morally wrong, and that it is forbidden by the Torah commandment "Do not go as a talebearer among your people" (Lev. 19:16).

The method of breaking the gossip habit would be to take the biblical verse "Do not go as a talebearer among your people" and repeat it every day for a twenty- to thirty-minute period, like a mantra. As one works on it, the message is gradually absorbed, and the self-control necessary to avoid gossip is attained.

Another effective technique is described by Rabbi Nachman of Bratslav. This technique consists in speaking to various parts of the body. If a person wishes to change a certain trait, he can talk to the part of the body associated with that trait, and in this way change his actions.

Taking the above example of gossip, a person could use Rabbi Nachman's technique and speak to his tongue, telling it never to say anything against another person. If one does this for a fixed amount of time every day, this, too, can be an effective form of meditation.

Let us say that you want to lose weight. You can use Musar and other meditative techniques in various ways. You can simply use the phrase "I am going to lose weight" as a mantra. You can speak to your body and tell it that you want it to be slim. You can also use an imaging technique: imagine yourself slim, what you would look like, and how it would feel to be carrying less weight. Gradually your self-image will start to change. You can speak to your mouth, telling it not to eat so much, and to your stomach, telling it to crave less food. A combination of techniques can be effective even in overcoming lifelong habits.

There are several hints that the Musar schools give to make any self-improvement program more effective. The first is not to try to make too many changes at once. A Talmudic teaching—"If one tries to grasp too much, one grasps nothing"—is taken as a watchword. Better to be successful in making small changes than to fail at making big ones. If one succeeds in making a small change in one's life, it is easy to build on this success.

The important message is that success breeds success and failure breeds failure. People often try to effect a change in their life-style and make the attempt many times, only to meet with failure. This is particularly true of people who have tried to lose weight or give up smoking.

Take as an example the person who resolves to quit smoking. He keeps his resolution for a few weeks, but then feels that he cannot go for the rest of his life without a cigarette and reverts back to his bad habit. He has experienced a failure, which makes stopping all the more difficult the next time around. After a number of such failures, people give up and feel that the habit in question is beyond their control.

The Musar approach would be to give up smoking for a specified period of time, say thirty days. At the end of the thirty-day period, one could begin smoking again. This is the key to success. During this thirty-day period, a person would not have to confront the fact that he will never taste a cigarette again or that he will have to maintain this level of self-control for years to come. The time of abstinence is manageable because it has a limit.

The point of this technique is that at the end of the thirty-day period, a person is free to choose whether or not to begin smoking again. If he resumes smoking, he does not have to feel like a failure. Quite to the contrary: he has been successful in maintaining his thirty-day abstinence and therefore has a success upon which to build. Later, he can stop for another thirty-day period. After doing this a number of times, he may find that the desire to smoke has waned.

Of course, at the end of any of these thirty-day periods, he may decide not to resume smoking. If one thirty-day period was a success, the second thirty-day period will be even easier. By taking one thirty-day period after another, a person can continually weaken the habit until it ceases to exist.

This is particularly true if, during the period of abstinence, one uses the Musar meditational techniques discussed earlier. One can use the expression "I want to stop smoking" as a mantra to help strengthen one's will, so that by the end of the thirty-day period, the desire to smoke will be diminished. Other meditational techniques can also be helpful.

The idea of using thirty-day periods is a very powerful tool in spiritual growth. Many moral or ethical habits are easier to break than smoking or eating habits, since in the latter one must deal with the body as well as the mind. Many bad moral or ethical habits can be overcome in a thirty-day period.

You can work on a relatively large number of character traits over the course of years and thus continually grow, both spiritually and morally. You can in fact remold yourself into the good and righteous person you wish to be. Where you are is not as important as where you are heading. If you are willing to devote your life to continued growth, there are virtually no limits to the levels you can reach.